MASCULINITIES IN CONTEMPORARY AFRICA

LA MASCULINTÉ EN AFRIQUE CONTEMPORAINE

Edited by/Édité par

Egodi Uchendu

CODESRIA

Council for the Development
of Social Science Research in Africa

Conseil pour le développement de
la recherche en sciences sociales en Afrique

ISBN: 978-2-86978-227-3

Typeset by Daouda Thiam
Cover image designed by Ibrahima Fofana
Printed by Imprimerie Saint-Paul, Dakar, Sénégal

Distributed in Africa by CODESRIA

Distributed elsewhere by African Books Collective, Oxford, UK.
Website: www.africanbookscollective.com

CODESRIA would like to express its gratitude to the Swedish International Development Cooperation Agency (SIDA/SAREC), the International Development Research Centre (IDRC), Ford Foundation, MacArthur Foundation, Carnegie Corporation, (NORAD), Norwegian Agency for Development Cooperation the Danish Agency for International Development (DANIDA), the French Ministry of Cooperation, the United Nations Development Programme (UNDP), the Netherlands Ministry of Foreign Affairs, Rockefeller Foundation, FINIDA, CIDA, IIEP/ADEA, OECD, OXFAM America, UNICEF and the Government of Senegal for supporting its research, training and publication programmes.

Le CODESRIA exprime sa profonde gratitude à la Swedish International Development Corporation Agency (SIDA/SAREC), au Centre de Recherche pour le Développement International (CRDI), à la Ford Foundation, à la Fondation MacArthur, à la Carnegie Corporation, au NORAD, à l'Agence Danoise pour le Développement International (DANIDA), au Ministère Français de la Coopération, au Programme des Nations-Unies pour le Développement (PNUD), au Ministère des Affaires Etrangères des Pays-Bas, à la Fondation Rockefeller, à FINIDA, CIDA, IIEP/ ADEA, à l'OCDE, à Oxfam America, à l'UNICEF, ainsi qu'au Gouvernement du Sénégal pour le soutien apporté aux programmes de recherche, de formation et de publication du Conseil.

Contents/Sommaire

Acknowledgement

Africa is intriguing for its environmental, climatic, racial, cultural, political and other diversities. Its range of historical experiences is wide, even within regional specificities. Yet, within the diversities are many similarities. A major point of unity is membership in a defined geographical zone. Non-Africans may divide the continent and its peoples into two: the Maghreb (Africa north of the Sahara) and the Black Africa (areas south of the Sahara, popularly identified as sub-Saharan Africa). But to the peoples of the continent, we are one; we are Africans. This does not ignore or injure our racial, political, religious and other differences; rather, it emphasizes our unity in our joint location and our general sense of belonging in the continent.

This volume celebrates Africa's unity as well as its diversities. It comprises chapters on various expressions of Africa's masculinities from different regions of the continent. The papers in this volume were initially presented and discussed at CODESRIA's 2005 Gender Institute. The contributors are gender scholars drawn from various disciplines in the wide fields of Humanities and Social Sciences, but interested in the critical study of men in Africa.

I am greatly indebted to many individuals who helped in one way or another to bring this project to fruition. CODESRIA set the ball rolling when it chose the theme 'Masculinities in Contemporary Africa' for its 2005 Gender Institute; the choice of masculinities was a clear departure from the normal gender issues that raise concerns specific to the interests of women, by turning the attention to men. This volume concentrates on issues that range from expressions of maleness to masculine associations with power. I thank the anonymous reviewers, both French and English, who read the papers and offered many helpful hints towards their improvement. I also thank all the contributors for their exemplary cooperation. The contributors to this volume, however, accept responsibility for any mistakes in their respective papers.

Egodi Uchendu

Notes on Contributors

Egodi Uchendu teaches at the Department of History/International Studies, University of Nigeria, Nsukka, specializing in gender and women's history. She has held a number of prestigious fellowships, most recently at the Centre of African Studies, School of Oriental and African Studies, University of London. Dr Uchendu has published articles and chapters in various journals and edited volumes. She is the author of *Women and Conflict in the Nigerian Civil War* (2007).

Kopano Ratele is a Professor at the Institute of Social and Health Sciences (ISHS) University of South Africa. He has a range of scholarly interests spanning the areas of violence and fatal injury, critical psychology, sexuality, culture, men and masculinities, and research methodology. Prior to ISHS, Ratele was a professor in the Department of Psychology and in Women and Gender Studies, University of Western Cape. Among others, he has edited or co-edited the books *From Boys to Men: Social Construction of Masculinities in Contemporary Society* and *Inter-group Relations - South African Perspectives*.

Egara Kabaji is a Senior Lecturer in Literature and Communication at Western University College of Science and Technology (WUCST), Kenya. His published works include *Women in Development* (1997), *Jomo Kenyatta* (2002), *A Guide to Francis Imbuga's Aminata* (2002) and *The Strange Bird of Navuhi* (2005). His research interests include Gender and Masculinity Studies, and Cultural Discourses.

James Ogola Onyango is a Senior Lecturer in the Department of Literature, Languages and Linguistics, Egerton University, Kenya. He holds a PhD in Applied Linguistics from the University of Vienna. His research and publication areas include Discourse-Historical Approach Theory, Discursive Masculinities and Feminities, Language Policy and Kiswahili Studies.

Abdessamad Dialmy est professeur en sociologie. Il est le directeur du Laboratoire Interdisciplinaire des Etudes sur la Santé et le Population (LIDESP) à l'Université de Fez. Il est membre du conseil d'administration de *Social Compass,* la Revue Internationale de la Sociologie de la Religion (Université de Louvain-La Neuve/Sage Publications). Il est aussi membre de l'Association Mondiale de la Sexologie, et a servi comme consultant pour plusieurs organisations internationales, notamment l'OMS, l'UNICEF, le Conseil sur la Population, USAID et l'Union Européenne. Il a publié plusieurs œuvres sur le genre, la sexualité, la santé et l'Islam en Arabe, Français et Anglais.

Svetlana Roubailo Koudolo est enseignante/chercheur dans le département d'Anthropologie de l'Université de Lomé. Elle a fait partie du personnel scientifique de l'Institut de l'Anthropologie et de l'Ethnographie de l'Académie des Sciences à Saint Petersburg en Russie de 1971 à 1979. Elle a aussi la directrice de recherche au Centre de Formation Permanente pour l'Action et la Recherche Pédagogique à Lomé au Togo de 1984 à 1999.

Claire Kelly is the Research Co-ordinator for Intercultural and Diversity Studies and a junior lecturer in Race, Class and Gender at the University of Cape Town (UCT). She completed her Master's degree in Diversity Studies at UCT in 2005, with a focus on white masculinities in South Africa. Her other research interests include organisational transformation, diversity and questions of social justice. She is currently working on her PhD in Psychology, with a focus on Identity and Social Transformation.

Ibrahim Mouiche est assistant professeur au département des Sciences Politiques de l'Université de Yaoundé II au Cameroun. Il est actuellement chercheur au CNWS, Ecole de Recherche des Etudes Asiatiques, Africaines et Latines Américaines à l'Université Leyde en Hollande. La plupart de ses travaux sont sur l'ethnicité, la démocratisation et les chefs traditionnels.

Wanjiku Chiuri is a Senior Lecturer in Environmental Science at Egerton University, Kenya. She is a researcher, consultant and scholar on Gender, Planning, Community Development and Sustainable Development. She has published widely on Gender Analysis and Poverty Studies.

Charity Mwangi-Chemnjor teaches at Egerton University, Laikipia College Campus, Kenya. She has an MA (Education) from Dalhousie University, Canada, and is currently pursuing a PhD at the University of South Africa. Her research interests include Education Management, Policy Studies in Education and Gender Studies.

Inês M. Raimundo is a Lecturer, Researcher and Head of the Department of Population Studies, Centre for Policies Analysis, Faculty of Arts and Social Sciences, Eduardo Mondlane University. He is also a PhD candidate at the University of the Witwatersrand, Johannesburg, South Africa.

Lilian Ndangam is an independent Researcher based in Toronto, Canada. This article was submitted whilst she was Andrew Mellon Postdoctoral Research Fellow at the School of Journalism and Media Studies, Rhodes University, South Africa.

Raïssa Edwige Koutouma Nsona est membre de Interdisciplinaire groupe de recherche sur l' Afrique contemporaine (IGRAC) à la Faculté des Lettres et des Sciences Humaines à l' université Marien Ngouabi.

Zahia Benabdallah est Détentrice d'un magister en Sociologie avec option : « Sociologie du changement social ». Elle a travaillé en tant que Chercheur permanent dans le Centre National de Recherche en Anthropologie Sociale et Culturelle (CRASC). Elle est actuellement chercheur permanent au Centre National de recherches en préhistoire et anthropologie historique (CNRPAH) à Alger. Elle prépare un doctorat en anthropologie sur les enjeux de l'idéal corporel dans le milieu estudiantin : « Approche genre », dans le cadre de l'école doctorale organisée par le CRASC et l'université d'Oran en Algérie.

1

Introduction

Are African Males Men?
Sketching African Masculinities

Egodi Uchendu

> The stupid inertness of the puzzled negro is duller than that of an oxen; a dog would grasp your meaning in one half the time. 'Men and brothers'! They may be brothers, but they certainly are not men. (Robert Baden-Powell, cited in Hyman 1993: 278).

Of the Zulu, at the turn of the twentieth century, it was written:

> Throughout his life, the Zulu of the olden times was subjected to a remarkable system of unremitting discipline, but it was a discipline that 'Made him honest, brave and wise, respectful toward king and neighbour … He was a cunning and daring opponent, a keen logician and consummate diplomatist, not a mongrel but a man of repute, not a debased savage but an intelligent being. He was, in short, a man of right with an undeniably just and overwhelmingly strong claim to be dealt with as such', even by his conquerors and every other Whiteman living in Africa. (Stuart 1903: 13, cited in Binns 1975: 183).

The Boy Scouts' founder's view of African men and, by inference, expressions of masculinity on the African continent, seen in the first quote follows the Eurocentric and colonial tradition of regarding Africans as lacking in almost every virtue. Nineteenth- and early twentieth-century European traders, missionaries and colonizers who operated on the African continent left a rich store of records, telling the world that Africa and its peoples, especially its men, were morally bankrupt, inept, barbaric, backward and doomed (McFarlan 1946; Middleton and Kershaw 1972). When colonial powers in Africa sponsored ethnographic studies of African societies, it was by no means a product of a sincere desire to understand Africa and Africans but an opportunity to collect materials to back up what they considered to be the disparity between the civilized and enlightened world on one hand and the barbaric and dark continent on the other (Hutchinson 1966; Wilson-Haffenden 1967: 95). Thus, colonial ethnography became the tool for serving colonial interests. It created unequal 'others', depicting Africa as the 'other world'. These early ethnographies often shared the perspectives of European commissioned officers who served in Colonial Africa. European societies became the standard against which Africans were judged and were found lacking (Cornwall and Lindisfarne 1994: 39).

Baden-Powell, a distinguished British colonial military officer, is not known as an anthropologist/ethnographer, but by dismissing African men as 'not men' he aptly exhibited western contempt for African manifestations of masculinity. He reached his conclusion because he looked at African masculinities from a certain lens; from all indications, a race-coated lens. To Baden-Powell, by deduction, masculinity should be measured in terms of 'intelligence' and 'action', and from his viewpoint nineteenth- and early twentieth century-African men lacked these attributes. They were not only 'stupid' – lacking in intelligence and insensible – but sluggish and lifeless (*Oxford English Dictionary* 1993: 763, 3111). Moreover, they were 'inert' – without inherent power of action or resistance (ibid. 1357). Incidentally, their stupidity and inertness were of such a magnitude to be at par with that of oxen – a castrated male animal. Even a dog was more intelligent than them. Simply put, they were not man enough!

Baden-Powell's comments imply some underlying awareness that masculinity had various shades, even in his own days. One form of it, a superior form obviously, was his European (more appropriately British) model, manifested through intelligence, quick wit, power and action. The other was his African model, identified by stupidity, dullness and inertness, not to mention a total lack of power and apparent unreliability. And yet, Baden-Powell acknowledged that they (Europeans) and them (Africans) both belonged to that universal stock of human males for he said: 'they may be brothers...' This awareness of the existence of various shades of masculinities was not applied to African men whom Baden-Powell judged, using his European lens, and fitted into an imaginary homogenized global form of deficient masculinity.

An issue that Baden-Powell did not grasp by the time he penned these sentences on African masculinity was the social construction of notions of maleness. That gender categories are socially constructed indicates the existence of varieties of masculinity within a society, across societies and across continents. In line with this, Baden-Powell also failed to understand how yardsticks for assessing manifestations of masculinity could differ from place to place and from continent to continent. One thing that must be said for these earlier yardsticks is that none was objective especially when applied across racial and geographical boundaries. To a reasonable extent, the same can be said of most stereotypical yardsticks still employed in the contemporary period. One puzzle is: how would Baden-Powell have categorized the Hua of Papua New Guinea, who see masculine subjects as highly placed but physically powerless and weak? And among whom masculinity is lost by men as they age but gained by women through childbearing? (Anselmi and Law 1998: 157). On Baden-Powell's summation of African men, Hyman (1993: 278) observes that 'Baden-Powell's outlook fitted in perfectly with the aggressive racial attitudes of the time. Although he denied being a "regular nigger-hater"….' he nonetheless subscribed to stereotyped notions of the African man's laziness and unreliability.

In this examination of African masculinities, it will serve us to remember that considerations of masculinity (and masculinities) are society-specific. Masculinity is what any given society accepts as features associated with the male gender and expressions of maleness. Masculinity speaks of those practices and ways of being that serve to validate a masculine subject's sense of itself as a male, boy or man (Whitehead 2002: 4). Race, culture, religion and belief systems, environmental realities and historical experiences influence notions of masculinities all over the world, not least in Africa. Moreover, these notions alter within different contexts: when in reference to females as a category and as belonging to different age groups; also when applied to men of diverse ages, social classes and from different societies. These facts should humble us when tempted to project on 'others' a particular notion or form of masculinity.

To begin our investigation of African masculinities, our first question is: who are African men? Broadly speaking, Africans are persons who are indigenous to and inhabit the African continent. They include all the races and racial mixtures that are harboured and continue to be harboured in Africa along with the inhabitants of islands on the Atlantic and Indian oceans who regard themselves as Africans and are duly recognized as such by the African Union. The male segment of these societies comprises African men whose masculinities are the focus of our discussion in this volume. These men vary according to their races and geographical placement within the continent. For the purpose of this discussion, I adopt the OAU/AU simplified geographical categorization of the African continent into North, West, East, Central and Southern Africa. Put together, they incorporate sections both north and south of the Sahara.

My definition identifying who African men are undoubtedly has contenders in individuals and groups that would want to dismember Africa to deny it any historical relevance. One such individual is C. T. Binns, who in *The Warrior People* (1975) traced the origins of some Southern African groups to Egypt. He asserts that Ancient Egyptians were a superior race different from indigenous African peoples whom they met when they arrived in Egypt, then subjugated and ended up amalgamating (1975: 20). In another part of his book, he wrote that the Ancient Egyptians and African peoples 'have many things in common', indicating 'that there must have been some link between these Ancient people and the Africans of today' (1975: 34). Whatever Binns wants us to believe, the fact remains that both the Ancient Egyptians and the African peoples they 'met', 'subjugated and amalgamated' ended up in Africa; thanks, according to Binns, to the famous great cataclysmic upheavals of many millions of years ago in Gondwanaland (Matthews 1973; Binns 1975: 18). If all mankind lived together in Gondwanaland before the great cataclysmic upheavals that scattered them over the many continents and isles as we know them today, those groups of peoples and races that afterwards congregated in specific sections of the globe should be regarded and treated as 'indigenous' to those places, since Gondwanaland no longer exists. Thus, Ancient Egyptians, whether indigenous Negro stock or not, who occupied Egypt since 5500 BC were bona fide Africans. They and their descendants presently occupying Egypt are treated in this examination as Africans. The same applies to white South Africans and peoples of Arabic and Asian ancestries found in the continent who claim citizenship of specific African countries.

Are African Males Men?

There are many ways of answering this question. It can be considered biologically and culturally. Biologically, what basically distinguishes a human male from a non-male is the presence of male genitals and accessory male sexual characteristics. Granted, Africa historically has had its share of human hermaphrodites and men castrated for purposes of military and domestic responsibilities. These are human species, which though manifesting a majority of male biological features, cannot be regarded as fully male because of natural and artificial interferences with the development of their male sexual organs. For hermaphrodites, only a medical assessment can prove their degree of maleness. Nevertheless, the presence of these 'sub-male' categories, as we may call them, does not imply that Africa is lacking in genetically masculine subjects or, as Baden-Powell informed the world, that African males are not men, implying not masculine enough to be aggressive, intelligent, powerful and assertive. Secondly, there are many cultural traits identified in African societies as evidence of masculinity. These traits can be considered on the basis of accounts from different African societies in the different regions of the continent and within specific historical periods.

The first dynasty of Ancient Egypt (3100–2800 BC) was known for a high degree of civilization with the art of writing so well established that Ancient Egyptians shared with the Sumerians, a pre-Babylonian people, the invention of this art. The Egyptian and Sumerian civilizations were the first known in the world (Binns 1975: 20; Shillington 1995: 20). Such a developed society as Ancient Egypt had from 3100 until 1100 BC was the product of many centuries of well-coordinated administration. Egypt was highly structured. The majority of the population was the peasants who sustained the nation through agriculture and supplied the labour that made Ancient Egypt great. At least, a thousand of these men built the Great Pyramid at Giza around 2400 BC. The government was run by a team of bureaucratic and well-educated civil servants (Shillington 1995: 23). Intelligence in all spheres was a marked feature of Egyptian men. Efforts to 'tame' their environment to their advantage resulted in a host of scientific inventions, including mathematics and astronomy, which have lasted to the present. Their men were also gifted in craftsmanship and developed a firmly established artistic culture. They were an active group and highly assertive as their trading exploits and their civilization indicate. Violence and martial prowess were not very pronounced in Ancient Egyptian society, and hence in their masculine subjects, for it was not until the empire was invaded during the Second Intermediate Period after the Middle Kingdom, in about 1670 BC, by foreign invaders (called Hyksos by Manetho, the Egyptian historian) from western Asia that a standing army was established and the empire 'extended by conquest' (Shillington 1995: 29). Many of the soldiers were non-Egyptians. It cannot be said with certainty what the family life of Ancient Egyptians was like and whether violence and aggressiveness were features of the private space during this period, even if not in external dealings.

Laziness was rebuked in Ancient Egyptian male youths. On a papyrus text dating to the end of the New Kingdom (1567–1085 BC), a teacher admonishes a lukewarm student as a lazy learner (Obenga 2004: 244). Intellectual life was highly esteemed above all professions. The life of a scribe was greatly preferred to those of the peasants and soldiers. The Egyptian scribe was 'a researcher, a seeker concerned first of all to guarantee the immortality of his name'; he was an intellectual with extraordinary value (ibid. 606). Scribes shaped Ancient Egyptian philosophy and for three thousand years maintained the moral, intellectual, cultural, spiritual, scientific and other values of Pharaonic society. Schools and training centres for boys existed to train achievers to become high government officials. The aim of learning was to acquire wisdom and therefore perfection. Virtue, from the development of the mind through intellectual activity, was compatible with wealth and political power. The architects who designed the pyramids and other grandiose constructions of civil and religious edifices were masters of a wide range of scientific disciplines (Shillington 1995; Obenga 2004). They must have possessed exceptional drive to have managed the vast numbers of men needed for their intricate projects.

The focus of the records on Ancient Egypt was on boys and men and their achievements, suggesting that Ancient Egypt was a male-dominated society. Little was recorded about women, who were called 'mistresses of the house'. Their domestic excellence could be gleaned from a comment in a papyrus text that described the scribe as 'like a woman cheerfully giving birth' (Obenga 2004: 246). In terms of gender relations and men's general views of women, we gain some ideas from Ptahhotep, the vizier under King Isesi of the Fifth Dynasty of the Old

Kingdom, writing about 2350 BC, who warned men to stay clear of women because of their ability to ensnare men in numerous ways and divert them 'from important goals into fleeting debauchery' (Obenga 2004: 595). Women constituted the other group, one that distracted the esteemed (masculine) category and of which the latter should be wary. In Pharaonic society, however, women were legal equals of men. They could own and use property and work as administrators or temple priestesses, but comparatively little attention was paid to them either as a group or as individuals. Few highly placed women were mentioned in the records, but by and large the references to women were for their erotic and entertainment qualities. Most likely, the number of women who were visible in the society must have been small. Male intellectuals and scribes and boy students all received attention in records on Ancient Egypt, but not so for women in similar positions. In Obenga's (2004) extensive work on Ancient Egypt, a mere six pages were devoted to issues about women and all dealt with nothing but their unresisting and dangerous sex appeal (2004: 595–600). Binns (1975) and Shillington (1995) had nothing to say about Ancient Egyptian women.

This academic silence throws much light on gender relations in Ancient Egyptian society and women's visibility within it. If women had much value besides their sexual and nurturing roles and there was more to be said about them Obenga's 671-page book, crafted from surviving hieroglyphic writings, should have had more than six pages on women and discourse on other issues than women's sexual prowess and mysteries. The argument here remains that Ancient Egypt was male-dominated. While the dominant masculinity was one that extolled intellectual prowess linked to action, it was nonetheless a masculinity predicated on domination even though women may have enjoyed a few privileges. This does not contradict my earlier claim that violence and martial prowess were not pronounced features of Ancient Egyptian dominant masculinity. Non-violence appears to have been the norm in external dealings until militarism, evidenced in the introduction of a standing army during the Second Intermediate Period (Shillington 1995: 24), became a part of Ancient Egyptian foreign policy. My argument on non-violence would not apply so simplistically to domestic affairs, if we take into consideration Ancient Egypt's dependence on forced labour.

Masculine expressions in Africa before 1880 and after, a phase that many African societies categorize as comprising pre-colonial and colonial periods, had distinctive features. These were a time of uncertainty and danger borne out of the dying yet smouldering embers of the international trade in slaves and the sudden imposition of alien rule in the form of colonialism on most African states and societies. We can look at the Zulu society of Natal in Southern Africa within these periods for an appreciation of how masculinity was constructed and what images of it can be identified. The Zulu kingdom in particular commenced its decline as an independent state in the 1880s after the defeat of its army and capture of its king, Cetswayo, by the British. In 1887, Zululand became a British colony (Shillington 1995: 320).

Binns (1975: 183), who at the turn of the twentieth century praised Zulu males so eloquently, as we saw in the second quotation on the opening page, was not particularly fond of Sub-Saharan African groups as a whole. For instance, he dismissed Central African ritual specialists as 'a bunch of unscrupulous and avaricious rascals whose practices were so inhuman and barbaric as to make the lives of their followers nothing but a daily round of fear…'. He regarded the Negro mind as too simple to grasp the doctrine of the Trinity (1975: 37, 41). Yet he found the Zulu, among whom he lived for fifty-nine years and in whose land he worked as a colonial education officer, an amazing crop of men whom he intensely admired.

Zulu masculine subjects were praised for their 'unremitting discipline' manifested in honesty, wisdom, bravery and respect for authority. These qualities were not intrinsic but learned. In other words, Zulu society during its pre-colonial period had articulated its ideas on masculinity and set in motion informal and formal structures, the most important being the family, to transfer, through learning and practice, these qualities to every male child. The Zulu boy of the late nineteenth and early twentieth centuries was not slothful. The father and the mother played complementary roles in training the male child to acquire the esteemed qualities appropriate for his gender. Binns (1975: 159) paid the following tribute to the Zulu family structure for its role in grooming boys into men:

> one cannot but stand rooted in amazement at the splendid type which was produced as a result of the 'stern family discipline' which every Zulu boy had to undergo from his earliest days to manhood.

Between the ages of 11 and 13, the society organized for boys the ceremony of the Piercing of the Ears, *Qhumbuza Izindlebe*, at which time the oldest man within an extended compound instructed initiates on appropriate daily conduct. They were taught to be totally obedient to their parents and elders, to pay careful attention to their duties, to be ready to help others and to display their masculinity, honesty, dependability and trustworthiness in all their doings. The ceremony was the boy's official step towards manhood (Binns 1975: 163–4).

An adolescent male's first nocturnal emission was a sign of his entering into manhood and indicated the right time for the most important male ritual, called the Thomba ceremony (Binns 1975: 174). The week-long event ended with an early morning bath to wash away the ways and habits of childhood and assume manhood. From then on, he would be attired as a man. 'Full' manhood, however, was attained around the age of 33, after about fifteen years of military service. It was at this point that the man could marry and undertake the responsibilities of a wife and children.

Strict discipline in childhood transformed a boy from around the age of 18 onwards into a man who was 'a cunning and daring opponent, a keen logician and consummate diplomatist', 'a man of repute' and 'an intelligent being'. Even Baden-Powell (1896), who spent some years in South Africa at the end of the nineteenth century, could not help but admire the physical beauty of Zulu warriors:

> ... the men themselves looked so splendid. They were as a rule fine, strong, muscular fellows with cheery, handsome faces of a rich bronze colour, and very smartly decked out with feathers and furs and cows' tails. Both the sight and the sound were intensely impressive.

Zulu men were assertive and aggressively individualistic. Their masculinity was expressed in militarism.

Zulu society was highly hierarchical and men enjoyed positions of power from the home and into the wider society. Maleness was superior; hence, men were served first and exclusively at all meals before women and children. Within the male group existed varieties of masculinities along age lines, although it should also be assumed that there was no uniform expression of masculinity within any given age category. But the preferred masculinity, by Zulu standards, combined martial prowess with honesty; high morality, as shown in the absence of pre-marital penetrative sexual interaction with a female subject even though intimate encounters were allowed; loyalty; aggression; a sense of responsibility; courage; self-reliance; athleticism; alertness; endurance; and absence of emotions (Bryant 1949; Roberts 1974).

Penetrative sexual encounters of any kind before marriage were unmasculine acts. It was inappropriate behaviour to prove one's masculinity through sexual conquest. A Zulu masculine subject must not deflower a girl: where he did, it brought public shame as well as severe repercussions to him and his family. The act was punished by the confiscation of his father's cattle, his own disinheritance, banishment or even death (Roberts 1974).

Zulu masculinity had a domestic side. The foundation was laid in childhood as boys were taught to clean the home and cook meals for their fathers. Before the age of 30, the purpose of their domestic lessons would have become obvious: they enabled the young warrior to face the rigours of military life. Masculine domesticity was for moments when the individual was alone and with no female subject nearby. It was therefore for personal survival. Much of one's youth and the early stages of adulthood were expended in military campaigns. Towards middle age, the male subject leaves the military to start a family and to begin to exercise authority over his family members. A father must prove his ability to control. Roberts (1974) and Binns (1975) described Zulu fathers as despotic rulers of their households whose orders must be implicitly obeyed. It was their responsibility to produce strong, healthy, disciplined and civilized male offspring to replace them and to serve the land.

Notions of masculinity enhance and accord privileges to one gender group, but do the opposite for the other. Used in reference to Zulu women, masculinity assumed a negative connotation as something inferior and unbecoming. For being 'extremely purposeful', 'self-willed and sharp-tongued', Nandi, the mother of Shaka, in pre-colonial Zululand was branded 'a masculine and savage woman', qualities that attracted much resentment towards her from men and women alike and also led to her estrangement from Shaka's father (Roberts 1974: 34). It was all right to be savage in pre-colonial and colonial Zululand if one was a man, but certainly not if a woman! Here is evidence that the lopsided preference that social constructions of masculinity in pre-colonial and early colonial patriarchal societies brought favoured status to males, but when applied to females brought disfavour.

The impacts of colonialism on African masculinities are seen in Shire's (1994) childhood recollections of colonial Shona society. The Shona are the original inhabitants of former Southern Rhodesia, now Zimbabwe. Shona society was gendered, with men and women having defined spaces that rarely overlapped. Both held positions, hence power relations were in a neatly single-sex hierarchical structure (Shire 1994: 149). Pre-colonial Shona masculinity was determined by an ability to 'perform', actually to manifest verbal skills. A young boy who could 'perform' by speaking convincingly and winning arguments was a man, while an older male person lacking verbal skills was a child and was often excluded in male gatherings.

Colonial experience compelled Shona men to internalize a masculinity intended to transform and place them in a subordinate position in relation to the colonial officers. British patriarchal masculinity, spread through the vehicle of colonial discourses, was projected by warfare and phallocentrism. These became part of Shona social reality during colonial occupation and led to concepts of masculinities that depended on weapon-centred notions, provoking a tendency to look to militant societies like the Zulu as models. Colonial legislation further eroded the bases of Shona masculinities, leading individual males to construct new identities that revolved around foreign ideas that promoted martial qualities. Shona traditional masculine ideals were undermined at the same time that the masculinities of the colonial class were upgraded. These 'new' masculinities became the bases for determining the real man. Shire recalls how resistance to colonial domination contributed to the emergence of multiple and changing masculinities, the dominant one manifested in male domination (Shire 1994: 150).

Colonial wage labour in particular had its own impact on the confused masculinities of Shona youth. As young Shona men left the rural (African) areas for the urban (European) areas in search of employment, they disengaged from their elders and the influence they exerted, and imbibed new masculine images and traits that predominated in the urban areas, features of which differed from what existed in the rural areas. Rural–urban migration, which commenced in

1931 after the division of the colony into African areas and European areas (Weinrich 1971: 4), undermined Shona masculine values. Being colonial subjects, Shona men lacked autonomy over the type of work they did. Thus, some had very limited options and worked in such capacities as domestics to colonial officers, a feminine task they would not perform in the rural areas (Shire 1994: 152) because of the predominance of indigenous practices. Meanwhile, the women left behind in the villages became more assertive through keeping the home front and doing things that men would have done and, gradually, women's deference to male authority diminished. In the long run, male control in the home lost its potency just as it did in the wider society where the colonial administrators took over the public political space and initiated a political structure intended, according to official colonial report, to 'break indigenous methods of control' and 'to make Africans directly dependent on European administrators' (Weinrich 1971: 11). The dwindling masculine control in the family apparently triggered gender clashes in attempts to re-establish it. In the long run, a medley of masculinities, fashioned from many conflicting models, occurred among urban Shona men and submerged their original masculinities.

Africa is not completely patriarchal and all lineages are not patrilineages. Patrilineal systems differ in detail but with a good deal in common all over the world. Of matrilineal groups, even within Africa, there are wide differences. The basic rule is that descent and inheritance claims are transmitted through women (Mair 1974: 67). Africa has no definitive evidence of a fully matriarchal society outside what exists in myths like the popular Kikuyu legend, which told of a time 'when women … ruled the country for many generations … [until] deposed from power by men …' (Kenyatta 1942: 7). However, Africa has significant areas that are matrilineal, particularly in Central and East Africa, with other matrilineal groups in North Africa (in Algeria) and West Africa (in Ghana and Nigeria).

In Africa's twentieth-century matrilineal societies, almost all important offices were held by men but because women in such groups determined the group affiliation of their children and were of great formal significance in establishing a man's rights (he claimed political office through his mother), women commonly attained a freedom of action and a degree of public significance that was difficult for them to acquire in patrilineal kin groups (Kenyatta 1942; Mair 1974; Roberts 1976; *Encyclopaedia Britannica* 2003: 804). Women's enhanced social status as the determinant of the group affiliation of their male relations had implications for masculine expression in Africa's matrilineal societies, including Muslim matrilineal communities like the Tuareg (singular Targui).

Between 1948 and 1968, the Tuareg nomads of Algeria lived in tents and mobile camps in the desert. They had no villages or towns but their principal centre was Tamanrasset. Male Tuareg have intrigued observers for their supposedly misleading 'feminine' exterior. They painted their eyes and were veiled instead of female Tuareg, quite unlike other Muslim groups where women were veiled. The culture of hiding the male face began at puberty and continued till death, with very few laws of exemption. Thus, whether eating or drinking, riding or sleeping, alone or accompanied, the face was covered with the exception of the eyes. Where at all it should be revealed, just part of the nose was shown (Keenan 1977: 128).

Wearing a veil at puberty for the first time called for family celebration to mark the adolescent's initiation into adulthood. The veil was an expression of Tuareg masculinity and group identity. It seems to hold more secrets of the Tuareg society's notions and expressions of masculinity than other symbols and behavioural traits. Without doubt, veiling by male Tuareg had no association with any form of gender inferiority nor was it used to show allegiance to women by whom power is passed to men. The veil obviously helped to conceal emotions and had the effect of lending anonymity to male Tuareg. While outside the group, the veil projects an aloofness and inherent superiority over other people (Keenan 1977: 137), its use would suggest a subtle and subdued masculinity within the group where little aggressiveness was shown. But, outside the group, it did not prevent manifestations of generally recognized masculine qualities. For example, prior to the colonization of Algeria in 1948, a colonization that for many years had little impact on desert-Tuareg nomads, male Tuareg were famed as 'head-strong warriors, camel raiders and slave traders' (Gunther 1955: 133). From these words we can extrapolate the following masculine traits: determination, aggressiveness, domination, fearlessness, martial prowess and violence.

The matrilineal Tuareg were no less masculine than their patrilineal Zulu counterparts. But, unlike the Zulu, they showed some degree of deference to women. They would not smoke, eat or receive money in front of women for reasons not quite clearly stated other than it being inconsistent with their masculine identity to do such things before women. Male Tuareg were public figures who dominated communal politics although deriving their power to control from their female relatives (Keenan 1977: 134–5). While, unlike a good many other matrilineal societies such as the Ashanti of Ghana, women were sidelined from the power source because of menstrual taboos forbidding contact with sacred objects, the Tuareg recall a famous queen who once ruled a sub-group of them. But there was not more than this one reference to such an occurrence. Tuareg women owned slaves and livestock in their own right and were prominent in social life, leading Murdock to conclude that Algerian Tuareg society was a matriarchy (Murdock 1959: 408; Keenan 1977: 107). Yet, power was structured among male Tuareg and along class lines. Male nobles controlled the vassals, male and female, and other members of the group.

Tuareg sexuality was for the most part heterosexual in its expression. (They were also monogamous, quite unlike Muslim societies of their day.) Their sexuality was not ascribed by their religious culture. Men married late as a rule and there was no regulation for abstinence when unmarried. Also, during the time under investigation, Tuareg girls were among the few women in the Islamic world free to express their sexuality before marriage. Keenan (1977: 107) and Gunther (1955: 134) observed that females were allowed to flirt and did so unreservedly. However, female nobles enjoyed greater immunity from sexual exploitation than vassals. Tuareg males had physical appeal. They were portrayed to be majestic, tall, with a splendid bearing and proud (Gunther 1955). Make-up, especially the use of eye paint to ring the lids, was part of Tuareg masculine dressing just as a tattoo was an indispensable feature for women. The masculinity of the noble class was shown in a relative life of leisure. Nobles did not work, work being solely the responsibility of vassals. Success was not determined by wealth, for the Tuareg were not wealthy by modern standards and their frugal lifestyle is an indication of the absence of materialistic preoccupation. Mair (1974: 67) observes that one rarely finds matrilineal groups where there is any kind of significant property to inherit. Although it is dangerous to apply this across the board, the story of the Tuareg and other colonial matrilineal societies seem to lend some credence to it. Tuareg masculinity does not fit perfectly into the popular mould. It combines contradictory features and, with respect to its expressions towards women, lacks a rigid hegemonic quality, perhaps out of deference to the women for their privilege in determining men's social and political positions.

Tuareg male vassals constitute another and different masculine category within the larger Tuareg society. Theirs was a reticent and dependent masculinity. Isolated 'naturally' as it were, from political and social privileges, they were men but without the cultural backing to manifest most conventional Tuareg masculine qualities. They were servants to the noble class of whom control over vassals was of utmost importance (Keenan 1977: 32). Even the vassal headman had little or no judicial, political or military authority over his descent group. He was merely a representative of a noble king for whom he collected taxes and tributes. In spite of the reticent nature of Tuareg male vassals' masculinity, they nonetheless exercised some control over their women at the family level. In relation to Tuareg female vassals, male vassals had political advantage, but in relation to nobles and to other vassals as a group, they exhibited a reticent masculinity.

The repressed and dependent masculinity of the Tuareg male vassals was somewhat replicated by Lele males found on the edge of the equatorial rain forest in Zaire, now the Democratic Republic of the Congo, before 1970. However, there were very clear differences in male subjects' expressions of masculinity between these two matrilineal groups. Young Lele men prior to marriage served as servants to their elders, both their father's and mother's brothers; and remained dependent on their mothers for their wellbeing. Lacking in personal independence and assertiveness, owing to a gender structure that disfavoured them, life was one of discomfort and hardship for these men (Mair 1974: 70).

When they eventually married, it was first a joint affair in which an age group of ten to twelve men were jointly committed to one wife. In other words, polyandry was the norm. In such arrangements, the woman was the privileged personality in the relationship. She controlled her group of husbands and regulated sexual interaction among them to her advantage. Meanwhile, she did no domestic or any other type of work for her husbands who, on the other hand, were obliged to serve her parents as sons-in-law, to please her in order to remain married to her and to give her gifts that went to her marriage payment. Moreover, men left their communities at marriage to join their wives' communities. Children born by a woman when married by a group of husbands belonged to none of the prospective fathers but to the wife's village. Control by a father over the children and their mother was almost non-existent at this time. Lele men were constrained to prove their masculinity through service to parents-in-law and the wife's community. Virility was shown by sexual conquests of other men's wives.

When a woman was ready to settle down to raise a family, she selected four or five of her husbands to live with; this number eventually diminishes to three. It was for this small crop of husbands that she performed traditional wifely duties (Mair 1974: 72). From this time onwards, husband domination began. Prior to this time, authority over a female subject resided with whoever had the right to give her in marriage, namely the father. But, besides that, he had little control over the daughter who belonged not to his own lineage but to her mother's. Lele community was organized with the oldest man at the helm but there was a total lack of coercive power at the communal level. The system of polyandry was legislated against by the colonial authority and it eventually withered away. Moreover, with the growing popularity of Christian ethics, most Lele men disengaged from traditional matrilineal practices, favouring Christian patriarchal tendencies.

There was more than one way of being a man and more than one type of masculinity. In all the societies discussed, men in patriarchal settings were irrefutably the favoured class: an esteemed group that grew from childhood to manhood culturally imbued with notions that made them believe they were superior and had multiple privileges, including inherent rights to dominate. Where matrilinealism diffused such masculine confidence, colonialism, which was uniformly patriarchal in its verbal and non-verbal expressions and social exportations in the continent, undermined non-patriarchal hegemonic masculinities. Other factors, however, strengthened the colonial impact. In answer to the question: 'Are African males men?' we have enough data from the foregoing to arrive at our individual conclusions. This collection has a goal of celebrating Africa's diversities as well as its unity through critical examinations of various shades and ramifications of Africa's masculinities and what these portend for the peoples of Africa and gender relations on the continent.

Contemporary Masculinities

So much has changed regarding notions and expressions of masculinities in Africa since ancient times. Many aspects of modern masculinities were fashioned during the colonial period and after. Different aspects of contemporary African masculinities are addressed by each of the contributors to this volume. Although it has been the preoccupation of scholars, male and female alike, to study men; such an academic exercise requires a new tilt. What is needed, argues Ratele in this volume, is a critical study of masculine subjects. This new dimension to African gender scholarship will interrogate issues about men and dominance much more directly than mainstream gender studies approached from a feminist perspective have done. Masculinities scholars are engaged in gender scholarship. They must be familiar with feminist theories in, and place of an implicit focus, should accord specific attention to men and masculinities, showing recognition of men and masculinities as social and cultural productions that differ within contexts, nations and continents. In this lies the departure from non-critical studies of men often conducted by non-gender-conscious men who see their works as a response to the establishment of feminist thought and women's liberation, with the aim of giving men something similar to what women's studies have given women. Un-critical studies of men globally are more popular and tend to restore traditional values of womanhood; hence, Ratele's call for critical studies of men, especially in Africa where masculinities studies are at an early stage.

Kabaji's discussion of the bullfighting ceremony among the Luhyia, Kenya, provides an appreciation of how masculine images are portrayed in mundane activities, including games. The language of the game embeds masculine desires and aspirations of the Luhyia. It is used to prove the degree to which an adult male has achieved the masculine ideal. The phallus is celebrated in this game as an estimable symbol of masculinity. Male fascination with sex and the predilection to violence were themes projected through the medium of the bullfight. Sexual identity and expression are integral in understanding masculinity in this society. Still on the theme of male sexuality, Onyango concentrates on rape as a weapon of masculine domination also in Kenya. Griffin (in Herman 1984: 20) equates rape to a kind of terrorism that severely limits the freedom of women, making them dependent on men. In Kenya, as Onyango demonstrates, rape against women is rooted in societal ideological and power structures related to hegemonic masculinities and which supports men's sexual aggression against women. Ideologies of masculine sexuality appear so pervading that all categories of men, including law enforcement officers, fathers, brothers, teachers, top government officials and so on, are implicated in rape crimes. Here, too, as in Kabaji's study, language is used to construct images of male sexual domination as one form of overall domination of women. Onyango uses newspaper reports to illustrate how language serves as a tool for perpetuating rape violence, while embedding practices of domination and discrimination simultaneously. Domination is a masculine quality that transcends social boundaries and which is institutionalized in patriarchal societies.

Drawing from various authorities, Dialmy outlines some observations on Moroccan male subjects' masculinities, which in some ways and given the dominant Islamic religious culture, is symptomatic of much of North Africa. He discusses the goals of religious and sexual socialization in Morocco, which include: the avoidance of every manifestation of femininity; constructing an image of the male as powerful to prepare him for the public space; and esteeming phallic virility, aggressiveness and competitiveness. Religious socialization in particular contributes to a construction of gender relations where masculinity is socially privileged and where heterosexuality is projected. Homosexuality has long been a common practice in North Africa (Gunther 1955; Mernissi 1996) and is predicated in religious socialization. The absence of social contacts and close and intimate interactions with young girls of one's milieu prior to marriage predisposes male youths to homosexual practices, if they do not seek sexual outlet with prostitutes. Dialmy provides insight into the effect of legal changes in favour of female public visibility on Moroccan masculinities. But, in contrast to these developments, religious fundamentalism seeks to maintain traditional masculine privileges in the name of the sacred.

Masculine ideologies are learned by male human beings beginning from childhood. This is the argument of Koudolo, who identifies the family, mass and audio-visual media, religion, education and interpersonal interactions as among the factors that contribute to the development of any particular brand of masculinity in a Togolese male subject. Koudolo discusses how these factors oscillate between tradition and modernity to produce masculine stereotypes, sometimes combining indigenous and foreign models. Examining the socialization process for Togolese male subjects, she exposes the dynamics in the formation of culturally appropriate masculine qualities.

Kelly's study of white South African youths shows how similar their ideas on their masculinities are to those of black South Africans, even while these are expressed differently. Like Ratele, Kelly considers it very necessary that African scholars study white masculinities along with black masculinities because of the many versions that are embedded in the former. Importantly, white masculinities entrenched white male privileges by projecting the exclusion of African masculinities. Colonialism, she notes, played a crucial role in entrenching white male privilege in South Africa. But colonialism was not the sole factor. Along with it went racism, by which such hereditary characteristics as skin colour became the distinguishing factor for assessing and categorizing 'superior' as well as 'inferior' masculinities. Consequently, the dismantling of Apartheid has, to some extent, removed boundaries separating white and black segments of the society and subsequently gave rise to white male population's reconsiderations of their privileges, but the new versions of white masculinities that seem to emerge in post-apartheid South Africa somehow continue to project the supremacy of white masculinities over black masculinities. Kelly's study informs us how historical experiences determine social experiences. In this case, the ideologies backing certain types of masculinities were punctured because of their irrelevance in a specific era.

Political masculinity that projects public patriarchy is the thrust of Mouiche's paper. Mouiche tells us how, and on what bases, the African state is masculine and incorporates gender disequilibrium. The evolution of the African political milieu and associated rights were fundamentally influenced by colonialism, which left it considerably masculinized and appropriated as a male sphere. Mouiche demonstrates how colonial power, which was highly repressive, was responsible for entrenching post-colonial political masculinity. Under colonialism, the administrative, military and other personnel were male. This meant that the colonial authorities banned perspectives that were open to women in certain regions to escape masculine domination. Colonial patriarchal ideologies in association with indigenous patriarchal ideologies reinforced subordination, exploitation and oppression of women. In post-colonial Africa, political masculinity consists of a quantitative dimension, comprising an inflated male domination at the highest state positions, and a qualitative dimension, referring to the nature of political power manifested, namely, violence, authoritarianism, war, personalization of power and so on. Often, politics is confused with war, and the war imperative makes it more of a male institution. Mouiche's study further shows how women, through apathy and other self-defeating factors, contributed to the institutionalization of post-independence political sexism in Africa.

Lastly, Chiuri's paper exposes masculine irresponsibility in rural Kenya, which contributes to persistent poverty. Chiuri's thesis – that rural Kenyan males' lack of accountability, influenced by a hegemonic masculine ideology, is responsible for gross poverty in rural Kenya – can be applied to many countries in Africa with a predominantly agricultural economy. Africa is the one continent where, despite all attempts, there is as yet no improvement in the level of poverty crippling individual countries. From Chiuri, we understand that one factor for Africa's deep-seated poverty is masculine inefficiency: men's failure to efficiently use their time and invest their labour along with women. Using gender daily calendars from participatory rural appraisals and other tools, Chiuri argues that if rural men would invest eight hours daily on productive farm labour, one of the forms of poorly paid unskilled work, Africa would break out of the scourge of poverty. In effect, Africa can generate wealth in place of poverty when individual countries emphasize masculine productivity, and not depend solely on women who historically are acknowledged as supplying the bulk of the labour in the subsistence sector.

These papers individually contribute to the construction of masculinities while demonstrating commonalities that show their interconnectedness. Embedded in the discussions are issues requiring further and broader-based investigations if we are to understand, as much as possible, African men and their masculinities along with the impact of the latter on the continent.

References

Anselmi, D. L. and Law, A. L., eds., 1998, *Questions of Gender: Perspectives and Paradoxes*, New York: McGraw Hill.

Baden-Powell, R., 1896, *Lessons from the Varsity of Life*, Montana: Stevens Publishing.

Binns, C. T., 1975, *The Warrior People*, London: Robert Hale.

Bryant, A. T., 1949, *The Zulu People*, Pietermaritzburg: Shuter and Shooter.

Cornwall, A. and Lindisfarne, N., 1994, 'Dislocating Masculinity: Gender, Power and Anthropology', in A. Cornwall and N. Lindisfarne, eds., *Dislocating Masculinity: Comparative Ethnographies*, London: Routledge.

Davidson, B., 1968, *Black Mother*, London: Victor Gollancz.

Encyclopaedia Britannica, 2003, London: Encyclopaedia Britannica.

Gunther, J., 1955, *Inside Africa*, London: Hamish Hamilton.

Herman, D., 1984, 'The Rape Culture', in J. Freeman, ed., *Women: A Feminist Perspective*, 3rd edn, Mountain View: Mayfield Publishing Company.

Hutchinson, T., J., 1966, *Narrative of the Niger, Tshadda, and Binue Exploration*, London: Frank Cass.

Hyman, R., 1993, *Britain's Imperial Century, 1815–1914*, London: Macmillan.

Keenan, J., 1977, *The Tuareg*, Harmondsworth: Penguin Books.

Kenyatta, J., 1942, *My People of Kikuyu*, Nairobi: Oxford University Press.

Mair, L., 1974, *African Societies*, London: Cambridge University Press.

Matthews, S. W., 1973, 'This Changing Earth', *National Geographic Magazine*, January.

McFarlan, D. M., 1946, *Calabar*, London: Thomas Nelson & Sons.

Mernissi, F., 1996, *Islam and Democracy: Fear of the Modern World*. London: Virago Books.

Middleton, J. and Kershaw, G., 1972, *The Kikuyu and Kamba of Kenya*. London: International African Institute.

Murdock, G. P., 1959, *Africa: Its People and their Culture History*, New York: McGraw Hill.

Obenga, T., 2004, *African Philosophy: The Pharaonic Period, 2780–330 BC*. Popenguine: Per Ankh.

Roberts, A., 1976, *A History of Zambia*, London: Heinemann.

Roberts, B., 1974, *The Zulu Kings*, London: Hamish Hamilton.

Shillington, K., 1995, *History of Africa*, New York: St Martin's Press.

Shire, C., 1994, 'Men Don't Go to the Moon: Language, Space and Masculinities in Zimbabwe', in A. Cornwall and N. Lindisfarne, eds., *Dislocating Masculinity: Comparative Ethnographies*, London: Routledge.

The New Shorter Oxford English Dictionary, 1993, Vols 1 and 2, Oxford: Clarendon Press.

Stuart, J., 1903, *Boyhood Among the Zulus* [pamphlet].

Weinrich, A. K. H., 1971, *Chiefs and Councils in Rhodesia*, Nairobi: Heinemann.

Whitehead, S. M., 2003, *Men and Masculinities: Key Themes and New Directions*, Malden, MA: Blackwell Publishers.

Wilson-Haffenden, J. R., 1967, *The Red Men of Nigeria*, London: Frank Cass.

2

Studying Men in Africa Critically

Kopano Ratele

How vital is it to study men? My purpose in this study is to show that it is as essential to investigate a Mopedi or Sudanese man (as instances) as one of the Bapedi ethnic group or the Sudanese nation as it is to look at them as *men* of the Bapedi and *men* in Sudan. It is equally important to study a man as a part of the group called men as is to study them as ethnic or national subjects.

Then again, perhaps one ought to pose the question directly: whether there is anything of consequence that gets lost from studying men *indirectly*. I mean by this, whether there is something of significance we miss if we adopt a lens that, for instance, places *women* at the centre in studying men, as feminist studies have done for long. I shall maintain that we do indeed tend to mis-appreciate some of the true forms and functions of psychic structures, the world of labour and capital, cultural forms and political landscape if we do not examine closely the deployment of masculinity in the structuring of psyches, in employment and money-making, in culture and politics.

It is important to stress that what I suspect is an ever-present possibility of mis-appreciation, not malevolence; I see the project of studying men as related to and supportive of radical gender transformation, at least in Africa. For anyone concerned with injustice around the world, a study of men cannot be underlined by the project of subverting male power, of reworking hegemonic masculinities and gendered superiority. In such a world as we have, authenticating manhood or finding the lost key to being a true male cannot be the driving purpose of our investigation of masculinity. Even as I seek to show the gain of investigating men as subject to gender power as much as they are of ethnic or linguistic power, race or national ideology, culture or class, I am at once going to allow myself to wonder whether it is best to do so by putting our energies towards building a discipline around a men's discipline that will be the dedicated vehicle for this task, or whether it will suffice to examine men as a unit of analysis, infusing masculinity within, for example, social and developmental psychology, economics, cultural studies, politics.

In this chapter, I draw a simple sketch, depicting researches and other interventions on men and their development around the continent. My intention is to work from this towards showing reasons that support further efforts to study men in Africa. Finally, I indicate what form I believe such studies ought to take and why.

I will begin by making a distinction of some import around orientation towards men. I then present and analyse a case of a letter to a newspaper. The letter is used to ground subsequent arguments about the form and contexts of our approaches in investigating men: approaches which, for the sake of argument, are here distinguished into two broad lines. I then go on to show that what the letter-writer (and indirectly, in his reception to the letter, the newspaper's editor) is intent on is buttressing or recuperating a particular form of masculinity, an *instance* of masculinity as this form of masculinity must not be regarded as the only masculinity in town, even though the masculinity being argued for by the letter is indeed the main masculinity. The point made in this section is that not to pay attention to insignificant matters within the idea of masculinity and a man contained in that letter is to continue in the direction of a massive submerged iceberg in the dark. The struggles for a just gender order requires pointing out why some work around men and boys needs to be viewed and brought even closer together rather than parallel to or away from struggles for women's liberation around the world, around the continent, and in local settings.

An Upsurge of Research

At the start one ought to take note of the fact that as a disciplinary formation, what I shall for my purposes call men's studies or critical studies of men, is non-existent on the continent. Nevertheless, it needs pointing out that there has in recent times been an upsurge of empirical studies, courses, conferences, symposia and institutes about men and masculinities. With this is meant that while critical studies of men or men's studies as a coherent body of knowledge, and activities constituted by practitioners, journals, dedicated professional associations or divisions within associations, departments or programmes, and students or a combination of these constituents does not exist, there are some students and teachers, there are departments of gender studies or others who offer modules or parts of modules on masculinities, and special editions of journals and books on the topic have been published (see *Agenda* 1998; *Journal of Southern African Studies* 1998; Dunbar Moodie with Ndatshe 1994; Luyt and Foster 2001; Morrell 2001; Reid and Walker 2004; Ouzgane and Morrell 2005).

On the other hand, there is great unevenness in the development of thinking, research and teaching about men's practices and lives from one country to another. Some countries exhibit certain of these aspects of disciplinary establishment while others still have to make a start. In general, however, developments around studies of men in Africa are still, in comparison to developments in Australia, parts of Europe and North America, at an early stage.

From Sympathy to Critical Engagement with Men

In any talk of studying men, there is a crucial differentiation to be made. This I have already suggested above in reference to men's studies *or* critical studies of men *or* masculinities. These names actually bear different meanings. And herein lies the beam on which male agony, or male leadership or other skills, or male ways of doing things, or any possible discussion of aspects of males' lives is balanced; it is a beam that separates groups of observers of male behaviour from each other.

One group of observers looks at male behaviour and says, for example, events and phenomena such as the Industrial Revolution, anti-colonial wars and the emancipation of women have caused grief and confusion in men's lives. These material and psychosocial assaults have 'stiffed' males. Boy-children, young males who would be husbands, fathers and men on the shop floor, most of us are confused if not terrified about the changes these historic events have brought into our lives. For a long time, but much more so in the last few decades, there are very few individual males who are still certain about what their roles and place in society are. Only a handful of males can say with confidence who they are and what they can and cannot do in their relations to women, children and other males. The result of this has been confusion, even a loss of true manhood. This lost masculinity, this puzzlement about what men really are, which tends to erupt in different forms of negative acts, is what needs diagnosing and fixing.

War has its less enjoyable sides, and Africa has not had a great time in symbolic and physical wars waged on its people by European imperialists, home-grown dictators, army generals and capitalists. This is what the second broad group of observers might say. In war people lose their lives, actually or psychologically. It is true then that individuals and groups of males might and do experience suffering from wars as from the vagaries of capital, the residues of imperial domination, racism and ethnocentrism. However, on the whole, it tends to be males who wage war on other males and everybody else; it is men who hold social and political power in most societies. Indeed, there have been no female dictators or coup leaders in Africa. Hence, this second group of thinkers would argue, forms of masculinity and gendered social and political relations that encourage war are what need engaging with and transforming.

There is another reason why we need to mark out men's studies from the critical variety of studies of men and masculinities. That reason is that there has in fact been much debate about what to call this field that studies men. Some writers opt for men's studies while others think this is an unsuitable name (Hearn and Lattu 2002). The important distinction is therefore one of *orientation*. It is a distinction of groups of observers in terms of how they *perceive what men do*, whether they are naively sympathetic or just critical. A simple example might make this clear.

Say a teenage girl gets pregnant by an older married man who for one reason or another does not own up. The teenager begets a boy. Alone and as best as she can, she raises him. The boy grows up to be a strong man. At 40-something, now a happily married and successful businessman, he in turn gets a young woman pregnant. For reasons different from his unknown father's he also is unable to own up. How might different observers of men's practices understand this scenario?

The first group of observers would approach the 40-something man, and perhaps his father, as harbouring the pain that most men in post-colonial capitalist societies carry around with them. It is this male pain that makes older men chat up teenage females for sex. It is this hurt, which most men will recognize but rarely admit to, that leads them not to use condoms when they have casual sex. It is this unacknowledged and deep suffering that lies behind men not taking responsibility for their 'illegitimate' children. These observers therefore tend to look for reasons why an older man would like casual, condomless sex with a younger woman but not be too happy to play father were she to fall pregnant and say the pain is what post-colonialism and capitalism do to good men.

Another group of observers might say, look at that teenage mother who raised the boy who became the 40-something, happily married, successful businessman: she was the first to get a raw deal. They might say, let us examine the conditions that would force a teenage girl to want to have unprotected sex with an older man. They might say, these conditions are probably the same ones that allow older men to bend young women's will to having unprotected sex with them as well as manage to abandon their part in raising the offspring of this coupling, conditions that include laws, culture and economy. These observers might argue that there seems to be a power that the young females do not seem to have and the men do. They might also point out that this gender power, as other forms of power tend to be, is entwined in the example with age-power and perhaps money-power. Therefore, in this approach what are sought are the circumstances that render it possible for men to leave, and for women to be left carrying the baby.

Motivators, preachers, programme leaders, scholars and writers who work from a position we have referred to as men's studies, or perhaps more appropriately men's consciousness thought, tend to walk the first way outlined above. This group sees its work as analogous to and a response to the establishment of feminist thought and women's liberation, as the poet Robert Bly has averred. In the preface to his popular book *Iron John*, Bly said:

> I want to make clear that this book does not seek to turn men against women, nor to return men to the domineering mode that has led to repression of women and their values for centuries. The thought in this book does not constitute a challenge to the women's movement. The two movements are related to each other, but each moves on a separate timetable. *The grief in men has been increasing steadily* since the start of the Industrial Revolution and *the grief has reached a depth that cannot be ignored.* (1990: x, emphasis original)

Where Bly spoke of meek men who need to get iron into their bellies and psyches, someone like Théun Mares (1999), who follows Bly in using the myth of a lost or hidden key, perceives the problem of masculinity as one of a world gone haywire; of men and women not knowing their rightful places. In this world women act like men, and men, like the one in our example, have turned into juveniles who actually want but resent being mothered. That is where it all starts. The problem with society is that men are no longer true to their male stuff and that women reign.

> This is exactly what has happened in the world today. Because men have been acting helpless, the mother in females has taken over, and to such an extent that the world is being dominated by women who are becoming ever more aggressive, as men are becoming ever more weak and self-indulgent. (Mares 1999: 51)

The aim of men's consciousness thought is to give men something along the lines of what 'Women's Studies' gave to women: self-knowledge. Men's consciousness thought puts men at the centre, just like women's liberation struggle put women are the forefront.

For our purposes here, this is what might be named *sympathetic* men's studies. It ought to be admitted that talking this way about men and women does pull in the crowds. It seems that when one says the problem is boys need fathers, women need to submit to husbands to right the order of things, and males must stand like real men, there are more men and women who are going to be listening. More than the other sort of studies of men, sympathetic men's studies have been successful in spilling out of journal pages, symposia and lecture halls into popular knowledge, women and men's magazines, church gatherings and men's groups. Leading figures, though they may not work as scholars themselves, who are associable with men's consciousness thinking, or at least work from a view of men's anguish or a loss of true manhood as central to the enmeshed problematics of gendered relations and men's lives, include Bly, James Dobson, Théun Mares and Steve Biddulph. Many more books, articles and other media are produced from within a men's consciousness thought-influenced orientation than there are from what we have identified as the second strand of studying men.

This second course in studying men is followed by scholars who prefer to talk of *critical* studies of men and masculinities. Where the idea of men as under attack from gender stuff or confused about what they need to be or in pain from absent fathers has received considerable attention in the media, business boot-camps and government, the critical tendencies continue to battle against dominant forms of social, economic and political life. They also battle about showing that in spite of the apparent attack on straight men, the identity diffusion and the depression caused by being born male, men as a group still control society. Some of the writers in this area include the Australian Robert Connell, the Finland-based British scholar Jeff Hearn, the South African Robert Morrell and Michael Kimmel from the USA. These and other scholars working from this orientation are not likely to be discomfited by being referred to as feminist, and all of them will have little trouble with the label pro-feminist. As such, their body of work might also be filed under pro-feminist studies. Researchers in Critical Studies of Men tend to be familiar with feminist theory and research and get inspiration from, to use that old but more appropriate term, women's liberation struggles. Some of them tend to work side by side with feminist teachers in Gender Departments and Women's Studies Programmes.

What I want to do next is to give another example and analyse it to show one version of masculinity. In this way, I want to further animate the distinction I have made between the two streams in understanding men. This example also grounds my comments on why there has not been a great deal of development around studying men and masculinities in Africa, be it from sympathetic perspective or critical vantage point, as well as towards arguing why heroic efforts are necessary to develop this field in Africa.

Money for Your Winning Points

The *Daily Sun* of Friday 7 January 2005 carried a letter signed by Thembinkosi-ka-Mthwana, Dobsonville, Soweto. The name indicates a writer of Nguni ancestry. The tabloid at that time held the distinction of being the newest and the highest-selling South African newspaper. It remains the biggest seller. Ka-Mthwana's letter was entitled, 'What is happening to South Africa?', a rephrasing by one of the paper's editorial team of a line from the published letter.

The letter itself is printed with accompanying large white lettering on a red-box background, with the heading: 'This letter of the day wins R100. WELL DONE!' Then, in bold letters at the bottom of the letter, the editor writes: 'You certainly have raised some interesting points. What do other *Daily Sun* readers think? In the meantime, please accept R100 for the winning letter of the day.'

Here is the first reason why this letter is worth some of our time. For a letter to win a prize, however meagre, alerts us to the fact that this letter contains winning views about, in this case, manhood, the gender order and the general social structure in South Africa in 2005. For a poor man, or woman, in a post-apartheid neo-liberal country with a very high unemployment level to read that *this* letter has won a hundred rand could motivate him or her to see whether its winning formulations might be replicated, especially given that the editor is encouraging the escalation of its contents. For all who read this letter, whether they agree or not with its positions, it could also have crossed their mind that manhood, the gender order and South African social structure may or may not be in need of fixing as the editor appears to suggest, but the editor clearly thinks the readers of the *Daily Sun* may be interested to contemplate the subject.

Alternatively, in that letter is drawn a society that critical readers of the tabloid cannot but seek to challenge. However, it is of course possible that the editor may be drawing us out. Let us play along then. If we do, we are led to the second reason for the noteworthiness of the letter: what it says. Let us consider its views and assumptions about its objects. In other words, what views or penmanship won Ka-Mthwana that R100? In view of its brevity, 131 words in all, let me quote the letter in full.

> Oh my lawless country! Allow me to express my views on my beloved country, South Africa. This country is lawless. Other countries enforce their laws whether the community is for or against them. In other countries everything is in order. The community knows what one may or may not do. If you do something wrong, you will bear responsibility. Why is it not so in my country? Or is this democracy, the ruler of my beloved country, right or wrong?
>
> • Abortion is legalized.
>
> • Gay marriage is legalized.
>
> • Children are allowed to lay charges against their parents.
>
> • Men no longer rule over their families.

What is up with this beautiful country of mine? It is getting totally out of the hand of God? Please God, save South Africa.

One Man's Masculinity and Another's Pain

Evidence exists that there is more than just one letter-writer and possibly more than one editor who share the view that South Africa is a country in trouble. It is not uncommon to hear callers to radio and television talk-shows articulating feelings and thoughts congruent with those of the writer of the letter. Studies have also shown how democracy is something that still has to infect homes and hearts, that it needs to be made practical in daily existence and not simply a right on the Bill of Rights (see Abrahams, Jewkes and Laubsher 1999). You would therefore not be too far-off if you believed this is a society where the gender order has completely broken down. From this perspective, public and private life, families and cultures, are all in a mess. As Ka-Mthwana puts it, this putative disarray derives from the fact that unlike in other countries in South Africa, termination of pregnancy – specifically, of certain categories of pregnancies and before a certain time – is now permitted, same-sex marriage may soon become a reality (it is not yet law), abused children are encouraged by activists, schools and the police to report such abuse even if it is their fathers who abuse them, and 33 per cent of households, as at 2001, have females as heads and the source of the largest income in the home (Statistics South Africa 2002).

At this point, it becomes crucial to emphasize that the letter expresses *a specific form* of masculinity. What Ka-Mthwana is assuming to be how men are in South Africa is in fact *not* the only masculinity in that country. In fact, there are men who are pro-choice and believe that women have a right to their own bodies; males who have sex with other males and may want to marry each other; normal grown men who do not long to rule over a family, do not wish to reproduce, and believe that children have rights; there are men, as there are women, who do not believe in God but in Allah, Yahweh or Jah; and there are others who are atheist. Having said that, it is vital to recognize that a heterosexual patriarchal capitalist masculinity is the hegemonic form of masculinity in South Africa.

Contradictory to its presumption of a single masculinity, one cannot miss a sense of nostalgia in the letter for an era that is melting away when all men were powerful and straight. In other words, even while he posits one true masculinity there is melancholia in the man's words about a bygone putative era and place when the fact of one masculinity in town was incontestable. Psychoanalysis would speak about disavowal here, that the letter-writer holds two incompatible beliefs at the same time: one where men have always ruled over women, which would fit in with Ka-Mthwana's wish, and another, which fits in reality, where there are homosexual men and women have a right to their bodies.

In spite of all the worrying and contradictions in his letter, more of the house that male power built remains intact and very well looked after than Ka-Mthwana allows. By this I mean masculine domination has built a house, or if you will a world, which suits itself and which can perpetuate itself. This dominant masculinity that the letter highlights, in other words, is trussed to a certain architecture of society and the world. In this account of life between males and females and the world in which they interact, 'the male is the one who, firstly, provides the lead; secondly, points out the direction; thirdly, prescribes the method to be employed'

(Mares 1999: 58). From within this world, the letter-writer, (like the last author), tries to bring to our attention, and strings together, a number of related elements, central among which is a certain way to be a man and which if threatened will endanger the world itself. Both speakers claim true manhood is heteromasculinity, true manhood is revered, for it is only true men who can rule, and all of this is because true manhood is, the suggestion goes, decreed by a certain spirit; and hence, in this view, the social order is near collapse because a great gender and sexual upheaval is under way.

There is evidence of confusion, even pain and despair, in what Thembinkosi-ka-Mthwana is saying. This must not be derided out of hand. Reasons why some men in South Africa might be experiencing bewilderment, distress and despondency are not in short supply. Some of them are objective, others intra-individual. Similar social facts and personal pains that trouble males are evident in other parts of the continent and the world. With respect to the USA, in an interview by George Myers on why the story of Iron John found such fertile ground among contemporary North American men, Bly's answer was that it had to do with different kinds and moments of psychic abandonment that have impacted on male lives and identities that society did not take care to repair. He said, given this state of affairs, men had to get together with other men to repair to the wilds, as it were, learn to be their own fathers, and with the help of the old stories, find the key that would lead them from being boys to men:

> I was thinking this weekend, after doing a couple of days [speaking at a conference] for men out in Colorado, that men have had three abandonments. From the time after the Industrial Revolution, men have felt abandoned by their fathers and that abandonment is quite real. Then they are abandoned by their grandfathers, because their grandfathers have gone to Phoenix, or they're just plain gone and there's no one to tell the younger men stories, and so on. To some extent, men also have been abandoned by women. You can feel that men have depended on women to initiate them or help them in some way. So in a certain way, men have been abandoned by women in the last 34 years. I don't think that's a bad thing because the women have been doing a lot of caretaking – more than they ought to have been doing. Nevertheless, those three abandonments float around in the men's psyche and they're not quite recognized. So what all that really means is that, to move from boy to man, you're not going to get help from the father, you're not going to get it from your grandfather, and you're not going to get it from the women. Therefore, where do you get it? Well, you're going to have to get it from other men, but the knowledge is not stored in the other men. The knowledge is stored in the stories. Two things happen by getting at the knowledge in this way. We go back to the stories that have stood the test of time and, by getting together, men are

able to help themselves, to be each other's fathers and grandfathers. (Myers 1992)

Returning to South Africa, the last fifteen years have seen the country undergo tremendous political, economic and social changes. Surely, these shifts must have an impact on how males and females see themselves and each other. Surely, the fact that white masculine political power has been challenged by ideas of racial and gender democracy has implications on how white men see themselves, women and other men. Surely, the new constitutional order must mean that the old way of exercising power, the brute power that prevailed apartheid, needed to find a new subtle way of expressing itself. And surely, the Bill of Rights and other laws and policies that set out the principles of non-sexism, gender justice and equity challenge masculinities fundamentally. All this cannot be overlooked in reading Ka-Mthwana's letter and the newspaper approbation.

That is not all. Globalization has also had an equally confusing effect on social and economic relations, as well as specifically gendered life and masculinities; an effect that is at times felicitous but at others has been devastating. For example, the continuing changing fortunes of the South African currency and the rise of interest rates early in the new century have had untoward effect, especially on the poor. The country has seen a fall in employment in low-skill sectors, including mining and manufacturing, leaving many a man without a job. Where men derived their sense of worth and identity from earning a salary, paying for children to go to school and having women look after the house, the loss of employment and daily spectre of unmet needs would have a serious effect on these men's masculinity.

There is, however, a sense in which the sentiments in the letter, as much as Bly's and Mares's work, are as unsafe as going to a shebeen (a place of drinking in a township) carrying a homemade gun. If firearms are responsible for a lot of deaths in South Africa and so need to be regulated much more stringently, firearms clumsily made at home are just murder/suicide walking the streets, meaning they have a tendency to backfire or go off when simply being stroked. To carry such an unreliable weapon to an illegal drinking rendezvous makes it multiply unsafe. More than just the intended target might get hurt.

The relevance of this image to masculinity, gender and society is that you cannot go around with half-baked, ahistorical, dangerous ideas about men, women and children whose intention is simply to blame others (women, children, LGBTQI [lesbians, gays, bisexuals, transgendered, queers and intersexed]), for whatever pain or sense of powerlessness men are experiencing. Is this not like blaming women for being raped, children for being abused, queers etc. for being discriminated against?

However, about the social order being challenged, and of there being under way attempts to change the gender and sexual regimes, there is no disagreement. It is true that there is a change, at times stressful, occurring in South African society. Yet, in a country where there were tens of thousands of reported cases of rape each year for the last few years and a long history of persecution of gays and state-sanctioned disrespect of the 'rights of others', it cannot be women and girls and anyone else except heterosexual males who cause this distress. How can it be those who were legally historically oppressed (who still mostly informally continue to be marginalized) who are responsible for the disorientation experienced by 'once warrior heterosexual men'?

It is true that when one realizes that those who argue this position are indeed serious, one might get stumped. Yet, again, if it *is* true that straight males are experiencing uncertainty and pain for no longer being in power or being truly men because of local and global changes, why, I would ask, would their grief and confusion be more than that of others, more than of queers, the poor and women? Indeed, then, what this seems to suggest is that men as a group, alongside the poor, women and homosexuals, should engage the state to step up its effort of protecting and legitimating those who were not given protection and beyond the pale before the advent of new constitutional order, without denigrating the rights of heterosexual men.

Contrary to the letter-writer's claim, therefore, South Africa is not lawless because good men are under attack. Rather, whatever lawlessness is perceived or actually evident is because violence against women and children, for a long while at astronomical levels, was not regarded as a social problem but at best individualized. Having historically believed that respect is theirs by natural right and that they did not have to earn it, men are the group that has tended to resort to and escalate violence both against each other and against children, in addition to sexual violence to restore the 'law'. Social disorder is not a consequence of the fact that homosexuals can marry (this is not true, yet) or that women can now decide about their bodies with constitutional protection, and that only prayer can help bring gays and females under control, but rather that the practices of men and gender relations, despite changes in the legal and constitutional order, have generally refused to change that much. Whatever pain and confusion a man such as Ka-Mthwana may be experiencing then, there is an equal, if not more, of a case to be made for working for the transformation of masculinities and relations between African men and women.

The Gender Iceberg

Given the troubles Africa faces, such as the government-sponsored, ethnic-motivated destruction of Darfur, deepening poverty throughout the continent, the crisis that erupted in Togo and the mind-numbing rates of HIV/AIDS in Southern Africa, it is perhaps hard to think of much else than trying to deal with these problems. There seems to be little time to give thought to an insignificant, ranting, letter-writing man. However, to overlook the writing would be an error.

For one, I would argue that such ideas as contained in the letter inform the daily lives of some men and women and underpin this troubling picture of the continent. Such 'winning' assumptions about gender, masculinity and sexuality, and relations between adults and children as read in the newspaper are the submerged iceberg whose visible tip is of cultural and political intolerance, state violence, sponsored inter-ethnic hatred, widening inequalities and deepening poverty, different national crises around the continent and the rates of HIV/AIDS.

Women's and Men's Intersecting Struggles

Given the foregoing, it needs to be made known that there are many organizations and individuals in Africa whose work seeks to show that doing good towards children, females and homosexual citizens, and generally towards those on the margins of or outside society, is what a society should do. Some of these individuals and organizations have recently held dialogues on and been rewarded for showing the genderedness of different aspects of society, economics, politics and culture that would take up all the space given for this chapter. I should still like to mention a few:

1. A conference held at Fort Hare in July 2004, aimed at providing a range of stakeholders with an opportunity to exchange information on gender equality in health;

2. Two conferences, one on Gender and Visuality in August 2004, hosted by University of Western Cape History Department and Women & Gender Studies, and the other, Writing African Women, at the same university;

3. 2005 CODESRIA annual Gender Institute, with Masculinities as theme for the year;

4. The second Sexuality Leadership Development Fellowship, held by the Lagos-based African Regional Sexuality Resource Centre hosting fellows from Egypt, Kenya, South Africa and Nigeria on Sexuality and Masculinity, its chosen topic for the congress;

5. Perhaps there is no better signpost of the advances and encouragement for the continuance of gender equity and transformation work than the efforts of Wangari Maathai who was awarded the 2004 Nobel Peace Prize for leading the Green Belt Movement. The singularity of the award was not only for being given to the first African woman; it was also in highlighting the importance of seeing the interwoven nature of environmental concerns, peace and gender struggles. On receiving the prize, and after noting to Marika Griehsel on behalf of the Nobel Foundation website that it is not incidental to power and struggles around it that it is men who have power, Maathai also said:

I'm quite sure that, with this kind of a prize, a lot of prejudices against women are automatically removed. I can say without exaggeration that everybody in this country (Kenya), and I'm sure many people in Africa, are extremely happy and are associating themselves with the prize – both men and women. And I'm sure that, at such a time, men appreciate the role that women can play. I know that, for many men in this country, they're very proud. And they associate themselves with what the women have been doing. And this is something that I had already seen in the work that many men associate themselves with. So, I think that, at a certain level, when women are dealing too with real issues, and when those issues are recognized, that there is no longer the gender bias, and that both men and the women converge in their appreciation.

Side by side with these struggles around women's gendered lives, there has also been a build-up of work around men and boys. These efforts are focused on critiquing ideas such as those contained in the letter we have examined. More generally, these men's intellectual and material struggles have posed questions on the production of masculinities as well as working on how males can be mobilized into working towards *gender and sexual justice*, and not simply being warriors. For example, in 1997 scholars gathered in Durban, South Africa, to talk about masculinities. Since then there have been three other conferences on the same theme: one hosted by the Gender Education and Training Network, a non-governmental organization based in Cape Town, in 2003, another at Wits University in 2004 in Braamfontein, and the third at Western Cape University in 2005.

Along with these opportunities to share critical work around men, there has also been developing a body of research and programmes on masculinities. In a context where sexual and gender-based rights still raise the hackles of editors and letter-writers, it seems crucial to make note of these advances. Rather than merely pointing to them, of even greater import is to stress the importance of how work on masculinities cannot but show the centrality of gendered and sexual politics and practices.

But Why Men?

The last point brings us back to the question of why study men. I have suggested that the emergence of research, activist work and programmes around masculinities in some parts of Africa follows the trend around the world. From different areas, some of that attention has been focused on what has been called a crisis of masculinities. The nature of the crisis has not always been made clear, though. Some men's movements and scholars within men's consciousness thought have argued for restoring traditional values of manhood. Other scholars such as those in critical studies of men and masculinities have posited a different view. There are thus varying motivations for the engagement with men's genders. Nevertheless, there does appear to be some consensus that there is a problematic that has to do with being a man. And the problematization of manhood is visible in several spheres, from activism to the state and scholarship. In scholarship, the attention can be seen across many disciplines, from African studies to theology and history, and straddling concerns from the HIV/AIDS epidemic to sociological, psychological and historical themes.

Men, Situations and Flux

It is scholars within the broad tradition of critical studies who have noted (again, elaborating a point made by feminist epistemologists and methodologists) that masculinities and men have never been absent from academic writing, as they have not been from the centre of economy, culture and politics. Again, following feministic critiques, these scholars have pointed out that academics have traditionally had a habit of presenting the world from a male perspective. Male power has always been embedded in political hierarchies, social order and family structures, as they have been in intellectual work.

How the current interest is different from what men have been doing for a long time is in its focus on men *as a gender*, *'not-one'*, *situated* and *ever-changing*. In addition to differentiating between the sexes, one of the key insights from critical studies on men is that each gender is *internally* differentiated and unfixed. To get back to where we started and use an example: critical scholars of men's lives would say there is some value in investigating a man of the Bapedi ethnic group or one from Sudan as equally or firstly a *man*, as part of a group called men, which is distinguishable from women, just as it is to study Bapedi or Sudanese with the analytical lens of ethnicity or nationalism. Such scholarship would go on to say that a Bapedi man's manly practices are unlike say, a Sudanese man's gendered behaviours and ideologies. They would also maintain that in studying a Bapedi or Sudanese masculinity living in the twenty-first century, there is a good probability of soon finding out that such an object is different from what it was in the nineteenth century.

In summary then, critical studies on men and masculinities seek to distinguish themselves by putting a specific rather than an implicit focus on men and masculinities; taking into account feminist, gay and critical gender scholarship; showing recognition of men and masculinities as explicitly gendered; indicating an understanding of men and masculinities as socially produced; seeing men and masculinities as differing from context to context such as Europe to Africa, country to country, one period to another; stressing men's and masculinities' relations to gender power; by spanning both the material and the discursive in analyses; and interrogating the intersection of gender and other social divisions such as race, class and rural/urban in the making of men and masculinities (Kimmel, Hearn and Connell 2005: 3).

It may be that the horse has bolted the stable, but I think work around men and masculinities in Africa can be conducted quite comfortably in old disciplines such as law, anthropology, economics, politics and psychology and others like African Studies, business and management studies, and cultural studies; and in fact, that this is the preferred route to pursue. At best, I think owing to the tradition in which critical scholars of masculinities and men's lives position themselves, such work can, and ought to take its place alongside feminist or women and gender studies. While there may in the future arise debates about whether or not to have local or regional associations or departments, what one might say with confidence is that scholars and teachers around the continent who would study men can do little harm in their researches and classes by engaging in an approach that seeks to point out that it was not simply *African* people who were oppressed under colonial rule, but instead that it was Africans as *at the same time* subjects of *gender* and *sexual orders*; that there is a relation between African men and African women that fails to be fully comprehended if it is not *also* referred back to gender *power*; that African masculinities and men do not grow naturally from the ground, so to say, but are *produced in relationship* between people, and between individuals and structures; and that there are *differences* between men, over *time*, over *villages and national borders*, and because of their divergent desires, biographies and life developments.

What all of this simply seems to point to is that any analysis of political or economic disadvantage gains immeasurably from a focusing on sexual and gender practices/subjectivities of males, history, power and context. The advantage in politicizing and historicizing men's practices/subjectivities, in looking closely at the doing of masculinity, is realizing their tenuous hold on and struggles around the demands to be 'the' man. But it has been clear to anyone who is interested that, for example, there have always been rich old gay men who are in a different position from rich old heterosexual men, and violent straight white urbanites in contrast to pacifist bisexual Muslim villagers. The politics and psychologies of men's gender thus reveal the instability of masculinities, the idea of there being vital distinctions among men. In other words, when society is looked at through the view of men as transgendered, bisexual, straight or HIV-positive subjects, in addition to being poor/rich, African/American, it is enabled to understand that masculinity changes with circumstance, history and culture, that in fact one can only talk about several masculinities within a society. Politicizing masculinities offers society a way to see that, at any point in time, there is no single idea of how to be a man. Knowing that there are dominant masculinities, and alternative and subordinate ones, a challenge can then be mounted.

References

Abrahams, N., Jewkes, R. and Laubsher, R., 1999, '*I Do Not Believe in Democracy in the Home*': *Men's Relationships With and Abuse of Women*, Tygerberg: Medical Research Council.

Agenda, 1998, 'The New Men?', *Agenda,* No. 37.

Bank, L., 1999, 'Men with Cookers: Transformations in Migrant Culture, Domesticity and Identity in Duncan Village, East London', *Journal of Southern African Studies*, Vol. 25, No. 3, pp. 393–416.

Bly, R., 1990, *Iron John. A Book about Men*, Shaftesbury, Dorset: Element.

Dunbar Moodie, T. with Ndatshe, V. 1994, *Going for Gold: Men, Mines and Migration*, Berkeley: University of California Press.

Hearn, J. and Lattu, E., 2002, 'Gender, Men and Masculinities', *NORA: Nordic Journal of Women's Studies*, Vol. 10, No. 1, pp. 3–5.

Journal of Southern African Studies, 1998, Special Issue on Masculinities in Southern Africa, *Journal of Southern African Studies*, Vol. 24, No. 4.

Kimmel, M., Hearn, J. and Connell, R.W., 2005, *Handbook of Studies of Men and Masculinities*, London: Sage.

Luyt, R. and Foster, D., 2001, 'Hegemonic Masculine Conceptualisation in Gang Culture', *South African Journal of Psychology*, Vol. 31, No. 3, pp. 1–11.

Mares, T., 1999, *The Quest for Maleness: Avoiding Emasculation; Releasing the Powers of the True Male*. Cape Town: Lionheart.

Morrel, R., 2001, ed., *Changing Men in Southern Africa*, Durban: Zed/University of Natal Press.

Myers Jr, G., 1992, *"Iron John": An Interview with Robert Bly*', Literary Review, Vol. 35, No. 3 (available online on *Academic Search Premier Database*).

Ouzgane, L. and Morrell, R., 2005, eds., *African Masculinities: Men in Africa from the Late Nineteenth Century to the Present*, Scottsville: University of KwaZulu-Natal Press.

Reid, G. and Walker, L., eds., 2004, *Men Behaving Differently: South African Men Since 1994*, Cape Town: Double Storey.

Statistics South Africa, 2002, *Women and Men in South Africa: Five Years On*, Pretoria: Statistics South Africa.

3

Masculinity and Ritual Violence: A Study of Bullfighting among the Luhyia of Western Kenya

Egara Kabaji

Gender relations are constructed in terms of the relations of power and dominance that determine the opportunities and circumstances of both men and women. Nevertheless, gender research in Africa has tended to focus only on women. This skewed attention has given rise to the popular but fallacious attitude that gender issues are synonymous with women's issues. This study demonstrates a shift in focus and discusses the images and symbols of masculinity in bullfighting contests among the Luhyia of Western Kenya. It seeks to present a critical analysis of the game in order to uncover its overt and covert features that point to the hidden masculine desires, values, ideals and aspirations of the Luhyia. This study further directs inquiry into the construction of masculine metaphors that define standards of masculinity and maleness in the Luhyia society.

The Luhyia type of bullfighting is different from the kind of bullfighting exhibited in other parts of the world, especially in terms of its structure and form and the personae involved. In Spain, Portugal and Mexico, for example, protagonists in bullfighting are human beings and bulls. The Spanish version pairs off the bull and the matador, with the matador obliged to demonstrate his bravery in risky and daring acts. Luhyia bullfighting is a matter of an animal-to-animal fight. I argue here that the bulls are symbolic male proxies that outdo one another in a violent contest as the owners watch in self-fulfilling gratification.

Bullfighting contests are very popular among the Luhyia of Western Kenya. They are performed on Saturdays to the excitement of multitudes of spectators from within and outside the community. As early as five in the morning, spectators begin to pour into the village arenas and stadiums to participate in this popular game. Many Luhyia men breed prized bulls that they present during these contests. My respondents revealed that lack of a bull is a mark of extreme poverty and unmanliness only expected perhaps from men 'castrated' and feminized by the teachings of some Christian sects. In fact, it signals some degree of social and sexual redundancy (Beynon 2002: 79).

The bulls are nourished both physically and psychologically in preparation for the contests. Undue excitement and a sense of expectation grip the audience on these occasions. Traffic on the major roads leading to the venues of the contests is temporarily interrupted as the animals are led by their owners and fans dance to the venues. The celebration continues into the evening when a drinking spree ensues in specific homesteads, the famed drink being the locally brewed beer. Bullfighting contests are also staged on burial occasions of warriors to celebrate their lives.

This discussion is focused on bullfighting contests that are staged during weekends for pure entertainment. I examine bullfighting in terms of its structural and psychological significance within the Luhyia culture by first offering an empirical ethnographic description of the game and secondly by presenting a psychoanalytic reading of the game as a signifying cultural text I directly inquire into the salient features of the contests and the motives they seek to fulfil among the participants. Central to this study is the folklore generated and performed during bullfights and how this defines masculinity and gender relations in this society. I argue here that there are basic benchmarks within which the masculinities of its male members function. Failure to fall within these defined parameters makes one unmasculine. Through bullfighting, these masculine values are generated and disseminated to members of this society. The folklore produced is largely misogynistic and seems to suggest that being peaceable and uninterested in sexual conquest is a demonstration of unmasculine behaviour. Masculinity does not, however, exist except in contrast to femininity (Connell 2004). I therefore find it necessary also to direct inquiry into images of femininity. The Luhyia, through bullfighting rituals, set standards, a marking scheme of sorts, on which Luhyia men aspire to score highest. At the bottom of this structure is femininity and at the apex is ideal masculinity. In an attempt to reach these standards, men arrive at various degrees of masculinity, and this is what convinces me that even within a neat cultural entity it is safe and in order only to talk about masculinities. Bullfighting is therefore a male contest that tests the degree to which one has achieved the masculine ideal. This is appreciated through examination of symbolic frames of masculine qualities exhibited within the polarity of ideal masculinity and femininity. In this semiotic opposition of masculinity and femininity, the phallus appears to be the master signifier, and femininity is symbolically defined by lack of a phallus (Connell 2004). Though indulged in by adults, the bullfighting game is a psychological replay of childhood boys' contests. It offers nothing but imperatives dictated by male rivalry: the 'strongest' being the one who has the best 'hard-on', the longest, the biggest, the stiffest penis or even the one who pees the farthest (Irigaray 1995:1 21).

This cultural ritual game is characterized by violence, which is apparently a masculine virtue associated with the ideal masculine man. It manifests itself in two ways: physical and verbal. This public display of violence can best be understood in the Freudian perspective that sees cultural practices as a form of expressing what cannot be articulated in direct ways. Bullfighting as a cultural ritual game is partly a socially sanctioned outlet for the expression of taboo and anxiety-provoking behaviour (Dundes 1997). There are very many icons that disguise the seriousness of this theme. Luhyia men, for instance, sing the following song:

> Haa hooyi
>
> Haa hooyi
>
> Haa haa hoyo
>
> Sere Vuzwa
>
> *English*
>
> Haa hooyi
>
> Haa hooyi
>
> Haa hooyi
>
> It is just a game

In psychoanalytic term, disguising it as a harmless game makes it easy to explore anxieties without feeling a sense of guilt. We may say that through this game the community indulges in things otherwise proscribed in everyday life. Thus, bullfighting is a projection of what is actually within the minds of participants: their obsession with sex. The theoretical postulations in this inquiry pay attention to various frames of signification within the Luhyia cultural imperatives. The contest is visualized as a text. As a literary and cultural text, bullfighting is interrogated to reveal the micro-structures of power in the society and their intersection with ideology. The gendered structure of bullfighting and the misogynistic frames of masculine hegemony show a kind of violence approved and appropriated as manly in this society.

The primary data for this research was collected from Western Province of Kenya. This is the traditional Luhyia country. The data was collected through oral interviews, observation and participation in bullfighting.

Men, Their Bulls, Cows and Women

The intimate relationship between bulls and their male owners in Luhyia land is unmistakable. This is discernible not only in Luhyia idioms and proverbs, but also in all that the bull symbolizes. In reference to live earthly possessions, the Luhyia men use the word *Imirugo*, which includes cows, chickens wives and children as symbolizing one's wealth. But Luhyia men demonstrate a deep psychological identification with bulls, which define their sense of masculinity. Bulls are to a large extent symbolic of the men. It may be argued that among the Luhyia, bulls – like cocks in Balinese culture – are viewed as detachable, self-operating penises, ambulant genitals with a life of their own (Geertz 2002: 81).

As masculine symbols *par excellence*, the bulls provide the Luhyia language with raw materials for metaphoric postulations on the nature of life and how it should be lived. A man who is referred to as *Ijirichi* or a bull is perceived as virile, powerful, tough and a womanizer (a highly positive virtue). Some women will be heard boasting: *Ndavahira ku Ijirichi*, I am married to a bull. A man fondly referred to as a bull is not only feared but also revered. The Luhyia say one can only talk ill of such a man out of his earshot. Luhyia politicians vying for positions of leadership struggle to get the bull or any other masculine icon as their symbol. A politician recognized as a bull is accorded respect and is always given an opportunity to address people in any gathering he attends. A sick man on the verge of death will be told; 'a bull dies with grass in its mouth'. Through this statement, the sick man is asked to have sex with his wife even if he is sick in order to prove that sickness has not feminized him. If the men want to establish if the sick man will die, they ask his wife: 'does the bull ever taste porridge?' This is a euphemistic reference to sex. In this respect, masculinity is therefore a function of sexual activity.

The intimacy of the men with their cows and bulls is also visible in the bulls' feeding and grooming. A Luhyia man treats the bull as his pal and will spend time observing his animal eat. Even in modern times when land sizes are diminishing, most homes with less than an acre of land have at least a cow tethered in the homestead. Cows are a mark of wealth and affluence. A Luhyia marriage is made legal through payment of cattle in the form of dowry. Many of my respondents announced that they have no marriage certificate and that they do not need them because bridewealth in the form of cattle was paid, and this is a better certificate than writings on a piece of paper. Dowry negotiations centre on how many cows one should pay. In some Luhyia communities the number to be paid is already predetermined. Thirteen cows are prescribed for a virgin but a woman with a child out of wedlock or a divorcee will attract less. This requirement of virginity does not however apply to the men in equal measure. A man with a child out of wedlock is at best praised as a bull that 'started early'. Out of all the cattle paid for dowry, the most important is the last one. This has to be a bull. The bull presented as the last instalment of dowry is a symbolic prayer for the woman to produce male children who will one by one obtain bulls from their maternal uncles once they get circumcised.

There are instances when the bulls act as cleansers who fight dark forces of destruction. As noted earlier, bullfights are staged for two reasons: to celebrate the life of a hero and for entertainment. Although the focus in this study is on the entertainment aspect, it is important to note that bullfights are sometimes staged in a ceremony known as *eshiremba*, which marks the life of a warrior. It is held on the day of the burial of the warrior and is done within his compound. To be a hero worthy of the ritual of *eshiremba*, one must have fought in a war and killed a man in a war situation. It is important to define a man here. A man is a mature circumcised male. Killing an uncircumcised man, woman or a child is not considered a heroic deed. In a war situation in traditional Luhyia land, this was in fact an abomination, an unmanly and cowardly act. It was a stupid act of blind rage attributed to demented males. During the *eshiremba*, bulls fight at the graveside and spread the soil from the grave all over the compound. Essentially, this is to help the spirit of the warrior fight the spirits of the men he killed in order to enter the world of the ancestors. It is this power appropriated to the bull that the Luhyia men aspire to possess.

Preparation for the Contest

To have full knowledge of this masculine ritual, we have to look at the etymology of the word 'contest' itself. The Luhyia talk of the bullfight as *khurwanya tsi Jirichi*. The verb *kurwanya* is the equivalent of contest, competition or fight. 'Contest' in English means, literally, *con* (with) *testis* (testicle) (Ong 1989). It is therefore an activity for those with testicles, and it involves male ego at its best in an attempt to conquer and subdue the opponent. This combat necessitates elaborate preparation. Events prior to the fight attest to this. Although the fight itself may take as little as five minutes, the highly structured and detailed pattern of events point to a gendered cosmic perception of reality. The physical and psychological conditioning of the bull is extraneous though culturally sanctioned. The bull reared specifically for fighting lives a life of isolation throughout its fighting life, being completely separated from other cows in the homestead. This separation serves a number of purposes. First, it makes it easy for the owner of the bull to condition and socialize his animal to imbibe extreme aggressiveness towards other bulls. There is also no competition for food with less prized animals. This is another masculine ideal that Luhyia men aspire to. An ideal Luhyia man does not struggle for food. He eats alone while his wife eats together with the children. This fact convinces me to look at the bull as a form of surrogate man. The bull does not get the opportunity to mate for it is believed that this would diminish its power to fight. It is a common belief among the Luhyia that one preparing for any form of competition or contest should abstain from sex. In essence contact with the vagina is believed to weaken a man. Hence, in Kenya, footballers are asked to abstain from sex when preparing for a match.

Nothing exemplifies the violent nature of this game than the act of sharpening of the bull's horns three days before the day of the contest. The owner undertakes this exercise as he talks to the bull in an ironic monologue that goes on for a long time. If it were just a mere game as the song quoted above says, why then endanger the life of the bulls through this act? The fact that the owners find it necessary to sharpen the horns signifies a masculine virtue inspired by the sublimation of sexual desires. In this culture, what is dangerous is masculine. It also ricochets with elements of the ritual of circumcision that are meant to make a man virile, dangerous and lethal. It is my contention that the game is meant to make one male demonstrate his virility against another. The victory will entail a form of penetration. In these opposing polarities, the one who penetrates feminizes the one penetrated and makes him less of a man.

Once the professional matchmakers announce the day and venue of the contest, preparations start in earnest. Matchmakers organize contests by considering the weight and experience of the contesting bulls. There may be only one main fight, but other fights between lightweight bulls serve as curtain-raisers. The night before the fight witnesses a celebration of songs and dances. The bull's fans arrive in the home in the evening and dance around the bull for some time before dispersing to go and sleep. They wake up very early around 3am to start dancing and psyching the bull once again. The bull responds to these efforts by bellowing repeatedly. This is interpreted as a sign that it is accepting the instructions being given to it.

Something has to be said about bellowing among the Luhyia. *Khukumula* – to bellow – is a masculine activity. In official gatherings, respectable people are not asked to talk but to bellow. Bellowing is an act of authority, force, relevance and power. The bull may, however, refuse to bellow if certain imperatives, such as sexual abstinence are not observed. Because of this, on the pre-contest night, the owner of the bull and all its fans abstain from sex. It is believed that if the owner indulges in sex, the bull may be defeated or it may turn against the owner. Indeed, my respondents cited cases where bulls had attacked their owners and killed them. A case in point involved a man called Mabonga from Shikoti village in Kakamega District who was stamped to death by a bull in 2003.

Departure from the shed to the arena follows a well-defined pattern of patriarchal hegemonic values. The bull has to leave its shed to the arena amid dances and songs by its fans, like a great man leaving or arriving home. Except for the bull owner's wife, no other woman should cross its path at this moment. Having avoided sex that night, she is considered a step above femininity and therefore could contribute to the preparation of the bull. In this case, she assumes some degree of masculinity by association. If she is the one who feeds it, then she is under an obligation to wake up very early in the morning, take off her underpants and beat the back of the bull with them while urging it to be brave, saying: 'go and put up a good fight and win. I do not like being let down.' The symbolic relevance of this act can best be understood as a projective impulse. Removal of the panties is a symbolic invitation to a penetrative act. Through this act, the bull is conditioned to go and penetrate the opponent in order to feminize it with the 'erect horns'. It is only after this that the entourage departs to the venue, which could be as far as five kilometres away. Some bull owners confessed to me that they visit the grave of a warrior with their bulls prior to the contests and give instructions to the beasts while standing on the grave. This reinforces the belief that the bulls have supernatural powers not derived from this world.

The journey to the venue is even more eventful and action-packed. Whistles rend the air as enthusiastic fans release shouts reminiscent of war cries amid vows to crush and destroy the opponents. Traffic on the main highways in this part of Kenya is considerably slowed down on these occasions. Motorists are warned not to overtake the bull and its fans lest the fans stone them. As they travel to the venue, the sticks and clubs of the fans remain raised. This in Freudian terms is a phallic symbol imitating an erect penis. This reading makes sense in the Freudian perspective when we consider the assertion that anything vertical is symbolically phallic. Freud extended this contention to more mundane images such as the tie. He argued that a tie, being an object that hangs down and is not worn by women, is clearly a male symbol (Dundes 1997: ix). The raised sticks and clubs, it is said, encourage the bull to fight hard and not 'withdraw.' But as the team approaches the venue, sometimes they consider it necessary to take a detour from the main entrance to avoid being tricked by opponents who may bewitch the bull through charms buried on its way.

The Bull

As a human male surrogate, the bull is conditioned to behave in a certain way throughout its life. To produce hatred towards other bulls, this surrogate is isolated from other animals. It is a fact of life that hate between men comes from cutting ourselves off from each other (Wittgenstein 1980). This conditioning can best be understood from the power relations in Luhyia society. The main axis of power in Luhyia land is the subordination of what is considered feminine. Masculinity is infused within a collection of practices, symbols, discourses and ideologies associated with the category 'man'. In the same way that the Luhyia expect of a 'real man', the bull is reserved, reticent and uncommunicative, especially in regard to showing emotions unless they are those of anger. The fighting bull spends most of its time alone since it is separated from other animals in the homestead, and it is never tethered for fear of being contaminated with femininity. It is only the owner, his wife or any other special person drawn from the same basket of taboo and imperatives of tradition that may attend it. If it is the owner's wife who feeds it, she needs to observe a wide range of taboos – for instance, she should not feed it during her menses. This, it is believed, would weaken the bull. The same is applicable to Luhyia men who are asked to keep away from women at such times. The bull should never be castrated. To castrate it is to weaken it so that it can never fight. These are other pointers indicating that the bull is a surrogate male human being. Luhyia men look down on a castrated man and consider him a woman. The bull is bred solely for the purpose of fighting and serves no other purpose. Using it as an ox is not allowed, and would in fact be an abuse of its integrity. This range of taboos requires explanation.

Freud once observed that whenever man sets up a taboo, he fears some danger. It cannot be disputed that a generalized dread of women is expressed in all these rules of avoidance associated with the bull. Men create taboos because they are afraid of being weakened by a woman and thereby tainted with femininity (Kabaji 2002). The best way man found to express his fears was through myths and rituals highly infused with rules of avoidance. I suggest that bullfighting rituals project psychological inner realities of the masculine mind. Carl Jung (1963) recognized the power of myth when he observed that myths represent fantasies of the group and that this material may be interpreted psychologically to yield information related to hidden psychological realities (Kabaji 2002). It is therefore possible to construe taboos related to women and menstruation as a twin product of dread and as a protective device for hegemonic masculinity.

Combat as a Contest of Masculinities

Crowds of predominantly males pour into the arena, as drumbeats grow louder. Fans appropriate ownership of the bulls so it becomes 'our phalluses versus theirs'. Each owner of a bull begs his animal to 'open up'. To open up in the language of Luhyia bullfighting is to urinate. A bull is only ready for combat after urinating, which means accepting the challenge. The Lyhyia also observe other instances when a cow has to urinate for a ritual to be complete. So, in the case of dowry, when the cows are taken to the bride's home, the ceremony can only begin after the cows urinate. This, it is believed, is a sign that the bride will be fertile and give birth to male children. It is only after a contesting bull has urinated that its owner can urge it to charge forward and fight. In response to the activities around them, the bulls snort, sway their heads from side to side and dig their hooves into the ground, signs that they are spoiling for the fight. Meanwhile, the owners of the bulls tirelessly continue to praise them by reminding them of past victories and conquests.

As contending bulls close on each another, the spectators' clubs and sticks remain raised while they cheer their bull to victory. The clubs also protect the spectators who use them to ward off charging bulls. And indeed there are moments when the bulls charge towards the crowds before continuing with the contest. At such times, the spectators are forced to scamper to safety until the beasts retreat.

Fights can last just five minutes and sometimes, they may take up to twenty minutes. The victor is determined when the defeated bull takes to its feet, running away from the opponent. At this juncture, the owners of the victorious bull guide it out of the arena with songs and dances. The defeated bull is also driven out of the arena by its fans with a subdued fanfare as they sing to console it. The victorious bull is returned home where the owner and its fans celebrate the victory by eating and drinking beer. It is also important that the fans are given some little money, say about 10 shillings (U$ 2 cents), and it is believed that the bull would know if the fans are not treated well and may not perform well in the next contest.

Naming Contests

As noted earlier, the bulls are proxy male human beings. They are further personified by being given names that describe their best qualities or at least the expectations of their owners. Every fighting bull has a name. The names given are determined by the characteristics of the bull, expectations of the owner, circumstances of its birth or in tribute to a bull that won many battles. This pattern of bull-naming is also used in naming children among the Luhyia. I would like to look more closely at the names of five bulls whose fights I witnessed. These were: Osama bin Laden, Mike Tyson, NARC, *Nyati* and *Eminyi*.

From the outset, I have to say that the names given epitomize what the Luhyia consider masculine values. The fact that Osama bin Laden's name is given to a bull signals an intimate relationship between the Luhyia perception of power and Osama bin Laden's ideals and exercise of power. As al-Qaeda's chief ideologue, Osama, more than anyone else, is considered the most dangerous international terrorist because of his jihad strategy. He is reputed to have masterminded the terrorist bombing of the twin towers in New York City, the American Embassy in Nairobi and Paradise Hotel in Mombasa, Kenya. The fact that Osama is recognized as a hero in these villages, even after leaving a trail of destruction in Kenya, is worth our curiosity in the context of the sense of power and influence in Luhyia. Osama is lethal, unsympathetic, anti-American and committed to his cause. The fact that he pulls unimaginable stunts against the mighty USA makes him an object of admiration by the poor members of the society whose pleasure come through a psychological process of identification. What seems to attract these people to Osama is not the logical understanding of what he stands for, but his power to destroy and to defend his position. It is with such fervour that they fight to preserve their hegemony.

Mike Tyson is considered by some to be one of the greatest heavyweight boxers of our time. Tyson's story has been heard in these villages through the radio to which the people have an almost romantic attachment as the conveyer of 'truth'. Tyson, in his prime, routinely defeated prominent opponents in a devastating manner and was once one of the most dreaded fighters. The bull owners give his name to the bulls because of the prowess that Tyson displayed during his heyday as the king of the ring. His punches were powerful and most often sent opponents out of the ring within minutes. But there is another side of Tyson with which the Luhyia identify. Like most of them, Tyson received minimal formal education. As a youth, he was expelled from high school and spent some time in juvenile detention centres. In addition, he has had serious problems in his marriages and has served jail terms for rape and assault. The identification with Tyson is partly a function of these attributes, which to the Luhyia are masculine. To them he is a hero, a man whom they would like to emulate.

Nyati is a Kiswahili word for buffalo. The admiration of the buffalo can perhaps be linked to its fearlessness and scary appearance.

But even more intriguing is the name NARC, which is an acronym for National Rainbow Collision. This is the party that won the elections in Kenya in 2002 and brought to an end the forty years' rule of the Kenya African National Union (KANU). KANU's defeat in the elections was effected through a coalition of parties that fielded one presidential candidate, Mwai Kibaki. In psychoanalytic terms, the coalition, in a way, gang-raped KANU and feminized it, hence the admiration for it.

Eminyi is a type of bird found in this part of Kenya. Known for its bravery and cunning nature, *Eminyi* is difficult to trap. It flies high in a zigzag way. Luhyia mythology holds birds in high esteem, taking them as emissaries to the supernatural world. When they appear in folktales, they have uncanny male-like behaviour. *Eminyi* exhibits behaviour that the Luhyia consider masculine.

Bullfighting Songs

A lot of singing is done in connection with bullfighting. Most of the songs despise and feminize opponents while others are infused with sexual symbols, glorifying the virility of the bull and his owner. In some songs, it is difficult to distinguish references to either the bull or its owner, for they are treated as one and the same. The songs reinforce idealized images of masculinity in relation to images of femininity. They epitomize the Luhyia understanding of the role of a man in the society and carry sexual innuendos. The hegemonic ideal of masculinity in Luhyia land projects men as risk-takers, aggressive, heterosexual, rational and powerful personalities. The songs uphold these ideals, reminding participants of them. The songs perpetuate images of toughness and endurance of hardships. This, clearly, is not peculiar to the Luhyia. In his study of the hegemonic masculinity of the US Navy, for example, Barrett (2004) found similar traits.

Let me direct the spotlight on some of the songs sung and the sex imagery and metaphorical insinuations of masculine attributes. The active participant is the reputed winner who performs the prestigious male role of 'penetrating' the loser. On the other hand, the passive participant is the loser who assumes the non-prestigious 'female' role as the penetrated (Dundes 1997: 31).

Song 1

Fala Ekondomu (Wear a Condom)

Mama Mama Mama

Fala ekondomu

Nomyola Mukana fala ekondomu

Fala ekondomu

Fala ekondomu

Gushere gwu mundu fala ekondomu

Sisa sisa ku madamu

Sisa sisa ku madamu

Nomnyola ling'ang'ule fala

Nomnyola ling'ang'ule fala

Sisa sisa lingangule

Fala ekondomu

English

Mother mother mother

Wear a condom

When you get a lady wear a condom

Wear a condom

Wear a condom

When you get someone's wife wear a condom

Massage it on a madam

Massage it on a madam

If you get a prostitute wear a condom

If you get a prostitute wear a condom

Massage it on prostitute

Wear a condom

Wear a condom

The song begins by invoking the title mother, which reflects what happens when one is in trouble. Usually, the natural reaction for many in such situations is to call out to their mother. 'Mother, mother, mother' in the first line suggests the seriousness of the message to come. The song then implores men to always wear a condom. This line is repeated for emphasis. This song asks men to massage it (penis) on a variety of categories of women: madam (school teacher), other people's wives and prostitutes, but concludes that this has to be done while one is wearing a condom. In general, the song glorifies extra-marital sexual relationships only if it is safe for the man.

It should be noted that there are moments when the drums are played without vocal accompaniment. After the singers have finished the last line, the soloist steps in front of the group, raises his hands in an apparently excited but controlled gesture, to signal to the instrumentalists to play the male drum while the playing of the female drum (small drum) is suspended. At this juncture, the soloist shouts the praises of various men amid employing vocal gymnastics that make up the repertoire of performers' tricks. The mood of controlled frenzy is given form by the shouts loaded with phallic signals, insinuations of sexuality and almost pervasive body jerks. This affords the soloist the opportunity to exalt men, within the crowd, known for their sexual prowess. By the use of sexual imagery, he likens such men to bulls that never tire, among other superlatives. He plays on the vanity and emotions of these men, indirectly castigating women, playing out men's anxieties and exalting masculinity by repeating percussive phrases.

Images abound in all songs extolling male sexuality. Let us consider another song:

Song 2

A Club to Seduce

Mbe ShikongoShanje

Vakoji mbe shikongo shange

Nzie kuserere Shinyalu

Utasera dave

Urasira kumtego

English

Give me my club

My Vakoji [partner during circumcision] give me my club

Give me my club

So that I go and seduce in Shinyalu

Do not get excited

You will be trapped

In this song, the soloist asks for a club (an obvious phallic symbol) from his friend with whom he was circumcised. For better understanding of this song, we have noted that among the Luhyia, circumcised boys are kept apart for a month before they emerge from the seclusion area. One of the items a boy is asked to make for himself is a club, which he is expected to keep until old age. Elders can still be seen carrying these clubs. This culture is not restricted to the Luhyia. The Masai and Kalenjin of Kenya also carry clubs as cultural icons of masculinity and authority. In the Luhyia culture this signifies virility, authority and power. The former president of Kenya, Daniel Arap Moi, carried his club about while in power and still carries it anywhere he goes.

The symbolic significance of the club in this song cannot be gainsaid. When the singer implores his mate to give him a club in order to go to Shinyalu and seduce women, we realize that he is out for sexual exploits. Shinyalu is a market centre that boasts of beautiful girls in the Western Province of Kenya. But the singer goes ahead to warn the men not to be excited because they can be trapped. This is a direct reference to marriage. The singer is therefore castigating men who were trapped in marriage before enjoying free sexual exploits as proof of their masculinity.

Other songs are misogynistic. They are used to despise opponents as persons not ready for sexual exploits. We see this from the following songs:

Song 3

Unanjiri shi go? (Why did you call me?)

Unangirangi kii

Unangirangi kigu

Unangirashigo kastiri

Shinangangwa viswa

Shinanga vutswa

Unanjiri gahiri?

English

Why did you call me?

Why did you call me?

Why did you call me if you are not ready?

I am not called for nothing

What is the matter you called me for?

Song 4

Munyororo (Caged Males)

Yoo haa

Ve gavandu

Vasieveranga munyololo gwagumira

English

Yoo haa

These people

Those threatening me are caged.

Song 5

Mbeere Ngoteve (Let Me Ask You)

Mbere Ngoteve

Mbere ngoteve

Wava wadira kukindu cha mundu

English

I want to ask you

I want to ask you

Have you ever trespassed on someone's wife?

Song 6

Engo'mbe Niyananga (When a Cow Bellows)

Engombe ne niyananga

Yakwesa yakwesa

Engombe ne niyananga

Yakwesa yakwesa

Yakwesa yakwesa munyororo yonyene

Eeeh vane lelo luno

Saaaaaa

Engombe ne niyananga

Yakwesa yakwesa

Engombe ne niyananga

Yakwesa yakwesa

Yakwesa yakwesa munyororo yonyene

Waaa kutsie kutsie kutsie

English

When a cow bellows

It pulls it pulls

When a cow bellows

It is pulling it is pulling

It pulls the rope alone without help

Eh my people

Today is the day

Cheers

When a cow bellows

It pulls, it pulls

When a cow bellows

It pulls the rope alone

Waaa let's go let's go

Song 7

Engo'mbe (A Cow)

Engombee mama engombe
weeee

Engombee mama engombe

Engombe ya mavere

Mama engombe

Engombe ya masingu

Mama engome

Engombe yo kukhywa

Mama engombe

Engombe ye nyama

Mama engombe

Engombe yo kulwana

Engombe mama engombe

Engombe yo mubucha

English

A cow mother a cow

Hey hey

A cow mother a cow

A cow for milk

Mother a cow

A cow for cow dung

Mother a cow

A cow for dowry

Mother a cow

A cow for meat

Mother a cow

A cow for bull fighting

A cow for the butchery

I agree with Dundes (1980) that whatever is contained in a song is meaningful, even if we do not have full insight into what the meanings may be. The projective impulse, that tendency to attribute to another person or to the environment what is actually within oneself, is at work in a number of the songs sung during Luhyia bullfighting. What is attributed is usually some internal impulse or taboo or feeling, which may be painful or unacceptable. This ascription of feelings and qualities of one's own to an external source is accomplished without the individuals being consciously aware of that fact. The individual perceives the external object as possessing the taboo tendencies without recognizing their source in himself.

In song 3, for example, the singer wonders why he was called for the contest. He boasts that he is only called for a contest in which the rival is ready. Being ready in this case is having imbibed masculine qualities of toughness and aggression. He spits out at the opponent as not ready and therefore uncircumcised. The song indicates that not being tough and aggressive are reflections of femininity and therefore worthlessness. Song 4 continues with this theme and regards the opponent as caged. The metaphor draws from power relations of gender in the Luhyia society. A man who is considered caged is not free from the control of his wife. He is perceived here as one who has been bewitched by his wife. Song 5 picks up the theme of adultery in an attempt to project on to another person what is inherent in the singers. The song asks those who have at any time trespassed on another man's wife to come out and be cleansed. This is in reference to a popular belief among the people that if such a person is in the crowd, the bull can turn against him and maul him to death. It is ironic that they sing this song after Song 1, which glorifies adultery and fornication. In essence, the crowd achieves a psychological cleansing through this song. Song 6 exalts the virtues of autonomy and freedom. A cow, in this case a bull, is said to work alone and does not seek help in accomplishing tasks. This becomes ideal masculine behaviour whereas to seek help is to be feminine. Song 7 enumerates the importance and usefulness of a cow. Among other things, it provides milk, it is used for paying dowry, it has a role in bullfighting and makes meat when sold to a butcher. All these are what a man needs to do and possess in order to be considered masculine.

The Metaphor of the Female Underpants and the Vagina Curse

Before this discussion ends, it is important to discuss, albeit briefly, the metaphor of a woman's underpants in the bullfighting ritual in relation to a dreadful curse in Luhyia land, the curse of the vagina. The underpants acquire potency from what they are meant to cover, the vagina. I noted above that the woman who feeds the bull has to abstain from feeding it when in her menses, and that when the bull is leaving the animal house to go and fight, the woman has to bless it by beating it with already used underwear as she commands it to go and conquer. But there is another practice that is equally significant in understanding the symbolic nature of a woman's underpants. If a cow or bull is so tough and aggressive to members of the family, the wife of the owner (women do not own cows) has a way of making it docile. It is believed that what she needs to do is to wash her underwear and pour the dirty water on the bull's face. This makes the bull docile and easy to tame.

In all these instances, the panties seem to perform various functions. They can inspire courage and enable the bull to win a contest, but they can also make cows docile and inactive. It is my contention that the underpants are symbolic of the supposed negative feminine feared by Luhyia men. The power that the underpants have is through its association with the vagina whose mysteries have never failed to astound Luhyia men. Just as the vagina is feared, it is also revered as a life-giving organ, but one that can be used to destroy a man. This reminds us of Freud's assertions on penis envy. In this sense, the men fear that the vagina can swallow the penis, and these anxieties of its mysteries are discussed in symbolic terms in Luhyia folklore. The meaning in this folkloristic fantasy is somewhat unclear, but it provides a socially sanctioned outlet for what cannot be directly articulated. It is in shouts, songs, proverbs, games and gestures that these anxieties are vented.

The ritual of the bullfight, therefore, mirrors the unconscious operation of the minds of Luhyia men cast in an arena in which they have to aspire to a certain kind of masculinity. The folklore created is like other myths in raising issues of gender and contests for power. They discuss gender in the same fashion as myths and folklore from other cultures. The most well-known myths driven by misogynistic attitudes are actually found in holy books. In the Biblical story of creation, for instance, which draws from Jewish mythology and involves Adam and Eve, the gender question is raised and settled after the creation of the universe. Here, we are told that Yahweh created woman only as an afterthought, because Adam could not find a suitable helpmate among the animals. Yahweh decided to mould her from one of Adam's ribs. Logically, this is ridiculous. Rudimentary knowledge about human anatomy reveals that a single rib is superfluous, almost unneeded. The removal of one has very little effect on the health and muscular function of the individual. Had Yahweh fashioned woman out of man's genitals, the lung or heart or right hand, it would add weight to the position of the woman. Made out of an inconsequential rib, the woman's function in society and in life is to support man (Kabaji 2002). Bullfighting folklore presents the woman in similar ways: as subordinate, an object of pleasure, dangerous and mysterious with dark powers that can either destroy or make a man.

Conclusion

At the beginning of this study, I stated that I would present a critical analysis of bullfighting to uncover the covert and overt meaning of the Luhyia game. In the words of Le Roux (2005: 19), I was going to study the *non-dit*, what is not said or what is said in a manner that conceals the meaning. It has become apparent that bullfighting is popular because it provides a psychological venue through which anxieties of violent sexual tendencies are vented. The bull, as a masculine symbol, is perceived as embodying the aggression and power associated with virility and conquest.

Although my respondents confided that they rear bulls for prestige, it comes out clearly from my analysis that the game is a masculine activity that reinforces what the Luhyia consider masculine or feminine. It is also clear from the data that bullfighting is one avenue of exploring the anxieties and fears of men at a time when the very elements that made one masculine are being challenged and contested. It is also to some degree a way of connecting with the now ever-dwindling ideal of masculinity. It becomes clear that male aggressiveness is learned and acquired in a context in which men learn that it is both rewarding and expected to behave in an assertive way. Boys grow up in environments that encourage certain kinds of conduct instead of others. They learn to be 'men'. Aggression from this point of view is a response to specific kinds of experience. Men will only behave aggressively if they have learned that it is appropriate to do so (Brittan 1997: 114).

The Luhyia argue that they participate in the game partly because *Msabwa*, the ancestors of the group, said they should. Again, it is noticeable that there is a way in which the Luhyia yearn for togetherness with other men, the dead and their Gods. Many of my respondents argued that some churches are hostile to the game. They particularly cited the Friends Church (Quakers). Those who attend this church and many other modern churches are dissuaded from attending and participating in the bullfighting ritual. The ritual, however, gives us an avenue through which we observe the Luhyia projecting anxieties over their masculinity.

References

Barrett, F., 2004, 'Hegemonic Masculinity: The US Navy', in S. Whitehead and J. Barrett, eds., *The Masculinities Reader*, Oxford: Blackwell Publishers.

Beynon, J., 2002, *Masculinities and Culture*, Buckingham and Philadelphia: Open University Press.

Brittan, A., 1989, *Masculinity and Power*, Oxford: Basil Blackwell.

Connell, R. W., 2004, 'The Social Organisation of Masculinity', in S. Whitehead and J. Barrett, eds., *The Masculinities Reader*, Oxford: Blackwell Publishers.

Dundes, A., 1997, *From Game to War, and Other Psychoanalytic Essays on Folklore*, Lexington: The University Press of Kentucky.

Dundes, A., 1980, *Interpreting Folklore*, Bloomington: Indiana University Press.

Geertz, C., 2002, 'Deep Play Notes on the Balinese Cock Fight', in R. Adams and D. Savran, eds., *The Masculinity Studies Reader*, Malden, MA: Blackwell Publishers.

Irigaray, L., 1985, *This Sex Which is Not One*, Ithaca: Cornell University Press.

Jung, C., 1963, *Memories, Dreams and Reflections*, New York: Random House.

Kabaji, E., 2002, 'Mysteries of the Masculine Mind', *The East African Standard*, 4 August.

Le Roux, E., 2005, 'Imaginary Evidence: Finding the *Non-Dit* in Fiction', in *Gender, Literature and Religion in Africa*, Gender Series, Vol. 4, Dakar: CODESRIA.

Ong, W., 1989, *Fighting for Life: Contest, Sexuality and Consciousness*, Amherst: University of Massachusetts Press.

Wittgenstein, L., 1980, quoted in H. Brod and M. Kaufman, *Theorizing Masculinity*, 1994. London: Sage.

4

The Masculine Discursive Construction of Rape in the Kenyan Press

James Ogola Onyango

Rape is an act where the victim is violently forced into sexual activity against his or her will. In this study, rape is viewed as an act of brutal sexual domination by men over women. Broadly speaking, it can be vaginal, anal, oral or penetration with an object, and rape can take place even when the victim is asleep or in a trance (see httpp//www.rapecrisisonline.com/articles.htm). Because of the violence that is associated with rape, it can have tragic consequences. Although we are aware that rape can be perpetrated by women on men, in Kenya the overwhelming number of rape cases are perpetrated by men on women. Indeed, it is this type of rape that falls within our study because it is rooted in societal power and ideological structures that are related to hegemonic masculinity.

In Kenya, rape against women has increased remarkably in the last fifteen years or more. Analysis of the cases over these years reveals that all types of men are involved: fathers, brothers, cousins, schoolmates, teachers, policemen, top government officials and so on. Apart from rape on women, rape on children (defilement) is common. The 1 July 2005 edition of *Daily Nation* carried statistics showing that fathers take the lead when it comes to defiling their girl children. Police reports in the press in July 2005 also indicate that rape against women is the number one crime in Kenya. Table 1 shows how rape has steadily grown since 1990.

Table 1: Number of Reported Rape Cases in Kenya, 1990–2004

Year	Number of Reported Rape Cases on Women
1990	515
1991	943
1992	590
1993	989
1994	1050
1995	958
1996	1368
1997	1050
1998	1329
1999	1465
2000	1675
2001	1987
2002	2013
2003	2308
2004 (July)	1653

Source: Kenya Police Headquarters. Reported in *East African Standard*, 30 April 2000 (for 1991–2000) and *Daily Nation*, 27 July 2005 (for 2000-2004).

The table, disregarding fluctuations, shows how the number of rape cases on women in Kenya grew fourfold in fifteen years. It is even more disturbing when one takes into account the fact that because of the stigma and the secrecy attached to sex matters in general, and rape in particular, the reported cases do not reflect the true record. Further, as Wachira (1994) correctly observes, the law concerning rape in Kenya is weighed down by masculine overtones. The whole process of rape trials is tantamount to the victim going through a rape ordeal for a second time. Thus, very few women actively want to report a rape case. At present, extremely few women can talk about their rape ordeal in public.

The remarkable increase in the number of cases of women raped in Kenya has resulted in the emergence of pressure groups, human rights groups and groups against torture and rape victims, who have come up strongly against such acts of injustice. Moreover, defilement and rape have attracted remarkable debate in public discourse. In terms of positive action, the most resounding step has come in the form of the proposed sex crimes' bill, which has far-reaching recommendations such as castration for rapists. Despite this, however, the number of cases of raped women remains on the increase and men's talk on rape in public ignores the issues at stake.

Despite the spirited efforts of gender activists in Kenya in the past three and a half decades, masculine ideologies that enhance the domination of men over women in Kenya remain strong. Apart from the fact that the number of rape crimes perpetrated by men in Kenya is dismayingly persistent and on the increase, male public utterances on rape are little changed. Seemingly, since many communities in Kenya are overwhelmingly patriarchal, the masculine discursive construction of rape in the press appears to be a projection of the dominant ideology and the power structures in those communities that place a premium on hegemonic masculinity.

The present study has three objectives. The first is to discuss the masculine construction of the word 'woman' in the Kenyan press. The second is to examine ideologies and power structures behind masculine discursive utterances on rape in the Kenyan press. The final one is to discursively construct the form of argument and the argumentation strategies used in masculine utterances on rape in the Kenyan press.

The advent of serious gender studies in Africa, in the last three and a half decades, has triggered off discussions over unequal power relations between men and women, the domination of men over women and ideologies that reflect male points of view (Mama 1996). One theme that has attracted serious attention is gendered violence (for example, Abane 2000; Muchera 2000; Bammeke 2000; Atinmo 2000; Nwagbara 2000, and Adjekophori 2000). Issues on gender violence are diverse. They range from wife-beating and the cultural underpinnings thereof (Abane 2000) to violence against women in conflicts (Nwagbara 2000) and rape (Griffen 1999; Tibatemwa-Ekirikubinza 1999). Gendered violence takes various forms, including men against women, women against women, and youth against the old (Muchera 2000). Although it is true that both men and women are involved in gendered violence, women are usually on the receiving end.

Rape is an extreme edge of gendered violence, and is much more a male crime than a female crime. Masculine stereotypes still appear in masculine discourse such as: 'the woman who is raped asked for it', and 'it is the bad girls who are raped' (Griffen 1999). This underlines the masculine ideology characteristic of patriarchal societies in many parts of the world.

Gendered violence is a dominant preoccupation in masculinities studies, and it seems incontestable that violence is more common to men than women (Frosh, Phoenix and Pattman 2004; Luyt 2005). One area that is emerging in connection with masculine violence is sexual violence against women. It has been argued that the male genitalia have far-reaching ramifications on the conceptualization of masculinities in the context of sexual violence (Izugbara 2005; Plummer 2005). In this connection, Plummer says about men:

> They are much more likely to feel that they can assert themselves to take sex when they want it, not just in obvious rape situations, but more routinely with their wives (wife rape), girl friends (date rape), children (son or daughter rape) and other men (homosexual rape). They are much more likely than women to feel they have a *specific turn on* – a little out of the ordinary – which must be met (Plummer 2005: 179).

Plummer argues that a man is inherently more likely to rape because of the inclination to want to assert himself through sex. Thus, sexual activity is an important feature in masculinities, particularly in the prism of domination. It is in this context that Izugbara (2005) has theorized that the erect penis is central to any attempt at hypothesizing on hegemonic masculinity. In many Kenyan societies, when a man impregnates a woman, he boasts that he has broken her leg. In other words, he is saying that he has disabled her to some extent, hence indicating his ability to dominate.

While the theme of gendered violence has been meaningfully addressed in gender studies, the question of discursive construction of violence has been relatively neglected. This implies that the role of language in perpetuating the myriad forms of violence such as rape requires further analysis.

Since the advent of Critical Discourse Analysis (hereafter CDA) it has been correctly observed that language embeds practices of domination and discrimination and aspects of power. Indeed, CDA has been used in a number of research topics, for example on racism, discrimination and xenophobia in Europe (Wodak 2001c). Here, the goal has been to make transparent discursive practices that are racist, discriminatory and xenophobic. It is in this prism that CDA is important in analysing the male discourse on rape, with a view to exposing the dominant masculine ideologies and the masculine argumentation strategies embedded in such utterances.

The importance of CDA in the study of power and discriminative discursive practices is well explained by Wodak. She rightly says:

> Power is about relations in difference, and particularly about the effects of differences in social structures. The constant unity of language and other social matters ensures that language is entwined in social power in a number of ways: language indexes power, expresses power, is involved where there is contention over and a challenge to power. Power does not derive from language, but language can be used to challenge power, to subvert it, to alter distributions of power in the short and the long term. Language provides a finely articulated means for differences in power in social

hierarchical structures. Very few linguistic forms have not at some stage been pressed into the service of the expression of power by a process of syntactic or textual metaphor. CDA takes an interest in the ways in which linguistic forms are used in various expressions and manipulations of power. Power is signalled, not only by grammatical forms within a text, but also by a person's control of a social occasion by means of the genre of a text. (Wodak 2001b: 11)

Language is definitely entwined with societal structures that embed unequal power relations such as those of sexual violence. Thus, an utterance can be analysed to reveal its discriminatory import and the ideological base. This is what has made CDA a versatile conceptual framework in the analysis of discrimination in racist utterances.

Theoretical Framework

Critical Discourse Analysis and the Hegemonic Masculinity Hypothesis offer insightful approaches to our topic. An offshoot of CDA, known as the Disco-Historical Approach (Wodak 2001c), enables men's utterances to be critically analysed to expose the dominating masculine ideologies and male point of view in argumentation strategies. The Hegemonic Masculinity Hypothesis highlights the importance of the penis in the question of male domination over women, examining how men use a penis physically as well as the symbolic value attached to it as literally a tool of domination. The leading proponents of CDA are Ruth Wodak, Teun van Dijk, Norman Fairclough, Gunther Kress and Theo van Leeuwen, while the literature of CDA shows how it has become a highly versatile theory for analysing discourse (e.g. Wodak 1989, 1996a, 1996b, 2000a, 2000b, 2000c, 2001a, 2000b, 2001c; Wodak and de Cillia 1998; Wodak and van Dijk 2000; Wodak, de Cillia, Reisigl and Liebhart 1999, and Fairclough 1989).

CDA rests on certain assumptions. For the sake of this research, the following are underscored:

- Language is a social phenomenon.
- Not only individuals, but also institutions and social groupings, have specific meanings and values that are expressed through language in systematic ways.
- Texts are the relevant units of language in communication.
- Readers/hearers are not passive recipients in their relationship to texts. (Kress, in Wodak 2001b: 6)

CDA maintains that language is not merely an instrument of communication, but ideologies and power are indexed in language. CDA draws attention to the three elements of criticality, ideology, and power. Criticality basically entails distancing from the data. So, when we have an utterance on rape, the important task at hand is not activism but rather to uncover as critically as possible the unequal power connotations of the utterance.

Ideology, which can be defined as the way meaning is constructed and conveyed by symbolic forms of various kinds (Wodak 2001b), in the realm of CDA is seen as implicit in establishing and maintaining unequal power relations. The importance of ideology in shaping a people's worldview is emphasized by Mumby:

> Ideology does not simply provide people with a belief system through which they orient themselves to the world, but instead, it plays a much more fundamental role in the process by which social actors create reality of the world in which they live. (Mumby 1988: 71)

On power, in the context of a male-dominated society, CDA critically analyses the language of men as it unfairly refers to women. So, CDA has its focus on enhancing the position of women who are in a disadvantaged position. Thus, here CDA is interested in improving the condition of women. In the case of rape, after revealing the negative male power embedded in utterances, CDA also becomes an important means of exposing the ideological orientation that is embedded in the utterances.

The Hegemonic Masculinity Hypothesis (HMH) underscores the centrality of the penis and the cultural attachments thereof in questions revolving around men's desire to dominate women (Friedman, in Izugbara 2005; Izugbara 2005). According to Izugbara (2005: 13–14), HMH has its beginnings in the primitive background (in relation to men) where a penis gained cultural significance, such that those who possess one ought to behave, that is, they are supposed to accomplish certain things with the penis. Succinctly, Izugbara delineates two understandings about the penis that have relevant ramifications on the question of power, as attached to masculinity: the physical activities of the penis and its symbolic functions. In physical or expressive terms, Izugbara says that to a primitive mind (real male mind) the erect penis has power: it is hard, bold and strong; it is also an element of domination. In Izugbara's words:

> The invasive nature of the penis derived from primitive understanding of the meaning of penetration. The liquid (semen), which it emits during ejaculation, was also viewed as a sort of venom which weakened women. It registered as a tool with which to demobilise, invade and disvalue women. (Izugbara 2005: 14)

Although Izugbara contends that it is a primitive understanding that bestows the penis with such accolades, certain men are still socialized to believe these accolades, as implied in the Gikuyu myth, which we are going to discuss later. In terms of what the penis signifies, Izugbara explains that it has been bestowed with the significance of life and death: '… the major outcomes associated with the penile activity and penetration centred on loss of virginity and pregnancy, thereby inscribing on the penis the power of life and death' (ibid.).

It is apparent that to many men who place a special premium on the penis, it is the most important means of enhancing the domination of men over women. This perception of the penis has dangerous consequences in terms of hegemonic masculinity (mainly symbolized by the penis), because as Izugbara (ibid.) rightly observes, this type of masculinity is the cultural ideology that 'inscribes superiority, power, vigour, strength and brutality to men'. It is in this context that we can vividly locate discursive violence, such as when a man warns men from a different community that if they continue supporting multiparty politics, their women will be raped (because his community is the ruling class and multiparty politics is a threat to its privilege). We shall discuss this utterance later. Implicit here is the desire to protect privileges and enhance domination through the penis. It is also the kind of hegemony that encourages men to mete out sexual violence on women, in what some men value as vigorous sexual intercourse.

Using the principled criteria of CDA and HMH, we analysed the masculine ideological and power base of the Kenyan society. We also looked at the masculine connotations of the term rape in selected Kenyan communities. Thirdly, we collected and analysed samples of male public utterances on women and rape in the Kenyan press.

On the analysis of male utterances, we were interested in answering the following questions:

- How are women named and referred to linguistically?

- What traits, characteristics, qualities and features are attributed to them?

- By means of what arguments and argumentation do men justify and legitimise rape in their utterances in the Kenyan press?

- From what point of view are arguments, labels and attributions expressed? (adapted from Wodak 2001c: 72)

Ideology, Power and Sexual Violence

The forty to forty-five Kenyan communities are predominantly patriarchal societies. In these societies, the male worldview is predominant and decisive. Such idioms as 'if you are man enough…' (from almost all Kenyan societies) and *mkono wa kiume* (a Kiswahili term meaning the right hand) are a few examples that explain this.

In terms of social psychology, the masculine element has been highly pervasive. Kenya's national symbols are the cock and the bull. The former ruling party had, and still has, its eulogised symbol in the cock. The symbol of the bull is very popular in many Kenyan communities. Thus, among the Luhya community (Samia dialect) of Western Kenya, a revered man is called *esurusi* (the bull). Similarly, among the Luo (Nyanza Province), *ruath* (the bull) is a respected reference. Even in the widely used Kiswahili language, a tough man is called *dume* (a male animal). The bull, the cock and *dume* have one obvious thing in common: they are symbols of virility. It is instructive to note that there are no revered female sexual symbols in Kenya.

The male genitalia have been portrayed as a symbol of domination in Kenya. As earlier mentioned with regard to a number of communities, impregnating a woman is metaphorically expressed as breaking her leg. In other words, the man who impregnates a lady has somewhat disabled her. A Gikuyu myth (Central Province) illustrates this. The myth claims that at one time women were very powerful in the community. One day, men conspired to reduce the women's power, and all agreed to impregnate them. From that day, their women were regarded as being disabled by pregnancy. The strong message in this myth is that a man's penis can be an important instrument of enhancing a man's domination over a woman or invariably of bringing women under subjection (cf. Izugbara 2005). In sum, in Kenya, female sexuality invites scorn and male sexuality invites celebrity.

Against this backdrop of placing a premium on the male genitalia, rape has been common in many Kenyan communities for a very long time. In the many pre-colonial communal clashes, one of the common punishments inflicted on a vanquished community by the victorious army was abduction of their women who were savagely raped. During colonialism, one of the excesses of colonial rule was the rape of women by Europeans. Writing on the crimes of colonial rule in Kenya, Elkins (2005) identifies rape. Moreover, the process of marriage in some communities concealed what was in actual fact rape. Apart from marriage that was procedural where the bride was peacefully released after agreement between both parties, the other form, no less popular, was that of abduction. In this case, the wife-to-be was abducted and forced into marriage. She was raped but this rape was made to look normal after she had become a 'wife'. The import of this example is that a woman was there for the purpose of fulfilling a man's sexuality, whether she liked it or not.

Accruing from this ideology, rape for a long time passed as a 'normal' happening in Kenya. This is particularly evident when we critically look at many of the words that describe rape in selected communities as shown in Table 2 below:

Table 2: Translations of the Term Rape in Selected Kenyan Languages

Language	Meaning[1]
Gikuyu	*Kunyita na hinya*: to get by force
Luhya	*Okhukwaho*: to catch by force
Luo	*Diyo*: grabbing and pinning down
Ekegusii	*Gotachera inse*: to pin down.
Kidabida	*Kudidika*: to catch by force
Kalenjin	*Koborien kwondo*: to fight with a woman
Turkana	*Atikonor*: to push somebody when she does not want it

Source: Field Data, 2005

If we subject the above translations of rape to PEGITOSCA (a good yardstick of translation) – namely, precision, economy, generativity, internationality, anti-obscenity, systemacity, consistency and appropriateness (Kiingi, in Mwaro 2000)[2] – what becomes clear is that they are not precise equivalents. They are low on economy, transparency and appropriateness. This in itself points to one thing: these societies do not have an appropriate term for rape. The reason for this is not hard to find. Rape was taken for granted or simply treated as 'normal'. Serious reporting of rape in the press is just a few decades old in Kenya. For a long time, it was the abnormal and extreme cases, considered beyond social norms, that were reported. The rest were treated as normal.

The Masculine Construction of a Woman in the Press

At the height of the multiparty politics agitation in Kenya, at the beginning of the last decade, men went for each other by using metaphors of women. We look at a few of them listed below. A Kenya African National Union (KANU) minister of the then ruling party accused Members of Forum for Restoration of Democracy (FORD) of groping:

1) 'like women rejected by men and have been going to Chester House like prostitutes trying to attract men clients.' (*Daily Nation*, 18 October 1991)

In another statement, the speaker compared people who decamped from KANU to a wife estranged from her husband:

2) 'If she does not want you and you do not want her, you let her go… there is a name we use for such women which I can not say here…' (uttered by a KANU politician, *Daily Nation*, 18 October 1991)

An individual supposedly speaking positively about women said:

3) 'women are the flowers in our lives. They bear us, they feed us, give us comfort and tender love, so when some of us turn around and abuse them something must be wrong.' (uttered by a pastor, reacting to the first two comments, *Daily Nation,* 18 October 1991)

The first utterance starts with a masculine presupposition, that it is men who reject women. The converse is that women do not reject men. Secondly, it refers to women as prostitutes and men as clients. In terms of power, the opening masculine presupposition bestows power to a man for it is a man who has the power to reject a woman. On the question of prostitution, it is vividly a case of positive self-image presentation and negative 'other' representation. The *topos* (plural *topoi*),[3] presented here is that of definition, name or interpretation. The explanation of this *topos* goes like this: 'if an action, a thing or person (group of persons) is named/designated (as) X, the action, thing or person (group of persons) carries or should carry the qualities /traits/attributes contained in the (literal) meaning of X' (Wodak 2001c: 75). Prostitution is derided in Kenyan society, and in moral terms a prostitute is one who goes against the straight moral fabric of society. On the other hand, the label 'client' in reference to men is positive. It can be used in a number of positive contexts, including those in which normal business is involved.

The idea of discursively constructing women in negative terms and men in positive images can be traced to the dominating masculine ideologies in many Kenyan societies. In line with this, a man who engages in prostitution is a hero (as very virile). One who engages in multiple sexual relationships is seen as a worthwhile bull, cock or *dume*. Conversely, a woman who engages in multiple sex relationships is seen as a prostitute! In reality both men and women who are involved in serious sexual promiscuity, either for commercial gain or otherwise, are actually prostitutes. But the male-dominated society still sees women as prostitutes and excludes men. This ideology has held sway in East African society for a considerable time. In 1967, one critical Tanzanian poet condemned the idea of labelling only women as prostitutes. In the last stanza of one of his poems he wrote:

Tungesema na kupima mwanzo wa hii hekaya

Nani mbele na wa nyuma, katika hiyo himaya?

Ni yule mtoa vyuma, katika hiyo himaya

Wanaume ndiyo malaya watoaji wa milungura.

(Mnyampala 1967: 142)

If we were to critically look at this fable,

Who is at the forefront and who is in the backyard?

It is the one who gives silver who is at the forefront

Men are the prostitutes, they are the ones who bribe their way.

As this poet correctly observes, when a tree withers, you look for the reasons in the roots and not in the leaves. Men initiate prostitution. They are the ones who pay for the services, so they share as much of the blame as women. It is important to note that the question of prostitution has implications for rape. Kenyan society believes less in the rape of a woman who is considered a prostitute. The assumption is: she is used to violent sex and therefore can only be seen to be acting if she says she has been raped. This is actually implied in the Kenyan law on rape (Wachira 1994).

In the second utterance involving the image of the estranged woman, the male speaker did not give the exact label. But the implication is there: that such a label cannot be said in public. What cannot be said in public must be negative or horrible. Once again in this utterance, the male point of view is projected. The baseline is that both the man and the woman are in mutual agreement that they do not need each other. However, out of masculine socialisation, the male speaker believes it is the woman who should carry a very bad label that he cannot dare utter in public.

When men portray women as prostitutes or other things that they cannot say in public, they are simply laying grounds to justify their excesses against them. It is plausible to observe that such negatively skewed ideological images of women constructed by men are the precursors to gendered violence against women by men.

At first glance, the third utterance about women may look positive. However, it still reflects that archetype that regards a woman as the source of a man's pleasure. When women are referred to as flowers, it is again a case of the *topos* of definition, name and interpretation. A flower is a fancy symbol that is colourful and picturesque. In terms of function, it is the ultimate other to thorns. In this context, a woman is seen as one who is supposed to give colour to the world of a man.

The sentiment about women bearing men, feeding them and giving them comfort and tender love bring to the fore the *topos* of burden. Why should a woman be so burdened with all the above for the sake of a man? However, this type of utterance does have a background in Kenya. For example, in Kenyan music and oral and written literature, prior to the advent of gender consciousness, a woman was traditionally seen as a good mother, a man's subservient sexual object and a man's property (see Matteru 1982). Thus, songs about the woman with 'secretary bird's legs', 'sexy lips', 'attractive eyes', 'sharp neck' and so on are not a rarity. The relevant question is, why these properties? To go back to our original statement, why should women be so distinctly identified with tender love and comfort? The unfortunate thing in this context is that this tender love and comfort has to be given to men, but it does not matter if they do not give it back. Actually it is this type of argument that has been the background of the image of a woman as an object of a man's pleasure, implying mainly sexual pleasure.

The first two utterances have something in common: when we make a tacit actor analysis, we see the positively constructed man and the negatively constructed woman. And in the third utterance, the woman is seen in decorative terms, meant to beautify a man's life. A woman is not seen as an equal partner. The negative image of a woman constructed by a man is not logical, but all the same can be understood in terms of the dominant belief system of Kenyan society; for, in the case of a female prostitute, how does she become a prostitute without interacting with a male prostitute? In simple terms, no male prostitutes, no female prostitutes; or to leave it in its original ironic form, no male clients, no female prostitutes.

The Masculine Discursive Construction of Rape in the Press

After looking at the ideological and power positions of men as a necessary background, we now move on to the masculine construction of rape. The following utterances explain this:

> 1)All Kikuyu women will be raped if the community continues to support multiparty advocates.' (by a KANU male politician and quoted in *Daily Nation,* 18 October 1991)

This statement was later disowned by the person who uttered it (a very common happening among Kenyan politicians and one of the reasons why reporters use tape recorders these days), but was only after a spirited response by other leaders.

As disturbing as it is, and leaving aside the politics of whether the statement was made or not, the truth is that this statement has been actualized many times in Kenya. What is important here is that rape is clearly portrayed as an important angle in the domination of men over women. And even more absurd is that if a man wants to vanquish another man, then raping his woman is the ultimate sanction. This happened in many inter-tribal wars before colonialism, in the colonial punitive expeditions and more recently in the massacre in the Marsabit district, in Eastern Kenya, where rival clans were involved (*Daily Nation*, 15 July 2005).

In this context, rape is portrayed as an extreme edge of tragic domination. It means that, first, a man knocks out another man, before he gets down to rape the women of the vanquished man. At the heart of this is hegemonic masculinity that eulogizes the penis. Here, the penis is depicted as the ultimate instrument for perpetuating humiliation.

The picture of masculine ideology in the construction of rape in the Kenyan press continues to be painted in the two next statements. The first is:

> 2)'Donors are behaving like people raping a woman who is already too willing.' (*Daily Nation,* 10 February 2003)

It is important to be aware of the context. This sentence was uttered by the Kenyan minister in charge of justice. The press reported that he also laughed at his 'joke'. Judging from the ideological and power network that we have traced above, many men in Kenya would have said the same thing. The outrage that this statement attracted for three days, before an apology was tendered, was overwhelmingly expressed by women groups. Male leaders did not come out convincingly in condemning the comment.

Let us get back to the statement. In the utterance, the 'people' (men) who are raping are many. This implies gang-rape. Even among die-hard male chauvinists in Kenya, this is not very popular. But in the minister's statement 'people' was used in the plural, suggesting gang-rape. This is absurd. What is commonplace in Kenya is the assumption in the last part of the statement, that a victim of rape can be willing but pretends she is in pain. The addition 'too willing' is indeed the absurd gloss on the ideological position.

There is an explanation behind this. There are some men in Kenyan communities who think this way. For example, among the Luhya of Western Kenya, it is held that when a woman says no she is actually willing. This was the reason behind the 'willingness' as expressed by the cabinet minister (a Meru from Eastern Kenya). In other words, it is implied that women never say yes openly to matters of sex. If there is any substance in this, then the answer is found in the brutal way men have dominated women in such societies. It is in this context that we locate acts of sexuality where a woman's pain is a man's pleasure, as seen, for example, in the various forms of female genital mutilation common among many Kenyan communities. Genital mutilation is a brutal and painful act, with at best agonising repercussions and at worst tragic consequences, and yet because of deep-seated masculine ideological connotations, it is still practised despite spirited campaigns against it.

In a community like the Luhya, a woman is supposed to feign pain in sexual activity. Admittedly, this is a truism for a less educated rural woman, but again she is in the category of the majority. If she openly shows that she is genuinely enjoying it, she is dubbed an unsuitable wife. Alongside this, many patriarchal societies socialize women to pretend that they are being hurt during sexual intercourse just to reinforce the sexual ego of a man. In such societies women pretend they are getting hurt to make a man reach the peak of his love-making.

Going back to the statement above, the press that reported it was not totally free from portraying the masculine viewpoint. After reporting what the cabinet minister said, the reporter added that 'he laughed at his own "joke"'. Seriously speaking, what the minister said can never pass as a joke, particularly in the eyes of a woman who has undergone the trauma of rape.

In some patriarchal societies, men are socialized to think that when they need sex from a woman, regardless of the feelings of the woman, they can have it, and that this is not terribly wrong because it is 'normal'. But, as one of the placards of women demonstrators in Nairobi on the above minister's utterance read, 'Rape is not about sex, it is about torture'. The relevant question to ask here is: how can men be so insensitive about rape? The truth is that it looks normal when it is a distant occurrence, when it involves somebody not closely related to them. When a sister, a wife or a mother is the victim the pain is discernible to all. There can never be anything laughable about rape. No matter the circumstance, it can never be a joke.

After three days of intense pressure from demonstrations by women's groups and anti-rape organizations, the cabinet minister was forced to tender an apology thus: 'I unreservedly and sincerely apologise to all women who were offended by the remarks. I withdraw the remarks to the extent to which they referred to rape and willingness …' (*Daily Nation*, 12 February 2005).

In spite of the apology, one is left wondering why it took three days to come. Could it be a popular belief that men are not supposed to give in very quickly to women? Or more importantly, was the minister just like a host of other men who said nothing about this utterance, initially blinded by the dominant belief system on what he had said and, therefore, only offered an apology after persistent and intense pressure from women's groups? I would suggest the latter; for the truth is that, even if the utterance was made in the spirit of the dominant male ideology, after the immediate reaction it is to be expected that the minister in charge of justice and constitutional affairs should have immediately realized his mistake and apologized promptly.

The press also referred to the cabinet minister's utterance as 'remarks'. This looks like an understatement. The remarks were unfortunate, embarrassing and profoundly an ideological standpoint of men on women's sexuality. To lend credence to the fact that the dominant masculine ideological and power standpoint still continues to take for granted the pain of female victims of rape, a few months after this minister's comeuppance, a man convicted of one of the worst rape crimes in Kenyan history made another shocking utterance on rape in Kenya. He said:

> 3) 'Perhaps if it was rape, then rape was normal. But really I do not think that they needed to kill any one. I mean how could they? They were mere boys.' (*Daily Nation*, 13 July 2005)

This statement was from a man convicted of participation in gang-rape at St Kizito mixed secondary school on 19 July 1991. In just one night, seventy-one girls were raped and nineteen girls died under the rage of the marauding boys. Fourteen years later, a released convict, implicated in the most vicious recorded gang-rape in Kenya's history, in an interview on what happened in the school, told a reporter that rape was normal. He meant 'normal' in this case because of the way Kenyan society views rape. As we have seen, often women are raped and suffer in silence; rape cases are only reported by very daring women. According to this rapist, it was only murder that was not normal. This is an argumentation masked in very thick masculinity.

The other aspect is the *topos* that is employed: the boys should be excused for their tragic excesses because they were just boys. This euphemism implies that the fact that they were boys means they were harmless. This is ironic because those whom the interviewee calls 'mere boys' acted in a vicious enough way to kill nineteen girls after raping seventy-one.

Again, we recall the reference on rape as normal. If at all normal, it is normal to the male perpetrator. That is why he can execute such a barbaric act without a second thought and without thinking of the pain he has caused his victims. The idea that it is normal suggests that the woman is a willing partner. This largely comes from the way boys are socialized in almost all Kenyan societies to the intent that women should engage in sex on a man's terms.

As the reporter who covered the proceedings of this tragic case observed:

I have no doubt that the boys *had sex on their minds*. The boys who broke the door to the dormitory were intent on *having sexual fun and many thought the girls should happily join in. That is why some of them were calling out some girls by their names as they forcibly grabbed and flushed them out of the hostel. St Kizito should be a lesson to every man that rape is the worst crime against women.* (emphasis mine) (*Daily Nation*, 13 July 2005)

The words of the *Daily Nation* reporter help to illuminate important theoretical points put forward in this study. A man in Kenya is socialized explicitly or otherwise to engage a woman in sex for his own pleasure. There is the assumption that a woman is also always ready to join in the act otherwise regarded as fun by the man. For if the boys had thought it was such a bad crime, they would not have dared call out the innocent victims by name as they did during the assault. Lastly, the question of force is vividly captured. This is what completes the cycle of brutal domination. The bold call on all men in the reporter's observation is because of the tragic repercussions that were the end-result, and the emotions and the anger that gripped the nation in the wake of this calamity. But unfortunately, this call was never heeded.

Fourteen years later, one of the perpetrators of the crime still believes that rape was, and rape is, a normal thing. Knowledgeable Kenyans still believe women enjoy rape! This simply shows that little has changed in this regard and that such a ghoulish rape is still far from being unrepeatable. No matter the argument, rape can never be normal for any woman. The same reporter again emphasizes:

> St Kizito made me understand that, for women, the fear of rape is just as bad as the fear of death. But women would rather die than face the humiliation of rape – one of the worst crimes any one would visit on a woman. (*Daily Nation*, 13 July 2005)

In all senses, rape is the worst crime a man can visit on a woman. A woman can never willingly welcome it. It is only a man using brutal force, socialized by very unfair masculine ideologies who may think she is pretending to be in pain. Rape is a violent crime, no more and no less.

Conclusion

It has emerged in this study that rape perpetrated by men is on the increase in Kenya. This study has necessarily relied on rape cases reported to the police. However, by the very nature of Kenyan society, where matters dealing with sex are treated with utmost secrecy and rape is seen as a stigma, we can conclude that the numbers of women raped by men are actually far higher than what is reported. Related to this is the male view on rape neutrally expressed in the press. It is also abundantly clear that the *topoi* depicted in all the utterances on rape considered in this study are lopsided and conveniently portray men's perspectives: these include sentiments such as 'rape is normal' and the people who rape are 'mere boys'. The other unjustifiable argumentation is that women enjoy rape, and that the ones who say they are in pain are just pretending.

We have traced the reasons behind the male utterances on rape to the ideologies and the power structures that are intertwined with them. First some men view women in derogatory terms as prostitutes. This acts as the basis for unfair treatment such as sexual violence on a person who is not in tandem with the desired moral fabric of society. We also discussed labels that perpetuate a woman as an object of a man's comfort.

Unfortunately, in connection with rape, the Kenyan law that is supposed to protect women is still overwhelmingly dominated by a masculine point of view. Thus, when a female victim of rape comes up to defend herself in a Kenyan court of law, because of the masculine connotations in the existing law against rape, she ends up going through another form of traumatizing psychological rape in the courtrooms. In this way, the negative masculine ideological standpoints on rape are likely to be perpetuated. It is only fair that the law on rape should be fairer to the victim than is currently the case.

In the light of the statements that have been analysed, it is important to put in place a mechanism that will expose the negative ideological structures that occur in day-to-day talk in public. Verbal exorcism and radical verbal hygiene are necessary. And more importantly, just as the laws of Kenya allow somebody who incites the public to be charged in a court of law for incitement, so should the law severely punish those who make insensitive public utterances on rape. This will help to eliminate discursive violence related to rape. Also, perpetrators of rape crimes on women should be meaningfully punished as a deterrent to others. Currently there is the sex crimes' bill that, interestingly, has led to considerable debate particularly from male circles because of the suggestion that male rapists should be castrated. The kernel of the matter is simple. Rape is cruel, absurd and the worst form of intrusion on a woman's self (other forms of violence are not in any way slighted). If it is proved beyond any reasonable doubt that a man has perpetrated rape, very severe punishment such as life imprisonment is not unfair, especially in a society that eulogises all forms of male domination of women. The court is an important starting point in dismantling both the brutal exercise of hegemonic masculinity and its discursive expression as well.

Notes

1. The respondents who gave us meanings were native speakers and, where possible, linguists.
2. PEGITOSCA is an acronym or a terminology model developed by Kiingi that is realized as follows in full. P stands for Precision, a term that should not be problematic to the user. E stands for Economy, the brevity of the conglomerates of the term. G is for Generativity, the generative ability of the term. I is for Internationality, and T for Transparency, where the term should reflect the meaning. O stands for Anti-Obscenity. S is for Systemicity,, meaning that terms should not be developed with some pattern, e.g. phonemics, phonemic analysis, phonemic notation, phonemic transcription and phonemic overlapping. C stands for Consistency, so that the term should have an acceptable flow, e.g. epicarp and endocarp. A is for Appropriateness, the term being used relative to the culture, ecology, social structure, linguistics and phonetics of language in question (Mwaro 2000).
3. *Topos* refer to 'parts of argumentation which belong to the obligatory, either explicit or inferable premises. They are content-related warrants or "conclusion rules" which connect the argument or arguments to the conclusion' (Kienpointner, in Wodak 2001c: 74).

References

Abane, H., 2000, 'Toward Research into Wife Battering in Ghana: Some Methodological Issues', in F. Oyekanmi, ed., *Men, Women and Violence*. Dakar: CODESRIA.

Adjekophori, E. E., 2000, 'Aspects of Gender Violence in Urban Market Gardening in Metropolitan Lagos, Nigeria', in F. Oyekanmi, ed., *Men, Women and Violence*, Dakar: CODESRIA.

Atinmo, M., 2000, 'Sociocultural Implications of Wife Beating among the Yoruba in Ibadan City, in Nigeria', in F. Oyekanmi, ed.,, *Men, Women and Violence*, Dakar: CODESRIA.

Bammeke, F., 2000, 'Gender Differentials in Students' Perception and Participation in Violence: A Case Study of the University of Lagos', in F. Oyekanmi, ed., *Men, Women and Violence*, Dakar: CODESRIA.

Daily Nation, Nairobi, 18 October 1991; 10 February 2003; 10 and 12 February 2005; 1, 13, 15 and 27 July 2005.

East African Standard, Nairobi, 30 April 2000.

Elkins, C., 2005, *Imperial Reckoning: The Untold Story of Britain's Gulag in Kenya*, New York: Henry Holt.

Fairclough, N., 1989, *Language and Power*. London: Longman.

Frosh, S., Phoenix, A. and Pattman, B., 2004, *Young Masculinities: Understanding Boys in Contemporary Society*, New York: Palgrave.

Griffen, S., 1999, 'Rape: The All American Crime', in A. Kesselman, L. D. McNair and N. Schniewind, eds., *Women: Images and Realities*, London: Mayfield Publishing Company.

Izugbara, C. O., 2005, 'Hypothesis on the Origin of Hegemonic Masculinity', in *Sexuality in Africa Magazine*, Lagos: Africa Regional Sexuality Resource Centre, Vol. 2, No. 1, pp. 13–14.

Luyt, R., 2005, 'Masculinity and Aggression in South Africa', in *Sexuality in Africa Magazine*, Lagos: Africa Regional Sexuality Resource Centre, Vol. 2, No. 1, pp. 11–12.

Mama, A., 1996, *Women's Studies and Studies of Women in Africa During the 1990s*, Dakar: CODESRIA.

Matteru, M. B., 1982, 'The Image of a Woman in Tanzania's Oral Literature: A Survey', in M. M. Mulokozi, ed., *Kiswahili*, Dar es Salaam: TUKI, Vol. 49, No, 2, pp. 1–31.

Meyer, M., 2001, 'Between Theory, Method and Politics: Positioning of Approaches to CDA', in R. Wodak and M. Meyer, eds., *Methods of Critical Discourse Analysis: Introducing Qualitative Methods*, Thousand Oaks, CA, London and New Delhi: Sage Publications, pp. 14–31.

Mnyampala, M. E., 1967, *Diwani ya Mnyampala*. Nairobi: Kenya Literature Bureau.

Muchera, M., 2000, 'Domestic Violence in Kenya: A Survey of Newspaper Reports', in F. Oyekanmi, ed., *Men, Women and Violence*, Dakar: CODESRIA.

Mumby, D. K., 1988, *Communication and Power in Organizations: Discourse Ideology and Domination. Norwood,* NJ: Ablex Publishing Corporation.

Mwaro, A. G., 2000, 'Tathmini ya Nadharia za Uundaji wa Istilahi za Kiswahili', in J. S. Mdee na Masabo-Tumbo, eds., *Mulika*, Dar es Salaam: TUKI, Vol. 26, pp. 49–62.

Nwagbara, A. U., 2000, 'Women and Dialectic of War: A Comparative Study of the Portrayal of Women in the Nigerian Civil War Fiction', in F. Oyekanmi, ed., *Men, Women and Violence,* Dakar: CODESRIA.

Oyekanmi, F., ed., 2000, *Men, Women and Violence*, Dakar: CODESRIA.

Plummer, K., 2005, 'Male Sexualities', in M. S. Kimmel, J. Hearn and R. W. Connel, eds., *Handbook of Studies on Men and Masculinities*, Thousand Oaks, CA, London and New Delhi: Sage Publications.

Online definition of rape: see http://www.rapecrisisonline.com/articles.htm [last accessed 10 August 2005]

Tibatemwa-Ekirikubinza, L., 1999, *Womens's Violent Crime in Uganda: More Sinned Against than Sinning*, Kampala: Fountain Publishers.

Wachira, M., 1994, 'Kenyan Law as an Ideology of Male Power', in W. Kabira and W. Muthoni, eds., *The Road to Empowerment*, Nairobi: African Women's Development Communication Network.

Wodak, R., 1996a, *Disorders of Discourse*, London: Longman.

Wodak, R., 1996b, 'Critical Linguistics and Critical Discourse Analysis', in J. Verschueren, ed., *Handbook of Pragmatics*, Amsterdam: Benjamins, pp. 207–10.

Wodak, R., 1999, 'Introduction', in R. Wodak, ed., *Language Power and Ideology*, Amsterdam, Benjamins, pp. i–ix.

Wodak, R., 2000a, 'The Rise of Racism – An Austrian or a European Phenomenon?', *Discourse and Society*, Vol. 11, No. 1, pp. 5–6.

Wodak, R., 2000b, 'Wer echt, anständig und ordentlich ist bestimme ich! -wie Jörg Haider und die FPO die österreichische Vergangenheit, Gegenwart und Zukunft beurteilen', *Multimedia*, Vol. 20, No. 2, pp. 10–11.

Wodak, R., 2000c, 'Does Sociolinguistics Need Social Theory? New Perspectives on Critical Discourse Analysis', keynote speech at SS 2000, Bristol, April 2000 (shortened and published in *Discourse and Society*, Vol. 2, No. 3, pp. 123–47).

Wodak R., 2001a, 'Diskurs, Politik, Identität', in F. Brix, H. Goebl and O. Panagl, eds., *Der Mensch und Seine Sprache(n)*. Vienna: Böhlau, pp. 80–102.

Wodak, R., 2001b, 'What CDA is About – A Summary of its History, Important Concepts and Developments', in R. Wodak and M. Meyer, eds., *Methods of Critical Discourse Analysis: Introducing Qualitative Methods*, Thousand Oaks, CA, London and New Delhi: Sage Publications.

Wodak, R., 2001c, 'The Discourse-Historical Approach', in R. Wodak and M. Meyer, eds., *Methods of Critical Discourse Analysis: Introducing Qualitative Methods*, Thousand Oaks, CA, London and New Delhi: Sage Publications.

Wodak, R. and de Cillia R., 1988, 'Sprache und Antisemitimus. Ausstellungs-katalog', *Mitteilungen des Instituts für Wissenschaft und Kunst*, Vol. 3.

Wodak, R. and van Dijk, T. A., eds., 2000, *Racism at the Top: Parliamentary Discourses on Ethnic Issues in Six European States*, Klagenfurt: Drava.

Wodak, R., Menz, F., Mitten, R. and Stern, F., 1994, *Sprachen der Vergagenheiten. Öffentliches Gedenken in österreichischen und deutschen Medien*, Frankfurt: Suhrkamp.

Wodak, R., de Cillia, R., Reisigl, M. and Liebhart, K., 1999, *The Discursive Construction of National Identity*, Edinburgh: Edinburgh University Press.

Wodak, R., Nowak, Pelikan, J., Gruber, H., de Cillia, R. and Mitten, R., 1990, 'Wir sind alle unschuldige Täter', *Diskurshistorische Studien zum Nachkriegsantisemitimus*. Frankfurt: Suhrkamp.

Wodak, R., de Cillia, R., Reisigl, M., Liebhart, K., Hofstätter, K. and Kargl, M., 1998, *Zur diskursiven Konstruktion Nationaler Identität*, Frankfurt: Suhrkamp.

5

La masculinité au Maroc entre traditions, modernité et intégrisme

Abdessamad Dialmy

« Dans de nombreuses cultures, les hommes se battent quotidiennement pour se prouver à eux-mêmes et aux autres qu'ils sont qualifiés d'appartenir à la catégorie estimée de mâle. Ne pas être homme, c'est être réduit au statut de femme, ou pire c'est être pédéraste » (Heise 1997 : 411-434). Cette citation opère trois distinctions fondamentales : entre le mâle et l'homme, entre la catégorie « estimée » de l'homme et le statut « inférieur » des femmes, entre l'hétérosexuel et l'homosexuel. Ces distinctions débouchent sur les questionnements suivants : la masculinité est-elle une donnée biologique ou une construction idéologique? La masculinité est-elle toujours définissable en tant que supériorité (par rapport à la féminité)? Y a-t-il plusieurs formes de masculinité?

Face à ces questionnements, deux grandes réponses théoriques sont identifiables : le différencialisme et le constructivisme. Si pour les différentialistes, la masculinité est une donnée biologique, pour les constructivistes, elle n'est qu'une construction idéologique servant précisément à légitimer l'oppression des femmes. Pour les premiers, c'est la biologie qui définit en dernière analyse l'essence masculine et féminine. Ce point de vue a retrouvé une nouvelle jeunesse avec la sociobiologie, fondée en 1975 par E. O. Wilson : tous les comportements humains s'expliquent en termes d'hérédité génétique et de fonctionnement neuronal. Pour les seconds, « l'homme est une sorte d'artefact » selon l'expression de E. Badinter (1992 : 15). L'homme est constamment confronté à des devoirs, à des épreuves, à des preuves, et cette confrontation continue prouve que la masculinité est toujours une entité sociale à construire (et à maintenir).

Pour les différencialistes, la masculinité est, en tant que supériorité, ancrée et portée par le biologique. Pour Anaxagore, la détermination du sexe vient du

père : les garçons provenant du testicule droit, le plus chaud, les filles du gauche...
c'est une plus forte chaleur qui fait concevoir un mâle. Pour Freud, la femme est
d'abord un manque, un manque de pénis, une incomplétude d'où son statut second et inférieur. L'anatomie détermine donc le destin (social) de chaque sexe.
L'universalité de la suprématie masculine trouverait son explication ultime dans la
différence sexuelle de base biologique, dans la force masculine. La loi d'exogamie
elle-même, qui fonde toute société et qui est loi d'échange des femmes et de leur
pouvoir de fécondité entre les hommes, s'explique en dernière analyse par la
violence et la force masculines. Selon F. Héritier, « dans aucune société humaine,
les femmes n'ont échangé les hommes ». « Pourquoi cela ne s'est-il jamais produit » s'interroge J. Mitchel (1975 : 511). À l'intérieur de ce paradigme bio-
différencialiste, l'historien américain Thomas Laqueur décrit le passage, à la fin du
XVIIIe siècle, d'un modèle « unisexe » où « les hommes et les femmes étaient
rangés suivant leur degré de perfection métaphysique, leur chaleur vitale, le long
d'un axe dont le télos était mâle, à un nouveau modèle de dimorphisme radical,
de divergence biologique. Une anatomie et une physiologie de l'incommensura-
bilité remplacèrent une métaphysique de la hiérarchie dans la représentation de la
femme par rapport à l'homme » (Laqueur 1992 : 19).

Pour les constructivistes, « il n'y a pas un modèle masculin universel, valable
en tout temps et en tout lieu... La masculinité n'est pas une essence, mais une
idéologie qui tend à justifier la domination masculine » (Badinter 1992 : 48). Le
constructivisme remet en question la puissance explicative (et justificative) du sexe
biologique pour lever le voile sur la domination qui caractérise le rapport social
des sexes (Hurtig, Kail, Rouch 1991 : 11). Cette théorie se subdivise en deux courants, l'un appelé égalitariste et l'autre radical selon la terminologie de Cégolène
Frisque (1997). Le courant égalitariste affirme que le sexe social est construit à
partir du sexe biologique dans le sens où il y a une transformation de la différence
bio-sexuelle en rapport inégalitaire de domination au profit des hommes. Le
deuxième courant est appelé radical parce que pour lui les catégories sexuelles
elles-mêmes ne sont pas une simple donnée biologique mais un construit social en
fonction des rapports sociaux de domination masculine. Dans ce sens, Bourdieu
affirme que les corps sont façonnés par « la somatisation progressive des relations fondamentales qui sont constitutives de l'ordre social » (Bourdieu 1990 : 8).
En d'autres termes, c'est le genre comme rapport de pouvoir qui construit le sexe
biologique de la femme comme une entité négative, c'est-à-dire comme un être
privé des propriétés de l'homme, le pénis en l'occurrence. On ne naît donc pas
homme, on le devient suivant des modèles, à travers un apprentissage. L'acte viril
par excellence, c'est le meurtre de la mère, et « le premier devoir pour un homme
est de ne pas être femme » (Stoller 1989: 319-311). Sur le plan sexuel, la masculinité est alors construite comme hétérosexualité, comme pouvoir de pénétration
de l'autre, le féminin.

Quelle est la situation de la masculinité au Maroc ? Qu'est-ce qu'être homme au Maroc? Suffit-il de naître mâle pour être un homme ? En un mot, à quoi réfère l'identité masculine au Maroc? Pour répondre à ces questions, nous traiterons de quatre points qui nous semblent refléter la problématique marocaine de la masculinité : la socialisation sexuelle traditionnelle, les stratégies égalitaires modernistes, les régressions intégristes, les évolutions au niveau des représentations masculines de la masculinité.

Socialisation sexuelle traditionnelle

Dans le Maroc traditionnel, la socialisation sexuelle visait l'établissement de deux identités sexuelles distinctes et hiérarchisées. En effet, les rites de grossesse et de naissance, les jeux d'enfance et les rites du mariage révèlent tous un traitement discriminatoire et inégalitaire entre les sexes. La finalité de ces rites est d'arracher le garçon à la féminité et le construire comme homme-pouvoir. Si la petite fille naît femme et le reste (axe horizontal), le garçon est appelé à devenir homme, c'est à dire puissant (axe ascensionnel vertical). La naissance du garçon est l'occasion d'une satisfaction collective qui s'exprime dans un rituel plus étoffé : les youyous sont plus nombreux, le bain de la parturiente sept jours après l'accouchement est bien plus cérémonial... Car dans le système marocain de la parenté, patrilinéaire, la naissance du garçon assure la perpétuation de la lignée (c'est-à-dire la perpétuation du nom et de l'identité). « La maison où l'on ne donne naissance qu'à des filles est une maison déserte », affirme un proverbe d'arabe dialectal.

La violence et les risques caractérisent les jeux des garçons, tandis que la douceur, la prudence et le maternage accompagnent les jeux des filles. Une initiation intense de la fille aux travaux domestiques est entreprise très tôt dans l'espace privé et pour l'espace privé. Contrairement à cela, la formation du garçon se fait dans le sens d'une préparation à l'espace public comme espace de pouvoir, aussi cette socialisation se focalise-t-elle sur la valorisation de la virilité phallique, agressive et compétitive. Les frontières sexuelles sont donc des frontières spatiales. À chaque sexe son espace propre, l'espace du garçon étant celui du travail rémunéré, public et politique.

Le cheminement vers cet espace de pouvoir commence, pour le garçon, par le rite de la circoncision : cet acte symbolise l'arrachement au monde des femmes et le passage à l'espace masculin. En effet, la circoncision doit être comprise comme une intégration au monde viril des mâles. Après la circoncision, le garçon n'accompagne plus sa mère au bain des femmes, il bascule dans le monde des hommes. Du coup, le monde des femmes devient pour lui un lieu interdit et, par là un objet de désir et de fantasmes. Cette transformation de la femme en objet de désir sexuel rassure les parents sur la réussite de leur socialisation. Leur hantise d'avoir un garçon homosexuel (passif) est effectivement la pierre angulaire de leur construction de la masculinité. En conséquence, l'activité hétérosexuelle préconjugale des garçons, moins prohibée par l'interprétation socioculturelle de l'islam en comparaison avec l'homosexualité, reste une activité rassurante sur l'orientation sexuelle du garçon : un garçon hétérosexuel est sexuellement correct. Pour l'homme marocain, être sexuellement correct, c'est être hétérosexuel.

Cette hétérosexualité normalisante est testée lors du rite de la défloration. La nuit de l'entrée-pénétration (lilt al *dakhla*) est à la fois une épreuve de virilité pour l'homme qui devient homme (*rajel*) en réussissant la défloration, et une épreuve de virginité pour la fille (*bent*) qui accède au statut social valorisant de femme (*mra'*). Dans cette optique, il ne saurait être question pour la jeune fille d'une activité sexuelle préconjugale. Si elle n'est pas intégrée à la conjugalité, c'est-à-dire dépendante, la sexualité féminine est dite *fassad*, prostitution.

Dans le rite du premier mariage, le marié est appelé sultan pour signifier que « le marié devient *rajel* (homme) en devenant d'abord le mâle par excellence qu'est le roi... le marié devient symboliquement le roi au début des cérémonies et le reste jusqu'à leur achèvement, jusqu'à ce que le sang de l'épouse soit répandu... Le roi fait accéder l'époux à la masculinité, et l'époux fait pénétrer le roi dans son domaine privé, dans ce qui détermine son identité, le premier acte sexuel conjugal...» (Combs-Schilling 1996 : 76-85). En un mot, être homme, c'est être sultan, être sultan, c'est être homme. Être homme-sultan, c'est être viril, puissant. C'est dominer l'épouse, le pénis devenant ici l'instrument de la domination masculine. Par conséquent, la vie conjugale est le champ premier où l'homme doit exercer inconditionnellement sa domination. Le *rajel* (à la différence du *rouijel*, diminutif péjoratif de *rajel*), c'est l'homme qui maîtrise femme (s) et enfants. Ainsi, « le simple fait de manifester publiquement des signes de familiarité ou d'affection à l'égard de sa femme vaut parfois à un homme les qualificatifs péjoratifs de *rouijel* ou de *hnin*, l'affectueux, le tendre, ce qui serait contraire à la nature d'un *rajel*... » (CERED 1998 : 38). Le *rajel*, c'est l'homme dur, tandis que le *rouijel*, c'est l'homme mou. Le *rajel* ne se laisse pas guider sexuellement par l'épouse, il est le maître initiateur qui doit tout le temps contrôler la sexualité de la femme.

Stratégies égalitaires

Ce rapport social hiérarchique des sexes est actuellement en transition dans la mesure où la dichotomie traditionnelle entre deux identités sexuelles hiérarchiques est mise en crise par l'évolution de la société marocaine. Cette évolution se caractérise notamment par un accès de plus en plus grand de la femme à l'éducation et au marché de l'emploi. Un tel accès ne manque pas d'avoir un impact sur la sexualité, la reproduction et les rapports sociaux de sexe. Cette évolution transparaît aussi dans la révision du *Code du Statut Personnel* en 1993, révision qui va timidement dans le sens de la promotion de la femme grâce à un féminisme associatif très actif.

Dans le champ de la santé reproductive et sexuelle

L'ouverture du champ de la santé reproductive est surtout visible au niveau de la planification familiale (PF). La baisse de l'indice synthétique de fécondité (moins 4,8 points en 30 ans) signifie que les programmes de la PF constituent une réussite, et ce grâce à une aide internationale soutenue depuis la fin des années 1960. Dans ce même cadre, la société urbaine regarde désormais d'un mauvais oeil le mari qui empêche son épouse d'être examinée ou assistée par un médecin de sexe masculin lors de la grossesse et de l'accouchement. Plus loin encore, la sexualité féminine ose maintenant se faire (Dialmy 2000) et se dire (La revue mensuelle *Femmes du Maroc* ne manque pas de traiter le sujet de la sexualité féminine dans chacun de ses numéros), avec ou sans l'aval du mariage, sans qu'elle soit prostitution et sans porter atteinte à la masculinité des hommes. C'est une sexualité qui se désinstitutionnalise et qui revendique le droit de s'autodéterminer.

Les stratégies marocaines d'exécution du programme d'action de la CIPD consolident cette ouverture. Un ministère délégué auprès du premier ministre chargé de la population est créé en 1995. Trois ans après la CIPD, le ministère de l'Éducation Nationale affirme que «l'actualisation des curricula est en cours... » (FNUAP 1997 : 35). De son côté, le ministère de la Jeunesse et des Sports a sensibilisé 30 000 jeunes filles aux questions de la santé reproductive, tandis qu'« un livre de référence a été produit conformément aux recommandations de la CIPD, les thèmes relatifs à la santé de reproduction, MST-SIDA ont été introduits dans les modèles de formation » (FNUAP 1997 : 35).

Le ministère de la Santé Publique, en faisant état d'une « épidémie » MST inquiétante, en appelle à une éducation sanitaire préventive qui débouche insensiblement sur la nécessité d'une éducation sexuelle à l'adresse des deux sexes. Cette éducation vise une double prévention, celle des grossesses involontaires et celle des MST-VIH. Le principe de l'égalité des sexes s'avère être ici une condition indispensable à la réussite de cette double prévention.

De son côté, l'Association Marocaine de Planification Familiale (AMPF) défend le droit à la santé reproductive et sexuelle de chaque individu. Son action vise à rendre les femmes autonomes, à éduquer les jeunes, à rendre l'homme conscient de ses responsabilités. L'AMPF dispose de 20 cliniques à travers le royaume : IEC, *counseling*, consultations médicales concernant PF, distribution de pilules, préservatifs et pose de stérilets. Elle dispose d'une unité de production en matière de télévision qui a produit deux télé-feuilletons, *Aziza* et *Aïnek mizanek*. Dans sa stratégie 2000, la question de la jeunesse et de la sexualité est l'une des priorités de l'AMPF. Pour que la jeunesse ne recoure pas à l'avortement risqué et clandestin et ne contracte pas de MST, il est nécessaire de promouvoir une politique qui défende le droit des jeunes à l'information et qui établisse une IEC en matière de sexualité. « La sexualité des jeunes est souvent conjoncturelle et n'utilise pas les moyens de prévention comme le préservatif » (AMPF 2000). L'AMPF lutte également contre tous les éléments d'inégalité entre l'homme et la femme afin que la femme puisse décider elle-même de tout ce qui concerne sa santé sexuelle et reproductive.

Dans le champ du droit familial

Face à la lenteur partisane, les femmes militantes ne pouvaient que se sentir non véritablement représentées au sein des partis et par les partis. Aussi assiste-t-on à un éloignement progressif des femmes par rapport aux partis politiques, espace quasiment monopolisé par les hommes. Le discours naissant des droits de l'homme au début des années 1980 ne peut que séduire les femmes féministes, les droits des femmes faisant partie intégrante des droits de l'homme. Ce discours nouveau conduisit les femmes à s'organiser au sein d'associations institutionnellement autonomes qui leur permirent de dialoguer directement avec les pouvoirs publics. Parmi ces associations, citons l'Association Démocratique des Femmes Marocaines (1985), l'Union de l'Action Féminine (1987), l'Association Féminine des Femmes Progressistes (1992), l'Association Marocaine des Droits de la Femme (1992), Joussour (1997)… Il faut surtout voir dans l'institutionnalisation associative du mouvement féministe un passage à la démocratie participative (suite à l'échec de la démocratie représentative, les femmes étant largement exclues et marginalisées dans toutes les structures politiques). Les femmes prennent en main la question féminine dans des associations féminines tout en étant conscientes du fait que cette question n'est pas que féminine.

Pour ce féminisme associatif, il s'agit avant tout de créer une opinion publique solidaire autour d'une nouvelle conscience féminine qui approfondit le paradigme de l'insuffisance de la lettre de l'Islam et qui revendique de manière beaucoup plus active la révision du Code du Statut Personnel (Dialmy 2004 : 121-135). Eu égard au sous-développement de la population marocaine, le féminisme associatif adopte la voie de la réforme par l'*ijtihad*. Aucune association féministe ou des droits de l'homme n'opte ouvertement pour la sécularisation du droit de la famille. Dans le cadre de l'option « *ijtihad* » comme seule option associativement (et politiquement) correcte (Dialmy 2000 : 68-88 en arabe), l'année 1992 peut être considérée comme une année charnière. Elle a vu l'organisation d'un colloque national sur le CSP le 17 avril, la constitution d'un Comité de Coordination National (qui regroupe UAF, section féminine de l'USFP, Association Féminine des Femmes Progressistes, Association Marocaine des Droits de la Femme, AMDH), la campagne d'un million de signatures, et la soumission d'une proposition de réforme du CSP au parlement. Ce projet revendique le contrôle de la polygamie par le juge, la transformation de la dissolution du mariage en divorce judiciaire, l'institution d'un Conseil Supérieur de la Femme, la promulgation de textes constitutionnels pour affirmer les droits politiques, économiques sociaux et culturels des femmes.

Le 10 septembre 1993, une révision du CSP a eu lieu et couronne la pression du mouvement féministe marocain. « Cette révision a eu lieu le 10 septembre 1993, c'est-à-dire à une période de vide parlementaire, comme si le pouvoir signifiait par ce choix que la législation en matière de statut personnel, défini comme religieux et apolitique, échappe aux prérogatives du parlement. Le statut juridique de la femme n'a pas à être déterminé par les différents acteurs de la société civile, tel semble être le message de cet acte législatif méta-parlementaire et supra-politique » (Dialmy 1995 : 245-246). Mais cette révision ne touche que 09 articles, ce qui signifie que 207 articles sont restés intacts. Statistiquement, il s'agit d'une révision qui a touché 4,1 % du corpus du CSP. Quels sont les nouveaux articles qui sont produits et qui visent à réduire la masculinité comme pouvoir? Il s'agit des articles suivants :

- Article 5 : le consentement de l'épouse au mariage doit être explicite et public ;

- Article 6 : la suppression du droit de contrainte (que le père pouvait exercer sur sa fille pour la marier contre sa volonté) ;

- Article 6 : la possibilité de se passer du *wali* (tuteur matrimonial) dans le cas de la jeune fille raisonnable (*rashida*) orpheline de père ;

- Article 30 : la nécessité d'avertir la première épouse ainsi que la seconde dans le cas d'une intention de polygamie (afin d'avoir le consentement des deux). Par ailleurs, le juge doit autoriser la polygamie (au cas par cas) ;

- Article 48 : la présence des deux époux est obligatoire pour enregistrer la répudiation. Mais il est passé outre la présence de l'épouse si elle reçoit convocation et ne se présente pas et si le mari insiste sur la réalisation de la répudiation ;

- Article 148 : l'octroi à la mère du droit de la tutelle testamentaire après le père.

Tous ces changements limitent le pouvoir de la masculinité et tendent à rompre avec la masculinité comme pouvoir (et privilèges).

Tentatives de régressions intégristes

Avec le gouvernement d'alternance (1998), la lutte féministe pour la réforme du Code du Statut Personnel continue de manière plus radicale à travers le projet de « Plan National d'intégration de la Femme au Développement » (PNIFD). Annoncé le 19 mars 1999 par le Premier ministre, ce plan comprend les propositions radicales suivantes :

- élever l'âge du premier mariage à 18 ans,

- supprimer la tutelle matrimoniale,

- enregistrer l'enfant naturel sous le nom de famille de sa mère,

- transformer toute dissolution de mariage en divorce judiciaire,

- interdire la polygamie et non seulement la limiter par des conditions restrictives ; les cas exceptionnels doivent être soumis à l'accord de la première épouse et à l'évaluation du juge,

- le juge qui prononce le divorce doit partager les biens accumulés au cours de la vie conjugale et offrir à la femme la moitié des biens dont elle a participé à l'acquisition, soit par son travail domestique, soit par son travail salarié,

- reconnaître aux femmes le droit d'être juge en matière de statut personnel.

Le PNIFD s'est heurté à une très forte résistance religieuse (Dialmy 1999) (en arabe). Ouléma et intégristes ont réagi en promulguant des *fatawi* (avis juridiques musulmans) accusant toutes les forces féministes d'apostasie et d'athéisme. Ils ont été contre la proposition d'élever l'âge du premier mariage à 18 ans. Selon eux, cette mesure est un facteur de licence sexuelle (*fassad*) et fait rater beaucoup d'occasions de mariage à la jeune fille. La proposition de supprimer la tutelle matrimoniale a également été rejetée. La supprimer constitue à leurs yeux une atteinte à la structure de la famille musulmane et risque de créer une coupure entre les membres de la famille, une haine entre les ascendants et les descendants. De même, ils trouvent inconcevable d'inscrire un enfant naturel à l'état civil sous le nom de famille de sa mère. Pour eux, l'enfant naturel n'a pas de père et ne peut jouir d'un nom de famille. Ce nom n'appartient pas à la mère seule. De plus, donner un nom de famille à l'enfant naturel, c'est une manière d'encourager la fornication selon eux. Dans la même logique, ils refusent que toute dissolution de mariage soit transformée en divorce. En d'autres termes, ils sont pour le maintien de la répudiation. Car le demandeur du divorce doit fournir, selon eux, un plus grand effort (pour motiver sa demande) et doit par conséquent dévoiler les secrets de la vie conjugale. C'est aussi une procédure qui prive le mari de son droit à reprendre son épouse après la répudiation simple au cours du délai de viduité. De plus, compliquer les procédures de la dissolution du mariage, c'est les prolonger dans le temps et c'est faire vivre les conjoints dans un état de fornication (*sifah*). Quant à la polygamie, elle est pour eux un principe indiscutable au nom d'un verset coranique catégorique clair, verset ne pouvant faire l'objet d'une interprétation ou d'une suspension. Dieu a seulement recommandé d'être juste envers les co-épouses. Au niveau du partage des biens après la dissolution du mariage, la proposition est rejetée : chaque conjoint doit rester indépendant et autonome dans l'acquisition et la gestion de ses biens. Seul l'entretien est dû à l'épouse. À part l'entretien, l'accord de l'époux est obligatoire (pour donner à l'épouse un bien après la dissolution du mariage). Les islamistes refusent enfin de reconnaître à la femme le droit d'être juge en matière de statut personnel. Le motif de leur rejet est que la société musulmane n'accepte pas que la femme siège dans le poste du juge en matière de statut personnel. Car à partir de ce poste, on désigne les différents imam-prêcheurs. Ce juge est également le juge des mineurs et le tuteur des sans-tuteurs. La femme ne saurait être chargée de toutes ces missions selon le raisonnement intégriste.

Comme on le constate à travers ces rejets, il y a une volonté manifeste de défendre les privilèges de l'homme au nom du sacré. Selon le raisonnement islamiste, l'homme a islamiquement le droit de jouir du corps des femmes dès leur puberté (licéité du mariage de la jeune fille avant 18 ans), de contrôler le marché matrimonial (à travers le maintien de la règle du tutorat), d'épouser plus d'une femme, de répudier sans passer par un procès judiciaire, de garder la plus-value du travail domestique de l'épouse, de monopoliser la fonction du juge en matière de statut personnel. Ces droits islamiques sont devenus, dans le raisonnement islamiste, des attributs quasi naturels intouchables de l'homme musulman. Ils constituent la dimension juridique sacrale de la masculinité islamique.

Pour les islamistes, le PNIFD porte atteinte à la nature de la famille musulmane et vise sa destruction. Ce faisant, les islamistes ont estimé que la famille musulmane est définie une fois pour toutes comme une structure hiérarchique inégalitaire au profit de ses mâles. C'est là une manière de sacraliser la famille patriarcale et d'en faire un invariant. Toute autre forme que prendrait cette famille est considérée comme une déviance et une hérésie. Il y a eu donc un refus islamiste de voir que la famille musulmane contemporaine se nucléarise aussi (et est appelée par conséquent à se démocratiser). Ce mal de voir les a conduit à ne pas reconnaître la famille nucléaire égalitaire comme une famille islamique (Dialmy 2000 en arabe). Pour cette raison, les islamistes ont taxé les défenseurs du plan d'incroyance, d'impérialisme, de sionisme, de marxisme et de communisme. Personne n'a échappé à leur inquisition. « Le plan-projet n'a t-il pas été financé par la Banque Mondiale ? » s'écrient-ils. N'est-il pas présenté par un ministre dont le parti est le prolongement historique du parti communiste marocain ? Pour les *ouléma* et les islamistes, il y a incompatibilité irrémédiable et définitive entre le plan et l'islam.

Les islamistes perçoivent la domination masculine comme une évidence car la famille patriarcale étendue est leur référent « naturel ». Plus loin encore, ce modèle familial est valorisé comme une norme. La dominance statistique de la famille nucléaire dans le Maroc des années 1990 est ignorée : la famille nucléaire est considérée comme déviance si elle représente l'infrastructure de l'égalité des droits entre les conjoints. Pour cette raison, l'intégrisme ignore sciemment la nucléarisation de la famille comme une nouvelle source potentielle du droit familial. Pourquoi cette cécité ? Pourquoi ce mal de voir ? Pourquoi cette volonté de mal voir ?

La connivence entre ouléma marocains et classes dominantes est historique et s'explique par le fait que les ouléma sont eux-mêmes issus de ces classes sociales. Aussi le droit musulman a-t-il toujours opéré selon le modèle et les intérêts de ces classes et des familles étendues et riches qui en sont issues. Et c'est dans ces classes sociales que le modèle familial patriarcal est le plus et le mieux observé dans le sens où le mari est économiquement capable d'entretenir toutes les épouses, les concubines, les esclaves allaiteuses, les esclaves domestiques…

Cette base socio-économique de la législation islamique patriarcale est occultée. Le pouvoir de l'homme au sein de la famille est sacralisé quel que soit son statut socio-économique. Même pauvre, l'homme musulman s'accroche à ce pouvoir que lui confère la loi islamique. Et c'est surtout le musulman pauvre qui s'accroche à la sacralité du pouvoir masculin parce qu'il n'a plus les moyens économiques de l'exercer et de le justifier. L'homme islamiste ne veut pas repenser la loi à partir de sa situation fragile au sein d'une famille nucléaire où l'épouse prend de plus en plus de pouvoir. À cet homme, il ne reste plus que la loi sacrale pour exercer le pouvoir de sa masculinité et pour exercer la masculinité comme pouvoir de manière inconditionnelle. D'où l'attachement « sauvage » au caractère supra-historique et sacral de son pouvoir d'homme.

C'est le contexte de crise socio-économique induit par la politique d'ajustement structurel depuis 1983 qui conduit le marocain ordinaire à régresser vers les formes traditionnelles de la domination masculine. Le principe de l'égalité des sexes est la première victime de cette crise malgré tout l'effort que déploient féminisme associatif et féminisme d'État afin de dissocier entre égalité des sexes et essor économique. Dans ce contexte, les programmes de la santé reproductive ne peuvent avoir un impact suffisamment corrosif sur l'identité masculine « dure ». Les difficultés de ces programmes conduisent à une remise en cause de l'idéologie égalitariste qui les sous-tend. Et la phallocratie se révèle être ici le refoulé (dynamique) d'une modernité inachevée. Cette phallocratie se dit au nom de l'islam, tant scripturaire qu'intégriste : toutes les questions relatives à la santé reproductive doivent être traitées en conformité avec deux principes dits inamovibles d'une *Shari'â* dite préétablie une fois pour toutes, l'inégalité des sexes en matière de statut personnel et la subordination de la sexualité au mariage.

Évolutions

L'homme marocain est donc ballotté entre deux appels : celui des programmes de la santé reproductive et sexuelle, égalitaire et celui des traditionalismes identitaires, discriminatoire. Comment s'arrange-t-il pour concilier ces deux appels ? Pour répondre à une telle question, nous avons réalisé en 2000 une étude intitulée « Identité masculine et santé reproductive au Maroc » (Dialmy 2000)[1]. Quelques-uns de ses résultats vont être exposés en guise de réponse au dilemme que vit la masculinité au Maroc.

Profil juridique

Concernant la tutelle matrimoniale, une majorité absolue confortable lui reste favorable. Pour l'homme y tenir, c'est se définir comme contrôleur de l'échange des femmes. L'homme tient à rester celui qui donne ses femmes (fille, soeur, cousine, mère…) à d'autres hommes, d'abord pour exprimer son pouvoir (de contrôle sur le corps féminin), puis pour réaliser un bénéfice financier, social et symbolique. L'homme, en tenant à se définir comme tuteur matrimonial, tient à sa qualité de « protecteur » des femmes de la famille. C'est un protecteur intéressé dans le sens où le tuteur transforme ses femmes en biens d'échange.

Concernant la polygamie, l'opinion est divisée en deux camps quasiment égaux. L'écoute des justifications de chaque camp conduit à distinguer entre trois positions : la polygamie est une norme à maintenir (patriarcalisme radical), la polygamie est une nécessité psychosociale à permettre dans les cas d'exception (patriarcalisme mitigé), la polygamie est un archaïsme à interdire totalement (féminisme radical).

Concernant la répudiation aussi, l'opinion est partagée de manière quasi égale. Deux points d'écart seulement sont à l'avantage de l'opinion patriarcale qui consiste à refuser la transformation de la répudiation en divorce judiciaire. Les patriarcalistes ne conçoivent pas une *Shari'a* qui transformerait la répudiation en divorce judiciaire. Lenteur de la procédure judiciaire du divorce (qui amènerait les époux en instance de divorce à cohabiter de façon illégale dans le cas où le mari aurait prononcé une répudiation), honneur masculin (répudier étant un acte interprété comme un acte de masculinité), volonté de pouvoir (l'homme n'acceptant de rentrer dans l'institution conjugale que s'il a la certitude de pouvoir la dissoudre sans avoir à en référer à la justice), tels sont les trois motifs majeurs qui poussent l'homme ordinaire à se cramponner à la répudiation. La répudiation est un pouvoir exercé par l'homme au profit de l'homme que l'homme patriarcal intègre dans sa définition de l'homme. L'opinion adverse, celle disant que confier le divorce au juge n'amoindrit en rien la masculinité de l'homme, est tout aussi forte. La présence des deux conjoints lors de la dissolution du mariage apparaît tout aussi légitime que leur présence lors de sa conclusion. Dans le cadre de ce raisonnement, la transformation de la répudiation en divorce judiciaire est dite susceptible d'arrêter l'arbitraire du mari. Pour certains, la lenteur de la procédure du divorce est positive dans la mesure où elle comporte une chance de réconciliation.

En un mot, pour les hommes féministes, le pouvoir patriarcal de la masculinité doit cesser et, pour commencer, ne doit plus trouver dans la *Shari'a* sa légitimation sacrale (Dialmy 2000). Aussi l'effort créateur de lois nouvelles (*ijtihad*) est-il encouragé et sollicité. L'homme ordinaire le revendique aussi et montre ainsi que la masse est partie prenante d'une réforme égalitaire du code de la famille. Il s'ensuit que les politiques intégristes ne peuvent plus avancer le prétexte de la masse pour justifier leur conservatisme patriarcal. Ainsi, même si l'homme ordinaire n'arrive pas encore à définir l'identité masculine sans y incorporer le droit au tutorat matrimonial, il conçoit par contre de ne plus y incorporer le droit à la polygamie, à la répudiation. L'homme ordinaire commence à se concevoir comme homme en sacrifiant une part non négligeable du pouvoir patriarcal.

Profil psychosocial

Malgré la mise en relation de la masculinité et des traits qui signifient la supériorité et la suprématie, la définition de l'homme comme supériorité et suprématie est une définition qui est loin d'être majoritaire. Être homme ne signifie plus être meilleur que la femme. Les risques que la masculinité encourt eu égard à l'évolution sociale sont ressentis et exprimés. Dans cette perspective, les difficultés financières sont désignées comme responsables de la dé-masculinisation des jeunes, c'est-à-dire de leur perte des « qualités » patriarcales de l'identité masculine. Des pouvoirs sont enlevés à l'homme et l'homme commence à ne plus être hégémonique. Cette dé-traditionalisation constitue le point de départ d'un nouveau profil psychosocial de la masculinité. Et l'on avance que l'homme sentimental ne doit plus être considéré comme une femme, de même que l'homme qui aide sa femme dans les travaux domestiques. La tendresse et la gentillesse sont désormais concevables comme qualités masculines (Dialmy 2002 : 125-146). On en conclut que l'homme n'est pas une donnée sacrée et figée, qu'il n'est pas une essence immuable. Sans être explicitement utilisée par les enquêtés, la notion de genre construit est ici adéquate pour décrire leur mode de pensée. En définissant l'homme comme susceptible de remise en question, de changement et d'évolution, la conscience masculine devient effectivement constructiviste. Le genre masculin est de moins en moins représenté comme une identité fixe, statique et exclusive. De même, rejeter tout ce qui est construit comme féminin n'est plus un acte nécessaire dans la démonstration de la masculinité. Certes, les hommes subissent encore une plus grande pression pour assumer des prescriptions socioculturelles telles qu'être raisonnable, honnête et travailleur, mais cela se fait dans un sens moins hégémonique. Être un agent actif dans la construction et la reconstruction de l'identité masculine ne signifie plus reproduire mécaniquement les normes patriarcales de la masculinité qui définissent la masculinité comme domination. Ces normes ne sont plus totalement dominantes, et être homme ne signifie plus dominer (la femme) par le seul fait d'être un mâle.

Profil sexuel

Pour la majorité, être homme ne signifie pas nécessairement être fécond et viril. Un homme reste homme tout en étant impuissant et/ou stérile. De plus, fécondité et virilité sont nettement dissociées. La fécondité n'est plus le signe visible et la preuve matérielle de la virilité. Être viril ne signifie pas être fécond, être fécond ne signifie pas être viril (Dialmy 2002 : 132).

Face à la stérilité et l'impuissance, l'explication sociale combine entre morale et science d'une part, et entre magie et religion d'autre part. Science et morale tendent à accuser l'homme et à le responsabiliser en investissant des notions comme le microbe et la débauche. Par contre, la tradition magico-religieuse est récupérée pour déresponsabiliser l'homme stérile et/ou impuissant et le rassurer sur sa masculinité. Mais le mode d'explication identifié est en général un mixage entre ces quatre registres de telle sorte que, par exemple, le microbe est dit être attrapé à travers une débauche que Dieu utilise comme motif pour punir quelqu'un.

En cas d'échec d'une thérapie (magique ou biomédicale), la causalité divine est invoquée comme dernier recours pour réconcilier l'homme stérile ou impuissant avec lui-même. Fécondité et stérilité, virilité et impuissance, ce sont là des questions qui relèvent de Dieu ou du hasard, souligne-t-on. Dieu serait une version sacralisée du hasard, une version qui a l'avantage de déresponsabiliser l'homme et de panser les blessures narcissiques de son moi patriarcal. Cette version noble du hasard a en effet l'avantage sécurisant d'interpréter la stérilité comme une fatalité contre laquelle l'homme ne peut rien. Le pouvoir de fécondation est indépendant de la volonté humaine. En conséquence, « l'homme ne doit pas se battre contre son destin. L'homme stérile est un homme, Dieu l'a créé homme ». La stérilité ne diminue pas de la masculinité d'un homme qui croit vraiment en Dieu : c'est quand l'homme est ignorant de Dieu qu'il doute de sa masculinité. Plus loin encore, l'on souligne que même s'il est sexuellement impuissant, l'homme reste homme tant qu'il ne devient pas homosexuel. « Tant qu'il ne se laisse pas sodomiser, on ne peut pas l'enlever du trône de la masculinité ».

Par ailleurs, le danger d'une définition de la masculinité par la virilité est désormais clairement perçu par l'homme marocain. L'homme impuissant reste un homme, pense-t-on contre l'éthique sexuelle traditionnelle qui estime qu'un homme impuissant n'est pas un homme. La modernité de l'homme marocain réside ici dans le fait de refuser de définir l'homme à partir de son activité sexuelle : « l'homme n'est pas seulement le sexe ». L'on pense que cette définition de l'homme par l'activité sexuelle est réductrice et incorrecte car « la virilité, on la trouve même chez les animaux, surtout chez les animaux ».

La tradition est également rejetée quant elle enferme l'homme dans la nécessité d'avoir des garçons pour être considéré comme un homme. Pour la grande majorité, la masculinité ne consiste plus à avoir des garçons. Plus loin encore, on peut affirmer l'apparition d'une légère préférence des filles, par intérêt : les filles sont dites plus tendres, et même mariées, l'on pense qu'elles continuent de s'occuper de leurs parents, à la différence des garçons. On reconnaît aussi qu'elles peuvent être fortes, responsables.

Conclusion

Cette enquête a brisé le silence des hommes marocains sur eux-mêmes. L'homme n'est plus ici un sujet de discours sur un objet autre, sur l'objet femme, l'homme est ici un sujet qui se prend lui-même comme objet dans un mouvement de retour critique sur soi. Retour sur soi nécessaire, mise au point utile après le défi féministe que lance la modernité à la masculinité.

Certes, il reste tant de choses à faire concernant les femmes en vue d'améliorer leur condition. Mais pour y parvenir, il est très approprié de travailler sur les hommes afin de pousser l'homme à travailler sur lui-même et à comprendre mieux la revendication féministe. D'ailleurs, traiter de l'homme, c'est traiter du genre comme unité d'analyse, c'est traiter du genre en tant que relation sociale, c'est traiter de l'homme et de la femme dans un même mouvement de savoir. Le genre n'est-il pas principalement relation hétérosexuelle oppressive? Notre re-cherche a révélé une chose capitale : les hommes marocains sont perdus à propos de leurs rapports à la femme, de leurs rôles dans la famille et à propos du sens et de la signification de la masculinité. Ces hommes qui perdent leur pouvoir et leur statut et deviennent incapables de jouir de leurs privilèges habituels ; ces hommes se repensent ou font des femmes les principales victimes de leur perte d'identité. Ils deviennent l'obstacle à un développement équitable. En conséquence, changer les relations inéquitables de genre peut difficilement se faire sans travailler sur les hommes, sans travailler avec les hommes, sans le travail des hommes sur eux-mêmes. Si le genre traite des hommes et des femmes, la balance sexuée de pou-voir ne peut être changée par les femmes seules. L'implication des hommes est une nécessité et leur visibilité servira la crédibilité et la promotion du genre comme champ de recherche et d'action. Il faut donc faire du genre un problème masculin (aussi). L'inclusion des hommes dans cette problématique, en tant qu'alliés, est susceptible de conduire à la politisation des revendications féministes, c'est à dire à une plus grande efficience.

C'est à cette seule condition qu'il y a des chances de mettre fin à des relations intersexuelles inégales, hiérarchiques, autoritaires et violentes. Notre étude a révélé que l'homme marocain, dorénavant un mâle problématique, commence à se re-présenter la manière non patriarcale d'être homme, à la concevoir comme une possibilité, comme un scénario légitime, comme une histoire à faire. Notre étude a montré que la critique de la masculinité doit certes conduire à un changement des comportements masculins, mais aussi et surtout à une interrogation sur la signification de la masculinité. Aussi les politiques sexuelles et reproductives ne doivent-elles pas s'arrêter seulement aux questions de la vie personnelle et de l'identité, mais aborder également les questions de la justice sociale entre les sexes afin de créer des possibilités politiques et théoriques permettant de repenser l'homme et sa violence, la masculinité et sa domination.

Note

1. L'étude a été possible grâce au soutien du *Lebanese Center for Policy Studies* (LCPS, Beyrouth) dans le cadre de *Middle East Research Competition* (MERC). Mes remerciements et ma reconnaissance les plus sincères sont donc adressés au LCPS/MERC et très spécialement au Dr Oussama K. Safa, directeur du programme MERC. Le mérite de l'élargissement de l'enquête à des sites non initialement prévus revient au Dr Mostafa Tyane, directeur de la population au ministère marocain de la santé, au Dr Théo Lippelveld, directeur du projet JSI (USAID) et au Dr Najia Hajji, chef de la division de la planification familiale à la Direction de la Population.

Références

AMPF, 2000, Le cadre théorique de la stratégie 2000. Numéro spécial à l'occasion du 25e anniversaire de la constitution de l'AMPF (en arabe).

Badinter, Elisabeth, 1992, *XY, De l'identité masculine*. Paris : Odile Jacob, pp. 15 et 48.

Bourdieu, Pierre, 1990, « La domination masculine », in *Actes de la Recherche en Sciences Sociales*, n° 84, p. 8.

Frisque, Cégolène, 1997, *L'objet femme*. Paris : La Documentation Française.

CERED, 1998, *Genre et développement : aspects socio-démographiques et culturels de la différenciation sexuelle*, Rabat : Ministère du Plan, p. 38.

Combs-Schilling, Elaine, 1996, « La légitimation rituelle du pouvoir au Maroc », in *Femmes, culture et société au Maghreb*, Casablanca : Afrique-Orient, pp. 76-85.

Dialmy, A., 1995, *Logement, sexualité et islam*, Casablanca : Eddif, pp. 245-246.

Dialmy, A., 1999, « Un front islamique contre le féminisme du gouvernement d'alternance » Casablanca : *Al Ahdath al Maghribiya*, août 1999 (en arabe).

Dialmy, A., 2000, « De la continuité entre *Shari'a* islamique et *Shari'a* internationale en matière de droit de la famille » Casablanca : *Prologues*, Hors-Série, n°4, pp. 68-88 (en arabe).

Dialmy, A., 2000, *Identité masculine et santé reproductive au Maroc (Rapport)*, Beyrouth : LCPS/ *Middle East Research Competition*.

Dialmy, A., 2000, *Jeunesse, Sida et Islam au Maroc* (Préface de J. Benoist), Casablanca : Eddif.

Dialmy, A., 2000, « Le Plan National d'Intégration de la Femme au Développement ne contredit pas l'esprit de l'islam », Casablanca : *Al Ittihad al Ichtiraki*, 25 avril 2000 (en arabe).

Dialmy, A., 2002, « Pour un homme citoyen dans la famille, une masculinité nouvelle », *Famille et citoyenneté*, Rabat : Éditions Chaml/Friedrich Ebert Stiftung, pp. 125-146, 132.

Dialmy, A., 2004, « Le féminisme marocain et la modernisation du droit de la famille », dans *Femmes et État de Droit*, Rabat : Chaire UNESCO, pp. 121-135.

FNUAP, 1997, *Rapport d'analyse du programme d'élaboration de la stratégie*, Casablanca : Le Fennec, p. 35.

Heise, L. L., 1997, «Violence, sexuality and women's lives », in R.N Lancaster and M. di Leonardo (eds), *The Gender Sexuality Reader : Culture, History, Political Economy*, New York, and London : Routledge, pp. 411-34.

Hurtig M-C, Kail, M., et Rouch, H., 1991, *Sexe et genre*. Paris : CNRS, p. 11.

Laqueur, Thomas, 1992, *La fabrique du sexe. Essai sur le corps et le genre en Occident,* Paris : Gallimard, p. 19.

Mitchell, Juliet, 1975, *Psychanalyse et féminisme*, Paris : Édition des Femmes, p. 511.

Stoller, Robert, 1989, *Masculin ou féminin,* Paris : PUF, 1989, pp. 319-311.

6

La formation de la masculinité entre la tradition et la modernité (le cas du sud du togo)

Svetlana Roubailo Koudolo

Introduction

La formation de la masculinité, en tant que catégorie sociale, s'effectue au cours du processus de la socialisation des enfants. Depuis la fin de la Seconde Guerre mondiale, ce processus traverse des mutations accélérées dues aux changements socio-économiques et culturels continentaux et mondiaux. L'économie de marché, l'urbanisation croissante, la scolarisation massive de la jeune génération, la christianisation et les différentes formes d'acculturation ont influencé le mode de vie de la population. Les crises sociopolitiques et socio-économiques des années 80-90 qu'a connu le pays ont approfondi davantage les difficultés économiques, abaissé le niveau de vie. Dans l'ensemble, tous ces changements ont eu un impact sur le statut social de l'individu, sur les rapports du genre et sur le processus de la socialisation des enfants. Dans ces conditions socio-économiques précaires, la construction du genre s'aligne sur les exigences nouvelles de la vie. Elle produit, par conséquent, des stéréotypes de la masculinité et de la féminité qui reflètent le recul des modèles traditionnels au profit des constructions modernes. L'enculturation qui est à la base de la formation du genre a déjà assimilé les multiples traits de la culture universelle. Cependant, elle s'exprime différemment dans le milieu rural et urbain. Dans les zones rurales les instituts traditionnels jouent encore un rôle de détenteur de la tradition et participent plus activement dans la transmission culturelle. Par contre, en milieu urbain cette transmission se présente autrement : elle s'appuie plutôt sur les modèles et valeurs nouvelles.

Jusqu'à présent, le thème de la formation de la masculinité sur la côte du Golfe du Bénin, plus précisément au Togo, n'a pas attiré une attention particulière des chercheurs. Néanmoins, certains d'entre eux ont abordé quelques aspects de ce sujet. Parmi les œuvres les plus importantes, il faut citer *L'enfant et son milieu en Afrique Noire* de P. Erny, où l'auteur donne un large panorama de la socialisation africaine et soulève, entre autres, le problème de la formation de la masculinité. Les auteurs comme F. Agblemagnon, D. Houenassou-Huangbe ont aussi accordé un certain intérêt à l'éducation des enfants dans cette région où la question de la masculinité a été soulevée. Nos recherches précédentes, consacrées au processus de la socialisation des enfants en milieu ewe, ont abordé également les spécificités de la formation de la masculinité.

Des données sur les représentations symboliques du genre ont été obtenues également grâce aux ouvrages consacrés à la vie religieuse et socioculturelle de J. Speith et de C. Rivière.

Les ouvrages historiques de H. Kwakume, N. Gayibor nous ont fourni une vision globale sur la genèse de l'aire culturelle du sud du Togo dont les Ewe et les Guins sont ses deux principales composantes.

Les travaux de nombreux spécialistes du genre ont particulièrement enrichit notre étude sur le plan théorique. Les auteurs comme D. Gardey et I. Löwy, entre autres, ont présenté l'évolution de la conception du genre et de la masculinité à travers le temps. Au cours des époques précédentes, elle a été généralement enracinée dans la pensée naturaliste et s'est basée sur la vision binaire de la nature comme par exemple : la nuit et le jour, le haut et le bas, le mâle et la femelle. Cette pensée valorise l'homme, compte tenu de ses fonctions « extra-sociales » qui, selon Sherry B. Ortner, se trouvent en rupture avec la nature humaine. En même temps, cette doctrine dévalorise la femme par ses fonctions « inter–sociales », telles que la maternité, « l'élevage des enfants » ou la transformation des produits alimentaires, qui lient étroitement la femme à la nature (Gardey, Löwy 2000 : 110-111).

D'autres courants de pensée comme le constructivisme culturel, contredisent le premier et estiment que la réification de l'individu se fait à partir de la formation différentielle des deux sexes, imprégnée par le symbolisme et la sémiotique culturelle. À ce propos P. Bourdieu remarque :

> N'ayant d'existence que relationnelle, chacun des deux genres est le produit du travail de construction diacritique, à la fois théorique et pratique, qui est nécessaire pour le produire comme corps socialement différencié du genre opposé (de tous les points de vue culturellement pertinents), c'est-à-dire comme habitus viril, donc non féminin, ou féminin, donc non masculin (Bourdieu 1998 : 41).

Ainsi, la nature physique joue dans le processus de la formation du genre un rôle secondaire, tandis que les effets socioculturels d'une société à une période de son évolution, construisent des stéréotypes identitaires du genre. Et cela concerne, en premier lieu, la masculinité qui a été touchée, dans le passé, par plusieurs crises (Badinter 1998 : 25-41). De nos jours, la côte du Golfe du Bénin, et plus particulièrement le sud du Togo, affiche les preuves réelles de transformation du statut des genres qui entraîne, par conséquent, les modifications de la position sociale des hommes. Or, la construction de la masculinité, imprégnée par les concepts idéologiques et culturels de la société, évolue à partir de la naissance et se modèle tout au long de la croissance de l'individu qui s'inscrit, évidemment, dans le processus de la socialisation.

En dehors des œuvres monographiques, nous nous sommes appuyés sur l'analyse des documents socio-démographiques comme : « Famille, migration et urbanisation au Togo » effectuée entre 2000 et 2001 par l'Unité de Recherche Démographique (URD) de l'Université de Lomé, à laquelle l'auteur a pris part. Les résultats des enquêtes qualitatives et quantitatives de cette étude nous ont fourni une documentation riche pour la vision de la dynamique socio-économique, culturelle et éducative au Togo (URD I, URD II, URD III).

L'analyse de la tradition orale et du folklore de la région étudiée a aussi apporté un support enrichissant pour ce thème, car ils véhiculent les expressions socioculturelles et psychologiques du genre et plus particulièrement de la subculture des jeunes.

L'objectif de cette étude vise à montrer la dynamique de la formation de la masculinité. Elle cherche à identifier les influences qui agissent positivement sur sa formation harmonieuse et celles qui constituent ses obstacles. Cette étude permettra d'éclairer les fondements de la construction culturelle de la masculinité, d'analyser ses changements produits en milieu urbain et en milieu rural togolais. Elle pourra aussi fournir une meilleure compréhension de la psychologie, donc du comportement des garçons et jeunes gens, et donner une possibilité de suivre le développement socioculturel de l'individu (mâle) comme un porteur de sa culture spécifique. Enfin, cette étude pourra contribuer à l'élaboration d'une approche de solutions d'amélioration au processus de la formation de la masculinité dans le contexte socioculturel actuel.

La collecte des données relatives à ce thème s'est effectuée au sud du Togo dans le radius maximal de la capitale togolaise, Lomé, jusqu'à 150 kilomètres en milieu rural et urbain. Ces régions sont peuplées généralement par les ethnies ewe qui sont originaires d'Oyo au Nigeria actuel et guins originaires d'Accra au Ghana actuel (Gayibor 1996 : 67-91, 113-124). Ces populations rurales pratiquent l'agriculture et l'élevage des ruminants et des volailles. Certains groupes côtiers font la pêche maritime et d'autres s'occupent du commerce ou de l'artisanat. Les populations du milieu urbain sont constituées du mélange des autochtones, de ressortissants des diverses régions de la République togolaise et d'étrangers. Elles exercent dans le service public, dans le secteur privé, pratiquent très activement le commerce et les métiers artisanaux.

Les résultats de cette étude sont les fruits des recherches conduits au cours des années successives. Elles étaient consacrées aux questions de l'éducation familiale et scolaire, la camaraderie des enfants, l'éducation par les institutions religieuses traditionnelles, principes et modes d'éducation des genres. Certaines questions liées plus particulièrement aux notions de formation de la masculinité ont été abordées au cours de l'année 2005. Dans son ensemble, l'enquête a couvert vingt trois lieux de peuplement du sud du Togo. La population cible a été très diversifiée : les parents, les éducateurs, les personnes âgées, les personnalités choisis dans les milieux traditionnels et religieux, les responsables communautaires et les enfants. Nous avons accordé une grande attention à la population cible de l'âge de la socialisation, car elle est au centre de nos préoccupations.[1] Ces jeunes sont les porteurs de la subculture masculine, qui est marquée par des modifications très accélérées.

Les difficultés de recherche sont apparues aux cours de l'enquête des groupes des camarades qui forment leur société fermée et qui sont très hostiles aux interventions de personnes non-concernées. Cependant, grâce à l'observation prolongée de ces groupes, la collecte de leur folklore, les formes de communications et jeux, nous avons pu obtenir une information détaillée concernant le sujet.

Dans le souci de garantir la fiabilité de nos résultats et de répondre aux objectifs assignés à cette étude, nous avons opté pour une méthode qualitative. Pour recueillir l'ensemble des informations relatives à notre travail, nous avons mené une recherche sur le terrain en combinant deux méthodes d'approche : l'observation participante de type ethnographique (objective et subjective) par le regard d'une étrangère et l'enquête sous forme de sondage d'opinion par un questionnaire comportant des questions semi-ouvertes et ouvertes. En autres, les entretiens libres individuels ou collectifs de focus-groupe ont complété notre enquête.

L'interprétation des données a été basée sur l'analyse du contenu taxinomique et systématique. Le traitement et l'analyse des données des discussions avec les focus-groupes ont été effectués à l'aide du logiciel Ethnograph.[2]

Les résultats de recherche

Entretiens individuels ou collectifs

La formation de la masculinité offre un intérêt particulier pour la problématique du genre, car la personnalité masculine, par ses fonctions et les activités qu'exerce l'homme en dehors de son foyer, est plus exposée que la femme à toutes les innovations de la vie et aux influences d'acculturation. Par conséquent la personnalité masculine accumule dans son contenu identitaire, très rapidement, toute la dynamique socioculturelle d'une société donnée.

La formation de la masculinité est influencée par de multiples facteurs, parmi lesquels il faut noter, de prime abord, la pensée socioreligieuse, la famille, les groupes des camarades, l'école, les mass media et l'audiovisuel.

Notre étude abordera progressivement l'impact de ces facteurs sur la formation de la masculinité et présentera leurs expressions à travers la subculture des jeunes.

La pensée socioreligieuse incorporée dans la masculinité

À travers la pensée socioreligieuse des peuples de cette région se dessinent des notions du genre et de la masculinité selon lesquelles le ciel, qui est la divinité masculine « Dzia » et la terre, qui est la divinité féminine « Anyia » constituent une unité, représentée par deux parties de la calebasse. Le ciel est l'espace d'habitation du Dieu « Mawu » et d'autres divinités, parmi lesquels le « vodu Hebiesso », la divinité bisexuelle de la foudre et du tonnerre qui occupe une place primordiale. La foudre est masculine « So », appelé aussi « Sogble », le tonnerre est féminin « Sodja » (Speith 1911 : 15). Par son éclat énergétique, la foudre annonce la pluie, par qui le ciel fertilise la terre.

Donc, la notion de masculinité est associée, dans la pensée des peuples, avec la force et l'agressivité positive (dans le sens de la fertilisation) qui participent à la fécondation et à la multiplication des populations. Cette croyance agit jusqu'à présent sur la perception de l'enfant mâle qui, selon la pensée, par le truchement sacré du monde de l'au-delà, prend part précisément à la pérennisation de la famille et du lignage. C'est pour cette raison que chaque famille attend avec impatience la naissance d'au moins un fils, qui sera ainsi l'héritier de son père et le porteur du nom de la famille. Cette pensée s'applique aux notions socioculturelles où le mariage et la procréation paraissent des actes obligatoires. À ce propos, l'africaniste Françoise Héritier écrit : Mariage et procréation sont des devoirs à l'égard de ceux qui nous ont précédé dans l'existence. Mais l'absence de procréation est aussi un crime contre soi-même, ici-bas comme dans l'au-delà (Héritier 1996 : 260).

Ainsi, la naissance de l'enfant et surtout du garçon, provoque une joie intense dans la famille. Le rite de sortie « videto », consiste en la présentation de l'enfant au ciel, à la terre et à sa famille. La cérémonie se termine par la projection de l'eau lustrale sur le toit de la maison ; cette eau retombe ensuite sous forme de gouttes sur le corps et la tête de nouveau-né. Ce rite rappelle encore l'idée de la fertilisation de la terre par le ciel. Il se déroule sans aucune différenciation pour les garçons et les filles, car chaque nouveau-né est considéré comme porteur des attributs des deux sexes (Rivière 1979 : 123-149). Et seule la circoncision révèle chez le garçon son statut mâle. Cependant, la notion de la dualité sexuelle ne s'efface pas complètement dans les représentations socioculturelles des peuples de cette région. Elle s'exprime à travers la tradition orale, le folklore, les soins aux bébés, les comportements éducatifs et la structure sociale chez des différents peuples d'Afrique (Erny 1981 : 44). Par exemple, les relations familiales du système de la parenté classificatoire du Golfe du Bénin illustrent cette notion dualiste. D'auprès ce système de parenté, le même terme désigne non pas un seul individu, mais toute une classe de parents, donc la même personne peut jouer dans sa vie le rôle masculin ou féminin, compte tenu des contacts de parenté. Cette la terminologie de la parenté détermine des paramètres socio-psychologiques pour l'individu en formation en lui donnant une vision d'élasticité de masculinité et de féminité (Note N°2).

La tradition orale et, surtout, les proverbes des Ewe, soulignent souvent la supériorité masculine et illustrent en même temps l'infériorité féminine, par exemple : « Nyonu medea gbe abe nutsu ene o » – La femme ne donne pas d'ordre comme un homme, « Koklono mekua ato o » – La poule ne chante pas (Série Genre et développement 2000 : 7,10). Malgré cette dévalorisation de la femme, elle est toujours considérée par la société comme le symbole de la fertilité de la terre. Ainsi, la naissance d'une fille est perçue comme une bénédiction des ancêtres, le prolongement de la vie et la multiplication des richesses familiales (dans le sens d'enrichissement des parents par la perception de la dot). Si dans le temps passé, la fille a été exclusivement considérée comme « une clôture d'une autre maison » ; aujourd'hui, avec le changement du statut social de la femme, son image prend de plus en plus de la valeur pour sa propre famille. La fille est citée comme un membre actif de sa propre famille, les parents comptant sur ses capacités économiques et son aide pour leurs vieux jours (URD I 2002 : 44).

Ainsi, la perception des genres est encore profondément enracinée dans les représentations socioculturelles du milieu. Cependant les changements des conditions socio-économiques et culturelles agissent progressivement sur leur nouvelle conception qu'on a des filles et des garçons. Dès lors, la famille est obligée d'appliquer des principes et méthodes nouvelles dans l'éducation des enfants des différences sexes.

La formation de la masculinité en famille

Dans la famille, qui est un très important foyer de la socialisation des enfants, la formation du genre s'appuie sur les registres d'encadrement familiaux. Ces registres sont basés sur les valeurs socioculturelles traditionnelles et sur les valeurs qui apparaissent suite aux innovations de la vie.

Les valeurs masculines

Une vision des valeurs propres à la masculinité est apparue à partir de l'enquête qui a été réalisée par la méthode du focus-groupe dans les milieux rural, semi-urbain et urbain. Les groupes masculins des niveaux d'instruction primaire et secondaire ont été choisis afin de recueillir l'opinion assez large et populaire sur le thème de la masculinité. Les hommes de différentes tranches d'âge : des jeunes de 15-25 ans, des adultes de 35-50 ans et des âgés de 55-80 ans ont pris part aux discussions. Cette enquête a accordé une attention particulière aux valeurs et comportements masculins qui, selon l'ordre d'importance, se pressent comme tels : l'homme doit avoir une bonne moralité, être économiquement viable, avoir une bonne apparence et connaître la culture de son milieu.

Parmi les valeurs morales de la masculinité figurent dans l'ordre les multiples notions de : l'honnêteté, l'amabilité (amour du prochain), la tolérance, la dignité. En ce qui concerne le comportement lié à la moralité, les qualités suivantes sont appréciées : être responsable de soi même et de sa famille (être chef), tenir sa parole, savoir-vivre et savoir parler, être non agressif, actif, intelligent et « dure » (déterminé) comme « la noix de palme ».

En deuxième lieu, la valeur économique de l'homme apparaît comme une spécificité nécessaire. Ici, les hommes de tous les milieux estiment que chacun d'entre eux doit avoir des ressources économiques stables sous forme de gains ou de salaires qu'ils peuvent obtenir grâce à leurs études, à l'apprentissage professionnel ou à un travail intensif. L'accent a été mis sur le travail pour l'homme qui, selon leurs paroles, forme l'individu : « Do ye nye ame » - C'est le travail qui fait l'homme. Le travail et l'argent, d'après leurs espérances, leur permettront d'assurer la stabilité de la vie familiale : payer la dot, se marier, acheter un terrain et construire une maison.

En troisième lieu émerge l'idée d'apparence physique de l'homme, en tant que mâle. Tous les jeunes soulignent que l'homme doit avoir une musculature bien développée et être robuste, fort et impressionnant, ce qui démontre des qualités physiques (y compris sexuelles) ou sportives. Les adultes et les personnes âgées des milieux semi-urbain, urbain mettent l'accent sur l'apparence de l'homme, qui doit être présentable, porter des habits beaux et à l'occasion somptueux.

L'homme peut également utiliser un maquillage de circonstances cérémonielles. Les jeunes et les adultes du milieu rural estiment que l'homme doit être propre, avoir une tenue correcte mais simple et être bien coiffé. En milieu urbain, par contre, les jeunes ont une vision esthétique moderne de la masculinité qui se définit à partir des coiffures variées, comme le crâne rasé, les cheveux tressés ou rasta, des décorations au corps comme les tatouages, des habits en jeans, la veste « adja » et même la tenue de gangster !

Quant aux connaissances culturelles qui viennent ensuite selon l'ordre d'importance, elles sont assez vastes. Les hommes adultes et âgés du milieu rural et semi-urbain donnent plus d'importance aux connaissances culturelles traditionnelles. Selon eux, l'homme doit être associé aux traditions familiales et connaître la vie de ses ancêtres. Il doit savoir danser, chanter, s'habiller à la façon traditionnelle en nouant le pagne autour du corps, savoir faire les libations, pratiquer les rites, jouer au grand tam-tam « agblovu », savoir servir les boissons au cours des assises des grandes personnes. Les jeunes du milieu rural estiment qu'il est nécessaire de connaître la culture de leur localité et de leur région mais, en même temps, ils accordent un grand intérêt aux loisirs nouveaux. En milieu urbain, par contre, les jeunes et les hommes s'intéressent à la culture moderne, comme : la connaissance de la musique et des danses populaires, des pièces théâtrales et la fréquentation des lieux de loisir. Selon eux, l'homme doit pratiquer le sport, surtout le football, et être à la mode. Au dernier rang, les jeunes mettent l'idée de participation aux funérailles de leur milieu.

Les valeurs masculines liées exclusivement à la sexualité ne s'affichent pas très ouvertement à travers les discussions. Ce sujet tabou dans le temps, n'a été discuté plus ouvertement que face à l'épidémie du SIDA, qui oblige les gens à connaître les mesures de protection sexuelle.

Ainsi, les résultats de cette enquête reflètent les orientations socioculturelles de la formation de la masculinité au sein de la famille togolaise. Ces orientations touchent, tout d'abord, l'appropriation des valeurs morales. D'après les représentations traditionnelles, l'homme cherche à maintenir sa place de leader au sein de la famille, d'où l'apparence de force masculine et les habillements qui jouent aussi un rôle non négligeable. Cependant, malgré ses ambitions, la situation socio-économique aléatoire du pays ne permet plus à l'homme à maintenir la position de la supériorité et pour cela il compte de plus en plus sur le soutien financier de sa femme. À ce sujet les jeunes disent : « La femme doit travailler pour aider son mari à supporter les enfants », « La femme peut supporter l'homme si celui-ci n'a pas de boulot » (URDI 2002 : 71).

L'appropriation des valeurs culturelles de la masculinité montre déjà une tendance à la fragilité de sa transmission. Elle est illustrée par le comportement des jeunes qui ne savent plus s'habiller à la façon traditionnelle, bien danser, chanter, pratiquer les rites du milieu ou respecter les règles d'étiquette traditionnelle. En même temps, les jeunes assimilent rapidement la musique et les danses populaires modernes, pratiquent les jeux sportifs et modifient leurs apparences compte tenu des normes esthétiques nouvelles.

Dans le but d'assurer cette formation, la famille met en place toutes les méthodes éducatives possibles comme : la démonstration, l'explication, l'encouragement ou les jurons et la punition. Ces méthodes impliquent la pensée socioreligieuse, la tradition orale, le folklore, la musique moderne, ainsi que les mass media et l'audio visuel. Mais cet aspect de la formation masculine peut constituer l'objet d'une étude particulière.

Les rôles masculins

L'éducation familiale accorde une place spéciale à l'appropriation de rôles du genre marqués par la stratification sexuelle. A ce propos, les gens énoncent le proverbe : « Koklo mekpoa gbo nube wona o.»- La poule ne fait pas ce que fait la chèvre (Série genre et développement 2000 : 21). Dans la tradition africaine, certains travaux domestiques sont réservés aux garçons et d'autres aux filles. Au sein de la famille, les enfants, selon l'âge et le sexe, ont des taches bien déterminées à accomplir dans la journée. Les travaux agricoles, comme labour, le désherbage sont réservés aux garçons. Alors que d'autres travaux agricoles, comme les semis, les plantations et les récoltes occupent les enfants des deux sexes.

La division sexuelle du travail débute bien avant la stratification sexuelle des enfants. Dès que l'enfant commence à marcher et à communiquer, il imite les gestes et les activités des adultes de même sexe que lui. Mais la stratification sexuelle marque la vie des enfants à partir de 4-5 ans, quand en compagnie de personnes de différents sexes, ils commencent à approprier les codes culturels et des modes de comportement qu'ils observent. La division sexuelle conduit les garçons à suivre leur père, grands frères ou d'autres hommes de la famille, en imitant leur manière de parler, d'agir et de se comporter. Tandis que les filles, en entourage féminin s'associent rapidement aux modes de penser et de comportement féminin.

À l'âge de 11-12 ans, en milieu rural, le père attribue à son fils une parcelle de terrain, qu'il aura pour tache labourer pour son compte. Il travail individuellement, mais le plus souvent avec l'aide de ses camarades. À partir de cet âge, le garçon s'engage ainsi sérieusement dans la voie de la productivité masculine. L'étape suivante dans la vie du jeune homme, le conduit, par les voies éducatives et coutumières vers l'appropriation totale de son rôle et des responsabilités masculines.

La répartition des tâches domestiques et la polarisation des rôles selon le sexe de l'enfant, sont plus visibles en milieu rural. Les garçons participent moins dans les taches domestiques que les filles. Par exemple, sept garçons sur dix font le balayage de la cour, aident à la cuisine, s'occupent de la corvée d'eau. Par contre, les garçons font en plus l'entretien des chambres, le couvert de table, le repassage et accomplissent les commissions des adultes (URD II 2002 : 90-92). En milieu urbain la dichotomie de répartition des taches domestiques commence à s'effacer légèrement. Souvent, les parents du milieu urbain, estiment que les garçons et les filles peuvent faire les mêmes travaux et, par la suite, exercer des activités professionnelles identiques. À ce propos les hommes du milieu urbain remarquent : « C'est ainsi qu'aujourd'hui un garçon doit balayer la chambre dans laquelle il se couche. Les hommes arrivent aussi à puiser de l'eau pour la toilette ou bien pour la cuisine et je dis qu'aujourd'hui les hommes jouent pratiquement les mêmes rôles que les femmes. » « Je peux dire qu'il y a des changements puisque nous voyons des garçons qui font pratiquement tous les travaux réservés aux filles. Les garçons font de la coiffure, les filles dans les mécaniques, dans les conduites. Bref, tout le monde fait tout. »

Ainsi, l'appropriation des rôles masculins commence dès la petite enfance par l'imitation des grandes personnes. Puis, elle est guidée par les adultes de sa famille dans le sens de dichotomie sexuelle d'où l'enfant assimile les normes culturelles propres à sa personnalité du genre.

La formation du genre et de la masculinité est influencée par le contexte des différents types de familles et les attitudes de l'entourage vis à vis de l'enfant, que nous présentons plus bas.

Le fils au foyer monoparental

La modification de la structure et de la taille de la famille agit sur l'appropriation des rôles et des responsabilités par le genre. Dans la famille étendue, où cohabitent plusieurs générations et un grand nombre d'enfants, la transmission des codes de la masculinité et la polarisation des rôles sont encore plus conservatrices. Mais ce type de famille est déjà minoritaire (7 %) et persiste plus en milieu rural.[2] Par contre, au niveau de la famille élargie qui est composée généralement des parents, de leurs enfants et d'autres comme des petits frères, des sœurs, ce qui est largement répandue dans tous les milieux, les principes éducatifs se modifient davantage (Koudolo 2002 : 27-41).

Dans ce type de famille, la distribution des tâches domestiques se fait en tenant compte du nombre d'enfants plutôt que de la dichotomie des sexes. Le nouveau type de la famille nucléaire n'a pas encore gagner l'estime de la population togolaise, mais les types familiaux transitoires, comme la famille monoparentale dirigée par la femme, sont en train de se répandre rapidement, surtout en milieu urbain. Le nombre de ces ménages dépasse, par exemple actuellement à Lomé (Togo), trente pour cent (URD II 2002 : vii). Le statut matrimonial des femmes -chefs de ménage est varié : célibataire, divorcée, veuve, mariée (mais vivant seule) en absence temporaire de son mari ou mariée en régime de polygamie dispersée (Pilon 1997 167-191).

Dans la famille monoparentale, les enfants grandissent et se socialisent sous l'égide de leur mère. La femme-chef de ménage organise son foyer à la façon de la famille élargie, tout en s'entourant des membres de sa propre famille comme les petits frères, sœurs et neveux ou d'autres parents. Actuellement, la taille moyenne du ménage dirigé par la femme au Togo est de six personnes (URD III 2000 : 11, 20). Cependant, les rapports et les attitudes qui s'établissent entre les enfants et ces membres de la parenté maternelle se construisent et fonctionnent exclusivement dans le contexte féminin. Ce fait s'explique par le système classificatoire de parenté, où tous les parents maternels sont perçus dans la sémiotique maternelle et féminine, malgré leur différence sexuelle.[3]

Au foyer dirigé par la mère, les enfants, et surtout les garçons, rencontrent de multiples difficultés dans leur formation masculine. L'absence du père à la maison ou ses visites périodiques ne lui permettent pas d'assumer ses rôles éducatifs et d'effectuer correctement la transmission des codes et des stéréotypes de la masculinité à ses fils. Ce sujet a été abordé par E. Badinter qui a cité la pensée du psychanalyste G. Corneau :

> L'absence du père produit un complexe paternel négatif qui consiste en un manque de structures internes. Ses idées sont confuses, il ressent des difficultés lorsqu'il doit fixer un but, faire des choix, reconnaître ce qui est bon pour lui et identifier ses propres besoins.

Cet auteur souligne également que l'absence du père conduit l'enfant vers la construction d'un individu mou (Bandinter 1992 : 26).

Les effets du non-encadrement paternel sont encore peu étudiés dans la région de la côte du Golfe du Bénin et seulement des études spécifiques des différents contextes culturels pourront donner une vision claire de ce phénomène.

Pour assurer le meilleur encadrement de l'enfant vivant dans le foyer maternel, la société adopte des solutions spécifiques de transfert de l'adolescent dans la famille paternel ou au foyer d'un proche parent du père. Cette famille, tout d'abord, doit se charger de la scolarisation ou de la formation professionnelle qui pourront assurer à l'enfant son avenir socio-économique. D'autre part, le père ou les parents paternels l'initient à tout le complexe socioculturel et aux pratiques coutumières familiales et claniques. Les données quantitatives montrent qu'au sein de la famille se produisent des mouvements liés à ce transfert des adolescents, notamment le nombre d'enfants du conjoint qui s'agrandit (URD II 2002 : 89). Cette pratique touche, en majorité, des garçons qui, selon le contexte traditionnel, doivent devenir le porteur culturel de leur famille et de leur clan. Dans la famille paternelle, les relations « enfant »-père ou « enfant »-membres de parenté se traduisent en sémiotique masculine qui agissent sur l'individu en forgeant son caractère fortifié « d'homme ». Les garçons ou les filles, sans considération de sexe, traversent cet encadrement strict qui se produit surtout vers la fin de la période de la socialisation.[4] Cependant, les pratiques actuelles montrent que les filles sont, le plus souvent, retenues par leurs mères qui les associent à leurs activités professionnelles.

Le placement en tutelle des enfants et des adolescents, qui est traditionnellement pratiqué chez les peuples de cette région, va dans le même sens d'encadrement strict et de formation de l'endurance masculine, car selon la pensée éducative, « il risque de se gâter à côté de sa mère ». De nos jours, c'est plutôt la raison économique qui pousse les parents à placer leurs enfants dans des familles aisées (URD 1 2002 : 38-39).

Toutefois, l'instabilité de la famille actuelle, les relations complexes entre les parents de l'enfant, les contraintes économiques du père et le problème de logement constituent très souvent des obstacles pour ce transfert. Par conséquent, la mère continue à élever seule ou avec ses proches parents ses enfants. À cet effet, au sein de ce type de famille, l'appropriation des rôles et des responsabilités par l'enfant, ne s'inscrit pas dans le registre classique. La mère y assume le « triple rôle » basé sur la reproduction, les soins aux enfants et la production des biens, ce qui implique souvent sa participation à la gestion communautaire (Moser 2000 : 134-135). Cette inversion des rôles familiaux au sein du ménage monoparental produit, dès lors, des effets psychosociaux sur l'enfant en le libérant de certains critères de responsabilité masculine, ce qui constitue un préjudice à l'éducation maternelle.

Dans certains ménages dirigés par des femmes instruites, la réussite scolaire est élevée et dépasse celle de foyers dirigés par des hommes (URD I 2002 : 107). D'autres ménages monoparentaux au contraire, présentent des signes de détresse pour des raisons économiques et des occupations de la mère qui n'arrive pas à accorder assez de temps à l'éducation de ses enfants. Cela provoque des lacunes dans l'éducation maternelle et conduit quelquefois l'adolescent à rechercher un groupe masculin au sein duquel il pourra trouver la compréhension, exprimer librement son caractère masculin et ses expressions culturelles. Pourtant, ce groupe des nouveaux amis le guide parfois à la délinquance juvénile à travers laquelle s'expriment les différentes formes de la violence.

Les chercheurs remarquent que le niveau de la délinquance juvénile liée à l'agressivité de l'adolescence est plus développé en milieu urbain. Le degré de la violence dépend également de la situation socio-économique et politique qui enflamme ou apaise la jeunesse (Kon 2001 : 9-37). Par exemple, au Togo, comme dans les autres pays de la région, on constate l'accroissement spontané de la violence juvénile au cours des périodes électorales. Ces violences sont liées, la plupart du temps, aux rivalités multipartistes et régionalistes, donc évoquent des sentiments chauvins et nationalistes. Dans ce contexte, les jeunes hommes affichent leur « héroïsme » et leurs forces. Ainsi, en milieu urbain, et plus rarement en milieu rural, les jeunes affirment leur caractère masculin entre autres, à travers les manifestations de violence en groupes.

Or, le milieu rural de cette région conserve encore un mécanisme spécifique de socialisation qui canalise les expressions de violence et d'agressivité masculine. Ce trait particulier de la formation masculine sera présenté plus bas.

La camaraderie masculine

Les groupes des camarades représentent l'un des facteurs puissants de la socialisation des enfants et de la formation de la masculinité.[5] Sur la côte du Golfe du Bénin et particulièrement au Togo, les groupes des enfants (surtout des garçons) sont largement répandus, car ils se forment au niveau de chaque quartier de la localité.

La connaissance de l'organisation des groupes et de leur fonctionnement, de leurs distractions et de leur mode de communications permet de présenter les camarades du groupe comme les porteurs d'une subculture spécifique à travers laquelle s'expriment les notions du genre de la jeune génération.

La camaraderie des enfants, marquée par la stratification sexuelle (groupes des garçons et groupes des filles) et par la division en deux tranches d'âge (de 8 à 12 et de 12 à 16 ans), constitue une véritable société autonome, absolument indépendante des adultes.

Ces groupes non institutionnels par leur organisation et leur fonctionnement, se présentent comme un mécanisme spécifique d'encadrement et d'orientation socioculturelle masculine. En imitant la structure sociale du milieu, les groupes des garçons choisissent leur chef et les notables qui y exercent les rôles de responsabilité. Cette organisation impose le respect absolu des « règlements intérieurs » basés sur l'ordre hiérarchique, une discipline et un comportement exemplaire.

Au sein du groupe, les garçons se forment comme des futurs membres de leur communauté masculine, ce qui les conduit à l'appropriation des rôles sociaux de leur milieu. À ce propos P. Erny écrit :

> ...les premiers (garçons) constituent, en régime virilocal, l'élément de la population destiné à rester sur place, à s'enraciner, à constituer l'armature, la partie stable des lignages et des clans (Erny 1972 : 86).

La nécessité d'intégration conduit les garçons à un apprentissage approprié aux variations socioculturelles de leurs quartiers qui peuvent s'exprimer par l'ordre historique, religieux ou culturel. Les groupes de chaque quartier se donnent un nom particulier qui doit, selon eux, impressionner leurs adversaires, comme par exemple « le groupe de l'aigle », du « lion », du « scorpion ».

Souvent, entre les groupes de différents quartiers éclatent des bagarres, et alors, les camarades doivent montrer leur audace, leur combativité ou leur capacité à trouver les injures les plus percutantes. À cette occasion les garçons chantent les différentes chansons de guerre « avahawo ». Selon les mots de F. Agblemagnon : « Ces chants servent à redonner courage, à vanter les vertus mâles d'un individu ou du groupe » (Agblemagnon 1969 : 120).

Exemple d'une chanson :

Ne ko ade kple ko adewo kpe dzrea,

Miabla tu kple agbadza adu wo dzi.

Traduction :

Si entre les quartiers il y a des disputes,

Nous prenons nos fusils et ceignons nos

Cartouches pour les vaincre.

Cette chanson, illustre la résurgence de l'esprit guerrier propre à la masculinité en formation qui s'exprime à travers le folklore et les jeux chez les groupes des garçons.

Au sein du groupe chacun est désigné exclusivement par un surnom et non par son propre prénom, comme par exemple : « banane rouge », « sale dent », « poils de chèvre », « lézard ». Ces appellations dégradantes produisent un effet d'anonymat social, d'annulation des ambitions personnelles, et de l'égalité au sein du groupe. Très souvent les groupes élaborent un langage codé, des mimiques ou des signaux de communication en vue d'assurer le caractère fermé de leur cercle et l'ésotérisme de leurs actions. Ces formes de communication rappellent celles qui sont pratiquées par les sociétés secrètes et initiatiques, comme par exemple, le couvent du Vodu, qui sont répandues sur la côte du Golfe du Bénin (Rivière 1981 : 157-172).

Les garçons, en groupe, cherchent toujours à se distinguer des filles, en prouvant leur supériorité physique et en manifestant leur hostilité envers elles. À ce propos G. Falconnet, N. Lefaucheur écrivent :

> Les seconds (garçons) sont élevés à voir dans leur sexe le signe de leur pouvoir, à condition qu'ils acceptent de ne pas s'en servir n'importe quand et n'importe comment (Falconnet/Lefaucheur 1975 : 129).

Et pour montrer leur pouvoir, ils agressent les filles par des chansons de raillerie, des insultes, et parfois même, physiquement avec des jets de pierres ou des coups de bâtons. Par exemple, les garçons chantent pour dénigrer les filles :

Nutsuviwo dome, adzi vi ga ade tobolo.

Traduction :

En faisant la compagnie des garçons,

Vous risquez d'avoir un gros bébé.

Cet aspect de la distinction sexuelle, de la rupture avec la féminité, de la démonstration de force, de l'autodétermination et de l'identification masculine s'exprime au sein de toutes les sociétés initiatiques africaines et permet au garçon de s'identifier en tant qu'homme (Paulme 1971).

Ensemble, les camarades des groupes pratiquent des activités semi-productives comme la chasse, la pêche, la cueillette, le transport de petites marchandises et les travaux champêtres collectifs- « fidodo »-. Ces activités alternatives se présentent comme un aspect conservateur qui est encore vivace chez les groupes des garçons, alors que les adultes l'ont déjà abandonné depuis plus de cinquante ans. Les recettes de leur labeur sont destinées à la caisse commune. Les dépenses à partir de cette caisse sont toujours décidées ensemble, à l'unanimité. Tout d'abord, ils achètent un ballon et des maillots pour leur propre équipe de football, mais ils dépensent aussi pour l'achat de sandales, d'outils agricoles ou de fournitures scolaires. Ainsi, les travaux en groupe et la caisse commune renforcent la solidarité tout en préparant les garçons pour la future gestion de leur communauté.

Les garçons accordent beaucoup de temps aux distractions folkloriques, aux jeux et au sport qui sont des occasions pour démontrer des qualités comme le courage, l'initiative, la compétitivité et la force. À l'occasion des fêtes au village, les différents groupes des garçons organisent des compétitions sportives comme les matchs de football, les concours de natation, de saut et la marche sur des échasses. Les groupes des garçons forment un orchestre et une chorale qui reproduit les mélodies et les chansons spécifiques de leur milieu. Cet apprentissage se poursuit pendant l'adolescence quand les adultes confient aux jeunes des instruments musicaux afin de les former comme de futurs musiciens. Cette activité artistique a été spécialement remarquée par D. Houenassou-Houangbé qui écrit :

> Chaque type de musique a sa tradition sociale et chaque aspect du social a son système musical (chefferie, guerre, religion, culte, rituel de chasse, initiation). Ils constituent néanmoins des jeux pour les enfants qui s'y donnent (Houenassou-Houangbé 1981 : 61).

Ces distractions folkloriques intègrent graduellement les enfants dans l'ensemble de la sphère socioculturelle et assurent leur formation comme porteurs de la culture et de la psychologie traditionnelle. Au bout de quelques années les adolescents deviennent les jeunes adultes. A partir de cette l'étape de leur vie, leur camaraderie se décroît rapidement et les jeunes se dispersent. Ceux qui demeurent sur place, prennent désormais le chemin de l'appropriation de culture des adultes qui les conduit vers le rapprochement entre les genres, la souplesse de leurs relations et un changement de leur comportement. Dorénavant cette nouvelle culture exige des jeunes hommes des engagements économiques pour préparer le payement de la dot, elle les amène à élaborer un projet du mariage. C'est là, que prennent fin les distractions propres à l'adolescence.

Ainsi, au sein de leur société les garçons sont amenés à construire leur personnalité tout en préservant les codes et les stéréotypes de la masculinité de leur milieu d'origine. Cette constitution s'appuie sur les références du social, du militaire, de la production de biens, de gestion, du sport, du folklore et de la culture. Elle comprend un encadrement rigoureux des garçons qui s'effectue pratiquement au cours de sept ou huit ans dans un cadre très bouclé et strictement limité aux « hommes »- concernés. Dans son ensemble, cette « formation » n'est pas enregistrée par la conscience des peuples comme telle, mais considérée plutôt comme des distractions de jeunes mâles. Elle s'effectue au niveau de chaque génération par la transmission entre les enfants et assure, finalement, la reproduction socioculturelle de l'identité masculine. D'après les indices de l'expansion de ce phénomène sur la côte du Golfe du Bénin, la société des camarades peut être considérée, comme un modèle initiatique non institutionnel ou bien comme la survivance des pratiques initiatiques dont la structure et les actions se reproduisent chez la totalité de la population masculine de cette région.

Malgré un conservatisme culturel, ces groupes sont ouverts aux innovations qui modifient leurs points d'intérêt et les conduisent vers les contextes nouveaux. La scolarisation, l'apprentissage professionnelle, l'exode rural des adolescents, les activités productives et commerciales de la famille qui augmentent de jour en jour, tout cela agit négativement aujourd'hui sur la stabilité et la fréquentation de ces groupes, en affaiblissant la transmission culturelle de cette société autonome. Cette défaillance des groupes des camarades touche de plus en plus le milieu urbain.

En milieu urbain donc, l'organisation des groupes des camarades se réalise de façon périodique et fragmentaire. Ces groupes n'ont pas la possibilité de fonctionner de la même manière qu'en milieu rural. Ils doivent s'adapter à l'espace urbain et au temps disponible. Actuellement leurs champs d'activités sont généralement limités aux distractions sportives, plus rarement artistiques ou musicales, aux jeux et aux fréquentations des salles de cinéma, des vidéoclubs ou des discothèques. La composition des groupes est aussi variée. Parfois les amis vivent à des distances éloignées. D'autres fois ces groupes se forment entre les camarades de classe ou avec des adhérents de même confession religieuse. Dans de nombreux quartiers peuplés par des ressortissants de régions diverses, les groupes des camarades se constituent sur le principe d'appartenance ethnique ou religieuse, ce qui leur permet de préserver en quelque sorte, leurs valeurs culturelles et de se former en tant qu'identité culturelle. Par ailleurs, il apparaît également des groupes des enfants (garçons) issus des différentes régions ethniques, où le multiculturalisme s'exprime à travers la culture de ces jeunes.

Ainsi, la transmission des codes culturels de la masculinité se heurte aujourd'hui à un nouveau contexte urbain dans la rupture avec leur milieu d'origine, et, surtout aux influences culturelles modernes, parmi lesquelles l'école occupe une place primordiale.

La mixité dans la scolarisation

L'école, en tant qu'institution du système éducatif européen, a été considérée dans le passé, comme un facteur d'acculturation. Mais avec la scolarisation massive qui touche quatre-vingt-un pour-cent de la population scolarisable du Togo, elle a pris une place très importante dans la formation de l'individu, comme un mode d'enculturation qui modifie les rapports et le statut du genre dans la jeune génération et agit sur l'élaboration de stéréotypes nouveaux de la masculinité (URD II 2002 : xiii).

La scolarisation mixte contribue aux changements des rapports entre les genres qui apparaissent tout d'abord, en milieu scolaire et se répandent ensuite en dehors de son cercle dans la vie quotidienne. La progression de la scolarisation des filles et leur réussite scolaire met en évidence, pour les garçons, leur parité et parfois même leur supériorité. A ce propos les jeunes du milieu urbain disent :

Quand les filles s'habituent à tous faire, elles vont réussir mieux et après elles deviennent des femmes ministres, des directrices des grandes sociétés. Même à l'heure actuelle, les femmes cherchent à être présidente ! Si la femme fréquente, tous ses vœux aussi ne seront plus impossibles.

Ainsi, avec la scolarisation mixte une nouvelle perception de la féminité se développe au sein de l'école qui, par ricochet, affaiblit surestimation masculine et ses ambitions de leadership dans le contexte moderne. Cette scolarisation crée une prédominance psychologique d'égalité entre les jeunes des différents sexes et oriente les enfants à la construction sociale qui leur permettra d'accomplir les rôles professionnels identiques. Elle favorise également la compréhension réciproque chez les jeunes, ce qui leur aidera à établir des relations conjugales équitables au sein de leurs ménages.

L'éducation scolaire accentue l'influence de la transmission cofigurative des multiples connaissances entres les pairs qui ne prend plus en considération la distinction sexuelle.[6] Par exemple, les garçons et les filles pratiquent les jeux électroniques, échangent leurs connaissances en informatique, travaillent en groupe dans les cercles scientifiques, lisent et discutent toutes sortes de littérature. Le volume d'informations scientifiques que possèdent les élèves, surtout en milieu urbain, et qui circulent entre eux constitue un bagage intellectuel qui dépasse généralement ceux de leurs parents. Ainsi, la transmission inverse des connaissances des jeunes aux adultes constitue la pratique courante dans tous les milieux. Cette forme de transmission préfigurative favorise l'établissement de nouveaux rapports entre les parents et les enfants et trouble la transmission classique – post-figurative, du père au fils. Ces nouveaux rapports brisent réellement les cloisons du système de classes d'âges, établissent des relations d'égalité intellectuelle entre le père et le fils et poussent les jeunes à revaloriser les connaissances de la génération précédente.

La scolarisation par ses valeurs, sa compétitivité et ses orientations d'intégration dans la vie active, favorise la construction d'un nouveau stéréotype de la masculinité d'apparence d'intelligentsia : studieux, concentré, calme, portant parfois des lunettes. Ce jeune homme, grâce à ses compétences scolaires, universitaires expose aussi un modèle idéal de la masculinité, car à nos jours, il est capable de bien gagner sa vie et de réussir dans la vie active.

D'autres nouveaux facteurs de la socialisation, comme les mass média et l'audiovisuel participent à la formation de la masculinité. Ils conduisent les jeunes à la découverte des horizons divers qui présentent les relations et statuts sociaux du genre, aussi que les stéréotypes de la masculinité.

Les influences nouvelles

Les mass media, l'audiovisuel et l'internet contribuent à la formation du genre et donc, de la masculinité. La première rencontre de l'enfant avec les médias, surtout en milieu rural, se fait généralement à partir des manuels scolaires. Ils présentent à l'enfant des images positives du monde, d'une société pacifique et aussi de familles heureuses. Entre autres, ces manuels reflètent le statut social de la personnalité et les relations harmonieuses dans le genre. À mesure que l'enfant avance en âge, il (le garçon) consulte d'autres ouvrages comme des contes, des dessins animés, des magazines des jeunes africains ou étrangers qui poursuivent toujours l'idée d'harmonie sociale. Ces médias pour jeunes ont une grande popularité, mais ils ne sont généralement répandus qu'en milieu urbain. Les adolescents s'intéressent très vite aux publications d'origines africaines, européennes, américaines destinées aux adultes qui présentent déjà des modes, des cultures et des stéréotypes du genre.

Les émissions télévisées, les projections de films dans les salles de cinéma et surtout de vidéoclubs constituent les nouveaux loisirs pour les jeunes en milieu rural et urbain. Par exemple, un recensement de dix quartiers de Lomé à permis de compter 578 salles de vidéo projection (Sambiani 2002 : 51). Les vidéoclubs, à moindre prix, soit 25 francs, rassemblent souvent dans leurs auditoriums, en majorité, la clientèle masculine et surtout des jeunes. Le répertoire de ces lieux de projection se limite à des films d'action basés sur la violence, l'horreur, l'érotisme. À propos des effets de ces films, les jeunes remarquent : « En regardant ces films, les enfants développent leurs idées et souvent ils imitent ces actions. Ils répètent les mauvaises choses avec leurs sœurs. À 12-15 ans, ils deviennent voyous », « À travers la vidéo la fille découvre la prostitution » (URD I 2002 : 60).

Ces films d'action présentent une nouvelle image de la société, des codes moraux et des rapports de genre qui, par conséquent, agissent sur le comportement et les mœurs des jeunes. L'étude de D. Sambiani a montré que ces films provoquent, selon l'ordre d'importance : la baisse du temps consacré aux travaux ménagers, la puberté précoce, la perturbation de l'équilibre familiale par la rentrée tardive des enfants, les réactions impolis et récalcitrants, le vol, la violence, les dépravations, les imitations des images cinématographiques, la sexualité précoce, le comportement de rébellion (Sambiani 2002 : 54). À travers la production cinématographique se révèle également un nouveau cliché de la masculinité « matcho » illustré par un comportement, des expressions, des modes et symboliques. Les images audiovisuelles sont souvent contradictoires par rapport à celles des livres scolaires ou mass media pour jeunes et aux critères éducatifs de la société africaine, car elles présentent une masculinité plongée dans la violence.

Dans l'ensemble, les images cinématographiques véhiculent des éléments d'acculturation que s'approprie et imite la jeunesse et, surtout, le sexe masculin. Cette production audiovisuelle a un double impact sur les jeunes. D'une part, elle expose constamment les mœurs venant d'autres espaces et contextes culturels, ce qui provoque, par la suite, un certain effacement identitaire. Cela se traduit par l'américanisation ou l'européanisation des modes, de la musique, des jargons, par des modifications du comportement, des notions de la moralité et de sexualité chez les jeunes. D'autre part, cette production audiovisuelle enrichit leur vision socioculturelle et les associe aux modèles et aux critères de la mondialisation qui s'installent de plus en plus sur la côte du Golfe du Bénin.

L'impact de l'internet sur la formation de la masculinité dans cette région reste encore très faible. En milieu rural, son usage est presque inconnu, alors qu'en milieu urbain l'utilisation de l'internet est plus fréquente, grâce à l'installation des cybercafés et à l'apprentissage de l'informatique. Cependant, il est à remarquer que la fréquentation des centres informatiques et des cybercafés des villes, et particulièrement de Lomé, est limitée encore à la jeunesse scolaire, favorisée ou aux jeunes travailleurs qui ont reçu l'initiation informatique et qui disposent de l'argent nécessaire. Par ailleurs, les écoliers participent massivement aux séances de la navigation gratuite qu'organise souvent le Centre culturel français à Lomé.

Les mass media et l'audiovisuel entrent réellement dans le complexe de la socialisation des enfants et des adolescents togolais, comme de ceux de la côte du Golfe du Bénin. Leur impact sur la formation de l'identité du genre, et plus précisément de la masculinité, s'accroît quotidiennement et prend des ampleurs considérables qui s'expriment par les expressions socioculturelles des jeunes.

Conclusion

À notre époque la socialisation togolaise offre une gamme de références socioculturelles à la construction de la masculinité. Cette construction prend sa source dans les fondements socioreligieux traditionnels, se réalise au sein de la famille par l'éducation des enfants, se renforce et se forge avec un apprentissage socioculturel dans le groupe des camarades. En même temps, la construction de la masculinité s'enrichit par les apports modernes de mixité de la scolarisation, qui propose aux enfants des contenus scientifiques et des orientations égalitaires pour l'intégration du genre dans la vie active. Les influences médiatiques, pour leur part, suscitent activement des modifications dans l'identité masculine en poussant les jeunes à interpréter des stéréotypes proposés et à adapter leurs modèles.

Le nouveau cheminement de la formation de la masculinité est subordonné à une dynamique socio-économique et culturelle intervenant brutalement dans la construction du genre, sans prendre en considération les paramètres essentiels et opportuns pour la vie familiale et pour les rôles et responsabilités de ses membres. Cette dynamique croissante déstabilise la personnalité masculine, prend en otage son hégémonie sociale, affaiblit ses références socioculturelles et coutumières. Ainsi, la formation de la masculinité se forme encore d'une façon spontanée par le fait des contradictions ou des jonctions des sphères socioculturelles traditionnelles et modernes. Un tel processus, par conséquent, produit des identités fragmentées, qui oscillent entre deux pôles socioculturels, dont les jeunes hommes sont les porteurs. La subculture masculine de chaque tranche d'âge et de chaque milieu reflète ces variations et transformations qui s'expriment à travers leurs activités, le comportement et les notions liées à la masculinité idéale.

Malgré la complexité de cette formation, la jeunesse masculine cherche à se mettre à l'avant garde du développement et à répondre aux exigences de la vie.

Dans ce but, les jeunes hommes s'engagent très vite dans toutes les activités novatrices où ils peuvent utiliser leurs compétences et aussi gagner leur vie. Ces engagements nécessitent une concentration des forces physiques, intellectuelles et morales sur les nouveaux contextes qui par leur importance relèguent les références socioculturelles africaines. La transmission permanente des valeurs novatrices par les hommes, favorise ainsi, la diffusion des modèles socioculturels étrangers et conduit progressivement la personnalité masculine vers l'effacement des références identitaires. Dans cette situation, l'homme commence à jouer un nouveau rôle, celui de promoteur de la culture moderne.

À cet effet, se pose la problématique des futures orientations de la formation de la masculinité qui est exposée davantage à l'influence de l'acculturation. De nos jours, cette formation doit attirer particulièrement l'attention des équipes des chercheurs composés de scientifiques de différents domaines, de décideurs du développement et d'acteurs du social sur le terrain. Par des actions convergentes, ces spécialistes pourront élaborer un support théorique et pratique en vue de l'encadrement pédagogique et socioculturel de la personnalité masculine. Ce nouveau contexte doit nécessairement viser l'harmonie socioculturelle dans la personnalité masculine en y associant les meilleurs éléments du patrimoine africain à ceux de la culture universelle.

Notes

1. La notion de la socialisation a été longtemps discutée par les sciences sociales. À l'heure actuelle, elle est plus perçue « comme un modelage des personnalités suivant les traits les plus structurants des cultures jugées essentielles au fondement social » (Dubar 2000 : 65). D'après M. Mead, la socialisation s'étale de la naissance à l'âge de la puberté et jusqu'à l'intégration de l'individu dans la vie active (Mead 1973). Or, dans le contexte actuel de la côte du Golfe du Bénin, l'éducation scolaire se prolonge, en raison des multiples échecs et redoublements et s'étend parfois jusqu'à 24-25 ans. Et ceci ne permet pas de considérer un jeune homme comme mâture, donc adulte, avant la fin de ses études.

2. Ce phénomène culturel a été décrit par plusieurs anthropologues, dont D. P. Murdock (1949 : 119-219) qui en a fait une synthèse dans *Social structure* (1949, New York : The Free Press). À titre d'exemple, l'oncle maternel est appelé en guin « nyiné », ce qui peut se traduire par : « mère masculine ». Il établit avec son neveu des relations maternelles de douceur et de tendresse. Mais avec ses propres enfants ou ceux de son frère, il joue le rôle masculin et est appelé « ta » (père), « taga » (père plus âgé), « tavi » (père moins âgé). Les relations du père et des enfants sont caractérisées par les attitudes de rigueur et de fermeté. Tous les parents du père sont considérés par les enfants dans le sens masculin, ce qui explique que l'enfant appelle sa tante paternelle « tasi » – (père féminin) et impose des attitudes de caractère paternel. Mais les enfants de sa sœur, désignent la tante par l'appellation « naga » (mère plus âgée) ou « navi » (mère moins âgée). Celle-ci établit avec eux des relations maternelles de douceur et de sollicitudes.

3. L'éducation des enfants dans les différents types des familles a fait l'objet de l'une des

études de l'auteur en 1987, *Quelques aspects de la socialisation traditionnelle des enfants chez les ewe.* (Lomé : DIFOP, 52 p).

4. Dans la famille paternelle, l'éducation que reçoit l'enfant (garçon ou fille) comprend la formation à l'endurance qui se fait naturellement tout au long de sa croissance. Dans ce contexte familial plus la fille avance en âge, plus elle devient « tasi » (père féminin) par rapport à ces nombreux neveux et nièces, ce qui renforce ses qualités de la masculinité.

5. Ce thème a été étudié par l'auteur en 1995, *La société des camarades comme un facteur de la socialisation des enfants en milieu ewe*, Lomé : DIFOP, 86 p.

6. Ces termes de la transmission culturelle proposés par M. Mead, sont cités dans : Camilleri, C., 1985, *Anthropologie culturelle et éducation*, Paris : UNESCO, p.65.

Bibliographie

Agblemagnon, F. N.,1969, *Sociologie des sociétés orales d'Afrique noire*, Paris : Mouton.

Badinter, E., 1992, *XY de l'identité masculine*, Paris, Éd., Odile Jacob.

Bourdieu, P., 1998, *La domination masculine*, Paris : Seuil.

Camilleri, C., 1985, *Anthropologie culturelle et éducation*, Paris : UNESCO.

Dubar, C., 2000, *La socialisation*, Paris : Armand Colin.

Erny, P., 1972, *L'enfant et son milieu en Afrique noire*, Paris : Payot.

Erny, P., 1981, *Ethnologie de l'éducation*, Paris : PUF.

Falconnet, G. , Lefaucheur, N., 1975, *La fabrication des mâles*, Paris : Seuil.

Gardey, D. et Lowy, I., 2000, *L'invention du naturel. Les sciences et la fabrication du féminin et du masculin,* Paris : Éd. Archives contemporaines.

Gaybor, N., 1996, *Le peuplement du Togo. État actuel des connaissances historiques*, Lomé : Les Presses de l'UB.

Héritier, F., 1996, *Masculin/Féminin. La pensée de la différence*, Paris : Éd. Odile Jacob.

Kon, I, 2001, « Masculinité comme histoire », dans *Les problèmes du genre dans les sciences sociales*, Moscou : RAN.

Koudolo, S., 1987, *Quelques aspects de la socialisation traditionnelle des enfants chez les ewe.* Lomé : DIFOP, 52 p.

Koudolo, S., 2002, « L'éducation familiale en mutation », *Journal de la Recherche Scientifique*, 6, (1) p. 27-41, Lomé, UL.

Kwakume, H., 1948, *Précis d'histoire du peuple ewe*, Lomé : IEF.

Mead, M., 1973, Une éducation en Nouvelle-Guinée. Paris : Payot.

Moser, C., 2000, « Planification selon le genre dans le Tiers monde : comment satisfaire les besoins stratégiques selon le genre », dans *Le genre : outil nécessaire. Introduction à une problématique*, dirigé par Jeanne Bisilliat et Christine Verschuur, Paris : L' Harmattan.

Murdock, G., 1949, *Social structure*, New York : The Free Press.

Paulme, D., 1971, *Classe et associations d'âge en Afrique de l'ouest*, Paris : Payot.

Pilon, M., Mama, M., Tichit, C., 1997, « Les femmes chefs de ménage : aperçu général et études de cas », dans *Ménage et famille en Afrique*, Paris : CEPED.

Rivière, C., 1979, « Mythes et rites de la naissance chez les eve », *Annales de l'Université du Bénin*, N° spécial, Lomé, UB.

Rivière, C., 1981, *Anthropologie religieuse des Evé du Togo*, Lomé : NEA.

Roubailo-Koudolo, S.,1995, *La société des camarades comme un facteur de la socialisation des enfants en milieu ewe*, Lomé : DIFOP, 87 p.

Sambiani, D., 2002, « Les effets de la vidéo projection sur la socialisation des enfants dans la commune de Lomé », *Revue de CAMES*, Série B, Vol., 004, éd., Ouagadougou, CAMES.

Série Genre et développement, 2000, *Adages et mythes porteurs du genre en milieu ewe et mina*, Lomé : INADES-FORMATION.

Speith, J., 1911, *Die Religion der Ewe in Süd Togo*, Leipzig : Dietrich.

URD, 2002, *Famille, migrations et urbanisation au Togo*, Fascicule 1, *Résultats de l'enquête qualitative*, Lomé : URD. (URD I).

URD, 2002, *Famille, migrations et urbanisation au Togo*, Fascicule 2, *Résultats de l'enquête quantitative*, Lomé : URD. (URD II).

URD, 2000, *Famille, migrations et urbanisation au Togo*, Fascicule 3, *Structures familiales et conditions de vie des ménages*, Lomé : URD. (URD III).

7

White Men: An Exploration of Intersections of Masculinity, Whiteness and Colonialism and the Engagement of Counter-Hegemonic Projects[1]

Claire Kelly

This study presents the case for the study of white masculinities in South Africa. White men, long seen as hampering gender and race transformation in South Africa, are seen here as engaged as potential allies in an exercise which, while locating whiteness and masculinity in a particular history, allows for the notion of multiple masculinities and whitenesses, and for alternative ways of being a man and white to emerge. Through exploring life stories, this study presents moments that illustrate the intersections of masculinity, whiteness and colonial legacy in the construction of these men's identities. It illustrates how these identities are complex and contradictory and that the ascendance into hegemony is heavily weighted with cost. Furthermore, it shows how different men, at different moments, inhabit these intersections differently. Some challenge the master narratives of masculinity and whiteness, some accept and perpetuate them. These challenges may manifest in the simple naming of power to a call to action to challenge it. The most important thing, however, is that master narratives are being 'interrupted' and the hegemony challenged.

Academic and popular interest in the study of masculinities is growing worldwide. In March 2004, the United Nations Commission on the Status of Women released its first set of agreed conclusions on *The Role of Men and Boys in Achieving Gender Equality* (UN 2004). In South Africa, these processes are echoed by endeavours such as the Fatherhood Project headed by the Human Sciences Research Council. It is becoming accepted that gender equality 'demands that men take on the challenge of changing themselves' (Morrell 2003). The struggle for men to see the privilege they have is central to this process (Wildman and

Davis 2002; Steyn 2001; Frankenberg 1993), and it can only be achieved through the inclusion of men in the struggle towards gender justice.

Although radical feminisms have been criticized for the demonization and exclusion of men, more inclusive feminisms have emerged. These acknowledge the value of men's involvement in the project of realizing gender justice. A 'third wave' (Frankenberg 1993) of feminism has endeavoured to undertake this project in the context of other axes of oppression, especially race[2] and racism,[3] the driving rationale being that gender and race do not simply present versions of each other but actively constitute each other (Lerner 1997). African feminisms have pointed out that African women's realities are shaped by a 'plurality of values of which Africa consists' and that sound scholarship around gender needs to be 'located in that history' (Modupe-Kolawole 2000: 93). The reality of African women's oppression is criss-crossed by factors such as culture, nationalism, religion, globalization, colonialism[4] and race. Gender is but one layer in the fight for equality. Modupe-Kolawole (2000: 92) goes on to say 'feminism' is viewed by many African men as a 'divisive concept' employed by the West to undermine the struggle against racism. It is also viewed with scepticism by some women, perceived by some to have been imported to 'ruin nice African homes' (Aidoo, cited in Modupe-Kolawole 2000: 93). The concerns of African feminists 'draws attention to the diversity of experiences amongst women' (Morrell and Swart 2005: 99) and illustrates the very intersectional nature of gender and racial oppression. It also underlines the 'need to theorise multiple forms of oppression, particularly where inequalities of race, gender and class are evident' and 'the need to highlight imperialism' (Oyewumi 2002: 3) in the study of gender in Africa.

In the same way that mainstream academic focus is shifting from women as the 'problem', the 'problem' of race can no longer be seen as 'coming from blacks' (Lipsitz, cited in Steyn 2001: xxix) but rather needs to be 'located and addressed in the discourses, socialization, political and economic privilege of white people' (Steyn 2001: xxix). In the past the analysis of race has focused largely on black people (Giroux 1997) but as bell hooks (cited in Giroux 1997: 291) argues, very little has been done 'to investigate and justify all aspects of White culture from a standpoint of difference'. More recently, however, for those engaged in critical analysis, just as men have become gendered, whiteness has become raced (Steyn 2001; Frankenberg 1993) and the primary task of those whites who are committed to transformation is to 'deterritorialize the territory of the White, to expose, examine and disrupt ... so that, like other positions, it may be placed under critical analysis' (Nakayama and Krizek. cited in Giroux 1997: 292).

Furthermore, the active co-construction of race and gender suggests that we cannot explore one without firmly contextualizing it in relation to the other. Failing to do so means failing to engage the complexity of these positionalities (Lerner

1997; Frankenberg 1993). This work is located within a critical postmodern paradigm and stands at the intersection of work around masculinities and whiteness. It joins the increasingly broad scope of work that examines the social construction of the complexities of masculinities and whitenesses, the way in which they interact and the implications that these interactions have for power, and the realization of social justice.

This study draws from a Masters thesis I completed at the University of Cape Town in 2005. My thesis was broad. Here, however, I wish to explore those aspects of my findings that most actively contribute to the debates around masculinity, whiteness and (post)colonialism.[5] I also wish to present those instances that serve to disrupt the dominant narratives associated with white colonial masculinities. Before that, however, I will present the argument for the study of white masculinities in South Africa and the conceptual foundations on which this argument is built. As the methodology of my study was closely related to these theoretical foundations, I will briefly reflect on the methodology adopted to undertake this exploration. Finally, I will present the extracts from the men's stories and their analysis.

The Argument for the Study of White Masculinities in South Africa

Literature in the area of men's studies in South Africa has failed to address the complexities of men's gender projects (Morrell 2001; Shefer and Ruiters 1998; Oyegun 1998; Ratele 2001). This is particularly true for white masculinities, which seem to have slipped under the academic radar. A case in point was the Symposium on Manhood and Masculinities held at WISER (September 2004) in which only one out of twenty-five papers, presented over three days, focused on white masculinities while the rest were on black masculinities; Furthermore, a lot of the work, which was unnamed in terms of race, was about black masculinities. It may be that white masculine hegemony is still doing a pretty good job of not exposing itself, but it may also be that the complexity of that hegemony and challenges to it are not being adequately engaged.

More broadly however, some theorists have argued, the exercise of conceptualizing masculinity tends to result in the fitting of men's experiences into pre-existing frames (Ratele 2001). The result is that the masculine subject is not allowed to change. In fact, it can be argued that the rearticulation of problematic masculinities further entrenches them. At the aforementioned Symposium on Manhood and Masculinity, Robert Morrell cautioned against the unproblematized assumptions undergirding many men's studies, of what he calls the man/power and man/violence couplet. He argued that to engage in the study of men from this theoretical platform is to lock the understanding of gender into these dichotomous relationships. Furthermore, it means losing the complexity and nuance that characterizes gendered identities and relationships, and the complexity of the way in which power permeates them.

Although this argument has been made about masculinity, the same dynamic applies to whiteness. After Giroux (1997), Steyn (2001: xxx) argues that equating whiteness with racism 'is paralyzing for those whites who seek liberating subject positions'. Giroux (1997: 293) expands this point in arguing that what is necessary is an approach that gives whites the 'possibility of rearticulating Whiteness, rather than either simply accepting its dominant normative assumptions or rejecting it as a racist form of identity'. He further argues that the result of equating whiteness to racism is that white people have 'few resources to question and rearticulate whiteness' (ibid.: 296) and as a result retreat into a 'general sense of angst over racial politics' (ibid.). However, Steyn (2001: xxx) notes how Giroux makes the distinction between 'whiteness as a racial ideology and the many subject positions that are open to, and adopted by, white people'. The disaggregation of whiteness in this way allows the space for whites to 'reconceptualise their identities in eman-cipatory ways' (ibid.) and in so doing take on the responsibilities of social trans-formation. The same holds true for gender identities.

The purpose of this work is to explore some of the many subject positions that Steyn talks about and, in so doing, contribute to discourse around more 'emancipatory' ways of being both white and a man. Everything. But The Burden (2004: 2), a group of young white men doing anti-racist and anti-sexist work in the USA, makes the point that it would be very cynical to believe that 'most white heterosexual males, if given the choice would trade the health of the people and the world's ecosystems for their own wellbeing'. I also agree, however, that in the current climate of world affairs, white men actually stand in a unique position to bring about change. It is about white men working to dismantle the power that they have and in doing so 'inhabiting' it differently (Erasmus 2004). It is about shifting some of the responsibility for transformation to the centres. Crucial to this redistribution of responsibility is the productive engagement of those who are by virtue of historical legacy, centred, in this case, on white men. Lack of engagement and the ongoing construction of all white men as barriers to transformation have resulted, and will continue to result, in most white men disassociating themselves from responsibility in these processes. More problematically, it may cause in those white men who are already involved in transformative processes to disengage. Productive engagement, then, requires a complex appreciation of the nature of transformation and the relationship it has with identity:

> Change in practice… can be the long and difficult remaking of an inherited (determined) practical consciousness: a process often described as development but in practice a struggle at the roots of the mind – not casting off an ideology, or learning phrases about it, but confronting

hegemony in the fibres of the self and the hard practical substance of effective and continuing relationships. (Williams, cited in Sideris 2004: 88)

Sideris (2004: 89) goes on to argue that 'the pressure to conform to the dominant standard is not founded on an uncomplicated desire for power' but rather plays out in the conflict of identity and a coherent sense of self. The pressure to yield to the hegemonic is greatest when there is no social support for alternative practices (ibid.). The disaggregation of the hegemonies of white masculinity, by giving voice to those who critique and 'interrupt' them (Steyn 2001: xxviii), is central in the process of creating these alternative discursive spaces. It is these alternative spaces that my study served to explore, and in so doing contribute to the growing engagement of white men in processes of social transformation.

In order to embark on this task, however, it is important to be grounded in particular conceptual frameworks around masculinity, whiteness and their intersection. The following section lays that theoretical foundation.

Theorizing Masculinities

Assuming that gender is a project wrought of social resources, we are forced to reconsider the term masculinity and refer rather to 'multiple masculinities' (Connell 1995: 76) so as to appreciate the 'diversity of men's projects' (Wetherell 1996: 322). As Holland *et al.* (1994: 123) put it, there are various ways in which 'men do masculinity', and how they do that masculinity is determined by the cultural resources available to them (Edley and Wetherell 1997; Wetherell 1996; Morrell 1998). The disaggregation of masculine identity in this way is crucial in the realization of more 'emancipatory' ways of being.

One of the only things that can be generalized is that the 'patriarchal dividend' (Connell 1995: 82) does not pay out equally to all men. Connell (1995) defines the 'patriarchal dividend' as the accumulated advantage that men experience relative to women. This dividend is the result of hegemony. Hegemony is the 'cultural dynamic by which a group claims and sustains a leading position in social life' (ibid.: 77). Gender is one dimension of that position and it intersects identity with equally powerful axes, like race and class. Hegemony is a crucial concept, in that it captures the power of certain versions of masculinity over others. In the exercise of working towards more progressive versions and challenging the obstacles to them, this is an important tension.

Different versions of masculinity become dominant in different contexts. To assume that the Euro-American version of hegemonic masculinity (the homogeneity of such a concept itself being problematic) is *the* hegemonic version of masculinity is in itself an act of cultural hegemony in that it assumes that the Euro-American version is, by default, the dominant one. This is particularly problematic when, in a global context, we have Euro-American systems of meaning being superimposed over and 'explaining' other cultural experiences. In any given context, there may in fact be competing not only masculinities, but dominant forms of masculinity within different meaning systems. For the same reason then that we speak of masculinit*ies* we should speak of hegemon*ies* (Connell 2004). An important tool for exploring the nature of these hegemonies, and the relationships that they have with each other and other less dominant versions of masculinity, is that of subordination (Connell 1995). This is an important development in the conceptualization of this work in that white masculinity is not conceived as *the* hegemonic version of masculinity in South Africa, but as one of many. This allows for the conceptualization of more than one dominant way of being a man and white and in different contexts, further contributing to a more nuanced understanding of masculine identities. This is crucial in capturing *all* the ways in which *all* these versions of masculinity serve to entrench male privilege.

One of the central characteristics of hegemonies is that they are only likely to be established if they are linked with some form of institutional power (Connell 1995). It is for this reason that it is important to locate the subjective experience of being a white man in South Africa very firmly in the reality of current socio-economic arrangements. South Africa's long colonial history and Apartheid meant that institutional power and resources were for a long time in the hands of one particular group of men, white men. Although since the new dispensation this arrangement has been rendered more complex, it is largely still in place (Epstein 1998). For example, according to the South African Department of Labour's Employment Equity Report for 2003, white men still dominate top management positions at 67%, while Indian, African and Coloured men hold 18% and women (white 9% and black 6%) make up the rest. Furthermore, unskilled labour is dominated by African men, who make up 62% of the total unskilled labour market, and African women who make up 22%. White men and women make up 1% each (Department of Labour of South Africa 2003). The exercise of colonialism was one that relied on a particular version of masculinity to achieve its aims: one that was dominant and one that was white.

Theorizing Whitenesses

The colonial endeavour was based on the 'superiority' of the colonizers, which was physically marked by their paler skin colour and socially by their 'civilized' customs. Conversely, the 'inferiority' of the colonized was marked by darker skin colour and less 'civilized' customs (Steyn 2001). Furthermore, the existence and legitimacy of whiteness in Africa relied on the 'inferiority' of dark-skinned Africans. Whiteness represented civilization, progress and moral enlightenment, which Africa was seen as clearly lacking, and in need of (ibid.). With God and science on its side, whiteness could claim not only moral superiority but endogenous superiority to a continent perceived as further down the evolutionary ladder. Whiteness relied on the deprivation and assumed sub-human position of the African in order to stake its claim to Africa. This is an important theoretical point of entry in that it locates whiteness within a particular historical power dynamic.

The nature of the whiteness of the colonial project was that it constituted itself as infallible, as the only version of reality, the 'master narrative', the framework from within which all other versions of reality, narratives, were interpreted. This was achieved in large by the naturalization of the colonial order of things, dissociating it from the social and economic, and locating it in the endogenous characteristics of the groups. The effect that this had, however, was to mark the dominated as deviant from a norm that was 'naturally' located in the dominant positionality. When the dominated are thus marked 'the dominating position is unmarked, allowing freedom and greater possibilities, and simultaneously setting itself up as normal, positioned beyond any obligation to explain itself' (Steyn 2001: 21).

The power of whiteness in South Africa has been such that it has remained largely normative. White people have been able to ignore the way in which race has shaped their lives (Frankenberg 1993) and thus 'as the privileged group whites have tended to take their identity as the standard by which everyone else is measured' (Steyn 2001: xxvi). Giroux (1997: 294) argues that although whiteness is increasingly becoming an 'object of critical analysis', 'there have been few attempts to provide a theoretical language' for white people to view themselves as 'both White and anti-racist at the same time'. This is a valuable insight, in that it does not automatically equate whiteness with racism but, with full consciousness of the insidious nature of systematic racism and white privilege, endeavours to allow anti-racist subject positions to emerge. An important aspect of this undertaking is the examination of less centred varieties of whiteness, like white women (Ware 1992) and the inclusion of the experience of whites who seek alternative subjectivities to those presented by the master narrative (Steyn 2001).

Intersections of Whiteness and Masculinity and the Exercise of Imperialism

> Defence of manhood demanded, above all, the defence of the white goddess of civilisation against the black sex crazed, barbarians at the gates.
>
> (Hoch 2004: 100)

In their hegemonic forms, both whiteness and the masculine hold the 'centre' and, as such, employ similar dynamics to retain that dominant position. In fact, 'the very same mechanisms that were used to elevate whiteness, were utilized to elevate maleness as a natural category in opposition to women' (Steyn 2001: 20). The domination of women was an important mechanism for maintaining racial dominance (Frye, cited in Steyn 2001; Frankenberg 1993; Ware 1992; Hoch 2004). The protection of 'vulnerable' and 'precious' white women often served to justify oppressive relations between men, black men being constructed as sexually deviant and aggressive (Frankenberg 1993; Steyn 2001; Hoch 2004). Conversely, the construction of the black 'other' as a threat relied on the construction of white women as vulnerable. White women's sexuality was policed not only for their own protection, but also to ensure the continuation of the superior race. Lerner (1997) illustrates how this same logic, for the policing of white women's sexuality, was used to protect and entrench class privilege. Furthermore, the blatant and often violent 'appropriation' of black women by the colonizers marked their superiority and domination over black men (Frankenberg 1993; Steyn 2001; Ware 1992; Hoch 2004). Whiteness as conceived by the colonial master narrative is 'absolutely centred, unitary, masculine' (Owens, cited in Steyn 2001: 151). Moreover, in South Africa it can be argued that the masculinity as conceived by this colonial narrative is, unerringly, white and that whiteness remains a powerful narrative in the rendering of the gender project (Epstein 1998). 'Colonialism was a highly gendered process' (Morrell and Swart 2005: 91). According to Anne McClintock (cited in Morrell 2005: 92), in order 'to understand colonialism and postcolonialism, one must first recognise that race, gender and class are not "distinct realms of experience" but rather, they come into existence in relation to each other'. Connell (2005: 75) adds that by the late nineteenth century 'gender ideology tended to fuse with racism in forms that the twentieth century never untangled' and that 'the imperial social order created a scale of masculinities as it created a scale of communities and races' (ibid.).

Disaggregating Whitenesses and Masculinities

Although race remains a very powerful axis in the construction of gendered identity, Ratele (1998) and Epstein (1998) argue that it is necessary to reject the notions of a singular black or white masculinity, as neither are homogeneous. South Africa is a strongly racialized society, and this has shaped the types of masculinity available to black and white men (Epstein 1998; Morrell 2001; Ratele 2001), but it has not resulted in two homogeneous masculinities. What is required is the disaggregation of both whiteness and masculinity into whitness*es* and masculin*ities*. This is important in that where alternative versions of 'self' exist, subject positions can and do change. These changes depend on the investment a particular individual has in taking up a certain subject position and the subject positions available, the nature of each being a function of historical processes (Morrell 2001; Epstein 1998). With the political illegitimation of the colonial narrative, as marked by the new dispensation in South Africa, came the illegitimation of the masculinity with which it was associated. Not only was the colonial version of masculinity no longer viable but in the wake of its unravelling, alternative positionalities were made more viable. In the context of the changes that South Africa has undergone, the gender projects that white men are engaging in at the moment are particularly tricky (Epstein 1998). More than ever there are 'no clear models' for white men to follow (Frosh *et al* 2001: 1). Along with the reconstruction of the political system came the 'chance for the remaking of masculinities' (Epstein 1998: 50). 'Different masculinities become relevant, common or even possible, in different historical times, in different places and in different political situations' (ibid.: 49). This has never been truer than for white men in the new (post-Apartheid) South Africa.

A Reflection on Methodology

The thesis that this study draws on was informed by fourteen in-depth interviews. Two one-hour-long in-depth interviews were held with each of seven white middle-class men in Cape Town. This data was analysed drawing on two theoretical frames. First, Grounded Theory was used to explore themes emerging from the transcripts. This approach enabled close attention to be paid to the complexity of the men's voices and helped prevent the unproblematic reproduction of dominant constructions of whiteness and masculinity. Second, Critical Discourse Theory was used to explore the ideological positioning of and power dynamics implicated in the discursive resources accessed by these men. An important part of this process was the positioning of discourse emerging in the transcripts relative to 'master' narratives and the active exploration of counter-hegemonic discourse. Furthermore, intersections between race and gender were examined.

The methodology employed was rooted in a very particular understanding of the relationship between identity, culture and language. Theodore Sarbin (1986: 8) proposes that narrative is the organizing principle for human subjectivity, that 'human beings think, perceive, imagine and make moral choices according to narrative structures'. Riessman (1993: 4) adds that 'the primary way individuals make sense of experience is by casting it in narrative form'. In other words, it is through the telling of our life stories that subjectivities are constructed (Gergen 1994; Connell 1995; Hollway 1984; Frosh *et al* 2001; Mishler 1986a and b, 1995; Sarbin 1986; Riessman 1993). Furthermore, it is through our life stories that 'culture speaks itself' (Riessman 1993: 5) because in constructing our own narratives we draw off larger cultural narratives, and in turn rearticulate or disrupt the roles we play therein. The purpose of the present study is to examine the participants' stories within a critical discursive framework in order to explore how these stories are spoken to, and in turn speak and 'interrupt' (Steyn 2001), the cultural narratives of masculinity and whiteness. Connell (1995) identifies how these personal stories are central in contributing to a localized and particularized understanding of 'the material, cultural, and psychic practices and constraints that produce formations of masculinity' (Haywood and Mac an Ghaill 2003: 9).

One of the major characteristics of narratives is that they are constructed to be as coherent as possible, in terms of individual events, the overall point of the story and general cultural values (Agar and Hobbs, cited in Mishler 1986a and b).

This renders the subject position coherent and legitimate. Narratives need to fit into a cultural frame of reference to carry social weight. A legitimate story is constructed through mitigation with canonical narratives, that is, stories that have social legitimacy (Bruner 1990). Canons are, in a sense, like 'master narratives' that 'define rights and duties and incorporate the values of dominant social and political groups' and thereby 'conceal patterns of domination and submission' (Boje, cited in Mishler 1995: 115). Personal narratives are constructed relative to these master narratives and locate these personal experiences in relation to broader social processes (Steyn 2001). In this sense, narratives are not so much 'literal stories' but rather each is a means through which:

> Respondents organise their memories, make sense of recent events, imagine the motives of others as they create coherent plot lines, to explain racial [and gendered][6] relationships, engage in impression management, and use the cultural resources available to them to fashion identities under changing circumstances. (Steyn 2001: xxvii)

It was these stories that an in-depth interview methodology aimed to encourage. Participants were asked to reflect on their life stories and to identify those times in their lives that were most significant. More specifically questions were asked to participants around their earliest experiences of being a boy and a man and of being white. What is presented are extracts of these men's life stories and an analysis of how they are positioned relative to master narratives.

The Stories

It is from these stories that the following extracts were drawn. The segments of the stories represented here were selected as they most clearly articulate the complex relationship between whiteness, masculinity and the colonial project. The discussion is primarily located within the spheres of school and sport, which emerged as important sites for the construction of these identities. Further to this, extracts that illustrate alternative rearticulations of these relationships are presented. It is these rearticulations of what is masculine and white in South Africa that are at the heart of this work's aim of exploring counter-narrative to challenge the hegemonies whiteness and masculinity.

'Almost like Going to War'

> Going to a boys' only boarding school is almost like going to war, probably, because you do have to fend for yourself all on your own. At our school, for the first year, you weren't allowed to see your parents. That was the deal. So, you were to stand on your own two feet and get on with it. And there was a hell of a big seniority system in place which knocked you around if you stepped out of line. I'm not saying it was a good thing, but it was a good thing; I don't think that any beatings are necessarily a good

thing, but to have that system in place where you earn and learn respect for people (Andrew, Int. 1, 16/9/2004).

Within the frame of British imperialism, manhood is achieved through the enactment of rites that 'separated them [boys] from home and the familiar, most particularly from their mothers' care and influence', where they 'were to suffer the dominance of older boys with authority over them', and they 'were expected to stand on their own two feet until the time came for them to exercise authority and power in their turn' (Kanitkar 1994: 184). Andrew's account is almost a carbon copy of Kanitkar's textbook British imperial schooling system. His war metaphor – 'boarding school is almost like going to war' – is very appropriate, as these institutions' main purpose was to prepare boys for 'positions of military and civil leadership in the far flung British Empire' (ibid.) and to generate new loyalties, to school and sports teams, 'preparing boys for later, greater loyalties to regiment, nation and empire' (ibid.: 186).

The relationship between military and masculinity has been well documented (Dudink and Hageman 2004). 'Many aspects of modern masculinity were forged in the nexus of politics and war' (Dudink and Hageman 2004: 7). Politics and war allow for the exploration of different versions of masculinity and the power relations between them, including racial and colonial power (Horne 2004). The fact that Andrew draws the parallel between his school and this militarism illustrates the power of this narrative, with all its ramifications for racial and colonial power, in his own story.

In his work with South African boarding schools, Morrell (cited in Epstein 1998) illustrates how they are modelled on the British public school and serve to reproduce the same English-speaking upper-class masculinities. As Kanitkar (1994) points out, the nature of these masculinities is that they are inevitably white. The whiteness of the schooling system is illustrated in Andrew's strong emotional reaction – 'it's enough to make me cry' – to the postcolonial decentring of his whiteness by the fact that his school 'has gone completely black':

> And she told me that High School 2, which was another boys' only school that we were fairly competitive with, has gone completely black, there's not one white scholar there now and they celebrated last year by killing a goat in the centre of the school, our hall, their mess hall, slaughtering a goat. And I thought you know, jussus man, it's enough to make me cry to think that that school you know you do compete but at the end of the day you're pretty close and to think that that's going on now, slaughtering goats and celebrating (Andrew, Int. 1, 16/9/2004).

The incongruity of the African custom of slaughtering a goat occurring in the school hall is highly charged for him. It is this emotional chargedness that belies the extent of the disruption of his personal narrative and the extent to which it aligns with the master narratives of colonialism. The enactment of this African custom in the school hall signals a deep disruption of the colonial narrative. The image of the slaughtered animal and the accompanying celebration represents, within this narrative frame, an undermining of civilization and descent into 'barbarism' (Hoch 2004: 98). 'The call for upper caste white heroes to prove their manhood by exerting civilisation over the dark brutes' was 'the key rationale for the conquest and control of the "darker" peoples of Africa' (ibid.), and it was this control that was one of the 'firmest supports for ... colonialism, slavery and all succeeding doctrines of social and racial supremacy' (ibid.). In this case the reality of changing power dynamics, whereby African customs are legitimately undertaken in what were stongholds of colonialism, creates a dissonance in this personal narrative. What is challenged is not only his narrative of whiteness but also its accompanying masculinity.

'The Sporting Boy'
But within the school environment, the enactment of this imperial masculinity is most evident on the sports field (Kanitkar 1994). Hierarchy is put into place through a combination of age, academic success and sporting success (Morrell, cited in Epstein 1998). Justin, who attended a private boy's school in the KwaZulu-Natal Midlands (for a brief period), is very aware of how this hierarchy operates:

> Claire: In what ways do you think you'd be different if you had stayed in South Africa?
>
> Justin: I think I'd be a lot less sure of myself. The way you're measured as being successful at that age is to be either the brightest in the class. You know, if you're the brightest in the class but you're crap on the rugby field, that's okay, because you're the brightest in the class or the other way around but I was neither and I think I was probably whisked out at just the right time. I think my confidence would have been severely knocked (Justin, Int. 1, 4/8/2004).

He is also aware of the consequences of this intra-masculine hierarchy and recognizes that had he stayed there much longer, and was not 'whisked away', he would have been a lot less confident about himself. It is ironic, then, that the confidence that he would have been denied as a result of not meeting the requirements of sporting excellence in one context is reinstated by the very same dynamic, in another context:

> Well, I left South Africa when I was eleven and I was just in the C [third] team or something. And then when I got to England and I was in the A [first] Team for my age group and that was like massive! Again it was a paradigm shift for me because I thought, Wow! It was a huge ego boost,

a huge confidence boost for me, to realise that actually yes, I was someone. (Justin, Int.1, 4/8/2004)

In this environment he can meet the standards – 'I was in the A team' – as stipulated by the system that he finds himself in. More than a simple confidence booster, he can, as a result of being in the first team, validate his existence – 'I was someone'.

Sport provides a continuous play of men's bodies in motion' (Connell 1995: 54). Men's greater sporting prowess is that which serves to justify their dominance in all other social institutions and 'as symbolic proof of men's right to rule' (ibid.). Sports, especially the organized team sports like rugby, cricket and soccer, are an important site for the enactment of hegemonic masculinities (Morrell 2001). When we consider the relationship between the colonialism and the hegemonic masculinity it invoked, it is not surprising that 'the sporting boy' (Kanitkar 1994: 186) is a key trope around which imperial masculinities are constructed. If imperialism is the exercise of dominating the peoples of Africa and hegemonic masculinity the exercise of dominating women and other men, then sport is the stylized enactment of the 'superiority' that facilitates that domination.

This sentiment is supported in a particularly sensitive insight by Justin, who links beating girls at games as a child with his actions in his relationships with women. He tells the story of how he and his brothers beat a group of girls at an avocado pear fight:

> And there was something around we're better than them because we won,
>
> we won the avocado pear fight, right. So that was one incident (Justin, Int. 1, 4/8/2004).

He links winning the game to being 'better than' the girls, and, in a particularly insightful reflection, finds that it translates into him not taking women seriously:

> One of the things I notice is I don't take… in my automatic way of behaving, I don't take women very seriously…. So I'm thinking about how does that relate to as a boy… what's the word, demeaning or like an invalidation of girls because we can outgun them in the avo fight or we can, whatever, and being one of three boys as well (Justin, Int. 2, 15/9/ 2004)

He makes the direct link between being able to 'outgun' the girls 'in the avo fight' to not taking women seriously. The war metaphor – 'outgun' – is important here as there is a direct link made between sport, its implications for masculinity and a discourse of militarism. Jansen (2002: 196) argues that the conflation of 'Sport/ war tropes are crucial resources for mobilizing the hierarchical values that construct, mediate, maintain, and when necessary, reform or repair hegemonic forms of masculinity and femininity' (ibid.: 186). The result of the 'invalidation' of women through sport is important in that it has material consequences like all forms of oppression:

> Mark: Besides women being crap at sport, no (laughs).
>
> Claire: Have you thought that women are crap at sport?
>
> Mark: No just less powerful. I have a serious problem with for instance women's tennis where women complain that they don't get paid enough and they don't, then I think Well then why don't you play five games of tennis as well or five sets of tennis rather than three, things like that and it's just (laughs). I think equality is great and I think it's very important but then make it equality for equality's sake and not equality but you get special kind of preference or whatever. I think if it's equal then it should be equal all on the same playing field and I think the same about gender and race (Mark, Int. 2, 10/8/2004).

What Mark's comments imply is that because men are perceived as physically stronger and therefore play longer and harder, it is only right that they be paid more. What is interesting is that he links his gender argument to the same logic that prevails around racial equity in sport. His comments feed into discourse around standards and performance and do not question the way in which these standards actively serve to exclude women and other marginal groups through what Anderson and Accomando (2002: 505) call a false neutrality'. This false neutrality is constructed by reference to the fact that 'if it's equal then it should be equal all on the same playing field', which 'makes sense only if the larger context of male [and white][7] power is ignored' (ibid.).

Mark's conflation of gender and race in equity in sport is important. Sport is one of the markers of manhood not only because it is a show of superiority over girls and women but it is also a show of superiority among men:

> I definitely also feel that there was bigger competition between the boys only schools that were boarding and they looked at the boys only schools and or the co-ed school that were day boarding or day scholars as inferior because we always beat them at sport (Andrew, Int. 1, 16/9/2004).

Furthermore, 'class and race values are institutionalized on and through the sports field' (Kanitkar 1994: 186). This is most evident in the great rugby/soccer divide, which is clearly a racial one. Morrell (2001: 23) illustrates how soccer, with its emphasis on artistry, came to be the sport of black township boys while rugby, with its focus on 'physical confrontation, perseverance and skill' was 'equated with white masculinity'. The emphasis on artistry in the black sportsmen and skill in the white taps into a broader interpretative repertoire; artistry speaks to natural ability, while skill speaks to learnt technical ability (personal communication, Z. Erasmus, 15/03/2005). As Weaver (1994) illustrates, the rational and natural are diametrically opposed; that which is natural in a human sense can easily being equated with primitiveness. The construction of the 'other' as having 'natural' ability only serves to highlight our own technical ability and, by extension, rationality (Chabal 1996). The effect of locating black and white sportsmen in this dichotomy is that of locating black and white on opposite ends of a natural/primitive and skilled/rational continuum (Weaver 1994). This was an important distinction in the colonial project, the rational being one of the cornerstones of colonial domination. The racialized nature of this divide on the sports field is clearly articulated in some of the narratives:

> My major memories of that time were probably playing soccer, this guy [a black friend at school] knew how to dazzle with the ball (Mark, Int. 1, 23/7/2004).

> You go to rugby, I went to go and watch a UCT [University of Cape Town] first team rugby game on Tuesday night, they were playing Maties [Stellenbosch University] and like you look at the breakdowns [racial breakdown] and it's still the majority of the people, like the overwhelming majority, are white, that play rugby, and supporters. In terms of soccer we go play rugby at UCT quite a bit, and if you look at the soccer team it's completely the other way round (Bryan, Int. 2, 12/8/2004).

This demarcation of race through sport illustrates the very co-constructive nature of masculinities and race. The stylized enactment of rugby may produce the masculine but it also secures the white. This echoes with Justin's encounter with the West Indian cricket team (cricket being the domain of white colonial endeavour), which upset his racialized expectations of black men:

> Justin: I was going to say something round… because I love cricket and when I got here to England and then I saw these black guys who were West Indians playing cricket and it felt like such a mindfuck that these people should be subservient.

> Claire: Can you tell me a bit more about how you reacted to that and why?

> Justin: It was just so odd. It was, God, these guys can actually do things! I know they can dig ditches and they can do roads but, wow, they can do other things on a par with white people (Justin, Int. 1, 4/8/2004).

The fact that he knows 'they can dig ditches and they can do roads' speaks to the boy's expectations of what 'these guys' can do, 'be subservient'. The fact that 'these guys can actually do things' emerges in relation to a node around which colonial power was articulate and is significant for the depth of this experience. To see this symbolic enactment of power by black men who are expected to be labourers and servants, 'on a par with white people', truly is a 'mindfuck', in that it is, within the master narrative, a contradiction in terms.

Rough and Tough

The importance of 'manly sports' like rugby and other mechanisms, such as strong hierarchy and separation from families, 'which serve to toughen boys up' (Epstein 1998: 56), alludes to an important characteristic of the masculinity under construction. Through his use of the war metaphor, Andrew alerts us that these masculinities emerge in the context of violence. 'War was a reflection of the aggressive masculinity implicit in imperial policy' (Morrell 2001: 12), and school as the incubator of these imperial masculinities exhibits the same violence and aggression. One of the mechanisms of this institutional violence is 'organised bullying' (Epstein 1998: 56) perpetrated by both students and teachers. Andrew's account at the beginning of this section reflects this, as does Justin's, and it is no coincidence that this bullying occurs on the sports field:

> Claire: You also mentioned that when you got to England your confidence grew at school. What was it about the schools in South Africa that didn't allow that?

> Justin: Bullying. Bullying, really. I think it was that whole macho stuff. The headmaster we had when I was at school and obviously I'm only speaking from my experience, I can't speak for any other, but he was just a bloody sadist! Whipping people with a whistle, with the whistle end, if they wouldn't get down with their heads into the scrum (Justin, Int. 1, 4/8/2004).

There can be no doubt that the systems that Andrew and Justin have endured are brutal and damaging. What is significant here is the way in which they now engage with that brutality. It is worth revisiting Andrew's account:

> And there was a hell of a big seniority system in place which knocked you around if you stepped out of line. I'm not saying it was a good thing, but it was a good thing; I don't think that any beatings are necessarily a good thing, but to have that system in place where you earn and learn respect for people (Andrew, Int 1, 16/9/2004).

He is ambivalent, he oscillates between saying it wasn't a 'good thing' to saying that it was, and that although beatings are not necessarily good, they are there for a reason, in this case 'you earn and learn respect'. It is where you go to learn your 'life skills' and where you go to become a man:

> And you know what, I reckon if I had the choice now, I'd probably send my son to a boys only school because even if I just look at university and how the guys that went to boys only schools became men and the guys that went to co-ed [co–educational, i.e. boys and girls] schools, not that they didn't but just it wasn't as if you'd gone off somewhere and learnt your life skills, you'd remained in society (Andrew, Int. 1, 16/9/2004).

The payoffs are great, so much so that he would send his own son to a boy's-only school. But although Andrew colludes with this harsh system, Hardiman and Jackson (1997) alert us to the complexity of the dominant positionality. Those who are dominantly positioned exist in a paradox in that in the process of exercising dominance they themselves are dehumanized (Freire, cited in Hardiman and Jackson 1997). Andrew's experience talks to the dehumanization that dominant positionalities are subject to in that they are 'trapped by the system of social oppression that benefits them, and are confined to the roles and prescribed behaviour for their group' (Hardiman and Jackson 1997: 20). It is the costs of this brutal system that Justin engages in and confronts. His very articulation of the negative effects that it had on him – 'my confidence would have been severely knocked' – and his negative and emotive language – 'sadist' – suggests that he does not in any way see it as 'a good thing'. In doing so, he actively serves to challenge it.

Towards New Masculinities, Towards New Whitenesses

There are two points to be made about the masculinities and whitenesses that these men inhabit. First, engaging the violent hegemonic colonial masculinity that the contexts of school and sport perpetuate is not an uncomplicated and easy ascendancy into power. It is a sometimes painful trial that, although it reaps great rewards, also involves heavy costs to the humanity of these boys. The second point is that these men do not inhabit these positionalities in the same way. Some men, like Andrew, acquiesce and accept the system. Others, like Justin, are questioning and grappling with it, and those who do, do not inhabit their postionality comfortably.

Thus far, the co-construction of whiteness and masculinity and its relationship to the legacy of colonialism have been explored. What has also become evident is that, as Justin's last narrative clearly indicates, this interaction is not taken up unproblematically, and in the same way, by all these men. The following section explores the problematization of, and challenges to, the hegemonies of masculinity and whiteness. In one case these challenges manifest in an interrogation of positionality, in another as direct articulations of challenge to the master narratives. In another still, they emerge as a call to action. In all cases they 'expose, examine and disrupt', so that their positionalities 'may be placed under critical analysis' (Nakayama and Krizek, cited in Giroux 1997: 292) and in so doing contribute to the counter-hegemonic project.

Challenging the Hegemonies

Some of the men display a deeply sensitive understanding and interrogation of their positionalities. Adam is gay. According to Phillips (2005: 137) (who is also gay, white and a man), homosexuality 'interferes with the smooth assumption of many of the other manifestations of power in my life, jarring my easy occupancy of an otherwise ascendant identity within hegemonic structures'. But being gay also 'empowers me, as it forces me on to a liminal path from where centralised power and the singular absolutism of its truth are inevitably challenged' (ibid.). Like Phillips, Adam is at once in marginal and dominant positionality and these dimensions play out in different contexts. He feels relatively powerful to:

> Men who are younger than me; men who are physically smaller than me; men who are somewhat more gentle, I suppose would be the right word to use, I feel more power over if that's the right word. Ja, I feel like I'm the person in power and I enjoy that and sometimes – I wouldn't say I abuse it – but I use it to my advantage (Adam, Int. 2, 26/8/2004).

But disempowered to men who exhibit more hegemonic qualities:

> Men who are taller than me, men who are older than me, definitely straight men, sporty men, men who are hyper-masculine, twenty-two, twenty-three year old sporty post-grad students with some attitude and a sense of style – those men I feel disempowered by, if that makes any sense? There's a sense of less power and to some extent it's not quite the same with women (Adam, Int. 2, 26/8/2004).

It is not a power dynamic that he can transpose on to women. And when he considers his positionality vis-à-vis women he is very aware that 'simply the fact that I am a man gives me power over women' even if they are in positions of power:

> I'm more comfortable and I feel more empowered when I'm with a woman I regard as a competition. She can be the MD [managing director] of a company and I would be much less anxious if I had to meet with her professionally. So definitely, simply the fact that I am a man gives me power over women. And dare I say it, to some extent still the fact that I'm white gives me power over people who are not white (Adam, Int. 2, 26/8/2004).

He is also aware that his whiteness works in similar ways to his masculinity, in that it 'gives me power over people who are not white'. His is a complex positionality, which also occupies different sides of different binary oppositions (Ware 1992). These oppositions serve not only to create tensions between himself and others, but within himself as well. Through his experience of relationships, he is sensitively unpacking his positionality, and in so doing engaging in a fundamentally counter-hegemonic act – interrogating and exposing his power.

It is this interrogation and continuous vigilance that Justin exhibits:

> But I'm just so aware of how I've been brought up as a racist and how those old habits take a lifetime of breaking down. I have to confront my racism every single day. I was driving just now and there was this really

slow car in the middle lane and this woman was driving like this and it was a black woman and just in my head was all this tirade of real racist shit and I'm a grown man and I'm responsible for that and what's important is that I'm able to own it rather than it own me. But it's quite scary it is quite scary (Justin, Int. 2, 15/9/2004).

Owning one's racism, taking responsibility for it and confronting it daily are the greatest challenges to the colonial narrative. Justin's, like all the stories in this section, fall *Under African skies*, one of the five narratives of whiteness in South Africa identified by Steyn (2001). *Under African skies* is told by those whites 'who are moving away from their whiteness' and represents a place where there exists the potential for 'exciting new ways of being' and where the narrator is committed to his own 'potential for growth'. More importantly, it is a place where whiteness is 'blended, contradictory and complex' and thus 'hyphenated', no longer with the 'power to abuse' (Steyn 2001: 147).

Furthermore, it is a whiteness that can mobilize, that can 'stand up to white people', be accountable for its past – 'be aware of it, be very aware of it' – and work towards transformation. It is a whiteness aware of, but not paralysed by shame and guilt, and a whiteness that can therefore find a place *Under African skies*:

> It's my role to stand up to white people and say, Don't be ashamed of being white. Stop that bullshit! That time is gone. Ja, we did fucking bad things, make no mistake, but being ashamed of it is not going to change it. Be aware of it, be very aware of it, actually. Don't just stand here, I'm ashamed I'm white, it's not going to go anywhere (Carl, Int. 2, 11/8/2004).

Conclusion

This study has presented the case for the study of white masculinities in South Africa. White men, long seen as the barriers to gender and race transformation in South Africa, are here engaged as potential allies. Whiteness and masculinity are located in a particular history, that of colonialism, but, importantly, the approach adopted here also allows for the notion of multiple masculinities and whitenesses, and alternative ways of being a man and white to emerge.

Through exploring life stories, it has presented moments that illustrate the intersections of masculinity, whiteness and colonial legacy in the construction of these men's identities. It has illustrated how these identities are complex and contradictory and that the ascendancy into hegemony is heavily weighted with cost, which ranges from enduring humiliation and physical beating to psychic damage resulting from co-option into enacting brutality in turn. Furthermore, it has shown how different men, at different moments, inhabit these intersections differently. Some challenge the master narratives of masculinity and whiteness, some accept and perpetuate them. These challenges may manifest in the simple naming of power to a call to action to challenge it. The most important thing, however, is that master narratives are being 'interrupted' (Steyn 2001) and hegemonies challenged. Alternative discursive spaces around masculinities and whiteness do exist, and through the processes of exposure, examination and rearticulation, these are becoming more robust.

Notes

1. I would like to acknowledge Dr Zimitri Erasmus, who was my supervisor for the thesis on which this paper draws and therefore instrumental to its conception and completion.
2. In this study, the concept of race is recognized not as the biological and social criteria set out by Apartheid, but rather as a social reality (Lerner 1997; Frankenberg 1993; Erasmus, with De Wet 2003) defined, like class, by the social resources made available to one on the basis of certain criteria. In South Africa the criteria of skin colour, through Apartheid, has been 'overdetermined' (Epstein 1998: 52) to shape that reality.
3. 'Racism emerges not only as an ideology or political orientation chosen or rejected at will, but also as a system of material relationships with a set of ideas linked to and embedded in those material relations' (Frankenberg 1993: 70). Furthermore, it exists as 'everyday racism', which is 'expressed and contested in ordinary situations' (Essed 2002: 203). As such, this study 'relates day-to-day experiences of racial discrimination [both by target and agent] to the macrostructural context of group inequalities' (ibid.) and understands it as a means to determine social reality through the everyday exercise of ideological power.
4. In this study, I follow Morrell and Swart's (2005: 91) definition of colonialism as 'a phase in world history beginning in the early 16th century that, eventually, by 1914, saw Europe hold sway over more than 85% of the rest of the globe'. I also follow their further definition of colonialism as 'the political ideologies that legitimated the modern occupation and exploitation of already settled lands by external powers' (ibid.). Like Morrell and Swart, I recognize this concept to be contested.
5. I also follow Morrell and Swart's (2005: 91) understanding of postcolonialism as 'the period after colonialism'. After Morrell and Swart (ibid.: 92), I also acknowledge that it 'refers inexactly to a political and geographical terrain' and that 'it is used to denote a position against imperialism and Eurocentrism'.
6. My addition.
7. My addition.

References

Interviews

Adam (pseudonym). Adam's home, Cape Town, 26 August 2004.
Andrew (pseudonym). Andrew's home, Cape Town, 16 September 2004.
Bryan (pseudonym). Bryan's home, Cape Town, 12 August 2004.
Carl (pseudonym). Carl's office, Cape Town, 11 August 2004.
Justin (pseudonym). Justin's office, Cape Town, 4 August and 15 September 2004.
Mark (pseudonym). Mark's home, Cape Town, 23 July and 10 August 2004.

Other Sources

Anderson, K. J. and Accomando, C., 2002, 'Real Boys? Manufacturing and Erasing Privilege in Popular Books on Raising Boys', *Feminism and Psychology*, Vol. 12, No. 4, pp. 491–516.

Bruner, J., 1990, *Acts of Meaning*, Cambridge, MA: Harvard University Press.

Chabal, P., 1996, 'The African Crisis: Context and Interpretation', in P. Werbner and T. Ranger, eds., *Postcolonial Identities in Africa*,. London: Zed Books.

Connell, R. W., 1995, *Masculinities*, Berkeley: University of California Press.

Connell, R. W., 2004, Public ure presented at the Wits Institute for Social and Economic Research (WISER) Symposium on Manhood and Masculinity: Struggles with Change, 5–7 September 2004, University of the Witwatersrand, Johannesburg.

Connell, R. W., 2005, 'Globalisation, Imperialism and Masculinities', in M. Kimmel, J. Hearn and R. Connell, eds., *Handbook of Studies on Men and Masculinities*, Thousand Oaks, CA: Sage.

Department of Labour of South Africa, 2003, 'Employment Equity Report' (http://www.labour.gov.za/useful_docs/doc_display.jsp?id=9961)[accessed. 25 February 2005].

Dudink, S. and Hageman, K., 2004, 'Masculinity in Politics and War in the Age of Democratic Revolutions, 1750–1850', in S. Dudnik, K. Hageman and J. Tosh, eds., *Masculinities in Politics and War: Gendering Modern History*, Manchester: Manchester University Press.

E.B.T.B. (Everything But The Burden), 2004, *A Different Shade of White, Another Kind of Male: A Guide to Using Privilege Responsibly*, Electronic Books Series (One CD ROM). Available online at http://ebtbcrew.com/store.htm

Edley, N. and Wetherall, M., 1997, 'Jockeying for Position: The Construction of Masculine Identities', *Discourse in Society*, Vol. 8, pp. 203–17.

Epstein, D., 1998, 'Marked Men: Whiteness and Masculinity', *Agenda*, Vol. 37, pp. 49–59.

Erasmus, Z., 2004, 'Undoing the Yoke of "Race"', in D. Chidester, B. Tayob and W. Weisse, eds., *Religion and Society in Transition (Volume 6)*, Munster and New York: Waxmann Publishing.

Erasmus, Z. with De Wet, J., 2003, *Not Naming 'Race': Some Medical Students' Experiences and Perceptions of 'Race' and Racism at UCT's Health Sciences Faculty*, Research Report, University of Cape Town.

Essed, P., 2002, 'Everyday Racism', in D. Goldberg. and J. Solomos, eds., *A Companion to Racial and Ethnic Studies*, Malden, MA: Blackwell Publishing.

Frankenberg, R., 1993, *White Women, Race Matters: The Social Construction of Whiteness*, Minneapolis: University of Minnesota Press.

Frosh, S., Phoenix, A. and Pattman, R., 2001, *Young Masculinities*, Basingstoke: Palgrave.

Gallagher, C., 1995, 'White Reconstruction in the University', *Socialist Review,*, Vol. 94, pp. 165–87.

Gergen, M., 1994, 'The Construction of Personal Histories: Gendered Lives in Popular Autobiographies', in T. R. Sarbin and J. I. Kitsuse, eds., *Constructing the Social*, Thousand Oak, CA: Sage.

Giroux, H., 1997, 'Rewriting the Discourse of Racial Identity: Towards a Pedagogy and Politics of Whiteness', *Harvard Educational Review*, Vol 67, No. 2, pp. 285–320.

Hardiman, R. and Jackson, B. W., 1997, 'Conceptual Foundations for Social Justice Courses', in M. Adams, L. Bell and P. Griffin, eds., *Teaching for Diversity and Social Justice: A Sourcebook*, New York: Routledge.

Haywood, C. and Mac an Ghaill, M., 2003, *Men and Masculinities: Theory, Research and Social Practice*, Buckingham and Philadelphia: Open University Press.

Hoch, P., 2004, 'White Hero Black Beast: Racism, Sexism and the Mask of Masculinity', in P. Murphy, ed., *Feminism and Masculinities*, Oxford: Oxford University Press.

Holland, J., Ramanzanoglu, U., Sharpe, S. and Thompson, R., 1994, 'Achieving Masculine Sexuality: Young Men's Strategies for Managing Vulnerability', in L. Doyal, J. Naidoo and T. Wilton, eds., *AIDS: Setting a Feminist Agenda*, London: Taylor & Francis.

Hollway, W., 1984, 'Gender Difference and the Production of Subjectivity', in J. Henriques, W. Hollway, C. Urwin, C. Venn and V. Walkerdine, eds., *Changing The Subject: Psychology, Social Regulation and Subjectivity*, London: Methuen.

Horne, J., 2004, 'Masculinity in Politics and War in the Age of Nation States, 1850–1950', in S. Dudnik, K. Hageman and J. Tosh, eds., *Masculinities in Politics and War: Gendering Modern History*, Manchester: Manchester University Press.

Jansen, S. C., 2002, 'Football is More Than a Game: Masculinity, Sport and War', in S. C. Jansen, ed., *Critical Theory: Power, Media, Gender and Technology*, Oxford: Rowman and Littlefield Publishers.

Kanitkar, H., 1994, '"Real True Boys": Moulding the Cadets of Imperialism', in A. Cornwall and N. Lindisfarne, eds., *Dislocating Masculinity: Comparative Ethnographies*, London and New York: Routledge.

Lerner, G., 1997, *Why History Matters*, New York and Oxford: Oxford University Press.

Mishler, E. G., 1986a, *Research Interviewing: Context and Narrative*, Cambridge, MA: Harvard University Press.

Mishler, E. G., 1986b, 'The Analysis of Interview Narratives', in T .R. Sarbin, ed., *Narrative Psychology: The Storied Nature of Human Conduct*, New York: Praeger.

Mishler, E. G., 1995, 'Models of Narrative Analysis: A Typology', *Journal of Narrative and Life History*, No. 5, Vol. 2, pp. 87–123.

Modupe-Kolawole, M., 2002, 'Transcending Incongruities: Rethinking Feminisms and the Dynamics of Identity in Africa', *Agenda*, Vol. 54, pp. 92–121.

Morrell, R., 1998, 'The New Man?', *Agenda*, Vol. 37, pp. 7–12.

Morrell, R., 2001, 'The Times of Change: Men and Masculinity in South Africa', in R. Morrell, ed., *Changing Men in South Africa*, Pietermaritzburg: University of Natal Press.

Morrell, R., 2003, 'Are Men an Obstacle to Development?', *This Day*, 17/10/2003.

Morrell, R., 2004, Public Lecture presented at the Wits Institute for Social and Economic Research (WISER) Symposium, Manhood and Masculinity: Struggles with Change, 5–7 September 2004, University of the Witwatersrand, Johannesburg.

Morrell, R. and Swart, S., 2005, 'Men in the Third World: Postcolonial Perspectives on Masculinity', in M. Kimmel, J. Hearn and R. Connell, eds., *Handbook of Studies on Men and Masculinities*, Thousand Oaks, CA: Sage.

Oyegun, J., 1998, 'Working Masculinities Back into Gender', Agenda, Vol. 37, pp. 13–23.

Oyewumi, O., 2002, 'Conceptualising Gender: Eurocentric Foundations of Feminist Concepts and the Challenge of African Epistemologies', in *African Gender Scholarship: Concepts, Methodologies and Paradigms*, CODESRIA Gender Series 1, Dakar: CODESRIA.

Phillips, O., 2005, 'Ten White Men Thirteen Years Later: The Changing Constitution of Masculinities in South Africa, 1987–2000', in M. van Zyl and M. Steyn, eds., *Performing Queer: Shaping Sexualities 1994—-2004, Volume One*, Roggebaai: Kwela Books.

Ratele, K., 1998, 'The End of the Black Man', *Agenda*, Vol. 37, pp. 60–4.

Ratele, K., 2001, 'Between Ouens: Everyday Makings of Black Masculinity', in R. Morrell, ed., *Changing Men in South Africa*, Pietermaritzburg: University of Natal Press.

Riessman, C. K., 1993, *Narrative Analysis*, Newbury: Sage.

Sarbin, T. R., 1986, 'The Narrative as Root Metaphor for Psychology', in T. R. Sarbin, ed., *Narrative Psychology: The Storied Nature of Human Conduct*, New York: Praeger.

Shefer, T. and Ruiters, K., 1998, 'The Masculine Construct in Heterosex', *Agenda*, Vol. 37, pp. 39–45.

Sideris, T., 2004, 'Men, Identity and Power. A Case Study of the Re-invention of 'Tradition': Implications for Involving Men in Training and Education about Gender', *Agenda, Vol. 60, pp. 88–93*.

Steyn, M., 2001, '*Whiteness Just Isn't What It Used To Be': White Changing Identity in South Africa*, New York: State University of New York Press.

United Nations Commission on the Status of Women, 48th Session, 2004, *The Role of Men and Boys in Achieving Gender Equality*, http://www.un.org/womenwatch/daw/csw/csw48/Thematic1.html) [accessed 8 September 2004].

Ware, V., 1992, *Beyond the Pale: White Women, Racism and History*, London: Verso.

Weaver, G. R., 1994, 'Contrast Culture Continuum', in G. R. Weaver, ed., *Culture, Communication and Conflict: Readings in Intercultural Relations*, Needham Heights, MA: Simon & Schuster.

Wetherell, M., 1996, 'Life Histories/Social Histories', in M. Wetherell, ed., *Social Psychology: Identities, Groups and Social Issues*, London: Sage Publications.

8

L'État moderne africain et le patriarcat public

Ibrahim Mouiche

Introduction

L'État en tant que société politique est un phénomène récent. Né en Europe au XVIe siècle, il a été imposé au reste de la planète à travers la colonisation. Une fois que nous admettons cette altérité, une question nous vient à l'esprit : quels sont les fondements de l'État moderne africain ? À ce niveau, il est bon de rappeler avec Thomas Hodkin (1966 : 54-55) que l'Afrique à la fin du XIXe siècle, à l'époque du partage colonial n'était pas une table rase, un conglomérat de peuplades. L'Afrique précoloniale peut-être correctement représentée comme un système d'États, d'empires (les Empires d'Éthiopie et de Sokoto) et de sociétés « sans États » ayant des formes extrêmement diverses d'organisation politique et des principes moraux et politiques établis. On ne peut comprendre les institutions et les valeurs des sociétés africaines contemporaines si l'on ne se réfère à ce contexte historique. Toutefois, qu'on le veuille ou non, qu'on s'en réjouisse ou qu'on le déplore et sans que l'on tombe dans le piège de l'évolutionnisme unilinéaire de la philosophie du progrès du XIXᵉ siècle qui a imposé une théorie unilinéaire du développement social (la société industrielle comme la forme vers laquelle devraient nécessairement tendre les sociétés estimées moins avancées), l'évolution des sociétés politiques africaines, comme leurs droits a été profondément influencée par le phénomène colonial, entendu comme, « la domination imposée par une minorité étrangère, 'racialement' et culturellement différente, au nom d'une supériorité raciale (ou ethnique) et culturelle dogmatiquement affirmée, à une majorité autochtone matériellement inférieure ; la mise en rapport de civilisations hétérogènes : une civilisation à machinisme, à économie puissante, à rythme rapide et d'origine chrétienne s'imposant à des civilisations sans technique complexe, à économie retardée, à rythme lent et radicalement 'non chrétienne', le caractère antagoniste des relations intervenant entre les deux sociétés qui s'explique par le rôle d'instrument auquel est condamnée la société dominée, la nécessité pour maintenir la domination, et de recourir non seulement à la 'force' mais encore à un ensemble de pseudo-justifications et de comportements stéréotypés, etc. Cette énumération est cependant insuffisante », soutient Georges Balandier (1955 : 34-35).

La spécificité relative des sociétés africaines sur laquelle insiste une large littérature africaniste est indiscutablement d'ordre historique : elle provient peut-être de la prédominance dans les temps anciens, d'un modèle d'organisation sociale qui, sans ignorer le principe de l'État, en limitait la centralisation et les capacités d'extraction d'un surplus, par rapport à ce que l'on pouvait constater aux mêmes époques en Europe et en Asie. Le coût de cette trajectoire historique singulière a été la mise en dépendance précoce du sous-continent par des civilisations matériellement plus puissantes que lui : celles de l'Antiquité méditerranéenne, puis le monde arabo-musulman avant que l'Europe occidentale n'assure progressivement sa suprématie à partir du XVe siècle. À cet égard, la dynamique de l'État contemporain/moderne en Afrique noire est bien « orpheline » comme l'écrivent Bertrand Badié et Guy Hermet (1990 ; voir Mbembe 2000 : 22-23) : orpheline d'une grande tradition étatique similaire à celle de l'Occident, de l'Asie centrale et de l'Extrême-Orient. C'est dire combien l'hybridation entre les répertoires autochtones et les répertoires allogènes du politique, phénomène indissociable de la construction de l'État dans le Tiers-Monde, s'effectue en Afrique dans des conditions originales. Il est caractéristique de constater que, dans le passé, les empires n'avaient que peu touché à de très grandes parties des territoires sur lesquels s'étendait leur domination. En dehors des villes d'Asie mineure par exemple, nous savons que les Romains ont laissé intactes des structures communales très anciennes. L'intrusion des Occidentaux signifiait par contre, non seulement l'arrivée des Occidentaux, mais leurs institutions et dont l'État.

Les pages qui suivent portent sur cet État importé en Afrique et le patriarcat public. La question se décline de la manière suivante : l'État africain est-il ou non masculin ? Y a-t-il équilibre de genre ? Qu'est-ce que le patriarcat public ? Le texte se structure en quatre charpentes. Il s'ouvre d'abord par des remarques préalables sur la signification du patriarcat public que nous ramenons à l'essentiel à la masculinité du champ politique avec comme trait singulier, la distinction de la sphère publique de la sphère privée. Ensuite, parce que l'État moderne africain est intimement lié à l'épopée coloniale, nous allons tenter de trouver le fait générateur ou mieux, la genèse[1] de la masculinité du champ politique africain dans cette dichotomie qui a accompagné le processus de formation de l'État moderne européen au XVIe siècle; suivra le pouvoir colonial comme facteur historique de la masculinité du champ politique africain, puis, enfin, l'évolution du patriarcat public au sein de l'État postcolonial africain, de l'indépendance à nos jours. Dans cette tâche, il est nécessaire d'avoir à l'esprit que les États africains présentent chacun une complexité économique, sociale, politique, culturelle et religieuse trop grande pour autoriser des interprétations unifiantes et globalisantes de la masculinité du champ politique (Poirmeur 2000 : 324-325).

Du patriarcat public ou la masculinité du champ politique

Pendant longtemps, les études de science politique ont tourné autour de l'homme, ce dernier, au contraire de la femme, maîtrisant les institutions politiques formelles, ainsi que le relève avec pertinence Paul Nchoji Nkwi (1993 : 181).

« L'exercice du pouvoir politique a toujours été considéré comme une affaire d'hommes, dans la mesure où très peu de sociétés acceptent ou tolèrent que les femmes occupent des postes politiques même d'importance marginale. Que ce soit la *Mafo* de la société bamiléké, la *Nafoyn* du royaume de Kom au Cameroun[2], ou la reine d'Angleterre, elle demeure sous le contrôle des hommes. Ce qui est paradoxal c'est que, même dans les sociétés matrilinéaires, l'exercice effectif du pouvoir demeure entre les mains des hommes » (notre traduction).

Dans le même ordre d'idées, Michèle Alliot-Marie observait en 1983 que pour figurer au nombre des élites politiques en France, il faut faire reconnaître son savoir. Il faut être fonctionnaire, posséder des diplômes, appartenir à un grand corps ou les trois à la fois. « Mais tout d'abord, il vaut mieux ne pas être femme : les filières qui conduisent au pouvoir sont plus favorables aux candidats qu'aux candidates et la compétence des dirigeants inspire plus confiance que celle des dirigeantes » (Alliot-Marie 1983 : 82). Tout ceci explique pourquoi en dépit des engagements des États en faveur des femmes, celles-ci ne représentent que 13% des parlementaires et 14% des ministres dans le monde (Yongue Fouatou 2003 : 475). Certes, les femmes sont omniprésentes en bas de l'échelle de la vie politique (dans les pique-niques des partis politiques, dans l'urne, au téléphone, dans les meetings, à la collecte des contributions financières, etc.), mais en même temps, elles sont très peu représentées au sommet où se prennent les décisions affectant la vie de la communauté, de l'État et de la nation (Kirkpatrick 1974; Gaxie 1978, 1993). Voilà pourquoi il importe de distinguer entre les approches qui font de la participation politique une simple « influence », domaine de prédilection des femmes, de celles qui mettent l'accent sur la « gestion directe de la chose publique » , l'apanage des hommes. Cette exclusion de la femme dans le domaine politique n'est d'ailleurs qu'un aspect de leur marginalisation dans les autres secteurs; elles sont aussi rares dans les sommets des industries, de l'éducation que dans la politique. Et quand elles entreprennent une carrière politique, elles sont souvent chargées de « questions sociales ».

En Afrique, en dépit des avancées significatives observables dans quelques pays comme le Mozambique, la République sud africaine, le Rwanda ou l'Ouganda, où de nombreuses femmes occupent des hautes fonctions politiques pour des raisons que nous allons tenter d'explorer plus tard, le monopole masculin de l'autorité politique est une donne constante de la vie étatique. Prenons le cas du Cameroun ; ce pays compte aujourd'hui 59 hommes ministres, secrétaires d'État et assimilés contre six femmes, 165 députés contre 15, 330 hommes maires contre six pour les femmes ; 136 hommes leaders de partis contre deux femmes, cinq recteurs hommes contre un pour les femmes; 14 vice-recteurs contre un pour les femmes; seules six femmes sont secrétaires générales de ministère, une, secrétaire général d'université, une autre, ambassadeur, une, colonel et trois, commissaires divisionnaires. Dans le commandement territorial, jusqu'en 2004, aucune femme n'y avait jamais accédé aux fonctions d'autorités administratives (entendues, gouverneurs de province, préfets de départements, sous-préfets d'arrondissements, chefs de districts ou leurs adjoints). Ce qui faisait un total de 773 autorités administratives, toutes des hommes, soit 10 gouverneurs, 58 préfets, 116 adjoints préfectoraux, 268 sous-préfets, 268 adjoints d'arrondissements et 53 chefs de districts. C'est ce que Rachel-Claire Okani qualifie de « domaine d'exclusion », une « exclusion absolue »[3]. Aujourd'hui, trois femmes sont sous-préfetes, après s'être imprégnées de la tâche pendant deux ans, en occupant les fonctions secondaires d'adjointes préfectorales entre 2004-2006.

Quelles que soient les raisons que l'on puisse invoquer, ces chiffres révèlent le monopole masculin de l'exercice du pouvoir. L'on observe comme une phallocratie qui a pour corollaire, l'exclusion des femmes des cercles réels de l'État. Comme résultat, tous les programmes des formations politiques en Afrique annoncent à l'envi une promotion de la femme dans les instances politiques supérieures : la répétition monotone de la formule, litanie permanente à l'adresse de l'électorat féminin qui est majoritaire, suffirait à établir, sans même l'éloquente précision des chiffres, l'avantage du sexe masculin quand il s'agit d'entrer dans le groupe des décideurs. Mais il est surprenant d'apprendre que tant de hérauts de l'égalité des hommes et des femmes n'ont pas réussi, lorsqu'ils ont eux-mêmes accédé au pouvoir, à modifier la situation là où l'on peut penser qu'il leur était relativement aisé de le faire, c'est-à-dire là où l'accès aux fonctions de décision résulte d'une nomination. Autant que pour les fonctions électives, la « misogynie » du corps social s'exprime pour celles qui donnent lieu à nomination. Cette domination masculine n'est pas le seul fait du corps électoral. Elle vient souvent des instances dirigeantes des partis qui invoquent le risque de voir l'électorat se détourner d'un candidat féminin pour écarter les femmes des circonscriptions peu sûres ou susceptibles d'être conquises ou des places intéressantes sur les listes. Elle résulte aussi du conservatisme du corps électoral (voir Alliot-Marie 1983 : 82-83). Dès lors, l'on peut à la suite de Slavenka Drakulic et Julia Slazai, deux activistes de l'Europe de l'Est parler de « démocratisation masculine » et de « démocratisation à visage masculin ». Raison pour laquelle certains spécialistes des sciences sociales d'orientation féministe qualifient l'État de patriarcal et emploient l'expression « patriarcat public ou patriarcat social » pour désigner les États contemporains. Suivant le paradigme patriarcal, la dépendance des femmes à l'égard des hommes s'est muée en dépendance envers l'État ; ce qui semble créditer les arguments du féminisme radical qui a une vision a-temporelle de la domination masculine fondée sur le réductionnisme biologique.

Pour les tenants du biologisme, toutes les sociétés établissent une distinction entre les tâches habituellement attribuées aux hommes et celles dévolues aux femmes. La division sexuelle du travail est universelle : certains pouvoirs spécifiques sont presque partout attribués aux hommes, d'autres aux femmes. Les hommes sont toujours les guerriers ; ils sont responsables de la protection physique du groupe contre les menaces externes et internes ; ils exercent un contrôle sur toutes les ressources importantes, y compris les femmes ; les activités les plus valorisées et les mieux rétribuées sont remplies par les hommes. En contraste, les tâches féminines sont les mêmes dans le monde entier et ne sont pas aussi diversifiées que les tâches masculines : les femmes sont le plus souvent limitées aux tâches domestiques de la cuisine quotidienne, des soins et de l'éducation des bébés et des jeunes enfants, elles sont exclues de certaines activités ; jamais, elles ne chassent le gros gibier (Friedl 1978 : 24-25 ; Mazrui 1977 : 69-81 ; Randall 1982 : 12-16). Pour expliquer cette division « universelle » du travail, les tenants du biologisme ont recours au dimorphisme sexuel caractéristique de l'Homo Sapiens. Les différences physiques le plus souvent citées sont que les hommes sont plus grands et plus forts que les femmes ; que l'anatomie adaptée à la grossesse empêche les femmes de courir aussi vite que les hommes ; que les hormones mâles incitent au comportement agressif, à la violence. Le rythme hormonal menstruel entraîne des variations dans l'acuité de la perception, dans la coordination musculaire et dans la capacité de concentration intellectuelle. En outre, la grossesse, la naissance et l'allaitement, joints à la longue période d'incapacité des nourrissons et d'immaturité des jeunes humains expliquent que les femmes soient absorbées par les enfants et qu'elles prennent moins de part aux affaires publiques, notamment la guerre et la politique. D'où on en conclut aisément que les femmes sont automatiquement et nécessairement exclues du pouvoir social public (Friedl 1978 : 25 ; Bourdieu 1998 : 22-23).

À côté de cet argument biologiste, les culturalistes qui s'appellent aujourd'hui « constructivistes » aux États-Unis, soutiennent que la masculinité serait plutôt une construction idéologique. En effet, le devenir masculin met en jeu des facteurs psychologiques, sociaux et culturels qui n'ont rien à voir avec la génétique mais jouent un rôle non moins déterminant, sinon plus. Mieux, les caractéristiques physiques et émotives des hommes et des femmes autorisent une grande liberté dans la définition des tâches et des relations. Et cette liberté doit être utilisée au maximum pour éliminer toute différence entre les rôles masculins et féminins. De ce second point de vue, les sociétés contemporaines et ici africaines n'ont pas suffisamment divergé de ce qui est à tort considéré comme les rôles « naturels » et c'est pourquoi la domination masculine demeure constante. Quand l'on transpose ces traits physiques de caractère dans l'art de gouverner les sociétés africaines effectivement, il se dégage deux dimensions : une dimension quantitative qui renvoie à l'inflation du personnel masculin dans les hautes fonctions étatiques ; une autre, qualitative faisant référence à la nature du pouvoir : le leader charismatique, la guerre, la mystique du chef, la personnalisation du pouvoir, sa concentration, l'autoritarisme étatique, la violence, la répression, la fermeté, la militarisation, etc. Dans cette perspective, les références aux notions de « héros de l'indépendance », de « grand camarade », du « père de la nation », etc. qui accompagnent ou ont accompagné l'exercice du pouvoir en Afrique ne sont en réalité que des manifestations de cette masculinité du champ politique.

De la genèse du patriarcat public au sein de l'État moderne africain : la dichotomie sphère publique / sphère privée dans la formation de l'État européen

L'État moderne africain étant un avatar de la colonisation est informé par l'idéologie qui a accompagné la formation de l'État européen au XVIe siècle. Du point de vue de l'analyse de genre, quels sont les ressorts de cette idéologie ? Sue Ellen M. Charlton (1989 : 20-43) nous offre des développements intéressants sur le diptyque, formation de l'État européen et masculinité du champ politique. Pour cet auteur, le développement de l'État moderne en Europe est lié de façon inextricable à la distinction de la sphère publique de la sphère privée. Cette dichotomie n'est pas demeurée statique; elle a subi de nombreuses mutations en même temps que se transformaient les sociétés européennes. Ce qui est resté par contre constant, c'est l'absence de la femme de la sphère publique, de la délibération, de la politique, confinée qu'elle est dans la sphère privée d'où relève la famille. Cette exclusion résulte de deux dynamiques donc l'une interne et l'autre externe ; celles-ci vont amener les États européens à bâtir leurs appareils administratifs sous un moule coercitif. D'une part, il s'agissait pour les royautés européennes d'asseoir leur légitimité intérieure en mettant à leur profit le monopole de la violence légitime, en réprimant les révoltes des forces centrifuges; de l'autre, il était question de se défendre dans un contexte de guerre endémique et de rivalités entre États.

Le XVIe siècle et la naissance de l'État en Europe : guerres, contradictions sociales et nécessité d'un pouvoir fort et coercitif

Le fait marquant du XVIe siècle en Europe, c'est la naissance de l'État et l'apparition de l'idée de l'absolutisme royal. Le roi incarne l'idéal national et possède en droit comme en fait tous les attributs traditionnels de la souveraineté. Cette idée de monarchie absolue vient s'ajouter aux anciennes idées de contrat et de coutume qui réglaient autrefois les relations des rois avec leurs sujets et leurs vassaux.

Mais ces idées subsistent. La doctrine de l'absolutisme naît du besoin de la société elle-même. Il semble à tous nécessaire d'avoir un pouvoir puissant pour des raisons multiples : tout d'abord, c'est l'époque de constitution des nations qui entrent en guerre les unes avec les autres : la guerre impose le renforcement de l'autorité et un pouvoir capable de décisions rapides. Puis il y a le problème de guerres intérieures, de religion, de conflits des grandes familles seigneuriales et des clans qui réveillent les sentiments du Moyen-âge et mettent en jeu l'unité des royaumes. Il y a enfin, le conflit entre la bourgeoisie riche et la noblesse. La situation internationale et nationale renforce donc le pouvoir du roi. D'autre part, le développement des théories de l'État absolu et de la monarchie de droit divin n'est pas si contradictoire qu'il peut paraître avec les doctrines dominantes de l'humanisme et de la renaissance. En réalité, l'homme devenu mesure de toute chose tend à s'incarner dans le type achevé, exemplaire de l'homme, le héros, c'est-à-dire le surhomme. Et c'est très exactement cela que le roi va représenter (Ellul 1969 : 28-29). Des auteurs tels que Machiavel et Jean Bodin viendront à grand renfort de théories pour contribuer à l'édification de cet État guerrier et belliciste, renforçant ce faisant la dichotomie sphère publique/sphère privée. Cet impératif militaire va exclure la femme et la connivence sera vite établie entre la guerre et le développement des institutions étatiques aussi bien militaires que civiles. La politique qui va se confondre alors avec l'usage de la force va devenir le domaine exclusif de l'État et celui-ci va se muer en une institution mâle. Ni le capitalisme et, *a fortiori,* le libéralisme ne modifieront plus tard ce biais sexiste.

Capitalisme, libéralisme, principe démocratique, « dangerosité » et « faiblesse » des femmes et protection de la masculinité du champ politique

Vers le XVIIIe siècle en Europe, la femme était depuis longtemps déjà exclue de la sphère de la délibération, de la citoyenneté (en tant que sans-propriétés) mais aussi de nouvelles institutions créées par les monarques pour protéger leur souveraineté extérieure et assurer leur unité nationale. L'avènement du capitalisme et du libéralisme va apporter un bémol à ce discours politique de l'époque et ouvrir une brèche pour l'émergence des premiers mouvements féministes occidentaux sans cependant créer des conditions favorables pour la libération des femmes des institutions mâles. Le capitalisme, puis le libéralisme vont d'ailleurs se révéler plus tard comme hostiles à l'émancipation de celles-ci. En effet, l'État libéral qui émerge en Europe au XIXe siècle est un État bourgeois, non pas seulement en raison de l'existence de la propriété privée des moyens de production, mais surtout du fait de l'unique circonstance qui fera de la bourgeoisie (par opposition à l'aristocratie), la nouvelle classe dominante dont les intérêts coïncideront avec ceux de l'État dans un contexte de représentation politique. Mais comme dans l'État capitaliste, le mâle est propriétaire, c'est la domination patriarcale qui sera restaurée, matérialisant ainsi l'un des paradoxes de l'État libéral des XIXe et XXe siècles. C'est pourquoi les femmes vont arriver dans le monde capitaliste en parents pauvres cela, aussi bien dans le monde du travail où elles seront reléguées au bas de l'échelle (leur travail en dehors du ménage étant d'ailleurs considéré comme une aberration) que dans celui de la politique. Ni les partis politiques, ni les syndicats ne répondront avec vigueur aux problèmes de genre (Charlton 1989 : 20-43).

Il faut d'ailleurs préciser pour la France que la révolution française avait plutôt mis un terme à l'évolution de la condition féminine. En effet, le sexe fut aussi un champ de bataille majeur de cette révolution : « un affrontement entre masculin et féminin dans lequel la création révolutionnaire de la culture politique par la bourgeoisie devait valider la culture politique des hommes et culpabiliser celle des femmes ». Si brouillées que pussent être les frontières de classes, « celles entre hommes et femmes devaient à tout prix être rendues visibles ». Les promesses de la Révolution française (qu'il était possible de régénérer l'humanité dans toutes ses relations sociales et culturelles, que les femmes avaient droit non seulement aux libertés civiques mais aussi aux libertés personnelles, qu'il était possible de rénover de fond en comble la famille, la morale et les rapports entre personnes) donnèrent naissance à un authentique nouveau féminisme, mais aussi à un antiféminisme d'un nouveau genre, à une nouvelle peur des femmes et à des frontières politiques qui engendrèrent des barrières sexuelles correspondantes (Laqueur 1990 : 222).

Aussi, lorsque les femmes demandent publiquement leurs droits de citoyennes, la Convention d'une seule voix les leur refuse-t-elle. Les députés qui n'ont guère connu les douceurs de l 'Ancien Régime, réaffirment avec force la séparation des sexes et le différentialisme radical. Proximité, similitude et confrontation leur font horreur et suscitent des réactions autoritaires, voire menaçantes. Hors du foyer, les femmes sont dangereuses pour l'ordre public. On les appelle à ne pas se mélanger aux hommes et on leur interdit la moindre fonction extra-ménagère ou extra-maternelle. « Renforcé par le Code Napoléon et entériné par l'idéologie du XIXe siècle, le dualisme perdurera pendant cent ans, jusqu'à l'apparition d'une nouvelle crise de la masculinité plus étendue et plus profonde que la précédente » opine Elisabeth Badinter (1992 : 29). Autrement dit, la création d'une sphère publique bourgeoise souleva avec d'autant plus d'acuité la question du (ou des) sexe (s) légitimement habilités à l'occuper. Et partout, la biologie s'immisça dans le discours. De toute évidence, les adversaires d'un pouvoir civil et privé accru pour les femmes (c'est-à-dire l'immense majorité des hommes qui se faisaient entendre) ne manquèrent pas de produire des preuves de l'inaptitude physique et mentale des femmes à de tels progrès : leur corps les rendait impropres à occuper les espaces chimériques qu'avait ouvert par inadvertance la Révolution (Laqueur 1990 : 222). Dès qu'apparaît l'idée démocratique, se pose en effet la question de savoir qui appartient au peuple souverain. Égalité et exclusion (des non-nationaux, des pauvres, des « incapables », de tout port et, bien entendu, des femmes) vont devoir être pensées, nous dit Sonia Dayan-Herzbrun. On pourrait s'étonner alors que des femmes aient pu accéder à des positions de pouvoir dans ce type de sociétés, tandis que l'ensemble des femmes se trouvait exclu de l'espace public et du champ politique. La cause, c'est que dans les sociétés strictement hiérarchisées, où l'accès à l'espace politique est réservé à un groupe très restreint se limitant parfois à quelques familles, mieux vaut encore confier le pouvoir à une femme que de le laisser sortir du clan. Au demeurant, il semble bien que l'enseignement des « technologies et de la politique » se transmette à l'intérieur du cercle familial (Dayan-Herzbrun 1992 : 292 et ss).

Les femmes politiques, héritières et reproductrices de la pratique politique au masculin

C'est un mode de légitimation par les liens de sang ou du lit[4] (conjugal ou adultère) qui a permis l'accès au pouvoir de quelques femmes. Il semble bien qu'aujourd'hui encore, contrairement à ce qui se passe pour les hommes, ces règles de la tradition s'appliquent toujours pour elles. Benazir Bhutto est la fille d'un Chef d'État comme l'ont été Indira Ghandi et bien avant dans l'histoire, Elisabeth I ou Marie Tudor, ou encore la princesse Fatimide Sitt-al-Mulk dont le nom signifie « la dame du pouvoir » qui, fille de Khalife, dirigea l'Empire, mais il est vrai au nom de son neveu de 1020 à 1024. Dans une étude réalisée en 1988, Mariette Sineau note que 55,3% des femmes politiques qu'elle avait interviewées en France bénéficiaient de ce qu'elle appelle une « hérédité » politique, tenant pour la plupart à un lien de filiation. Le mariage, même (ou surtout) rompu par le décès de l'époux, donne lui aussi accès à la politique. Aux régentes du passé ont succédé les veuves : après la mort accidentelle de son mari, Marie France Stirbois avait été élue en France au poste de député qu'il occupait, et ce sont deux veuves aussi qui ont dirigé le Nicaragua (Violeta Chamorro) et les Philippines (Cory Aquino). Pendant la très longue période d'emprisonnement de son mari, Winnie Mandela a joué un rôle de pseudo-veuve qui lui a conféré une légitimité politique se trouvant ravalée au rôle de compagne sitôt Nelson Mandela libéré. Si l'on étudiait de très près la biographie de toutes ces femmes, on constaterait qu'elles sont prises dans des réseaux serrés de filiation et d'alliance avec des hommes de pouvoir. Leur situation exceptionnelle dans le champ politique ne modifie en rien la condition de l'ensemble des femmes des pays auxquels elles appartiennent ; c'est parfois même le contraire qui se produit : on sait par exemple que Benazir Butto avait été contrainte d'accepter la stricte application de la loi islamique, la charia au Pakistan (Dayan-Herzbrun 1992 : 291; voir Curell 1974 : 164 et ss.) Plus près de nous en Afrique, Philomena Okeke (1998 :16-19) dénonce cela au Nigeria, en termes de « syndrome de la « première dame » ou « la corruption administrative au féminin ». Amina Mama (1995 : 37-58) de son côté, qualifie cette pratique nigériane de « fémocratie » (femocracy). La politique reste alors une affaire d'hommes. Le destin exceptionnel de quelques unes d'entre elles n'enlève pas la règle de l'exclusion de l'ensemble des femmes. Il permet seulement d'établir que l'exercice des fonctions politiques par les femmes n'est pas de l'ordre de l'absolument impossible.

La colonisation européenne comme facteur historique de la masculinité du champ politique au sein de l'État moderne africain

Comment la colonisation a-t-elle transposé en Afrique la dichotomie de la sphère publique et de la sphère privée qui a marqué le processus de formation de l'État européen? Quelles sont les conséquences de la colonisation sur le problème de genre en Afrique ? Dans quelle mesure l'Afrique coloniale était-elle ou non égalitaire ? Il serait excessif de tomber dans une généralisation à la limite abusive pour trouver l'origine de la masculinité du champ politique en Afrique contemporaine dans la colonisation. En effet, la relation entre le pouvoir d'État, le colonialisme et l'idéologie de genre est tellement complexe qu'une telle assertion mérite quelques réserves. La condition féminine dans l'Afrique précoloniale fut une réalité complexe et mouvante non exempte de contradictions où les femmes furent parfois appelées à jouer plusieurs rôles (voir Barbier 1993 ; Ba Konaré 1991). Des chercheurs ont montré que les femmes ont participé activement à la politique précoloniale, tant directement comme dirigeantes et au sein d'espaces perçus comme le domaine des femmes, qu'indirectement comme mères, épouses, sœurs, filles et compagnes d'hommes puissants. Les femmes se sont engagées dans la vie militaire, aussi bien en accompagnant individuellement les troupes d'hommes qu'en constituant de groupes de combattantes effectives (Zeleza 2000 : 116). La colonisation n'a toutefois pas gommé les systèmes d'inégalité et de domination antérieurs en Afrique qui poursuivent leur devenir historique et se trouvent transposés au sein des appareils politiques et économiques des États (Bayart 1985). Par contre, en apportant la distinction entre la sphère publique et la sphère privée, elle a permis aux administrateurs coloniaux, aux missionnaires et aux chefs indigènes d'imposer davantage le contrôle masculin de la sexualité et du travail féminins (Staudt 1989 : 68-85).

Ceci ne signifie pas que les sociétés africaines précoloniales étaient égalitaires, mais, que le pouvoir colonial étouffa dans l'œuf les quelques perspectives qui furent ouvertes aux femmes dans certaines contrées pour échapper à la domination masculine; son souci ayant été de créer un espace public géré par des hommes. Mieux, les idéologies patriarcales coloniales, associées aux idéologies patriarcales autochtones, ont eu tendance à renforcer la subordination, l'exploitation et l'oppression des femmes. Prenons le cas du Mali dont parle Adame Ba Konaré. Cet auteur observe que la femme a joué un rôle politique important dans l'histoire (précoloniale) du Mali, mais qu'avec l'émergence d'États de type guerrier dont le modèle le plus perfectionné fut élaboré au début du XVIIIe siècle par les Bamanan de Ségou, la société malienne tombe dans la misogynie. Une nouvelle idéologie se crée, qui consacre la subordination de la femme à l'homme. A posteriori, l'on corrige le rôle joué par la femme dans le passé pour l'adapter à la nouvelle situation. Même les femmes qui ont tenu une place importante ne l'auront tenue que par rapport aux hommes (époux ou enfants). Ainsi par exemple, Sogolon serait née pour mettre Soundjata au monde et disparaître. Sounou, la mère de Biton, aurait favorisé l'ascension de son fils par son appui matériel. Cet efface-ment de la femme de l'arène politique ou plutôt cette déresponsabilisation de la femme, dont le corollaire sera son infantilisation, deviendra la donnée perma-nente du destin politique de la femme malienne. Aussi bien les hommes que les femmes s'y mettront à grand renfort d'idéologie mais aussi d'actions concrètes pour consolider cette position aliénante de la femme. Cette dernière ne saurait être que soutien de l'homme ; elle ne peut qu'agir au nom de l'homme (Ba Konaré 1991 : 1-2). L'on note un développement parallèle à Madagascar à en croire Mireille Rabenoro :

> It seems that the loss of women's high position in society began long before the colonial invasion by French troops, which resulted in Madagascar becoming a French colony in 1896. It began when local chiefs started organizing their chieftaincies into a State, in the late 18th century, and was gradually aggravated under Western influence, first through the Christian missionaries throughout the 19th century, then through the policies , attitudes and practices of the western-educated elite, after Independence in 1960 till nowadays (Rabenoro 2005 : 6).

Ceci dit, deux traits ont marqué la colonisation européenne en Afrique du point de vue de la relation genre/politique : un pouvoir empreint de violence ambiante et une administration quasiment masculine.

Du pouvoir colonial comme violence : de l'impératif de pacification et d'ordre

Analysant le développement de l'État moderne européen, nous avons vu que la conjonction des facteurs internes et exogènes au XVIe siècle va confondre la po-litique avec l'usage de la force pour devenir le domaine exclusif de l'État ; qu'à son tour celui-ci va se muer en une institution mâle. De la même manière, le génie masculiniste des colonisateurs est reflété dans la littérature populaire de l'époque. Dans le roman colonial, l'Afrique est décrite de façon métaphorique comme un corps féminin, que l'homme blanc cherche à dévoiler, à pénétrer et à piller (Amina 2000 : 79). Et du point de vue de l'analyse de genre, la théorie de la dépendance est le courant qui rend le mieux compte de cette masculinité (voir Tsikata 1991), parce que la colonisation est par essence conquête et domination. Cette domina-tion n'est pas seulement spirituelle ou culturelle, elle réside également dans la force militaire. Condition indispensable au succès de la conquête, cette force militaire fut également nécessaire pour déployer l'autorité de la nation colonisatrice sur le territoire conquis ; car, s'il n'y eut pas d'hostilité de principe des Noirs au début de la présence européenne sur les côtes africaines, elle « se manifesta dans l'arrière-pays quand les Blancs se muèrent en conquérants et quand à une fructueuse collaboration se substitua une domination brutale ». Un peu partout en Afrique occidentale notamment, l'entreprise coloniale, ici française, se heurta à des révoltes ou à des résistances : dans un premier temps, entre 1880 et 1900, elles correspondaient aux premières réactions africaines à la conquête coloniale ; elles s'inscrivaient dans le sillage des grands courants de résistance de la fin du XIXe siècle menés par des chefs militaires prestigieux tels El Hadj Omar, Samory, Ahmadou ou Mamadou Lamine. Dans un deuxième temps, au cours de la décennie précédant la Première Guerre mondiale (la période d'affermissement du pouvoir colonial), les révoltes se localisèrent au niveau des villages, mais dans certains cas, elles furent un facteur d'union des chefs à l'échelle d'une région tout entière. Dans la plupart des territoires conquis, la résistance armée précéda ou suivit la « résistance passive » qui se traduisit notamment par le refus de payer l'impôt ou le refus du chef de se rendre aux convocations des autorités. On ne peut donc pas dire que la soumission au pouvoir colonial fut partout immédiate et naturelle ; nulle part d'ailleurs, elle ne fut inconditionnelle. Mais la réponse aux révoltes indigènes ne se fit jamais attendre. Les opérations punitives dont la brutalité répondait au souci de l'exemplarité du châtiment brisèrent partout la résistance des populations indigènes. Il y eut alors « une série d'épuration éliminant les chefs récalcitrants » (voir Kamto 1987 : 265-266).

En outre, une fois que les territoires furent conquis, L'État colonisateur voulait y étendre sa souveraineté ; et là, il n'entendait pas que son autorité soit contestée ; c'est pourquoi il mit tout en œuvre, au besoin la force répressive, pour la préserver. Ensuite, le pouvoir colonial entend protéger les ressortissants de la métropole résidant en colonie, ainsi que leurs biens. Toute atteinte aux intérêts de la nation colonisatrice ou à ceux de ses ressortissants appelle une réponse rapide et énergique de sa part. L'ordre colonial est ainsi marqué jusqu'à la Première guerre mondiale par la réaction brutale du pouvoir aux mouvements de révolte des populations africaines et, au moins jusqu'à l'année charnière de 1946, par les excès de certains administrateurs de colonies et les brimades des miliciens indigènes. Toutefois, comme l'a indiqué Georges Balandier, c'est surtout en matière de contrôle politique s'exerçant directement ou indirectement que l'Administration coloniale agit avec le plus de force et accepte le moins d'être contestée. La répression brutale des mouvements politico-religieux et plus tard des mouvements nationalistes qui se multiplient à partir des années 1920, en particulier au Congo, est significatif. Au Congo belge, Simon Kimbangu, le prophète du Kimbanguisme, est arrêté en 1921, condamné à mort et déporté à Élisabeth au Katanga où il mourut en 1951.

Une sphère publique, une armée et une administration coloniales masculines

Le colonialisme s'est essentiellement développé à partir d'une culture et d'un système patriarcaux qui assujettissaient les femmes. Prenons le cas du Ghana. Dans ce pays, la politique économique coloniale était principalement axée sur les exportations de produits agricoles et le commerce, mais aussi sur l'exploitation minière. Ces activités avaient leurs racines dans le commerce transsaharien qui avait prévalu durant la période précoloniale. De nouveaux emplois ont été créés dans les mines, l'administration coloniale et l'industrie de la construction. Les personnes qui avaient accès à l'éducation ont pu profiter des opportunités d'emploi dans la bureaucratie. Tenir les femmes à l'écart de la bureaucratie a été une politique coloniale explicite. Les quelques rares femmes qui avaient accès à l'éducation étaient formées dans les tâches ménagères, ce qui leur enlevait toute possibilité de postuler à un travail de bureau ou administratif. Dans le contexte du développement de l'économie monétaire, il devenait de plus en plus important pour les deux sexes de gagner de l'argent, mais les femmes africaines étaient presque totalement exclues du marché du travail colonial, qui absorbait les hommes comme main-d'œuvre forcée et migrante, et laissait les femmes s'en sortir toutes seules, dans des situations de plus en plus difficiles. Il est également manifeste que les hommes ont parfois cherché à affirmer ou même à accroître leur autorité traditionnelle sur les femmes par des voies qui ont fait que beaucoup de jeunes femmes ont cherché fortune ailleurs, certaines (exclues du travail salarié) se livrant à la prostitution et à d'autres activités informelles semi-illicites dans les centres urbains. C'est ce schéma des femmes marginalisées et des hommes absorbés dans le monde de travail que propose une analyse de genre de la participation des Africains à l'État colonial : c'étaient des hommes, et non des femmes, qui étaient recrutés comme soldats coloniaux, employés dans les structures administratives coloniales et nommés chefs auxiliaires dans les systèmes de gouvernement indirect. L'État colonial était presque exclusivement masculin et, dans son développement, il a remplacé les systèmes politiques autochtones, dont certains accordaient aux femmes une participation importante dans la vie politique et religieuse de leurs communautés. Dans bon nombre d'endroits, cet appareil administratif et bureaucratique colonial, exclusivement masculin, s'est débarrassé des systèmes précoloniaux qui, bien que différenciés selon le genre, comportaient des fonctions et des titres politiques d'importance et d'influence diverses pour les femmes comme pour les hommes (Okonjo 1976 ; Lebeuf 1963).

Cependant, durant la dernière phase du régime colonial, les colonisateurs ont commencé à se préoccuper d'incorporer les femmes à la société coloniale au Ghana, mais par la « domestication », laquelle était plutôt une initiative sociale visant à former des épouses « convenables » pour les Africains travaillant dans l'État colonial. Les idéologies de genre prônées par le régime colonial telles que la domestication ont également facilité l'exploitation des hommes, qui pouvaient accepter des bas salaires, en partie parce qu'ils continuaient d'être aidés financièrement par le travail des femmes au sein du foyer, dans les économies rurales et dans le secteur informel urbain. Là où les hommes étaient logés dans des dortoirs et des camps pour hommes, les femmes se chargeaient de la restauration des hommes et d'autres services nécessaires à leur survie quotidienne (Amina 2000 : 82).

Sur le plan militaire, nous avons établi tout au long de cette étude, un lien historique entre d'un côté la politique et la guerre et de l'autre, entre la virilité et la violence. La colonisation fut largement l'œuvre de l'« armée noire » sans laquelle il n'y eut jamais de conquête. Pourtant, constate avec raison Ali A. Mazrui dans une étude sur tradition guerrière et masculinité de la guerre, durant la colonisation, les puissances coloniales avaient raté une grande opportunité qui aurait modifié la masculinité du champ politique, en propulsant au devant des armées impériales la gent féminine africaine :

> In the African colonies a great experimental opportunity was missed this century. Why did not British and the French imperial governments create colonial armies made up of African women? The experiment could have been of immense value for the human race as a whole. Since the imperial powers were disrupting local cultures in other ways in any case, it might have made sense also to attempt a disruption in one of the most perennial and obstinate aspects of human culture- the masculinity of warriorhood (Mazrui 1977 : 69-81).

Pis encore soutient le même auteur, les Français aidèrent à démanteler au XIXe siècle l'une des rares classes de guerrières en Afrique, les Amazones du Dahomey (devenu le Bénin) non sans doter ce territoire d'institutions étrangères à l'histoire de ses peuples. C'était le même son de cloche avec d'autres puissances coloniales. Pourtant, si les puissances coloniales avaient enrôlé les femmes dans les forces armées, cette « ingénierie sociale » aurait eu des conséquences positives sur l'intégration politique de la femme africaine ainsi que nous le verrons plus devant dans les cas du Mozambique, du Rwanda, Ouganda, etc. Malgré ce prisme masculiniste cependant, l'histoire de la colonisation en Afrique ne saurait être conclue seulement sous forme d'un bilan avec un actif et un passif. C'est une histoire multidimensionnelle, mais aussi une somme de paradoxes qui font à la fois sa richesse et sa complexité. La colonisation en Afrique est épreuve de force, mais elle ne tient pas seulement en un cliché du Blanc écrasant le Noir, d'autant qu'elle s'est faite avec le concours des Noirs. De plus, elle s'est heurtée constamment à la résistance déterminée des Africains. La colonisation est domination et souvent même excès et abus, mais elle n'est pas que violence. Elle se traduit par une situation historique où se mêlent idéalisme humanitaire et démocratique, contrainte répressive et outrage psychologique nous dit Maurice Kamto (1987 : 253). Dans une perspective du genre, elle est perçue comme ayant eu un impact contradictoire et différencié sur les hommes et les femmes, tout comme sur les femmes elles-mêmes. Par ce jeu contradictoire, il y eut une certaine crise de la masculinité conséquemment à l'évolution de la condition féminine dans certains secteurs de la vie publique. De fait, les écrits les plus nuancés révèlent que le statut de la plupart des femmes a certes décliné durant l'époque coloniale, mais que les femmes ont également pris des initiatives qui ont remodelé leur vie et remis en cause l'ordre colonial. En outre, le rôle de la femme s'est redressé à la faveur de certaines mesures coloniales qui ont permis aux femmes intellectuelles d'inscrire leur lutte sous le signe de la libération des traditions ancestrales rétrogrades. Certaines d'entre elles créèrent même des associations à caractère apolitique pour défendre leurs droits de femmes travailleuses ou pour lutter contre les traditions (Ba Konaré 1991 : 6). Les femmes ont également participé activement aux luttes nationalistes. Soit elles ont organisé leurs propres groupes et combattu les politiques coloniales qu'elles considéraient comme contraire à leurs intérêts, soit elles se sont jointes aux mouvements nationalistes dirigés par des hommes[12].

De la masculinité du champ politique en Afrique postcoloniale

L'État africain postcolonial bat le record des épithètes s'agissant de sa nature : État « mou », État « fort », État « segmentaire », État « patrimonialisé », État « prédateur », etc. Cependant, on oublie souvent l'essentiel : c'est aussi un État mâle quantitativement comme la plupart des États contemporains, mais aussi qualitativement, de par sa nature autoritaire. C'est cette masculinité qui est d'ailleurs à l'origine de tous les autres épithètes que nous venons d'énumérer. Certes, vis-à-vis des puissances occidentales et de l'Est, les États africains demeurent des entités féminines, comme pendant la colonisation où l'Afrique est décrite de façon métaphorique comme un corps féminin, que l'homme blanc cherche à dévoiler, à pénétrer et à piller ; mais à l'intérieur de ses frontières et dans ses relations avec la société, il apparaît clairement que les indépendances africaines ne constituent pas une rupture et le projet post-colonial ne s'inscrit pas hors du contexte colonial. Parce que dans l'agenda nationaliste, c'est l'indépendance qui était inscrite et non la démocratie. De fait, en 2002, l'Afrique subsaharienne venait en avant dernière position, devant les pays arabes au niveau de la représentativité parlementaire avec 13,6% et 5% pour les pays arabes ; 12% des maires étaient femmes au Niger en 1999 ; 9% au Ghana en 2000 ; 11,7% au Burkina Faso en 2002 et 6% au Bénin, etc. bien qu'il y ait des avancées significatives au Mozambique, en Afrique du Sud, au Rwanda voire en Ouganda.

Participation féminine aux luttes nationalistes, indépendance et protection de la masculinité du champ politique africain

Les études menées sur la participation des femmes à la politique étatique démontrent qu'elles ont été exclues et mises en marge du processus politique, en dépit de leur engagement actif dans les luttes d'indépendance en Afrique (Parpart et Staudt

1989). Si nous prenons le mouvement Mau-Mau comme exemple, nous pouvons voir que, prises individuellement, les femmes ont gagné le respect et qu'on leur a accordé des positions de grande autorité, mais que seulement 5% des combattants basés dans les forêts étaient des femmes. Les femmes n'étaient pas autorisées à assister aux massacres, car elles étaient considérées officiellement comme incapables de garder le secret, bien que beaucoup d'entre elles étaient des partisans engagés et assermentés. Les femmes ont beaucoup fait pour la survie du mouvement, mais leur participation s'est limitée à un rôle d'intendance : elles constituaient essentiellement une « armée civile » chargée de nourrir les combattants, de faire un travail de renseignements souvent dangereux, et de transporter du matériel pour les combattants dans la forêt (Kanogo 1987). L'adhésion à l'assignation traditionnelle des rôles selon le genre a perduré après la fin du colonialisme direct. Une fois l'indépendance conclue, les parlementaires des années 1960 au Kenya, se sont opposés à l'introduction d'un code de la famille qui aurait corrigé les anciennes lois britanniques, en arguant le fait que battre sa femme était un droit « traditionnel » (Wamalwa 1989).

Au Nigeria également, la participation des femmes à la politique des partis avant l'indépendance est restée fortement circonscrite par les relations de genre en vigueur. À ce titre, cette participation a différé d'une région à l'autre. Alors que dans le Sud, les femmes étaient extrêmement actives dans les partis, aussi bien directement qu'à travers des puissantes organisations des femmes, dans le Nord, il leur était interdit de s'engager dans la politique conformément au point de vue selon lequel elles devaient rester confinées, bien que cette région était multi-ethnique et multi-confessionnelle et que bon nombre de groupes n'observaient pas cette pratique. Les femmes qui s'obstinaient à être actives dans la vie politique étaient dénoncées comme « prostituées », subissaient des harcèlements et des intimidations, et parfois des centaines d'entre elles languissaient dans les prisons du Nord. Ces femmes n'ont eu droit de vote qu'en 1976, et ce droit leur a été accordé par décret militaire et plutôt que par assentiment public. Néanmoins, durant les années 1950-1960, des femmes telles que Alhaja Fatima ont adhéré au National Council of Nigeria (NCNC), alors que Ladi Shehu et Gambo Sawaba dirigeaient la section féminine du Northern Elements Progressive Union (NEPU). Ce tableau contraste avec celui des régions du Sud et de l'Est, où les femmes étaient libres de jouer un rôle actif dans tous les partis, bon nombre d'entre elles ayant été candidates à des élections locales et ayant eu une grande influence, aussi bien en tant que représentantes des associations des femmes, qu'à titre personnel. Mba (1982) » fait une analyse détaillée de l'activité politique des femmes du Nigeria du Sud. Cet auteur conclut qu'en dépit du haut niveau de participation des femmes, et bien que la situation ait été différente d'un parti à l'autre, il n'a pas été accordé aux femmes, dans l'ensemble, des positions aux niveaux les plus élevés des instances de prise de décision dans n'importe lequel de ces partis. Il est donc peu surprenant de voir que l'on continue de traiter les femmes de l'Afrique postcoloniale de façon à se conformer à l'idéal de la domesticité féminine et donc à perpétuer le statut marginal et inférieur qui leur était réservé dans la culture coloniale (Mama 2000 : 86-87).

Prenons aussi le cas du Ghana dont parle Dzodzi Tsikata (2000 : 373-403) : l'agitation anticoloniale prit de l'ampleur dans ce pays après la Seconde Guerre mondiale et aboutit à l'indépendance en 1957. Les forces anticoloniales constituaient une large coalition de classes et des groupes divers dans la colonie qui partageaient l'opinion que leurs intérêts étaient mieux servis par l'indépendance. À la fin des années 1940, cette coalition était dominée par le Convention Peoples Party (CPP). À ses débuts, le CPP était une organisation politique de masse, sous le leadership de Kwame Nkrumah. La majeure partie de ses membres était des jeunes qui avaient quitté l'école et les secteurs de la société n'appartenant pas à l'élite. Le mouvement pour l'indépendance n'avait pas de programme sérieux pour aborder la discrimination de genre. Cependant, les femmes des marchés et d'autres femmes particulières travaillaient inlassablement au sein du parti qu'elles appuyaient et finançaient, car l'indépendance était censée bénéficier à la population en général. Comme la justice sociale était un des principes clés du nationalisme propre au régime de Nkrumah, cette action fut reconnue et récompensée après l'indépendance. Celle-ci s'est reflétée dans la politique gouvernementale, y compris dans les composantes de ses politiques anti-sexistes. Il y a eu des tentatives pour contrer la discrimination de genre, à travers des mesures de discrimination positive dans les sphères politiques et sociales. Dix sièges spéciaux ont été réservés aux femmes à l'Assemblée nationale. Des femmes commissaires et une femme vice-ministre ont également été nommées. D'autres ont servi dans des conseils d'administration d'entreprises, d'écoles et de mairies, en récompense de leur loyauté au parti. Quelques unes sont devenues membres du Comité central du CPP.

Seulement, la décision gouvernementale de regrouper toutes les organisations populaires sous l'égide du parti dirigeant a eu, également, des implications pour la politique de genre. Le Trade Union Congress, le Farmers' Council et l'organisation des jeunes sont devenus des sections du parti dirigeant. La National Council of Ghana Women (NCGW), formée par le CPP, à partir de diverses organisations indépendantes de femmes opérant au cours de cette période, devint également une section du CPP. Ainsi, les organisations de femmes furent non seulement cooptées, mais subirent également le désagrément de devoir s'unir par la force. Les différences politiques possibles entre diverses organisations furent écartées comme étant des « querelles mineures ». Cette mainmise du parti au pouvoir sur les sections du mouvement de masse en est venue à influer de façon significative sur les pratiques politiques de ces organisations. Il en a résulté une perte de crédibilité et une faiblesse politique, qui ont abouti à la disparition de la plupart de ces organisations, après le renversement de la Première République. Bien plus, pour les femmes, il y a eu d'autres problèmes : les commerçantes soutenant le parti continuaient d'apporter leurs contributions financières et, en retour, avaient le contrôle de l'attribution des étals des marchés ainsi que de la distribution des biens de consommation. La dénonciation de ce système de patronage promu par le CPP, après la chute de la Première République, a contribué à ancrer dans la politique de genre au Ghana, l'image de la commerçante puissante et corrompue. Ce qui est significatif, c'est que la perception du pouvoir des femmes du marché dans la politique du CPP était exagérée. Des femmes prises individuellement ont joué des rôles primordiaux dans le parti. Cependant, la participation organisée des femmes dans la politique de masse après l'indépendance s'est résumée à des chants de louanges et à des danses au cours des meetings. Avec la dégénérescence du mouvement populaire après la cooptation des organisations, on aurait « vu les membres du NCGW étendre des pagnes sur le sol, pour que les dignitaires du parti marchent dessus au cours des meetings et harceler les opposants du parti et de ses politiques ».

Au Mali, les femmes s'organisèrent à la veille de l'indépendance au sein d'associations à caractère syndical et apolitique, préoccupées qu'elles étaient par le progrès social. Au sein de ces associations, elles menèrent des actions importantes dans le domaine de l'éducation socio-sanitaire et éducative. Si ces associations n'étaient pas politiques, il n'en demeure pas moins qu'elles exprimaient une position politique, celle de l'affirmation de soi, en fonction de ses besoins et de ses préoccupations. Elles contenaient les ferments du combat pour le pluralisme d'opinions et la mobilisation autour d'objectifs corporatistes. Elles furent cependant toutes dissoutes par le régime de l'US-RDA, qui considérait que leur caractère apolitique les éloignait du parti, aucun problème ne pouvait être évoqué en Afrique sans le lier au contexte politique. Mieux, les membres les plus influentes de ces associations furent dispersées par mesure répressive. À leur place, fut créée en 1962 une organisation unique des femmes, appelée commission sociale des femmes du Mali, conçue, comme son nom l'indique, tout juste comme une commission et non comme une véritable union. Cette commission est affiliée au parti ; elle y est représentée par sa secrétaire générale Aoua Keita. Tous ses membres, au nombre de 18, sont proches du pouvoir. Les époux de six d'entre elles sont en effet ministres. Sa présidente reste l'épouse du chef de l'État. L'UNFM, qui prend la place de la commission sociale des femmes après le coup d'État militaire du 19 novembre 1968, va s'inscrire dans cette tradition de la subordination des femmes aux hommes du pouvoir. Son vice fondamental reste son inféodation au parti et surtout au couple Moussa/Mariam. L'UNFM n'a servi qu'à asseoir le pouvoir personnel de Moussa Traoré et de son épouse précise Adame Ba Konaré (1991).

Au Cameroun enfin, la situation de la femme est restée un secteur des affaires sociales, qui en 1972 était une direction du ministère de la Santé publique, devenu en 1975 un ministère avec pour mission « la mise en œuvre de la politique de prévention et d'assistance sociale de l'individu, de la famille et de la mère ». Le VIe plan quinquennal (1986 - 1991) élaboré sous le régime du Renouveau du Président Biya ne remédiera pas à cette exclusion de la femme de la sphère de la délibération :

> La femme a toujours été intégrée dans notre processus de développement. Le Ve plan a vu la création d'un ministère de la condition féminine qui est la matérialisation de la ferme volonté des pouvoirs publics de souligner et de mettre en œuvre le concept de la promotion féminine…. Le VIe plan entend promouvoir mieux que les plans précédents l'intégration des femmes dans tous les secteurs de la vie nationale. (…) Il s'agira de chercher à réunir toutes les conditions pour une meilleure participation des femmes au développement dans tous les secteurs de l'économie (L'essentiel sur le VIe plan quinquenal de développement économique, social et culturel, 1986-1991 : 78-79).

D'ailleurs, il a fallu attendre le congrès de Bafoussam, en novembre - décembre 1965 pour assister à la naissance de l'organisation des femmes de l'Union nationale camerounaise (OFUC) (parti dominant à l'époque qui devait devenir le parti unique ou unifié sous le sigle de l'UNC en 1966), à la faveur du sabordage du Conseil national des femmes qui regroupait, au plan national, les associations issues de l'époque du multipartisme. Lors de la fondation de l'UNC, l'OFUC fut transformée en OFUNC, sans modification notable sur le fond. Cet organisme qualifié d'« annexe » s'était vu prescrire le rôle fonctionnel de « social ». C'est ainsi que pour les dirigeants, les réunions de l'OFUC ne pouvaient « revêtir qu'un caractère exclusivement social et apolitique, le militantisme politique des membres de l'OFUC ne s'exerçant que dans le cadre des cellules, comités de base, sous-sections et sections de l'UC ». Cette délimitation stricte des activités (que conserveront les statuts de l'UNC après 1966) répondait très certainement au souci de conjurer la politisation de la gent féminine et ainsi protéger le patriarcat public.

Du pouvoir fort incarné par un homme jusqu'en 1990 : de l'impératif de l'unité nationale et de développement économique

Si l'on ne peut ignorer le poids des traditions dans l'attitude des populations africaines vis-à-vis du pouvoir et du droit nouveaux, on ne peut non plus comprendre la nature de ce pouvoir ainsi que les fondements du constitutionnalisme en Afrique sans s'en référer à la genèse de ces deux phénomènes. Or, L'État et le pouvoir africain nouveau naissent de la situation coloniale, on l'a vu. Le fait colonial en lui-même ainsi que les rapports que les autorités coloniales entretiennent avec les populations locales préparent celles-ci à une crainte révérencielle du pouvoir et de tout ce qui se rattache à l'administration. Autrement dit, la situation coloniale crée chez le colonisé, une prédisposition à la soumission résignée à l'autorité publique, en même temps qu'elle leur inspire une représentation sublimée du pouvoir dans lequel ils trouvent l'explication de leur propre impuissance. Quant à l'accession à l'indépendance des États d'Afrique, elle intervient à un moment où l'on note une tendance généralisée à la personnalisation du pouvoir même dans les vieilles démocraties occidentales. Dans le périmètre francophone par exemple, elle coïncide surtout avec le retour au pouvoir du général de Gaulle en France. Si l'envergure, la forte personnalité et le charisme personnel du chef de la « France libre » fascinent la plupart de ses compatriotes, ils ne laissent pas indifférents les nouveaux chefs d'État de l'ensemble francophone d'Afrique noire. La personnalisation juridique du pouvoir qui se dégage des premières constitutions de ces États en est la preuve. La brièveté et l'échec du cycle parlementaire confirment cette tendance nette au monisme politique et monocentrisme du pouvoir. Une étape décisive est franchie avec l'avènement du parti unique dont l'on a constaté la généralisation à partir des années 1965-66. De fait, l'apparition du monopartisme dans la plupart de ces États ouvre l'ère de la glorification du chef de l'État.

En fait, les dirigeants des États indépendants doivent affronter une situation politique, sociale et économique qu'ils soupçonnaient à peine sous la colonisation. Pendant la période coloniale, le multipartisme pouvait s'analyser comme la mobilisation des forces politiques différentes en vue de la conquête de l'indépendance. Les partis politiques, souvent très nombreux, étaient sans doute différents dans leur démarche, mais leurs actions visaient, en général à la même finalité : l'émancipation politique du territoire. Les antagonismes entre partis étaient par conséquent, provisoirement atténués, voire évacués, et l'agressivité commune dirigée contre le pouvoir colonial. Or, l'indépendance supprime ce facteur de polarisation commune. Le combat pour l'indépendance se mue en combat pour la conquête du pouvoir nouveau, un combat auquel les forces politiques ne sont pas toujours bien préparées. Par ailleurs, les dirigeants des nouveaux États ne sont pas forcément compétents et capables de gouverner dans une démocratie ouverte. Dans certains cas, au Congo-Kinshasa par exemple, l'intervention des puissances étrangères motivées par des contraintes idéologiques, va précipiter la fin de l'expérience parlementaire. Mais le plus souvent, ce sont les antagonismes ethniques, les ambitions personnelles et les rivalités des personnes qui sonnent le glas de la démocratie parlementaire en Afrique noire.

La pression des facteurs politiques et socio-économiques est tout aussi importante. Une fois l'indépendance acquise, il faut construire l'État et bâtir la nation, assurer l'éducation des populations et le développement économique du pays. La tâche est gigantesque. Mais, à la vérité, au-delà de ces arguments repris par tous les auteurs, l'échec de la brève expérience du parlementarisme multipartisan dans les États africains est lié à une certaine conception du pouvoir. C'est l'expression de la défiance du pouvoir de l'État nouveau à l'égard du constitutionnalisme parlementaire, et plus largement à l'égard du constitutionnalisme classique. De fait, il correspond à l'apparition dans les régimes politiques de ces États, d'un pouvoir incarné, fondé sur un homme, éventuellement porteur d'un charisme, répugnant en tout cas au contrôle qu'implique le régime parlementaire, méfiant du droit, et plus exactement des contraintes et des limites qu'il impose : à la séparation du pouvoir, l'on préfère sa concentration, à l'autorité institutionnalisée, l'autorité personnalisée. Tout ce qui est susceptible de menacer l'unicité du pouvoir s'oppose par conséquent à la conception du pouvoir qui se dégage de la pensée des dirigeants de ces États. Le Président Houphouët-Boigny exprime cette conception dans un proverbe fort répandu en Afrique noire : « il ne peut y avoir deux caïmans mâles dans le même marigot ». Le refus du contrôle intervient en corollaire au refus du partage du pouvoir. Il s'agit, d'une conséquence logique du présidentialisme tel qu'il est mis en application dans les États considérés. Dans la mesure où il organise et consacre l'omnipotence d'un seul organe, et à vrai dire d'un seul homme, le président de la République, cette forme de gouvernement a pour conséquence d'aliéner les pouvoirs des organes formellement habilités à tempérer ceux de l'Exécutif au moyen du contrôle (Kamto 1987).

Libéralisation politique des années 1990, évolution de la condition féminine et crise du patriarcat public en Afrique

L'on note avec Valentine Moghadam (1994 : 115-133) l'évolution rapide et profonde des rôles des femmes au XXe siècle sous l'effet conjugué de plusieurs facteurs dont le recours accru à la main-d'œuvre féminine dans les économies nationales, d'abord en URSS, puis après la seconde guerre mondiale dans toute l'Europe (à l'Est comme à l'Ouest), en Amérique du Nord et dans les pays en développement, les efforts déployés par les organismes internationaux, notamment par l'ONU et ses institutions spécialisées pour mieux faire connaître la part prise par les femmes dans le développement national et améliorer leur situation juridique, les activités menées par les mouvements et les chercheurs féministes dans de nombreux pays et les progrès remarquables réalisés par les femmes dans les pays nordiques, spécialement en Finlande, en Norvège et en Suède, pays où la part des femmes dans la main-d'œuvre et leur participation au fonctionnement des institutions politiques ne sont guère moins importantes que celles des hommes. En plus, durant la décennie des Nations Unies pour les femmes (1975-1985), des gouvernements situés dans différentes parties du monde ont établi des ministères de la condition féminine ou des bureaux des femmes afin d'institutionnaliser et de légitimer leur préoccupation pour le statut des femmes. Même si leurs réalisations ont connu des succès relatifs, le seul fait que de tels mécanismes aient été établis témoigne d'une reconnaissance de plus en plus grande des besoins et préoccupations des femmes. L'effet cumulatif et combiné de cette évolution a été un dépassement de la dichotomie du public/privé, une prise de conscience croissante de par le monde du rôle joué par la femme en tant que travailleuse et citoyenne, acteur économique et politique, agent du développement.

Aussi après près de trois décennies de régimes autoritaires et répressifs, l'amorce des années 1990 a-t-elle été marquée en Afrique par des bouleversements politiques, sociaux et économiques qui ont poussé les États africains aux portes de la démocratisation. Cette nouvelle conjoncture a provoqué, selon plusieurs observateurs, l'entrée sur la scène politique et économique africaine de nouveaux acteurs jadis exclus du jeu politique et mettant en cause la masculinité du champ politique : les jeunes et surtout les femmes qui réinventent, en marge de la scène politique ou au cœur des dispositifs partisans, des affiliations contraires au sectarisme des organisations ethnico-religieuses des élites politiques, afin de re-créer un tissu social solidaire face aux logiques de fragmentation. Les femmes tout comme les jeunes, du fait même de leur exclusion durant la période nationaliste, élaborent désormais des activités communautaires construites sur des dynamiques d'inclusion, de contrôle et de responsabilité qui jurent avec les idiomes et du nationalisme et des nouveaux discours sur la gouvernance et la démocratie (Diouf 1997 : 140). Cette mobilisation des femmes sera d'autant plus significative qu'elle se traduira par une augmentation de la représentation féminine dans les organes politiques officiels.

Au Cameroun par exemple, l'on assiste depuis l'avènement du régime Biya en 1982 à un accroissement du rôle de la femme dans la société camerounaise malgré l'hégémonie politique masculine. D'abord avec la création en 1984 d'un ministère de la condition féminine chargé de « promouvoir les mœurs destinées à faire respecter les droits de la femme camerounaise dans la société, à faire cesser toute discrimination à son égard et à accroître les garanties d'égalité dans le domaine politique, économique, social et culturel ». [6] De ministère de la condition féminine, ce ministère vient encore de franchir un autre cap après la présidentielle de 2004, en devenant un ministère en charge de la promotion de la femme et de la famille. Ensuite, l'impulsion donnée à la condition de la femme au IIe congrès ordinaire du parti au pouvoir, le RDPC, des 17,18 et 19 décembre 1996, où les organisations des femmes et les jeunes du parti (OFRDPC et OJRDPC) sont passées du statut d'organismes « annexes » à celui d'organismes « spécialisés », l'OFRDPC étant dorénavant « chargée d'assurer leur entière intégration dans tous les domaines de la vie nationale. À cet effet, elle conçoit et met en œuvre des programmes à caractère économique, social, culturel et politique ». Il n'est pas inutile de mentionner que ce congrès a fixé à 30% le quota de représentation des femmes dans les différentes institutions de l'État. Enfin, au cours des trois décennies, des progrès remarquables ont été réalisés au Cameroun en matière de scolarisation des femmes à tous les niveaux du système éducatif et, de manière plus spécifique, en ce qui concerne l'accès à l'enseignement supérieur où elles constituaient environ 36% de l'effectif total des étudiants des six universités d'État au cours de l'année académique 2000-2001. Pour ce qui est des grandes écoles, l'exemple particulier de l'ENAM (École nationale d'administration et de magistrature) mérite d'être retenu. Il s'agit d'une des filières permettant d'accéder aux grands corps de l'État et l'une des voies royales vers la nomination aux postes de responsabilité. Au cours de l'année 1999-2000, les femmes constituaient 26,02% de la filière Administration générale où se recrutent les autorités administratives.

Même au Nigeria où les femmes ont été longtemps dominées pour ne pas dire complètement inexistantes sur les scènes politiques du pays, elles se sont mises au début de la décennie 1990 non seulement à briguer d'importantes positions de pouvoir, mais à enregistrer d'indéniables succès qui attirèrent l'attention. Plus manifestement que jamais en 1990, nombre d'entre elles avaient pu obtenir tantôt par voie d'élection, tantôt par nomination de très hauts postes de responsabilité au sein des partis, à la tête des États fédérés, des gouvernements locaux, des commissions (Daloz 1991 : 126 - 131). Au Mali, pour la première en 1991, une femme, Madame Sy Kakiatou, a été nommée gouverneur (Ba Konaré 1991 : 22). Sous un autre angle, Ali A. Mazrui dans son étude sur tradition guerrière et masculinité de la guerre arrive à la conclusion selon laquelle la prééminence politique masculine serait intimement liée à la masculinité de la guerre, à l'inscription de la guerre au panthéon du métier du genre masculin. De manière symétrique, cet auteur plaide pour une militarisation de la gent féminine en vue d'enrayer le prisme phallocratique qui accompagne l'exercice du pouvoir dans notre continent (Mazrui 1977 : 80-81).

Effectivement, en raison de ce rôle de militantes actives ou de combattantes armées, les femmes occupent des positions politiques importantes et en quantité aujourd'hui au Mozambique, en Afrique du Sud, au Rwanda, au Burundi et même en Ouganda, pays qui ont connu des expériences de luttes armées, lesquelles ont pu porter au pouvoir les conjurés. Ainsi, au Mozambique, l'actuel premier ministre est une femme. Avant d'être promue chef de gouvernement, cette dame est restée ministre des finances pendant 10 ans. Dans ce même pays certaines langues parlent de plus en plus de gouvernement « féminisé » : les ministères respectifs du travail, des affaires étrangères, de la culture et affaires sociales, pour ne citer que ceux-ci sont dirigés par des femmes tandis qu'une autre est ministre adjoint de l'important porte-feuille de l'administration territoriale. Trois femmes y sont également ambassadeurs auprès des pays et organisations internationales puissants (France, Union européenne et Union africaine). Au Rwanda, presque la moitié du parlement est occupée par des femmes. En Afrique du Sud, des jalons importants ont également été posés en matière d'intégration politique de la gent féminine : une femme vient d'y être promue vice-présidente de la République, de nombreuses femmes y sont ministres ou gouverneurs de provinces. Mais malgré ces jalons décisifs, l'on se demande toujours si dans ces pays, ces femmes sont des véritables femmes de pouvoir, car, comme le relève si bien Ali A. Mazrui, il convient toujours de distinguer entre pouvoir politique par délégation, pouvoir politique par dérivation et exercice direct du pouvoir : dans les deux premières hypothèses, les femmes politiques ne sont en réalité que des héritières ou des reproductrices de la pratique politique au masculin (Mazrui 1977 : 78). Il faudrait d'autres études pour démêler un tel écheveau.

Conclusion

Aujourd'hui, l'accès des femmes au travail en dehors du foyer, à l'exercice des fonctions et responsabilités dans la sphère politique place les débats concernant les femmes dans l'ensemble des évolutions que traverse le monde à l'aube du XXIe siècle (Aguessy 1995 : 58). En effet, il reste bien peu de tâches, dans la société moderne, qui ne puissent être accomplies par des femmes ; plus est, les femmes n'acceptent plus d'être la propriété de l'homme patriarcal ; aussi l'homme n'est plus l'Homme. Anthony Clare en vient à la conclusion de « phallus agonisant ». Mais si le pouvoir mâle est ainsi renversé, il reste que tout autour de la planète, les hommes continuent à occuper à une majorité écrasante les positions de pouvoir. Ils continuent à lancer des regards noirs aux femmes qui ont l'audace de vouloir briguer un poste autre que subalterne. Ils continuent à se pavaner dans les salles de conseil. Dans le monde en voie de développement et plus particulièrement en Afrique, les inégalités sont encore plus flagrantes. C'est qu'en vérité le monde contemporain est en grande partie divisé entre deux sphères : la sphère privée, occupée en majorité par les femmes et la sphère publique dans laquelle l'homme trouve et cultive son identité et affirme sa dominance. La puissance du patriarcat, cet ensemble de relations de pouvoir qui permettent aux hommes d'exercer un contrôle entier sur les femmes, est fondée sur la conviction que la sphère publique a préséance sur la sphère privée. Les femmes qui luttent pour briser les chaînes du patriarcat doivent affronter l'acceptation tacite de la valeur supérieure de la sphère publique, de l'emploi, de la profession et du lieu de travail, et la dévaluation de la sphère privée. Les hommes ne ressentent qu'un besoin modéré de réévaluer la priorité qu'ils accordent à la sphère publique. Il est évident qu'ils interprètent le désir des femmes d'établir leur propre légitimité comme une preuve supplémentaire de la supériorité de la sphère publique sur la sphère privée. Cette dernière peut donc être, d'une façon tout à fait légitime, considérée comme inférieure (Clare 2000 : 19 ; voir Phillips 1991). Or, la femme joue un rôle important dans l'émergence d'une autre culture, d'autres valeurs. À partir de leur rôle social, elles ont développé un certain nombre de compétences particulièrement utiles dans une perspective de management participatif. Parce qu'elles ont appris à cultiver l'harmonie dans leur vie familiale, elles se montrent généralement plus soucieuses de vaincre les difficultés relationnelles pouvant exister au sein d'une équipe de travail. On leur reconnaît volontiers des qualités d'écoute, d'ouverture aux autres et de tolérance. Les femmes rechercheraient aussi l'établissement des relations de solidarité avec leurs collaborateurs. Plus enclines à la délégation des pouvoirs, l'un des outils du management participatif, cette option aura pour conséquence une amélioration de l'ambiance du travail et une convivialité de nature à réduire la dimension stressante de la vie professionnelle (Etoga Eyili 2003 : 292). À elles de civiliser notre mondialité contemporaine.

Comme le chemin se trace en marchant, il est donc indispensable de prendre des décisions et de les appliquer pour opérer les transformations attendues. Seule l'introduction de dispositions contraignantes et décisoires peut contrarier les lois générales de la masculinité du champ politique. En introduisant par exemple des règles implicites ou explicites comme le quota minimal de représentation féminine ou la préférence donnée en France par le parti communiste aux cadres d'origine ouvrière ou populaire lors des promotions internes (Gaxie 1980 : 6), les États africains peuvent enrayer le prisme de la masculinité en politique. Des exemples venus du Rwanda, de l'Ouganda et maintenant du Burundi abondent dans ce sens. D'ailleurs, la transition démocratique en cours aujourd'hui en Afrique exige des hommes politiques, même si c'est à contrecœur, qu'ils attribuent aux femmes quelques postes de responsabilité, ne serait-ce que pour manifester leur bonne volonté et mettre au moins symboliquement en accord leurs paroles et leurs actes. Au-delà, on peut penser que, là comme ailleurs, l'apparition sur les marchés politiques d'un vote féminin, plus autonome, plus incertain, travaillé par des valeurs féministes, sensible à l'évolution de la condition féminine, peut inciter certains concurrents à reprendre dans leurs programmes et leurs discours les demandes formulées par les associations féministes pour le capter. Mais si la démocratisation ouvre le champ des possibles, les effets qu'elle peut induire, à travers les opportunités qu'elle offre aux femmes d'entrer en politique, d'influencer plus fortement le pouvoir masculin et de faire avancer leurs revendications, dépendent de l'existence d'autres conditions qui leur permettent de les saisir, comme par la formation d'élites féminines capables de revendiquer légitimement des positions de pouvoir politiques, administratives, économiques et sociales ou de l'introduction dans la société de nouvelles représentations des rapports entre hommes et les femmes (Poirmeur 2000 : 324-325).

Notes

1. Comme son nom l'indique, le facteur génétique cherche la genèse des événements, c'est-à-dire les antécédents. La génétique pose les questions : quand ? Pourquoi ? Comment ? Il s'agit d'un processus se déroulant dans le temps, c'est-à-dire d'une explication diachronique. Comme l'histoire, la génétique répond à la question quand… mais ses réponses au pourquoi et au comment ont un autre sens. Elles impliquent une histoire, mais ce n'est pas l'histoire succession. La notion de temps distingue, ici encore, l'explication historique de l'explication génétique. Pour la génétique, le temps est secondaire. C'est le sous-produit d'une genèse qui a son propre rythme et cherche une causalité dans les faits

eux-mêmes. Il s'agit de trouver la cause initiale, le fait générateur (Grawitz 1981 : 439-440).

2. En effet, chez les Bamiléké, la *mafo*, la mère du chef, est la femme qui occupe le grade le plus élevé chez les femmes. Son titre confère de nombreux privilèges réservés aux grands : s'asseoir sur un tabouret au pied sculpté en forme de panthère, pratiquer la divination, avoir des sièges dans des sociétés secrètes de la chefferie, entrer au *ntipla* et danser la danse de *nzu* avec une peau de panthère au dos. Les plus importantes des *mafo* ont des serviteurs et président une association des femmes, appelée *muesu* (mère de la houe), dont les membres se réunissent chez elles une fois par semaine. Après leur mort, une de leur fille ou, à défaut un de leur fils hérite de leur titre et de leurs biens. La mère du chef jouit ainsi d'un statut masculin de chef de lignage qui met un terme définitif à son statut d'épouse (de Latour 1991 : 184). Elle est selon Georges Balandier, « …femme-homme afin que s'articulent par elle les rapports sociaux de ' signe-mâle' » et ceux de 'signe-femelle' » (Balandier 1974 : 47). Son décès donne droit à des cérémonies aussi grandioses que celles du chef. Elle possède son domaine propre et peut librement l'agrandir par héritage, don ou achat. Dans certaines chefferies, elle ne peut être demandée en mariage. C'est elle qui choisit son mari. Elle a droit à l'adultère sans reproche de la part de son mari. Par contre, le mari n'a pas droit à l'adultère, même s'il peut être polygame (Warnier 1993). La *nafoyn* est la mère du chef chez les Kom.

3. S'agissant des domaines d'exclusion dans l'administration camerounaise, cet auteur distingue l'exclusion relative de l'exclusion absolue. Dans le premier cas de figure, l'Etat procède par un léger saupoudrage caractérisé par une nomination exceptionnelle qui conserve au poste ou à la branche d'activité sa nature originelle de chasse-gardée masculine. Cette tactique est de mise dans la diplomatie camerounaise où, à peine, une femme est ambassadeur. Dans la deuxième hypothèse, c'est-à-dire ici le commandement territorial, aucune apparence ou manœuvre ne vient semer le doute et créer une ambiguïté inutile dans le temps ou dans l'espace quant au sexe du métier en question. Rachel-Claire Okani « Le 'deuxième sexe' dans l'administration camerounaise » in Amama 2003 : 278.

4. Marvick et Nixon qualifient cette filiation de sang ou de lit de « famille politisée » (*politicized family*). Ici, la tradition du pouvoir et du service public fait partie du quotidien et l'enfant est toujours porté à l'activisme politique, à l'acquisition des connaissances et des informations politiques. Les discussions politiques sont fréquentes et ce conditionnement est indispensable pour créer des activités politiques des deux sexes. Dwaine Marvick et Charles R. Nixon, « Recruitment Contrasts in Rival Compaign Groups » in Marvick 1961 : 193-217.

5. Le sujet qui, de loin, a suscité le plus d'intérêt est celui de la résistance des femmes à la domination coloniale : le soulèvement des femmes anlu au Cameroun, les soulèvements spontanés des femmes d'Afrique du Sud à la fin des années 1950, et leur participation aux luttes contre l'apartheid en général ainsi que sur des analyses générales sur l'engagement des femmes dans les luttes nationalistes dans différents pays. Il est à présent tout à fait manifeste que les femmes ont activement participé aux guerres de libération nationale, telles que celles menées par les « Mau-Mau » au Kenya, dans les colonies portugaises, en Namibie et en Erythrée (voir Zeleza, op cit, 2000 : 116).

6. La quatrième Conférence mondiale sur les femmes (Beijing 1995) est un autre pas important dans la recherche par les Nations-Unies, de l'égalité pour les femmes en l'an

2000. Dans la plate - forme d'action adressée à cette conférence, « l'inégalité entre l'homme et la femme dans l'exercice du pouvoir et dans les processus décissionnels » qui fut d'ailleurs dénoncée dans presque tous les panels et ateliers et par toutes les délégations, figure en première ligne (voir *World Alliance of YMCAS Delegation Report*). Cette conférence a amené certains Etats de l'Afrique de l'Ouest à adopter des réformes facilitant l'accès des femmes à la prise décisions. Il s'agit notamment du Sénégal, du Cap-Vert et du Niger.

Références

Aguessy, D., 1995, « Femmes et démocratie », *Démocraties africaines,* 1 : 58-60.

Alliot-Marie, M., 1983, *La décision politique. Attention ! Une République peut en cacher une autre,* Paris : Puf, 1ᵉ édition.

Amama, B. (dir.), 2003, *20 Propos sur l'administration camerounaise,* Yaoundé : MINFORPA.

Asso, B., 1976, *Le chef d'État africain,* Paris : Albatros.

Badie, B. et Hermet, G., 1990, *Politique comparée,* Paris : PUF.

Badinter, E., 1994, *XY. De l'identité masculine,* Paris : Odile Jacob.

Badinter, E., 2003, *Fausse route,* Paris : Odile Jacob.

Ba Konaré, A., 1991, « Rôle et image de la femme dans l'histoire politique du Mali (1960-1991). Perspectives pour une meilleure participation de la femme au processus démocratique », CODESRIA, Workshop on Gender Analysis in African social science, Dakar 16-21 septembre.

Balandier, G., 1974, *Anthro-pologiques,* Paris : PUF.

Balandier, G., 1955, *Sociologie actuelle de l'Afrique noire,* Paris : PUF.

Barbier, J.-C. (dir.), 1993, *Femmes du Cameroun. Mères pacifiques, femmes rebelles,* Paris : ORSTOM-Karthala.

Bayart, J.-F., 1989, *L'Etat en Afrique. La politique du ventre,* Paris : Fayard.

Bayart, J.-F., 1985, *L'État au Cameroun,* Paris : Presses de la Fondation nationale des sciences politiques.

Bernard, J., 1974, *Women and the Public Interest. An Essay on Policy and Protest,* Chicago: Aldine Publishing Company, fourth printing.

Bienen, H., 1974, *Kenya: The Politics of Participation and Control,* Princeton: Princeton University Press.

Boudoux, C. et Zaidman, C. (dir), 1992, *Egalité entre les sexes. Mixité et démocratie,* Paris : L'Harmattan.

Bourdieu, P., 1998, *La domination masculine,* Paris : éditions du Seuil.

Breckenridge, K., 1998, "The allure of Violence: Men, Race and Masculinity on the South African Goldmines, 1900-1950", *Journal of southern African studies,* vol 24, no 4: 669-693.

Breine, I., Connell, R. et Eide, I. (dir), 2004, *Rôles masculins, masculinités et perspectives d'une culture de paix,* Paris : Éditions UNESCO.

Charlton, S. E. M., Everett, 1989, " Female Walfare and Political Exclusion in Western European Sates "in Charlton, S. E. M., Everett, J. & Staudt, K.A., 1989, (editors), *Women, the State, and Development,* New York: State University of New York Press., Chapter 2, pp. 20-43.

Charlton, S. E. M., Everett, J. & Staudt, K.A., 1989, (editors), *Women, the State and Development,* New York: State University of New York Press.

Clare, A., 2000, *Où sont les hommes. La masculinité en crise*, Paris : Les Éditions de l'Homme.

Coulon, C. et Martin, D.-C. (dir), 1991, *Les Afriques politiques*, Paris : La Découverte.

Currell, M. E., 1974, *Political Woman*, Croom Helm, London: Rowman & Littefield New Jersey.

Daloz, J.-P, 1991, « L'émergence des femmes politiques au Nigéria », *Politique africaine* n°42 : 126-131.

Diaw, A. et Touré, A., 1998, *Femmes, éthique et politique*, Dakar : Fondation Friedrich Ebert.

Diouf, M., 1997, « Libéralisation politique ou transition démocratique, perspectives africaines », in Gemdev, *Les avatars de l'État en Afrique*, Paris : Karthala.

Duverger, M., 1955, *La participation des femmes à la vie politique*, Paris : UNESCO.

Ellul, J., 1969, *Histoire des institutions 4*, Paris : Puf, 3ᵉ édition.

Esoavelomandroso, M. et Feltz, G. (dir), 1995, *Démocratie et développement : Mirage ou espoir raisonnable?* Paris : Karthala.

Etoga Eyili, Suzanne-Béatrice, 2003 « Pour une implication accrue des femmes dans l'administration publique camerounaise » in Amama, B. (dir.), *20 Propos sur l'administration camerounaise*, Yaoundé : MINFORPA, p. 292. 2003 : 292.

Friedl, E., 1978, « La prééminence masculine est-elle inévitable? » in Mendras H., *Eléments de sociologie. Textes*, Paris : A Colin : 23-44.

Gaxie, D., 1978, *Le sens caché*, Paris : Seuil.

Gaxie, D., 1993, *La démocratie représentative*, Paris : Montchrestien.

Grawitz, M, 1981, *Méthode des sciences sociales*, Paris : Dalloz.

Habomugisha, P., 1998, "Political Empowerment of Women in the Contemporary Uganda: Implication of the National Resistance Movement (NRM) Government", paper presented at CODESRIA 9th General Assembly, Dakar, Dec. 14-18.

Haywood, C. et Ghaill, M., 2003, *Men and Masculinities*, Buckingham-Philadelphia: Open University Press.

Hodkin, Thomas, 1966 , « Les idées 'occidentales' sont-elles applicables aux États africains » in Pennock, J. R., 1966, *Les jeunes États se gouvernent*, Paris: Nouveaux Horizons, pp. 54-55.

Imam, A., Mama, A. & Sow, F. (dir), 2000, *Sexe, genre et société. Engendrer les sciences sociales africaines*, Dakar/Paris : CODESRIA-Karthala.

Jones, K. B. & Jónasdóttir A. G. (edited by), 1998, *The Political Interests of Gender. Developing Theory and Resarch with a Feminist Face*, London: Sage Publications.

Kirkpatrick, J.J., 1974, *Political Woman*, New York: Center for the American Woman and Politics, the Eagleton Institute of Politics, Rutzers University, Library of Congress Catalog.

Kamto, M., 1987, *Pouvoir et droit en Afrique noire. Essai sur les fondements du constitutionnalisme dans les Etats d'Afrique noire francophone*, Paris : LGDJ.

Kanogo, T., 1987, "Kikuyu Women and the politics of Protest: Mau Mau" in Macdonald S. et al (edited by), *Images of Change and War. Cross-Cultural and Historical Perspectives*, Madison: University of Wisconsin: 78-99.

Labrecque, M. F. (dir), 1994, *L'égalité devant soi. Sexes, rapports sociaux et développement international*, Ottawa, Dakar, Johannesburg : Centre de recherches pour le développement international.

Laqueur, L., 1990, *La fabrique du sexe. Essai sur le corps et le genre en Occident*, Paris : Gallimard.

Lebeuf, A., 1963, « The Role of Women in the Political Organisation f Africain Societies » in

Paulme, D. (edited by), *Women of Tropical Africa*, Berkeley and Los Angeles: University of California: 93-120.

Lombard, J., 1967, *Autorités traditionnelles et pouvoirs européens en Afrique noire*, Paris : A. Colin.

Mama, A. 1995, « Feminism or Femocracy ? State Feminism and Democratization in Nigeria », *Africa Development*, XX (1): 37-58.

Marvick, D. (ed.), 1961, *Political Decision-Makers: Recruitment of Performance*, Glencoe, III: Free Press.

Marvick , Det Charles R. Nixon, « Recruitment Contrasts in Rival Compaign Groups » in Marvick, D. (ed.), 1961, *Political Decision-Makers: Recruitment of Performance*, Glencoe, III: Free Press, pp. 193-217.

Mazrui, A. A. (ed), 1978, *The Warrior Tradition in Modern Africa*, The Hague and Leiden: E.J. Brill.

Mazrui, A. A. 1977, « The Warrior Tradition and masculinity of War », *Journal of Asian and African Studies*, vol 12, no 1-4 (Jan-Oct): 69-81.

Mba, N., 1982, *Nigerian Women Mobilised: Women's Political Activity in Southern Nigeria, 1900-1945*, Berkeley: Institute of International Studies, University of California.

Mbembe, M., 2000, *De la postcolonie. Essai sur l'imagination politique dans l'Afrique contemporaine*, Paris : Karthala.

Meena, R., 1992, *Incorporation of Gender Analysis in the Discipline of Political Science*, Dakar: treports /CODESRIA.

Ministère du plan et de l'aménagement du territoire, *L'essentiel sur le VIe plan quinquenal de développement économique, social et culturel, 1986-1991*, Yaoundé : Minpat, 1993.

Moghadam, V., 1994, « Les femmes dans la société » in *Revue internationale des sciences sociales*, Paris : UNESCO/erès, XLVI (1) : 115-139.

Mueller, C. M. (edited by), 1988, *The Politics of the Gender Gap. The Social Construction of Political Influence*, Newbury Park: Sage Publications.

Nchoji Nkwi, Paul, 1995, « Traditional female militancy in a modern context » in Barbier, J.-C. (dir.), 1993, *Femmes du Cameroun. Mères pacifiques, femmes rebelles,* Paris: ORSTOM-Karthala, p. 181.

Nlep, R.-G., 1986, *L'administration publique camerounaise : contribution à l'étude des systèmes africains d'administration publique*, Paris : LGDJ.

Nyamnjoh, F. N., 2005, "Entertaining Repression: Music and Politics in Postcolonial Cameroon", *African affairs*, 104 (415): 251-274.

Okeke, P., 1998, « Nigeria : Le syndrome de la « première dame » ou la corruption administrative au féminin », *Bulletin du CODESRIA*, 3/4 : 16-19.

Okonjo, K., "The Dual sex Political System in Operation: Igbo Women and Community Politics in Mid-Western Nigeria" in Hafkin, N. and Bay E. (edited by), *Women in Africa*, Stanford: Stanford University Press, 1976: 45-58.

Parpart, J. and Staudt K. A. (edited by), 1989, *Women and the State in Africa*, Boulder: Lynne Riener.

Pennock, J. R., 1966, *Les jeunes Etats se gouvernent*, Paris : Nouveaux Horizons.

Phillips, A., 1991, *Engendering Democracy*, Pennsylvania: Pennsylvania State University Press.

Pradelles de Latour, C.-H., 1991, *L'ethnopsychanalyse en pays bamiléké*, Paris : E.P.E.L.

Poirmeur, 2000, « Conclusion générale. Domination masculine et politiques de genre. Dérivé à partir de l'exemple camerounais » in Sindjoun, L., (dir), 2000, *La biographie sociale du sexe. Genre, société et politique au Cameroun,* Paris : Karthala et Codesria, pp. 324-325.

Rabenoro, M., 2005, "Madagascar: The Lost Status of Women", *News from the Nordic Africa Institute,* no 2, May: 6-8.

Randall, V., 1982, *Women in Politics,* London, The Macmillan Press.

Sineau, M., 2001, *Profession : femme politique. Sexe et pouvoir sous la Cinquième Rép*ublique, Paris : Presses de la Fondation nationale des sciences politiques.

Sindjoun, L., (dir), 2000, *La biographie sociale du sexe. Genre, société et politique au Cameroun,* Paris : Karthala et Codesria.

Staudt , Kathleen, 1989, « The State and Gender in Colonial Africa », in Charlton, S. E. M., Everett, J. & Staudt, K.A. (editors), *Women, the State, and Development,* New York: State University of New York Press, Chapter 4: 68-85.

Sydie, R. A., 1987, *Natural Women, Cultured Men. A Feminist Perspective on Sociological Theory,* New York: New York University Press.

Tsikata, Dzodzi, 2000, « Égalité entre les sexes et État au Ghana : quelques questions de politique et de pratique », in Imam, A., Mama, A. & Sow, F. (dir), *Sexe, genre et société. Engendrer les sciences sociales africaines,* Dakar/Paris : CODESRIA-Karthala, pp. 373-403.

Tsikata, E., 1991, « Conceptualising the Postcolonial State : The Experience of Gender Analysis », paper presented at the CODESRIA Workshop on Gender Analysis and African Social Sciences, Dakar, Sept , pp.16-21.

Yongue Fouatou, Rose, 2003, « Femmes et gouvernance partagée contre la pauvreté » in Amama, B. (dir.), *20 Propos sur l'administration camerounaise,* Yaoundé : MINFORPA, p. 475

Walmawa, B.N., 1989, « Violence against Wives and the Law in Kenya » in Obes, M. A., and Ooke-Ombaka, O., (edited by), *Women and the Law in Kenya,* Nairobi: Public Law Institute.

Waetjen, T. and Maré, G., 1999, « Workers and warriors: Inkatha's Politics of Masculinity in the 1980s », *Journal of Contemporary African studies,* 17, 2: 197-216.

Whitehead, S. M., 2002, *Men and masculinities. Key Themes and new Directions,* Cambridge: Polity Press.

Zeleza, Tiyambe, 2000, « Discriminations de genre dans l'historiographie africaine », in Imam, A., Mama, A. & Sow, F. (dir), *Sexe, genre et société. Engendrer les sciences sociales africaines,* Dakar/Paris : CODESRIA-Karthala, p.116.

9

Men's Role in Persistent Rural Poverty: Lessons from Kenya

Wanjiku Chiuri

Masculinities can be described as methods that men use to justify their superior and exploitative positions in any society. In hegemonic masculinities, men's power has been legitimized to reproduce social relationships that generate their dominance. This legitimacy is normalized through culture and gendered social responsibilities with dual transcripts (Cornwall and Lindisfarne 1994). Mies and Bennholdt-Thomsen (1988) expound this further by arguing that,

> the various forms of asymmetric, hierarchical division of labour which were developed throughout history up to the stage where the whole world is now structured into one system of unequal division of labour under the dictates of capital accumulation, are based on the social paradigm of the predatory/hunter warrior who, without producing himself is able … to appropriate and subordinate other producers, their productive forces and their products. This extractive, non-reciprocal exploitative … nature remained the model for all other male modes of production…. The characteristic of this model is that those who control the production process and the products are themselves not producers but appropriators. Their so called productivity presupposes the existence and subjection of others – *those who sustain the non producers*. … (N)on producers appropriate and consume what others have produced. Man-the-hunter is basically a parasite not a producer. (Mies and Bennholdt-Thomsen 1988: 91–2)

This explains why Kenyan societies and others societies across the globe legitimize and concentrate power positions on men with exclusive control over decisions, access and manipulation of social order and resources. At the same time, mechanisms to reinforce the subordinate social positions are put in place, which is where most women, some men and children find themselves. As a result both women and men subscribe to this social order of rulers and ruled, owners and beggars, masters and subordinates. This order has brought the gender inequalities debate into the spotlight. There are various forums discussing hegemonic masculinities worldwide in terms of gender inequalities and inequities. The most current is contained in the Millennium Development Goals (MDG) report, which envisions an improved world by 2015. Improvement is measured in halving extreme poverty, reduction of child mortality and gender disparities, improved health and environment, and accelerated empowerment of women. The report states that,

> gender equality is important not only as a goal in itself, but also as a path
> towards achieving other goals. Gender inequality ... tends to lower the
> productivity of labour and the efficiency of labour allocations in households
> and the economy, intensifying the unequal distribution of resources. It also
> contributes to the non-monetary aspects of poverty – lack of security,
> opportunity and empowerment – that lower the quality of life for both
> men and women. While women and girls bear the largest and most direct
> costs of these inequalities, the costs cut broadly across society, ultimately
> *hindering development and poverty reduction.* (World Bank 2003: 1)

The gender inequality that hinders development and perpetuates poverty results from the prevalence of hegemonic notions of masculinities at various levels within Kenyan communities. The discussion below zeroes in on *'productivity of labour and the efficiency of labour allocation in households'*. This is the first place to look in understanding masculine subjects' role in perpetuating persistent rural poverty. While the rest of the world attempts to include their women in decision-making positions as well as challenge masculinities, Africa has been giving the debate little attention. By and large within the continent, male domination is escalating and female subordination is deteriorating. Consequently, poverty has been escalating.

Various studies by researchers and development agencies spell out the abject and persistent poverty in Africa, both within the urban centres and the countryside. There are several theories on why Africans, whether within the continent or in diasporas, are at the bottom of the list when it comes to wealth and at the top of the ladder when it comes to poverty. Some schools of thought argue that slavery, colonialism and neo-colonialism, unfair trade agreements and the continued exploitation of Africa's resources are to blame. Others argue that Africa's ills are not all of external origin: Africans and in particular African leaders, who are largely men, have contributed significantly to the continent's crises. In one sense we can say that hegemonic masculinities are responsible for perpetuating poverty especially in the rural areas. Men in the rural areas are therefore the subject of examination and discussion in this study because each one can make a contribution within his own household to disentangling his family from the persistent rural poverty cycle.

Theories and explanations exist on the whys and hows of getting Africans out of abject poverty. But the gap in this debate, to which the study contributes, is on what contributions men can make within their households in order to get their families out of abject poverty. The study is based on rural men in Subukia locality, Nakuru district, Kenya. However, this study group represents many rural communities in Kenya in particular and Africa in general. It is an examination of the hegemonic masculinities with parasitic tendencies. These need to be examined in order to understand why poverty is persistent in the continent.

This study was triggered by the 'Gender, Growth, and Poverty Reduction' World Bank Report by Mark Blackben and Chitra Bhanu. In 1999, before the final report was written, I had the honour of listening to Dr Bhanu present her impressive report in Nairobi. Gender inequality in Sub-Saharan Africa came out as one of the major factors hindering the region's economic growth in this globalizing era. None of those present could argue with that. Most of us were witnesses of this inequality in all spheres of our own lives and those of our sisters in all socio-political and economic spheres in the country. The report's gender analysis is convincing but the labour recommendation triggered the need to find out what men in rural areas were doing. In Bhanu's report, men's limited contribution is given attention, but the recommendation is to '… raise labour productivity in the household economy by reducing the time burden of domestic work…' (Blackben and Bhanu 1999: 46), and redirect women's labour to marketable production. But domestic chores keep rural households functioning. Therefore, the proposal that women divert some of their time and labour to marketable production from domestic chores may have serious negative impacts on the families. The question then is: *why not make men more active in subsistence and marketable production instead of asking that women shift their time from domestic work to marketable production?* I was prompted to examine such a possibility where men would put more time and hence labour in household production. However, such an idea required a survey to establish that there is underutilized male labour and time allocation within rural households. Consequently, a pilot survey was carried out in 2002 in Subukia area of Nakuru district in the Rift Valley Province in Kenya.

Gendered Time and Labour in Rural Households

Rural development studies in Kenya and other African societies show that African women are overworked. They put in long hours to produce most of the food in the continent while at the same time providing substantial labour for cash crop production (Mwaka 1993; Government of Kenya (GoK) 1994; Boserup 1970; Chambers 1983; Rathgeber and Kettel 1989). The question that has not been answered is: *when women were doing all this, what were men doing?* This is where gender analysis becomes important as a tool to help us examine the actual contributions of men and women and boys and girls in household production. Unfortunately, most gender studies give little analysis on men as a category. In this omission men are left free, as in the case of household production activities. Hence this study attempts to make men a factor of analysis in order to understand the role hegemonic masculinities play in men's attitudes towards work in contemporary farming communities in Kenya, and Africa in general. This may explain the causal factors in the production and maintenance of persistent rural poverty in Africa, using the lessons from Kenya.

What is Persistent Poverty?

Persistent poverty is 'the socio-economic phenomenon whereby the resources available to a society (or household) are used to satisfy the wants of the few while many do not have even their basic needs met' (Kurien 1978, cited in Friedmann 1992). That being the case, one can propose that within rural households, persistent poverty occurs where labour, time and other resources are skewed towards members of the masculine gender in rural households where, owing to hegemonic notions of masculinities, most men are in control of all other members' labour, time and the resources available. They take the lion's share while often making the most minimal contributions towards their household production. They do this because they '… inhabit positions of power *which* … legitimises and reproduces social relationships that generate their dominance' (Corrigan et al. 1985: 92, cited in Conwell and Lindsfarne 1994: 19). Hence, there is no gender equity in labour and time use or equality is resource distribution within the various levels of society.

The privileges inherent in hegemonic masculinities are in part responsible for women working long hours, sometimes with the help of children, to provide the bulk of the labour in rural households' production (see Table 4 below) while men do little within the same households. Unfortunately, the labour of women and children is not adequate to lift rural households out of poverty, because most of it is spent in domestic chores and subsistence production. That is why Blackden and Bhanu (1999) advocated that women release some of the time spent on domestic and subsistence production to marketable production, which is financially rewarding, in order for households to break the cycle of poverty. The drawback with this suggestion is that it plays into the prevailing masculine ideologies, which do not question why women are working long hours, why their labour revolves around domestic chores and the subsistence economy, and what men contribute either to the domestic and subsistence economy or to the marketable economy.

Rural poverty has persisted all over the world for various reasons including unfavourable agricultural policies and global trade swings among others. Little has changed in the daily experience of rural people except more poverty.

Hegemonic masculine notions sustain the systems of domination that result in gender inequalities at various levels of society including and starting from the household levels. Though women '… bear the largest and the most direct costs of these inequalities, … the costs cut more broadly across society ultimately harming everyone – *the household, the community and the nation at large*' (King and Andrew 2001: 1). In the process persistent rural poverty structures are maintained.

In Kenya the government estimated that in 2001 56% of the population, or 17 million people, were living below the poverty line. Three-quarters of these were in the rural areas, and were mostly women (GoK 2003). According to Thomas-Slayter, Rocheleau and Asamba (1995), about 74% of rural households are under the management of women on a full-time basis. Although some men move to urban areas in search of non-existent jobs, a considerable number remain within rural households. This is the group that this work zeroed in on to examine *why rural households with both spouses present are caught up in a cycle of poverty*. The discussion below is based on a sample of households with land as a basic resource from which families should eke out a living by engaging household members in farming activities.

Friedmann (1992: 46) describes a household as 'a pattern of relationships and processes that connect the household to extended family, neighbours, the market economy and civic and political associations'. It is the primary polity in human organization. A household socializes its members from one generation to the next about their gender roles, expectations and position within and outside the household. It also shapes the gender relations within it and the larger society as it socializes its new members. The household economy is central to civil society through which market and non-market relations are articulated. The household does this by continuously solving the problem of allocating time and hence labour of its individual members to different tasks and different rewards. The household here is taken to represent people living together in one familial compound composed of adults of both sexes and children.

Rural households are the unit of analysis in this discussion. They are taken here as the most important institutions in addressing persistent poverty because they do have a stake in how successful poverty alleviation programmes would be. Friedmann (1992) reinforces this by arguing that the household is the most important unit for empowerment. Using the household as the basic unit of analysis makes it possible to 'start with people and not things' (Chambers 1983). This is important in understanding persistent rural poverty because it forces one to examine what each individual member does or fails to do in creating wealth or perpetuating poverty within a household. This brings us to examine what men and boys in contrast to women and girls do to contribute to the household production because '… equal sharing of responsibilities and a harmonious partnership between men and women are critical to their wellbeing and that of their families...' (DAW 2004: 4).

Do those men who remain at home work along with the women to provide the basic needs within their households? The assumption is that time and male labour are abundant resources in these households. If the two are efficiently used, they could help a family to get out of poverty. If carried out by all the men in a locality, the chains of persistent poverty would be broken within that locality. The research purpose was to show that rural household have excess male time and labour, which if tapped could make differences in household production, breaking the poverty cycle. The intent was to show that there is underutilized male time and labour in rural households, which should be the target in alleviation of poverty/ wealth creation designs. The survey examined time and labour, the two factors that rural households with resident male members have in abundance, and which are within their authority to control and manage.

Research methods included a survey, focus group discussions and Participatory Rural Appraisal (PRA) gender calendar data from rural communities in Kenya, to establish that men had extra time or unused time and hence extra labour for rural household production activities. The survey used a structured questionnaire administered to 33 men in Subukia locality of Nakuru district. Sampling was purposeful to capture only those households where the men were at home most of the year. It also targeted men young enough to have children of primary school age. In addition six informal women group discussions on gendered time use were held in the area. Twelve gender daily calendar results from various PRAs from different parts of the country were also analysed, to enrich the results from the survey and the discussions. Only men were interviewed because existing gendered labour analysis focused mostly on women, omitting men. However, gender discourse has to balance both men and women (DAW 2004).

Households in rural Kenya operate in a fast-changing world but indigenous systems still dictate the conduct of the members. The man, whether ever-present or occasionally present, is still the *de facto* head of the household. Household members find themselves in a new patriarchal system – a hybrid of Judeo-Christian colonial form and the traditional African form. The current hegemonic masculinities operating in Kenya tolerate minimal male contributions in household productions. This in turn reinforces and promotes masculine power in rural Kenya in particular. The result is a new form of patriarchy where there is *authority with minimal responsibility*. Men in rural Kenya are rarely answerable to anyone within their respective households because they are the heads and hence the decision-makers. They can work if they so wish but there appears a lack of societal expectations from them within the rural social structure. Meanwhile, women are blamed if the family is poor, if there is not enough food, if the house is unkempt, if the farms are not properly cultivated and the yields are low and if children cannot go to school. When these things happen, it is the woman who is perceived as failing.

Under prevailing notions of masculinities in rural Kenya, men are allowed to withdraw from domestic production activities with little or no official criticism (Silberschmidt 1999; focus group discussions with women). This is how researchers, policy-makers and poverty eradication strategists miss the role men can play within their household production, including participating in both domestic, subsistence and marketable production work. In fact if men participated in domestic chores, then women could release their saved labour and time for marketable production, as Blackben and Bhanu advocated in their report.

However, this is not the case. Findings from this study confirmed what others have stated, that women in Kenyan rural households work on the farm, the house, the school, the church and on government projects. As Okot p'Bitek would ask in *Song of Lawino*, 'African woman what are you not?' Yet, it was not till 1970 when Esther Boserup published her work that the world began to appreciate the overworked African woman. Unfortunately, this knowledge has not been translated into policies and programmes that would make men in rural households become active in household economic activities. Gender inequalities at the household level are a block to effective use of excess labour and time, especially those of the men in these households.

Impact of Gender Inequalities on Household Labour Allocation

Africa's household relationships are characterized by inequality in the distribution of work, land, income, consumption and contribution to productivity (*use of time*), based on gender and age (Mwaka 1993; Blackben and Bhanu 1999). This inequality is most pronounced in the division of labour between men and women and boys and girls within the same household. It manifests in societal expectations of each member of the household. Inequality that allows little expectations from men and older boys creates enormous inefficiencies in family labour allocations and time use. This results in loss of opportunities to improve the household economy. As Blackben and Bhanu (1999) found, efficient labour allocation at the household level (that is, shifting women's labour from domestic chores to producing goods for sale) would increase yields by 20% in one year. Like many other economists and rural development scholars, they failed to note underutilized male labour and time. Hence the question, *what would be the economic impact of putting underutilized male labour into household production?* We will answer this by referring to a summary from twelve communities where PRA was conducted between 1999 and 2001 by the Environmental Science Department of Egerton University, Kenya.

Table 1: Gender Daily Calendars (12 Communities, 1999–2001)

Villages where PRA was conducted	Hours men spent working	Hours women spent working
Kihingo	2	16
Mutiume	6	15
Mwireri	5	15
Kwanjiku	5	16
Thiru	7	16
Mungetho	5	17
Sikokhe	4	14
Kerma-a	3	14
Kerma-b	9	14
Mutito-a	7	15
Dikale	4	19
Total	57	155
Average	5	13

Source: compiled from PRA Reports: PRA Programme, Egerton University, Kenya.

Gender daily calendars are produced by separating groups of men and women from a zone or locality. A male group and a female group are set apart and asked to record a regular day with their activities. The hours spent working were solicited from men and women who voluntarily indicated the number of hours they worked within the household.

Table 2: Male Time Used in Subukia

Respondent	1	2	3	4	5	6	7	8	9	10	11	12	13	14	15	16	17
Hrs worked	3	4	3	0	3	7	3	2	2	4	4	3	3	5	0	0	6
Respondent	18	19	20	21	22	23	24	25	26	27	28	29	30	31	32	33	
Hrs worked	7	0	6	4	6	5	1	2	0	4	5	2	4	6	5	8	

Average hours worked from 33 respondents was 4 hrs.

Source: Compiled by the author from the survey.

Table 2 shows the hours men admitted to have invested in household production in the Subukia area. These two tables confirmed that women in Subukia work longer hours. But they also tell us that men in the same households are spending too little time, an average of between four or five hours a day, in household production. Some of them were not engaged in any way at all in their respective household production. The interview results show that 12% of all those interviewed did not engage in any productive activities within their households and yet they eat, wash/bathe, dress, and some smoke and some drink. Their female partners largely provide for all these personal needs. These results portray the parasitic hegemonic masculinities within Kenya's rural households. This is not only traceable in Kenya, for most of Africa's agricultural communities are facing similar challenges (*New Internationalist* 1986).

What Does the Unequal Gender Time Allocation Mean?

To answer this question it was imperative to calculate family incomes pegged on unskilled farm labour costs. Table 3 shows us the rate of pay for unskilled farm labour.

The government wage limit for agricultural non-skilled labour is Ksh 1428.00 a month for an 8-hour day and a 5-day week (GoK-CBS 2001: 58), which is about Ksh 72.00 or USD 1.00 a day. If we assume that the two adult members of a household agree on selling/costing their labour, then they would make a total of Ksh 3400.00 (about $500) a month while working only five hours in a day on their farm or selling their labour to other farmers in the neighbourhood. The two adults would be able to earn about Ksh 113.00 per day (3400/30 = 113), just slightly above US$ 1.50 a day.

Table 3: Unskilled Farm Labour in Subukia Community

	Women		Men	
	Kenya shillings	US dollars	Kenya shillings	US dollars
Payments/day	70.00	1.00	100.00	1.50
Payments/hour	14.00	0.20	20.00	0.30
Money earned/ month	70 x 5 x 4 =	Approx.	100 x 5 x 4 =	
Approx	1400.00	20.00	2000.00	28.00

Source: Personal communication with labourers and farmers in the study community.

However, this is not the case because in most households men do less than 5 hours of productive work such as hoeing, weeding, milking, planting and other duties within a household (see Table 4 below), while women do more than 10 hours, most of which is in domestic chores like fetching water and firewood, cooking and cleaning, mending and attending communal duties, all of which do not contribute much to tangible production. But they are nonetheless important daily chores for family survival.

We may ask: what would happen if men in these households increased the time spent on productive work from 5 to 8 hours a day? This would increase the family income from Ksh 3400.00 to Ksh 5400.00 a month, which would translate into Ksh 180.00 a day (5400/30 = 180.00), the equivalent of US$ 2.25 per day. Such an increase would move the family from persistent poverty and from under the poverty line. An extra four hours invested by the man in the household would more than double the family income. If this happens, the family would make some savings and have a chance of breaking the cycle of persistent poverty. Thus if male time within the household is efficiently used, the family can create the needed wealth to escape the poverty trap. If those four hours would be spent on the marketable production that Blackben and Bhanu referred to, they might improve the household's income even more. It should be noted that the positive contribution of male labour discussed above is at the level of the most poorly paid unskilled farm labour.

Table 4 highlights gender labour contributions in rural households.

Table 4: Labour Contribution by Gender within Kenyan Households

Activity	Women's labour contribution	Men's labour contribution
Food processing	90%	10% (with children's assistance)
Reproduction and domestic chores	95%	5% (with children providing the bulk of support)
Transportation of marketable farm to market	60%	40% including motorized products fromtransportation
Food processing and storage	80%	20%
Hoeing and weeding	90%	10% (with children's assistance)
Harvesting and marketing	60%	40%
Average	82%	18%

Source: Adapted from Blackben and Bhanu (1999) and Government of Kenya (1994).

On the average, women's labour contribution constitutes 82% while men, assisted by children, provide the remaining 18%. This is because, as we have seen in

Tables 1 and 2, men spend considerably less time in household production activities. Thus, inability to engage excess male time and labour means the loss of opportunities to create wealth within those households.

Given the existing gender stereotypes in rural communities, it may be difficult to expect men and boys to engage in domestic chores. However, PRA discussions have enabled male participants to realize and acknowledge that they are not doing enough and that there is room for improvement. Few role models exist in those communities of men who are themselves substantially engaged in household production. Such families prove what contributions men and bigger boys in rural households can offer in creating wealth for their families and getting them out of abject persistent poverty.

Where Should Men Spend their Extra Time Within Rural Household Economies?

Those men with underutilized labour and time could engage themselves in harvesting and marketing, hoeing and weeding, processing, storage and transportation. As Table 4 shows, there are activities within rural households that underutilized male labour could be engaged in. If that happens, there will be extra labour from both genders to be engaged in marketable productions. In this way dominant hegemonic masculinities would be moderated to give room for gender equity.

What Did the Women Living with these Men Say?

The focus group discussions confirmed that many men in rural households have excess time and underutilized labour. Women reported that with the failure of most men to 'help', none of their chores is done well and often they are never completed. For example, they reported that preparing the gardens for planting is never done or if done is done very poorly as the women juggle all the other responsibilities in the home. Planting is occasionally late, weeding is never thorough and sometimes is done very late. Occasionally, the families incur substantial losses owing to lack of time. For instance, post-harvest losses are one consequence of poor preparation of the storage facilities in the family. This in turn causes food deficits for most families. Others are able to have just enough for household consumption in situations where excess for sale can be produced if the male adults within the households agree to work alongside the women and children on the farm.

When asked why this is so, women observed that the main problem is lack of help from most men and some of the bigger boys in the households who still require food and other personal needs that most times women have to provide. Do men produce anything? The women answered yes, but more often than not what they produce was for their personal use only. On other occasions, they help technically in order to claim or legitimize their control of the produce and its marketing.

As Table 3 shows, most men are mostly engaged in transportation and marketing activities, where they provide 40% of the labour, a fourfold contribution compared to hoeing and weeding, where they give only 10%. This is in spite of the fact that hoeing and weeding are the crucial chores in crop production.

In these group discussions, stories were shared of how men steal food and sell it. Some men will wait for the spouse to go to church or take a child to the clinic to sell what they have stolen. A female participant reported how she came home one day to discover that there was no single grain of maize in the granary to cook for the evening. All the ninety bags of harvested grain were gone, and the husband was gone too. Labour shortages in rural areas are more often than not attributed to labour migration into urban centres (Macharia 2002). Yet, rural neighbourhoods are littered with idle men on the roads and market centres in mid-morning, features of a distressing underutilization of masculine labour and time.

What Explanations Did Men in the Survey Give?

The survey sought men's explanations on their use of time and labour in household production. When asked why they do so little at home, men said that they expected to have jobs in offices. They blamed the government for failing to provide them with white-collar jobs as they were promised when they were growing up and going to school. When asked what should be the solution, they said that government must create jobs: that it is the government's responsibility to set up factories and industries for them to work in. The implication of this is that if work is in the fields as Table 4 indicates, this is meant for women and children. Masculine ideologies came out clearly in these interviews. The interviewees' perceptions of what being a masculine subject is all about were expressed in their laxity in engaging themselves in activities that would make their lives better simply because they were socialized to expect formal jobs after having been to school. To them, the drudgery of farming is for women.

The school and education per se in Kenya are major socializing agents. Unfortunately, they have so far served to reinforce hegemonic masculinities and stereotyped gender attributes in both male and female learners. And because Kenya's education system like many others within the continent was inherited from the colonial masters, it has not changed its primary goal of producing clerks for the colonial government. In 1985, Daniel Arap Moi, the then President of Kenya, pronounced a presidential decree for a changed education system whose goal was to inculcate basic skills for entrepreneurship among the nation's learners. The idea was good but poorly planned and implemented, and it did not achieve its noble goal. Today, this system, known as the 8–4–4 system, has gone through several incremental changes. It is serving the same purpose as the colonial system and the post-colonial system. As in any other region, men participate more in education than women. This seems to give them the licence to seek only formal employment and to look down on manual work. When formal clerical jobs are not available, they fail to acknowledge other options within their settings.

Women's Opinions on Men's Underutilized Labour

Women's opinions on men's underutilized labour were interesting. They blamed the government for being blind to masculine idleness. They recalled an administrative police officer in the local chief's office who hated idlers. He would arrest them and get the local chief to punish them. This made men work. Though they primarily worked for themselves, they made positive contributions to their household economies because women did not have to share their proceeds with them. By the time of the study, this was not happening and women wished there could be laws to force men to work on their farms. Subukia women's sentiments confirm those of Tanzanian women, as reported by Blackben and Bhanu (1999). Tanzanian women who were participating in a land bill workshop expressed interest in '… a bill that (*would*) force men to work harder so that they would be too tired in the evenings to beat their wives' (Blackben and Bhanu 1999: 83). Similar sentiments were expressed by women from Nyandarua district in Kenya when contributing to Kenya's Poverty Reduction Strategy Paper (PRSP) in 2000. They said that in order to reduce poverty in their district, men must work and that the government should introduce a personal tax that would force those men who are not very active to become fully engaged in order to pay the tax. This strategy, according to the Nyandarua women, would make the men work and contribute to household production (discussion with Nyandarua women at PRSP forums).

Conclusion

The aim of this study has been to establish that most men living in rural Kenya do not fully utilize their labour and time adequately to help in their household production in order to create wealth to raise their families out of abject poverty. In order to demonstrate this, it was imperative to establish that these men have excess labour and time, and also record the impact of efficient use of that excess labour and time towards generating family income. The gender daily calendar, interviews with men and focus group discussions with women all pointed out that dominant hegemonic masculinities pose specific obstacles to poverty alleviation and gender equity in Kenya. These masculine notions projecting male supremacy have perpetuated gender stereotyping and male domination in decision-making at all levels of society, particularly at the household level. Hence, other family members pay a heavy price because men tend to contribute minimally although they share equally with the producers the proceeds in those households.

Table 3 attempted to show the impact improved male contributions in family labour would make in creating wealth for the family and getting it out of the poverty trap. In this scenario, it is clear that what is needed is to encourage more men and bigger boys to be active participants in the responsibilities of their families and their households, and especially in areas where they can contribute significantly in the production of goods and services for subsistence and for marketing.

References

Blackben, M. and Bhanu, C., 1999, *Gender Growth, and Poverty Reduction: Special Program of Assistance for Africa*. Washington, DC: The World Bank.

Boserup, E., 1970, *Women's Role in Economic Development*, London: Allen & Unwin.

Chambers, R., 1983, *Rural Development: Putting the Last First*, Harlow: Longmans.

Cornwall, A. and Lindisfarne, N., eds., 1994, *Dislocating Masculinity: Comparative Ethnographies*. London: Routledge.

Division for the Advancement of Women (DAW), 2004, *The Role of Men and Boys in Achieving Gender Equality*, New York: DAW.

Egerton University PRA Programme, *1999–2001 Participatory Rural Appraisal Reports*, Njoro: Department of Environmental Science.

Friedmann, J., 1992, *Empowerment: The Politics of Alternative Development*, Cambridge, MA: Blackwell.

Gender and Development Group, 2003, *Gender Equality and The Millennium Development Goals*, Washington, DC: The World Bank.

Government of Kenya, 1994, *Development Plan 1994–96*, Nairobi: Government Printers.

Government of Kenya, 2001, *Statistical Abstracts*. Nairobi: Government Printers.

Government of Kenya, 2003, *Economic Recovery Strategy for Wealth and Employment Creation 2003–2007*, Nairobi: Government Printers.

King, M. and Andrew, M., 2001, *Engendering Development through Gender Equality in Rights, Resources and Voice*, Washington, DC: World Bank.

Macharia, K., 2003, 'Migration in Kenya and its Impact on the Labour Market', Paper prepared for Conference on African Migration in Comparative Perspective, Johannesburg, South Africa, 4–7 June. Downloaded on 27 April 2004 from http:// pum.Princeton.edu/ pumconference/papers/4-macharia.pdf

'Man-Made Famine', Video Documentary, 1986, *New Internationalist*.

Mies, M. and Bennholdt-Thomsen, V., 1988, *Women the Last Colony*, London: Zed Books.

Mwaka, M., 1993, 'Agricultural Production and Women's Time Budget in Uganda', in J. Momsen and V. Kinnaird, eds., *Different Places, Different Voices: Gender and Development in Africa, Asia and Latin America*, London: Routledge.

p'Bitek, Okot, 1969, *Song of Lawino: An African Lament*, New York: Meridian Books.

Rathgeber, E. and Kettel, B., 1989, *Women's Role in Natural Resource Management in Africa*, Ottawa: International Development Research Centre.

Thomas-Slayter, B., Roceheleau, D., Asamba, I. et al., 1995, *Gender, Environment, and Development in Kenya: A Grassroots Perspective*, Boulder, CO: Lynne Rienner.

10

Student Fathers and the Challenge to Masculinities in Kenyan Universities

Charity Mwangi-Chemnjor

Introduction

The increasing presence of students who are parents in universities and parents who become students in universities poses a challenge to educators and to the institutional policies and practices of the traditional university set-up. In Kenya, there has been both an increased demand for university education and an increase in the number of universities as a result of a policy of liberalization and privatization of university education. This has led to a diversification in the university student population. Into this diversity enters the issue of student parents and the considerable attention they attract. Two angles of this scenario are presented in this study. One is of students seen as clients attending university, with needs and expectations of equity and equality of opportunity for a quality education. The other angle is the university or institution, its policies, practices and/or support structures for this changing clientele, and the expectations of society in the provision of quality education.

Traditionally, public universities have admitted students who expect to be housed in university hostels. These students are presumed to be single, without children and unaccompanied by dependants. Various universities in Kenya have adopted different policies concerning student parents, and these will usually be found in the university student handbooks and manuals. A review of some public university handbooks was carried out. The handbook of Egerton University, for example, recommended that expectant students vacate the university halls of residence three months before delivery: 'Since pregnancy disrupts academic performance' (Egerton University 2004: 35). In another campus the orientation and information manual stated: 'Maternity services are not provided ... expecting students should vacate the halls of residence at least three months prior to the expected date of delivery' (Egerton University, Laikipia Campus 2004: 37). Another Kenyan public university handbook commented: 'in the event of pregnancy either before or after taking residence in the halls, students move out of the residence at least three months before confinement and reapply three months after delivery' (University of Nairobi 2001: 637).

The student who is expecting and soon to be a parent is left with very few options. One is deferment of studies for a semester or whole year. Alternatively, the student may choose to defer studies till the baby is old enough to be left on their own, usually at home with the students, parents or spouse, at which point the student may reapply to enter university hostel accommodations. Another option, which most student parents prefer, is to vacate their rooms in the halls of residence as per the university regulation, look for a place to reside around the campus and continue with classes after delivery. Then as soon as they are able physically to get through the lectures and the long day they resume classes. The implication of the second option is that they have the responsibility of looking for a place to reside around the campus. In many cases their resources can only allow for a small room. They also need to budget for a child minder. The consequences are a situation where student have to fend for themselves, child and child minder on money that they are advanced from their student loan, which caters for the upkeep of only one person.

Thus there has arisen a growing population of student parents in the neighbourhood of campuses with their young ones, infants and babies, living in conditions that leave a lot to be desired. Most are squalid, unhygienic and inadequate given the meagre budgets available. These conditions are not conducive to the mental and physical health of the student parents. Academic performance is affected since the social environment is not enabling for learning. Students who choose to be parents feel alienated or ostracized since they do not fit into the expectations of 'traditional' university policies and practice. The student parent has needs that the university has not been able to address and which it needs to take seriously.

Reasons for the Study

The student father in many cases is caught up in this situation and faces conflicting issues in terms of parenthood and studying. This study seeks to explore this predicament of student fathers as they attempt to take up their responsibilities as a parent, and facing choices that will have an impact on their life situations and on the course of their studies.

As earlier mentioned, following liberalization and privatization of university education in Kenya, public universities have found themselves in an increasingly competitive situation, with demands to be innovative and sustainable, and giving evidence of growth, efficiency and effectiveness so as to remain institutions of choice. In distinguishing between efficiency and effectiveness in an organization Barnard (in Hoy and Miskal 1991: 84) argues that efficiency is geared towards the person and the feelings of satisfaction derived from being a member of the organization, while effectiveness is geared towards the system and has to do with organizational goals. The university as an educational organization will be seen to be efficient when members of the organization are satisfied with their needs being attended to or met. The university itself as an organization will be seen to be effective when it is able to attain its goals as an organization. As the university attains its goals, one of which is provision of educational services to the community in innovative and sustainable ways, it will remain seen as an organization of choice leading to its growth and relevance to the society. Among these members who are looking to the university to address their needs are the student parents. On a rating scale of efficiency there is need for the public universities to assess where they rate and to correct or improve this rating as this is instrumental in their being a university of choice. On being effective, this is seen in how the goals of the organization are met, one of which is maintaining educational standards of students or clients. As the universities look for ways and means to help enrolled students attain high academic standards, the university will be seen to be effective, which will lead to the university being able to sustain itself and grow, with perceived relevance to the changing needs of the society.

Public organizations all over the world are increasingly being subjected to demands for efficiency and effectiveness, especially in the face of dwindling public resources. The universities are not exempted as they struggle to be sustainable in a fiercely competitive environment. The context of this study is a situation where government aid in form of grants is falling in public universities. Students are now entering an era where they choose specific universities for the programmes they are interested in as opposed to the past where the Joint Admission Board (JAB) selected and distributed students into various public universities. As students exercise their capacity to choose, the universities of choice will be those that are seen to be cost-effective and yet efficient in providing quality educational services, both academic and administrative.

As students are looking for universities that will address their needs, universities are being obliged to address a diversity of students seeking higher education. The universities face certain challenges in this changing landscape. One is sustainability. The public universities need resources to continue financing their activities. These resources will help in the university sustaining itself as a public entity, and in its being able to fulfil its role as a service provider of education, thus sustaining society. In this era students, including student parents, are assumed to be clients and are seen as resources, since they come in with money in the form of fees. Since the students enter the university and are willing to pay for the services provided, this in turn establishes the relevance of universities to society, since it proves the need and demand for these educational services. Therefore as more clients are willing to exchange money for educational services, this goes a long way in sustaining demand and driving improvement in university education. These clients or students have resources and as the university courts these resources, they have to prove themselves worthy. With the diversification of the student body to include other non-traditional entrants such as student parents, can universities show that they are the educational organizations of choice? Students who choose to be parents, or parents who chose to be students, will increasingly find themselves in positions where they can chose an institution that will offer quality education in addition to other academic and administrative services that support their needs and expectations. Universities that offer these educational services efficiently and effectively will increasingly be in a better position as universities of choice for student parents.

Kenyan public universities are not alone in rising to this challenge. In their important Africa-wide survey, Zeleza and Olukoshi (2004) emphasize that the trade in educational services is part of the modern university's survival strategy in the face of cutbacks in government spending to public universities and the agenda of liberalization of the World Trade Organization (p.596). In response to liberalization public organizations enter private education to offer education services. The public universities must prove themselves able to rise effectively and effectively to this challenge. The authors point out there are simultaneous challenges posed to African public universities, and it is into this debate that student parents, including student fathers, are introduced, in order to highlight this group visible among the various non-traditional students seeking higher education as part of an ongoing debate on access to quality higher education.

This topic therefore situates the challenges posed by this group of students to the public universities in Kenya in the context of other challenges confronting the public universities in the continent as regards growth of educational services in an era of liberalization and privatization of university education. The provision of administrative and academic services to public universities will be seen against the background of the agenda of liberalization, thus placing the African public universities in a national and international perspective. The public universities have therefore to work at improving the delivery of their services, so as to attract more students, even the non-traditional ones like the student fathers who are a significant component of the student parent group. Retaining clientele is a challenge not only to Kenyan public universities, but also to African universities more generally (Zeleza and Olukoshi 2004). Another challenge in this situation is to attract and retain more students who will bring in resources that can be used to bridge budget deficiencies (Abagi 1999).

Focusing on parenthood and its implications in Kenyan universities as a case in point, this study attempts to analyse the situation in which students become fathers and fathers are students. It broaches the question of the increasing number of student parents in the universities, and the impact of parenthood on the potential of these students to function simultaneously as fathers and students. Research on student parenting has tended to focus mainly on student mothers, and the impact on their educational potential, economic and social progress. For an assessment of the impact of interventions on student mothers to be effective, it will be impractical to exclude student fathers. This study attempts to bridge any such gaps.

It is argued that any measures taken should address the needs of both student fathers and student mothers in assessing the challenges to fatherhood. Any interventions that may be needed will require an assessment of the current polices and practices in the public universities and how they may influence the provision of academic and administrative services to student fathers. The argument running through this study concurs with the claim that men need to be incorporated in any attempt to redress change in any institution that will impact on both female and male. Men are often excluded from being part of the process of changing and confronting practices that are unequal. They will need to be encouraged to question their personal practices and the ideologies of masculinity they embody, otherwise the task of changing one part of gender practices will be made impossible (White 1997: 15, in Pease and Pringle 2001: 8). In addressing the process of change in any institution it is important to consider the dominant model of social relations in the specific group. In terms of student parents, one needs to answer the question where they are, and how they conceptualize student fatherhood and its implications.

Objectives

One of the objectives of this study is to highlight the phenomenon of student fatherhood in an attempt to facilitate any help that may be given to student fathers to impact positively on their academic and other progress in the university. Another objective is to try and locate and address the issue of student fathers on work around masculinities and parenting, and the interactions and implications on these student fathers' life choices and academic potential. In the assessment of the parenting discourse, hopefully questions will be raised as to the responsibilities and relations within the act or process of parenting through reaching into the major areas of social life of the participants. From the discussion, it is hoped there will be an increased understanding of the social dimensions of student fatherhood and the response mechanisms of the student fathers.

This study uses the context of hegemonic masculinities in studying the university student fathers. In focusing on student fatherhood and its implications for Kenyan universities, there is a need to reflect on the ways that the institution responds to these groups of students, since their needs differ markedly from the traditional populations that universities were designed to serve. Not only do these student fathers carry the burden of parenthood, but also they have to continue education at a time when public spending on higher education in Kenya is decreasing. Another objective of the study is to help clarify the role that universities can play in the management and provision of administrative and academic services to undergraduate student fathers, and show to what extent these services make a difference, thus making it easy to adapt the services to the needs of the student fathers.

A newspaper report on Kenyan primary and secondary schools has highlighted the increased incidence of student pregnancy, which invariably results in the emergence of student parents (Kigotho 2004). The report notes that the tremendous increase of school pregnancy has led to students being driven out of school. It also suggests that there may be other implications, including the limiting of the academic potential of the individual student. Measures taken in response to this trend should deal equally with male and female students for any effective and lasting solution to emerge. Attempts by university administrators to curtail this development motivated the original study, which attempted to discover how potential student fathers responded to the consequences of their actions: did they abandon their student female partners once pregnancy resulted or did they accept the responsibility of parenthood, becoming father, husband and student at the same time?

A comprehensive study carried out on school pregnancies in Kenya in 1988 showed that 45% of Kenyan schoolgirls aged nineteen were either pregnant or already mothers, and 70% of the girls dropped out of school owing to teenage pregnancy (Ferguson 2004). The figures given are for the primary education sector, but the secondary school sector attested to a similar trend. In the 2005 examinations at least five girls were in the news for delivering their babies during exam time, being brought their papers in the maternity ward in hospital (*Standard*, 10 November 2005). Such reports of secondary school student parents make it clear that this is part of the pool of students that university entrants are drawn from, in addition to other traditional entrants. In this study the pregnancy statistics given for girls in the primary and secondary level and the issue of student parents in the university would lead to a gap in the body of knowledge if the student fathers' experiences were excluded.

In the public universities a culture seems to be emerging whereby students enter into 'marriages' of convenience in response to economic pressures. Student entrants may not necessarily be assured of a student loan in the face of dwindling public funds. With money scarce various tactics are employed, including pooling resources, with male students contributing food and the female students doing housekeeping, cooking and laundry. As a result of parenting, the grades of these students are affected negatively once they combine the business of parenting with schooling. This situation is a concern both for the individual students who become parents and for the administrators of Kenya's universities, as evidenced by various reports. One such report is from an opening address of a public university vice-chancellor to first years, in which he encouraged them to be aware of such practices and their negative impact on academic performance (Maritim 2005). Another warning came from the academic dean of a different university, who decried such practices for their effect on the education standards of the individual student parent and subsequently on the provision of quality education in the university (Shitemi 2005). Other studies have documented the effect on the public universities of such practices (Bartoo 2005). In separate reports on the numbers of primary school pregnancies, two researchers have surveyed the assumptions and feelings of the general public and of educators on the issue of school pregnancy, concluding that there is a need to assess and address the effects of pregnancy and what measures can be useful in helping student parents achieve their potential (see Kigotho 2004; Ferguson 2004).

Methodology

Cultural texts and representations are important in exploring the possibilities available to individuals as they constitute themselves in a society (Cranny-Francis et al. 2003). For purposes of this study, texts, including published and unpublished representations, have been used in the effort to locate the student father in the social arena, bearing in mind that culture constitutes much of what we identify in society since we are cultured beings. In the analysis of texts (Cranny-Francis *et al.*) emphasize how this extends beyond the merely written in various forms to other ways of communicating such as in casual conversations, television, advertising, newspapers and parent/child interactions among others (p.92). These means are influential in locating others and ourselves in society.

The methodology used here includes the analysis of published and unpublished texts, oral conversations and other means used to communicate meanings to one another in society. There is a wealth of information yielded that may be useful in identifying the position of student fathers in the university, and the challenges they face in the area of masculinities in this location. In the discussions on parenting, masculinities and culture in the universities, the expectations of the student fathers and the expectations of the university organization towards them has been located in a cultural and social representation, thus helping us understand the relations and social dynamics operating in the life of the student fathers that lie behind their life choices.

Men are often excluded from being part of the process of change, especially when it deals with confronting the differences in treatment of male and female. In addressing any process of change in an institution, it is therefore important to address the dominant model of social relations in the specific group, so as to address changing men's practices in a globalized world (Pease and Pringle 2001: 8). In this issue of change great importance is placed on complementing localized orientation with a focus on whole countries and ultimately the whole world. In that way changing subjectivities and practices of men are incorporated and validated, reflecting the globalizing processes at work. The university needs to recognize that any local assessment or change in practice will be influenced by international changes and that any internal changes in the way policy and practice are viewed will be influenced by local orientation.

To be able to understand masculinities in specific local context, Pease and Pringle argue the importance of thinking in global terms, since that provides the possibility of exploring felt experiences, culture and social networks (Pease and Pringle 2001: 9). The different subjectivities and practices will then reflect the individual local contexts. In research one is able to see where they stand in comparison to another. By locating the present study in hegemonic masculinities, it will facilitate transformation of policy and practice in the public university setting. Student mothers do not exist in the abstract but in relation to student fathers. To understand the implications of this division between men and women, Pease and Pringle's research argues that whether or not an individual acknowledges this association, the outcome of the political debate will impact on them at the societal level. They suggest that men and women should be recognized as discursive subjects, existing within political categories across the social web. Failing to acknowledge this reality is to fail to acknowledge that others exist beyond the individual (Whitehead 2002: 63). Hegemonic masculinity is seen to encompass 'the dominant interpretations and definitions of being masculine as embedded in and sustained by male dominated social institutions such as the state, the family and educational institutions'. Analysing men's practices at home or their involvement in childcare will require an unpacking of the private in the personal so as to better understand the public–private dualism in which Whitehead (2002: 149) contends the individual cannot be completely separated from society.

Focus at the international and national levels on issues affecting girls and women has led to a corresponding analysis on men, since in analysing one group questions on the 'other' arise that may lead to gaps in knowledge if left unanswered. In the research on masculinities there has been an increase of studies exploring fatherhood and focusing on reviews of research, policies and practices. These studies have shown a shift from an emphasis on women to the incorporation of women into already established agendas, then to the emphasis on gender relations, social structures, process and relations in specific international and local factors (Pease and Pringle 2001: 7). The conscious focus on the recurring themes of masculinity and fatherhood in everyday reality from media to academia has led to expansion of the debate to take into account student fathers and practices in public universities. This has been necessitated by the global change in focus from female-only to inclusion both of male and female.

Body

With both the government and other world organizations pegging their grants to performance of the public university, simultaneous challenges are posed to the African public universities in meeting the demands of these two stakeholders. It is into this debate that the student father is introduced, in order to make him visible and capture this group in the ongoing debate of access to quality higher education facilitated by whatever support is available.

Research on student parents has primarily concentrated on the plight of student mothers. This may be as a result of the visibility of pregnancy as a sign of motherhood. Much more is known about student mothers than fathers, leading to a situation in which any academic or administrative support that may be offered to the student father is below what is expected. Through making visible the reality of this phenomenon and in the process of scrutinizing it, hopefully it will lead to ways of accommodating and or situating it in everyday social reality. In the book *Young Masculinities*, the authors show how student fathers are affected by the uncertainties over social role, identity and personal relationships among other issues. This is a situation replicated in most of the contemporary forms of masculinity. They argue that there are no clear models or images of masculinities (Frosh et al. 2002: 4). This then influences this study in that in trying to identify the position of the student father the identity of this group is drawn from the culturally available resources in social networks and in society. In the assessment of the parenting discourse, this study hopes to raise questions as to the responsibilities and relations within the act or process of parenting through reaching into the major areas of social life of the participants. For present purposes, parenting is seen to be work that involves childrearing, and this is taken to be a role involving both male and female parents. With the understanding that through each of the parents acknowledging and understanding expected responsibilities, the functions of bearing and rearing a child will be accomplished. In the literature on male parenting or fatherhood, contemporary theories help envision the diversity of fathering. These are based on regional, geographical and cultural spaces. There are rapid transformations, and Haywood and Mac an Ghaill (2003: 58) argue that there is need to combine theory with empirical studies of what the fathers are experiencing. The present study places fatherhood within the framework of hegemonic masculinities, and the social institution of fatherhood is seen against a background of gendered work of women and men in both private and public spheres. With this understanding, the student fathers should be able to locate themselves making responsibilities visible in an area that has been rendered invisible by dominant cultural practices.

Support services would include those that help students deal with factors interfering with their learning and performance in educational institutions. Most educationalists affirm that any such factors must be addressed if the education mission is to succeed (Adelman 1996: 431). There is need for services that enable students to benefit from instruction, and Adelman argues that these should be organized in an integrated approach. In this study the university would need to address the barriers to educational achievement as concerns student fathers. This goes to show their commitment to the success of all their students, and the provision of excellent and quality education services. In maintaining standards of excellence the university staff and administration would need to show evidence of their involvement in this respect. In one of the local daily newspapers, a student captured the experiences of student parents in the public universities in Kenya. The writer illustrates these as falling under academic, financial and social challenges. Some of these negative experiences include ill health, poor accommodation and diet, and lack of access to medical facilities on campus (Mutyanga 2003). Other challenges are associated with pressure from family and friends, including low self-esteem through rejection and stigma associated with single parenthood. All these factors combine to interfere with student parents' academic performance (Empowering Student Mothers 2004: 6). The issues identified by the female student parents in the public universities underline the oral data collected, showing that socially the culture and environment in the university are not student parent-friendly. These are among the issues that contribute to making fathering invisible. The student author argues for the need of advocacy of the interests and wellbeing of student parents, including student fathers.

Recent studies on fatherhood range from practices to policies of support. In the practice of fatherhood, the social dynamics that have resulted in the invisibility of student fathers on campus may be explained by the scarcity of studies into the subjective experiences or feelings of fathers (Russell 2001: 57). In addressing the burden of parenthood for student fathers and mothers, the question of defining involvement and support of student fathers needs to be established within frameworks that help individuals and the university ascertain father provision. These may include support services and education programmes where the participation of both student parents is required and encouraged.

Social policy works best with community-based support as seen in nations where initiatives have been taken to encourage fatherhood. In promoting student fathers' support and the resulting respite in the burden of parenthood for student mothers, the Kenyan public universities will need to become more active in evaluating practice by developing support programmes. Some of these programmes have proved fruitful elsewhere in helping unmarried and young males through issues such as 'job search/training and employment, parent training and school involvement', with the key theme being encouraging 'responsible fatherhood' (Russell 2001: 60).

In the provision of such services, the universities will not only be helping individual student parents and student fathers, but will also be actively involved in programmes that ultimately lead to them being universities of choice. Critics may argue that this is encouraging students to become parents on campus. But given the trends of a growing incidence of schoolgirl pregnancy as aforementioned, the university system is part of the wider social system, and each of these systems have to do their part in addressing the reality of social responsibility towards student parents. It is significant to note that responsible fatherhood is a theme reflected in various international social debates, as evidenced in the Promise Keepers USA and the Million Man March, the Men and Family Relationship Initiative in Australia and Fathers Direct in the UK (Russell 2001: 10), where these initiatives begin a shift away from fathers only as breadwinners and their financial responsibilities to their inclusion in policy and workplace initiatives, with most of them identifying better access to advice and education as necessary for fatherhood support.

This study is yet to identify examples from Africa on this social debate of fatherhood, but hopefully it will provoke a debate that will lead to inclusion in policy and inclusion in other institution initiatives. As centres of research and service providers the universities cannot afford to be left out in this paradigm shift. It is part of their responsibility to society to begin initiating debate on responsible fatherhood. They also need to begin implementation of social research that will be helpful in addressing the reality of fatherhood and how its implementation in the university's policies and practices can be used to encourage student fathers in the choices they need to take. Universities can position themselves and through this information be able to incorporate student fathers in their policies and practices thereby improving the services rendered to this group of the university community and wider society.

Other reports have identified various methods and contexts with which to address fatherhood. Public universities in Kenya would greatly benefit from these findings based on diversity programmes that incorporate fatherhood workshops and developing fatherhood programmes in response to needs assessed. Ongoing contributions to the debate on fatherhood and masculinities establish fatherhood as part of the sociology of masculinity. The concept of men and family is understood as a series of gendered interrelationships that are mutually constructed and maintain paternal masculinities, located in particular periods and geographical spaces (Haywood and Mac an Ghaill 2004: 44). Public universities will need to find their geographical space and how it has constituted fatherhood masculinities, and whether maintaining those gender relations is valuable and practical in this period. This research from other geographical spaces and periods show a 'conceptual shift from role reproduction to an active production of complex identity formations'. This would impact on public university practices and policies by acknowledging that in sex roles, emotions and desires of the individuals are just as important as rational thinking in shaping paternal behaviour. In addressing student fathers an assessment of these roles and desires would be very helpful since this would expand the working space to allow social psychological and interpersonal considerations as well as emotional and future aspirations. The universities as public educational organizations need to acknowledge the fact that at any one time they are dealing with the issue of the potential of youth and their future goals in society. Every organization that deals with the youth has a duty to nurture potential, and if that organization is rendering education services and dealing with the youth as the public university is doing, it will need to be able to effectively harness this power so as to be seen to provide effective service as a university of choice. In the search to develop initiatives that address men's own issues and their roles as fathers, the approaches have moved gradually from role-deficient approaches with a need for 'fixing' to approaches that more directly address men's own issues and their roles as fathers (Brown 2004: 113). Instead of looking to fix the 'problem' of student fathers, it would be more productive if the universities started off by exploring the felt needs of these student fathers. As the study of parenthood and fatherhood intensifies, the significance of this work to individual student fathers and the society has been well expressed by Dollatite, Hawkins and Brotherson (1997). In their study they take the concept of genera-tive fathering as caring for and contributing in the life of the next generation. Thus generative fathering would imply a positive influence in a child's life as being developmental and of importance not only to the child but also to the father. What positive developmental fathering can the universities begin exploring that would have beneficial results? This may take time but it would be time well invested. The goal would be a transformation of desires and reality over a period of time and a set of skills and behaviours to bring about this transformation that can be learned, depending on circumstances (Brown 2004: 113). This approach is crucial to student fathers in a culture where men are expected to be provider and protector, because they are not seen as a problem to be 'fixed' or as deficient in not measuring up to expectations, but rather as an opportunity for learning improvement. With this approach, then, the student father will not be 'penalized' but will be involved in unlearning old and learning new behaviour. For the individual student father, the notion of generative fathering with its positive implications may appear less confrontational than challenging the individual to 'fit'. Depending on the individual and the circumstances or demands the university will be able to put in place enabling structures to provide support services to individual student fathers thereby facilitating their work as fathers, and in the same way, help the university in uplifting educational standards of individual student fathers.

Conclusion

This study has focused on student fathers and the need to address administrative and academic support in a privatized, liberated and globalized world. In research on 'fatherwork' in the Caribbean, Brown concludes that when men start examining the negative as well as the positive effects of structured male privilege within their own lives, they advance their own fatherwork (p.117). She maintains that men recognize the limitations, brought about by 'narrow social definitions of manhood, and fatherhood', on their own development, but that support needed to broaden these concepts of fatherhood is limited. Using the assumption that Brown makes, public universities can begin addressing areas that have rendered student fathering a challenge in their academic performance and parenting duties. Though the scope of the literature is narrow, oral data indicates there is need for administrative and academic support. Debates about student fathers and the role of the public universities in addressing any academic and administrative support can be part of the broadening of debate that may provide the much-needed support to student fathers. From the onset this study has set out to address the rising number of university student parents, drawing attention to the student father. This has been projected against a background of changes in provision of educational services, accountability and accommodation in the provision of academic and administrative services. The factors that influence change in the provision of quality education services to various categories of students have been discussed. The case of student fathers was introduced with an emphasis on how masculinities influence student parenthood. This study has attempted a brief analysis of the policy practices and culture in the public universities as concerns parenting. It also raised the need for support structures for student fathers with suggestions on how they can be helped to confront the challenges posed by being both student and parent. All through, this study has stressed the need for recognition and anticipation of fulfilment of the role in father work by the student father, showing how it will significantly ease the burden for the student mother. Issues concerning the involvement of the university and the implications of this on the university of choice have been addressed. Various shifts in masculinities and internationally the involvement of both men and women in initiating social change have been mentioned. Suggestions of the ways others have addressed these socio-cultural changes have been presented, showing how the public universities in Kenya can benefit from them. In conclusion, it is hoped that work such as this will facilitate in any administrative and academic support strategies planned towards student fathers in educational organizations.

References

Abagi, O., 1999, 'Education Reform in Kenya for the Next Decade: Implementing Policies for Adjustment and Revitalisation'.
Available: http://www./par.or.ke/ed3.html [Accessed 9 April 2004].

Adelman, S. H., 1996, 'Restructuring Educational Support Services and Integrating Community Resources', *School Psychology Review*, Vol. 25, No. 4, pp. 431–6.

Alon. T., 2004, 'Parenting Realities at the University of California, Berkeley: Balancing Work, School and Parenting in Academia'.
Available: http://www.eec5.berkeley.edu/programs/grad/parentpolicy.html [Accessed 23 September 2005].

Bartoo, V., 2005, 'Varsity Rocked by "Couples Crises"', *East African Standard*, 24 January.

Brown, J., 2004, 'Fatherwork in the Caribbean', in *S*. Ruxton, ed., *Gender Equality and Men*, Oxford: Oxfam.

Cranny-Francis, A., Waring, W., Stravopoulous, P. and Kirby, J., 2003, *Gender Studies Terms and Debates*, New York: Palgrave Macmillan.

East African Standard, 2005, 'Candidates Sit Exams in Maternity Ward', 10 November: 18.

Egerton Newslink, 2004, 'Empowering Student Mothers for Improved Academic Performance and Personal Development', Graduation Special: 6.

Egerton University, Laikipia Campus, 2004, *Orientation and Information Manual*, Egerton University Press.

Egerton University, 2004, *Student Handbook*, Egerton University Press.

Ferguson, A., 2004, 'Teenage Motherhood: Epidemic Pushing Girls Out of School', *East African Standard*, 5 August: 6.

Frosh, S., Phoenix, A. and Pattman, R., 2002, *Young Masculinities*, New York: Palgrave.

Haywood, C. and Mac an Ghaill, M., 2003, *Men and Masculinities*, Buckingham and Phildelphia: Open University Press.

Hoy, W. and Miskal, C., 1991, *Education Administration: Theory, Research and Practise*, New York: McGraw-Hill Inc.

Kigotho, W., 2004, 'Silent Epidemic in Schools', *East African Standard*, 5 August: 5.

Maritim, E., 2004, First Year Orientation Address by Vice Chancellor, Egerton University.

Mutyanga, S., 2004, 'Student Mothers Face Tough Challenges at Universities', *daily Nation*, Blackboard, 5 September: 5.

Nyangena, T., 2004, Interview by author with Dean of Students, Egerton University, Laikipia Campus, 20 December.

Pease, B., and Pringle, K., eds., 2001, *A Man's World? Changing Men's Practices in a Globalized World*, New York: Palgrave.

Russell, G., 2001, 'Adopting a Global Perspective on Fatherhood', in B. Pease and K. Pringle, eds., *A Man's World?* New York: Palgrave, pp. 52–68..

Shitemi, N., 2005, 'Varsity Students Warned on "Campus Marriages"', *East African Standard*, 2 January, p. 14.

University of Nairobi, 2001–2003, *Calendar*, Nairobi University Press.

Wood, C. L., Nicholson, E. W. and Findley, D. G., 1979, *The Secondary School Principal: Manager and Supervisor*, Needham Heights, MA: Allyn & Bacon, Inc.

Zeleza, P. T. and Olukoshi, A., eds., 2004, *African Universities in the Twenty-first Century*, vol. 2: *Knowledge and Society*, Dakar: CODESRIA.

11

The Interaction of Gender and Migration Household Relations in Rural and Urban Mozambique

Inês M. Raimundo[1]

Introduction

The concept of migration has in the past been applied to two related but different indicators of population mobility: people in *movement*, and people as *movers* (Gould 1994; Oberai 1987). The concept of *movement* views migration as an event much like birth and death, while the concept of *movers* treats migration as a transition of status analogous to a change in marital or employment status (Gould 1994; Oberai 1987). It is argued that a fundamental aspect of migration is its ability to change over time (Chant 1998; Chant and Radcliff 1992). Migration is not only the consequence of unequal development, which could be the result of natural causes, such as the difference in the natural potential of different regions (Amin 1995). Migration is also in itself a part of unequal development, thus resulting in different impacts between females and males serving to reproduce or aggravate the socio-economic conditions in both sending and receiving areas (Chant 1998; Chant and Radcliff 1992).

In the decades 1980–2000, migration has became an important issue of study in respect of the increasing number of people on the move and people likely to move, particularly those who move forcibly as a result of persecution and economic instability, such as refugees and participants in the brain-drain phenomenon (Oucho 2001; Lubkemann 2000; Gould 1994; Parnwell 1993). In analysing gender migration scholars such as Dodson (2000; 2001), Gugler and Ludwar-Ene (1995) point out that relations of power and access to resources determine who moves where, when, how and why. The result is a pattern of different opportunities for migration between women and men. In terms of who has migrated in the last two decades Chant (1998) and Adepoju (1995) show an increase of women's migration from rural to urban areas and across international boundaries. This, of course, changes the traditional concept of 'migration being a male feature as a rite of passage for adult manhood' (Brydon 1989) while females were left behind and involved in reproductive activities (Chant 1998).

Dialmy[2] (2005), Kimmel (2004), Anderson and Accomando (2002) point out that different countries or societies construct a model of masculinity in which each man defines and measures himself as a man and gives the characteristics of who is a man and who is a woman. That hegemonic definition is constructed in relation to various social, economic aspects vis-à-vis women and other men. Any male who fails to conform to one of those so-called men's features is likely to be viewed as unworthy, incomplete and inferior (Dialmy 2005; Kimmel 2004). In all situations masculinity is constructed in relation to femininity and expresses the multiple ways in which gender identity is articulated through the process of power relations (Dialmy 2005; Kimmel 2004). Masculinity is an 'adaptable' and 'mobile' concept that varies according to psychological features, moral qualities, social indicators and political qualities (Dialmy 2005). It is because of that 'adaptability' that throughout generations 'new men' emerge (Gill 2001) The nature of that new man represents a shift in his attitudes in relation to the 'new' environment that has been produced by changes in the global economy and has intensified the movement of people, particularly the movement of females.

It is under this variability of the concept that I locate this chapter, including the extent that migration can be a factor that defines masculinity. The issue is: to what extent can migration be a masculine characteristic and how does female migration counteract this characteristic? Despite the growing volume of research on women's movement, there is still a lack of study focusing on the effect of the trend of men's masculinity. This study will highlight the new challenges for masculinity in the context of the increase in women's migration. It aims to discuss some of these trends of migration and the effects of some men's masculinity in Southern Mozambique.

Scope of the Study and Methodology

The study specifically aims to discuss how masculinity has been affected by the trend towards feminization of migration, and to determine to what extent the new trend of migration has affected the rural and urban household structure. It was carried out in the city of Maputo, capital of the Republic of Mozambique among adult females and adult males aged between 23 and 62 years. In individual interviews some of respondents were migrants (3) and some not (3). The collective interviews were a mix of migrants and non-migrants. The study largely focused on: a) the migration experience, b) the root linkages between migration and masculinity, c) respondents' views on the feminization of migration, and d) the impact of this feminization on men's masculinity.

Research Methodology

This study is a result of the administration of qualitative methodology comprising life histories and focus group discussions. A collection and analysis of six life histories comprised a fifty-fifty ratio and two focus groups (adult male and adult female) in the receiving area, the city of Maputo. These gave an idea of how migration has affected masculinity in both sending[3] and receiving[4] areas. The effect of the feminization of migration on men's masculinity is also discussed. This task was preceded by a review of literature on gendered migration in sub-Saharan Africa and other settings as well as literature on masculinity. The study was carried out in the neighbourhoods of Xiquelene (Urban District number IV, Maputo city) because of its concentration of the largest number of females resulting from rural–urban migration (see 1997 Census returns[5]).

The life histories focused on the migration experience, the decisions made for migration, as well as choices, vantages and constraints faced during the process of departure and integration in the receiving area. The issue of migration as a rite of passage for men was fully discussed during the focus group as well as the impact of the feminization of migration on an individual level. This data refers particularly to the changes on gender migration patterns, bearing in mind certain limitations to the study such as time constraints and limited data and literature in Mozambique. The focus group was mainly around the impact of migration within the community and the factors that impel people to move. Issues such as whether migration is a male or female feature were discussed in the target group, along with issues relating to how migration has contributed to the changing concept of masculinity. The focus group discussion was organized separately according to gender. The languages used were Portuguese (Mozambican official language) and Shangana and Ronga (national languages spoken in Maputo city).

General Pindings: Population Mobility and 'Feature' Towards a Definition of Masculinity

This study attempts to discuss population mobility as a masculine (macho) attribute by giving examples from Southern Mozambique's predominantly patrilineal society. As a socio-cultural concept, hegemonic masculinity defines the characteristics of being a 'real man'. A 'real man' can have several characteristics that define his ability to: provide food, build a good house, have a plot of land, have children, have a job, to some extent be able to provide support to more than one wife, defend the household and be the house protector (Dialmy 2005; Men's Focus Group discussion, Maputo, 22 July 2005). To what extent does migration attribute to this? How is a man seen if he does not migrate?

The population distribution by sex in the municipality of Maputo shows a gender imbalance (Table 1).

Table 1: Population Distribution by Sex in Municipal Districts according to the 1997 Census

Municipal District	Total	Male	Female
N (in thousands)	966,8	473,7	493,1
Total	100.0 (%)	100.0 (%)	100.0 (%)
I	16.0	16.4	15.6
II	16.8	16.9	16.8
III	21.8	21.7	21.8
IV	23.6	23.4	23.8
V	21.8	21.6	22.0

Source: Instituto Nacional de Estatísti, 1998.

The Instituto Nacional de Estatística (1999) explains this gender imbalance as a result of rural–urban migration. What makes women move, according to the people interviewed (Maputo, 21 July 2005), is mainly the search for employment, the pursuit of studies, the following of parents and military obligations. The trend of female concentration in the cities particularly in neighbouhood areas varies according to their social and economic status. A study of income done by Araújo on urban geography of Maputo (1999) indicates that this is the case.

Historians assert that migration is not a new phenomenon in Africa, but has occurred on a substantial scale in many instances (Aina 1995; O'Connor 1983). There are different factors that compel people to change their residences. Economic factors can be one motive that creates the need to migrate. The genesis of a migrant labour system that required large supplies of cheap labour through various techniques such as taxation, labour coercion and land alienation forced several men to move (Brown 1980). The perception of a link between migration and masculinity has its roots in the labour system (Maputo, Men's Focus Group discussion, 22 July 2005). Perhaps these men who were forced to move owing to the economic system turned this obligation into one of the elements that defined manhood (Maputo, Men's Focus Group discussion, 22 July 2005). The reason for this is mainly because of its connection to two elements: a) earning money that is used to provide family needs and b) the harsh conditions that these men were facing in those jobs (das Neves 1998; Covane 1996). '*Only men who were able to go into mine or spend several hours in the field (plantations) could support that suffering. Suffering is destined to men. Only men can afford such suffering in the mines. Only men have the superior physique'* (Maputo, Men's Focus Group discussion, 22 July 2005). This assumption has been rejected by Wright. In her analysis Wright (1995: 781) calls attention to the fact of the need to be cautious of the argument that mining is inherently male work owing to its physical demands, because women and children had gone down the mines. Empirical evidence in Mozambican history also shows that during the pre-colonial period in the Zambeze valley children and women were employed in mining (Cadernos de História de Moçambique 1980). Wright also argues that it was in the interests of African men to confine African women to the rural areas in order to benefit from their agricultural and domestic labour. This was of paramount importance for male chieftaincies struggling to manage rapid change to their best advantage. In this context women's mobility was controlled. This control was woman to woman, in the sense that women had the task of safeguarding the reputation of women who were left behind (Wright 1995); in other words they had a police-like function.

The emerging participation of African countries in the international economy, as raw material providers, led to an increase in the sexual division of labour (Todaro 2000; Chant 1998). Many men were obliged to leave their homeland in order to find paid jobs. *'Employed man is a real man'* (Maputo, Women's Focus Group discussion, 23 July 2005). Initially, women were absent in this process of migration (Wright 1995), but later in a worsening economic situation were involved in the process (see the example of Botswana). At this point a question arises: how does migration and masculinity interact? The primary focus of migration studies undertaken in Mozambique in the post-independence period is on labour migration.[6] This kind of migration was primarily connected with masculinity, especially that migration which was related to economic reasons. The focus group discussion and life histories can attest to the extent of the relationship between manhood and migration. *'My son, go to Joni[7] to be a man.'* The desire to go to *'Joni'* went beyond the colonial exigency of paying taxes because of the issue of manhood (Covane 1998). Young men were forced by society to challenge harsh mine conditions in order to gain their manhood status. Young men and adults were also attracted by friends and relatives who had returned well-dressed and carrying goods such as bicycles, motorbike, dresses, shoes, etc. However, because of long stays in *'Joni'* some of these men left behind young lonely wives and added to the wife's responsibilities. They became 'men' since they had to perform the traditional duties of men such as contracting workers to the fields and fixing houses. These men who stayed away for long periods were generally portrayed as conventional 'villains' because they left their families for long periods, and once away they married other wives, so forgetting their duties as breadwinners (see gender studies undertaken in Mozambique).

It is clear that, historically, migration in Africa has focused largely on the movement of men. In the past, in South and Southeast Asia, migrant flows have also tended to be male-dominated (Brydon 1995: 125). Nevertheless, since the 1970s, as a consequence of changes in the global economy, it has been noted that migration is no longer a male feature (Brydon 1995; Wright 1995). Patterns of migration involve those related to the changes of people from the north (Europe and America) to Africa, Asia and Latin America as well as from Asia, Africa and Latin America to northern countries, thus sharing no clear distinction of who moves in terms of social and economic stratus. However, this new economy, known as globalization, has created a shift from male migration to female migration, making migration more and more feminized (see UNDP reports of 2001, 2000). Although the data in Mozambique is not reliable, this trend is no different from what has been seen around the world (see Table 2).

Table 2: Population Distribution in the City of Maputo according to Place of Origin

Province of Origin	1980 Census			1997 Census	
	Total	Male	Female	Male	Female
Niassa	266	217	49	495	269
Cabo Delgado	447	382	65	475	329
Nampula	655	550	105	1,347	836
Zambezia	668	501	167	4,255	1,433
Tete	432	354	78	609	415
Manica	251	197	54	552	402
Sofala	773	587	186	2639	1,503
Inhambane	3,596	1,870	1,726	9,188	8,301
Gaza	6,167	2,870	3,297	5,729	6,955
Maputo province	2,907	1,290	1,617	5,466	7,224
Foreigners	303	190	113	6,567	3,726

Source: Instituto Nacional de Estatística, 1999; Direcção Nacional de Estatística, 1981.

The census of 1980 demonstrates that the Gaza and Inhambane provinces in Southern Mozambique represent the majority of migrants within the city. The data reveals the trend of rural–urban migration that started during the colonial period and gained more impetus with the increase of political instability in the late 1980s and the beginning of 1990s (Raimundo 2002; Araújo 1999; Muanamoha

1999). To a lesser extent, Northern provinces such as Cabo Delgado, Nampula and Zambezia have their citizens represented in the city. However, excepting for Cabo Delgado and Niassa provinces, the 1997 census shows an increase of population from the other provinces, led by Inhambane followed by Gaza, Maputo province and Zambezia (central region). What has caused the relative decline of population from Gaza to Maputo, or the rapid increase of people from Inhambane and Zambezia provinces is still unclear. People had to flee to secure areas, which are mainly urban, although some literature (Araújo 1999; Muanamoha 1999) points out the intensification of the armed attacks in these provinces during the civil war as the main factor of the rural–urban move. However, Knauder (2000) argues against using civil war as a factor to explain the rural–urban shift, referring instead to countries like Zambia, which experienced a rapid population growth in their cities, but not during the colonial period or in a civil war.

Brydon (1989) emphasizes the fact that the literature on women's migration has shown that most women have moved on their own initiative, without husbands. In many of the provinces where such women's migration is increasing, this change is associated with occupational roles for women in the urban economy, such as being house-workers. What makes the difference between women and men in this context of migration? Smith (1994) says that women are forced to flee poverty and patriarchal custom, and some migrate to accumulate the capital needed to set up independent households. In the meantime, Brydon (1995:128) shows that recent empirical studies on African women migrants indicate that women move for the same reason as men, namely to look for work. To my mind, however, it is necessary to know the differences between a young, unmarried or married woman deciding to go by herself to a city. To ordinary people such migration is linked to misbehaviour (prostitution and an easy life). Nevertheless, it is not clear how this movement of women has changed the relationship with men as traditional migrants. Also, it is not clear to what extent it has affected men's perception of their masculinity.

Even though there is a paucity of data, there are some observable impacts of feminization of migration on masculinity. Firstly, men interviewed said that '*because of the policy of woman's emancipation introduced by FRELIMO[6] in Mozambique after independence many things have changed. It is not surprising to have women migrating. What do we feel is not the feminization of migration per se, but the fact of women taking our traditional household duty such as feeding the family*' (Maputo, Men's Focus Group discussion, 22 July 2005). Beyond this affirmation there is a sense of inferiority showed by men. Secondly, '*What is important is not feminization of migration, but who can earn some money to feed the family. The cost of living has increased. Who can actually afford to pay school fees and guarantee food at home? In rural areas where we came from agriculture is no longer profitable and there is lack of rain and there are no jobs there*' (Maputo, Men's Focus Group discussion, 22 July 2005). Although it was not clear during the interviews, the assumption is that this 'new man' (who has been 'overthrown' in his traditional duties) in a subtle way uses strategies to hide the fact of being fed by a woman. This new man had two 'houses' or possessed two wives at home: one for traditional duties, classified as a 'normal' (as they classify) woman and the other to search for subsistence such as crossing borders as a cross-border trader.

The remarkable increases in the proportion of young single women in certain migrant streams were slow to be detected, and even now the dimensions and implications of these changes are poorly understood. Patterns of female migration are both a reflection and cause of some of the major social and economic transformations taking place in developing countries, particularly in Asia. Fawcett *et al.* (1984: 6), quoting Thadani and Todaro (1984), underline marriage as a factor of migration. They argue that marriage is a major avenue of upward social mobility for women, which may imply moving to an urban area in search of a higher-status husband. Large-scale migration of women to urban areas is not entirely a recent phenomenon, nor is it equally common in all parts of the world (Smith *et al.* 1984:16; see also data from the INE 1999). Smith *et al.* (1984) suggest that women in a European society were primarily short-distance migrants moving within the same province or country, usually because of marriage or in response to the demand for domestic servants in the cities. Men, by contrast, travelled longer distances, usually in search of better labour markets. Although most African migrants are male, there has been a shift in the gender composition of migration in recent years (Dodson 2001 and 2000; Ulick and Crush 2000). It is suggested that in Africa migration from village to city offers women an escape (Dodson 2001; Gugler and Ludwar-Ene 1995). There is an escape from a traditionally prescribed status, obedience to male kinsmen amd exceedingly hard work; the customary sanctions against unmarried mothers; and divorced women running away from unhappy conditions of life, and broken or barren marriages of young girls, usually from poor families. These women come to the city as live-in maids or babysitters (Chant 1998; Chant and Radcliff 1992).

Mozambique, like many other developing countries, has been impacted negatively by global economic changes. The rate of unemployment has increased (see UNDP reports of 2001, 2000, 1998). The situation deteriorated during the late 1970s when after independence the then government closed the borders with Southern Rhodesia (Zimbabwe) and South Africa decreed sanctions against Mozambique (Hanlon 1986). The consequence was a reduction of the recruitment of workers to the mines of Southern Mozambique with the consequent increase of unemployment (see UNDP 1998; Hanlon 1986).

It is a fact that civil war, besides displacing people and creating refugees, impacted negatively on the economy because the target was the family field and the total social and economic infrastructure, of schools, bridges, hospitals, railways, etc. (Hanlon 1986). Indeed, millions of people in Mozambique were driven from their homes in the political instability (Raimundo 2002; Lubkemann 2000; Hanlon 1986). The failure of the rural economy, mostly engaged in large-scale agriculture, to create sufficient employment opportunities in the rural areas as well as the failure of the villagization programmes,[9] contributed largely to a lack of jobs and unemployment (UNDP, 2001, 2000; Raimundo 2002; Hanlon 1986). Dialmy and Mouiche (2005)[10] argue that these transformations on the economy have produced a 'new man',who is male, but unemployed and fails to fulfil his traditional household obligations. According to people interviewed, the 'new man' is not a conventional male, but a female who now wears her husband's trousers: *'Due to her better ability to feed the family she becomes a man'* (Maputo, Men's Focus Group discussion, 22 July 2005). This new migrant, called 'woman-masculinized' in the common assertion that she feeds the family, is seen in the cities working as a house-maid or civil servants, or is involved in different spheres of the economy in an entrepreneurial form. As entrepreneurs they succeed in delivering products such as groceries, meat, vegetables, furniture, fruit, alcohol, etc. to the city of Maputo. They control the biggest informal markets of alcohol, vegetables, fruit and clothing alongside the markets of Malanga, Estrela Vermelha, Xipamanine, Xiquelene, Museu and Vulcano (Maputo, Women's Focus Group discussion, 23 July 2005). They are commonly known in Southern Mozambique as *'Mukheristas'*.[11] This situation provides important pointers for studies that include a gender perspective in order to help understand the structure of gendered relationship differences in the migration context.

Analyses of migration have been based almost entirely on information gathered from male migrants (Chant 1992; Chant and Radcliff 1992; Thadani and Todaro 1984). However, women represent a growing proportion of internal migrants in Africa, many of whom crossed borders and fled from socio-economic and political persecution (Lubkemann 2000; Gugler and Ludwar-Ene 1995; Thadani and Todaro 1984). In addition, when women migrate with their families as either parent or spouse they are assumed to be merely accompanying the primary migrant. However, most explanations of this increased momentum of female migration are related to family migration – the associational migration of wives or daughters accompanying the primary male migrant – or, in the case of unattached female migration, the existence of economic and employment opportunities in the urban areas (Thadani and Todaro 1984:38). When women reach the cities they are primarily engaged in domestic activities (Chant 1998; Gugler and Ludwar-Ene 1995; Thadani and Todaro 1984; Brown 1980).

The present contribution seeks to open up new ways of thinking about migration issues in Mozambique in terms of the interaction of gender and migration and the impact on changes in masculinity, based on migration as being a rite of passage to manhood. The reasons, motives and aims of migration need to be taken into account in order to understand how migrants are able to accept the often-severe conditions in the host area and how the phenomenon has impacted on masculine and feminine status in both sending and receiving areas.

Gendered approaches are pertinent to migration studies since women as well as men have been migrating to the cities in Mozambique and even to neighbouring countries such as South Africa, Zimbabwe and Swaziland. It is important that these studies focus on understanding the dynamic related to the changes that migration creates within the economy, the household structure and the variables of certain concepts in the light of new trends.

Migration in Mozambique: A Path to Manhood? Who Should Follow Whom?

As discussed earlier, masculinity in Africa is socially constructed and is fluid over time and different settings. To attain manhood in Africa is to achieve some level of financial independence, employment or a certain income in order to fulfil household needs. Relevant research (Kimmel 2004; Byron 2002; Gill 2001) and the author's fieldwork undertaken in the city of Maputo show that to become a man one has to have the following characteristics: be married with children, have a family to care for, be able to fulfil household needs, have enough money to get married, acquire employment, have access to land and support an extended family. *'Men's recognition and their sense of manhood suffer when they lack work or fail to feed the family'* (Maputo, Women's Focus Group discussion, 23 July 2005). I will discuss this topic through the following question: how is the creation of masculinity linked with migration? If migration is seen as the rite of passage, as a means of earning a living for a man who does not migrate, does it mean that his masculinity is useless? Women interviewed affirm that *'a man who is not a migrant is because his mother put him in a bottle because she is not interested to have her beloved away from her'* (Maputo, Women's Focus Group discussion, Maputo, 22 July 2005). One conclusion to be inferred from this is that women are not comfortable in these changes of role in the migration process. Beyond this there is a woman, his mother, who does 'not allow' the son to be away from her. To this extent it is not a matter of the change in the economy, but the fictitious prohibition from the mother.

Migration has been found to respond to rural–urban differences of expected income rather than actual earnings (Amin 1995). Migration, as Todaro (2000), Amin (1995) and Ricca (1989) point out, exacerbates the rural–urban structural imbalances in two major ways. First, on the supply side, internal migration disproportionately increases the growth rate of urban job seekers relative to urban population growth, which itself is at an historically unprecedented high level because of the high proportion of young people who dominate the migrant stream. Second, on the demand side, urban job creation is more difficult and costly to accomplish than rural employment creation. The reason is because of the need for substantial complementary resource input in most modern industrial jobs.

Todaro (2000) asserts that the effect of the migration process is more pervasive than its obvious accentuation of urban unemployment and underemployment. Lubkemann (2000) points out that migration in the case of Mozambique has resulted in a change in definition of the rights and obligations of social relations and in the distribution of power within social networks.

Migration, according to geographers, implies a change of residence. Thus, traditionally a woman migrates when she follows the husband, and thus marriage becomes a factor of migration (Thadani and Todaro 1984). Although I do not have substantial empirical data I would like to draw attention to the political situation of ministers in Mozambique. If we look at the women who constituted the new government of 2005, it is clear that the issue of not having a husband following a wife was taken into account. Except for the Minister of Labour, who came from Northern Mozambique, the remaining women ministers have been living in the city of Maputo for years. The media do not consider women, but the 'Guebuza's[12] men' (*Savana*[13] February 2005). There is still a sense that ministers' positions belong to men. There are 26 ministers including the Prime Minister (a woman) and 15 deputy ministers; 11 of these (27%) are women (seven ministers and four deputy ministers). In terms of governors among the 11 provinces two are women. These are the governors of Maputo city and Maputo province, meaning that these women did not have a need to move with their husbands because they lived in the capital or close to it. In contrast, some of these new governors have wives who used to hold higher political and economic positions and lived in the city of Maputo. Perhaps this fact attests to something akin to the sense of masculinity emerging during the constitution of the government. Also, it is still unthinkable to have a husband following a wife who is politically empowered without also giving him some power (as in the case of the Mozambican ambassadors of France and European Union). It seems that only a woman should follow or be attached to a man.

From Men's Migration As Rite of Passage to Women's Migration as a Survival Strategy

Historically, migration in Africa has been largely a matter of men moving in order to fulfil household's needs, as a result of the impact of colonization and capitalism that created migration and spatial differences in employment opportunities. A man is expected to take care of the family as the breadwinner. The gains from his current place of work are used to build houses, buy food, pay school fees, buy land, cattle, etc. The man who does not migrate or has never experienced migration is not a man (Maputo, Men's Focus Group discussion, 22 July 2005). People interviewed asserted that migration for a man is a rite of passage for male adulthood. It is through migration that man matures quickly. A man's migration serves to show his masculinity because he is able to provide food and fulfil his household needs and is able to face harsh conditions. Migration has impacted on women since she has become forced to become head of the household and has to carry out all houses duties, but with limited decision-making and long periods of loneliness owing to the absences of her husband. Some examples can be found on the following life history:

> Clementina Muchanga was born in 1959 in Chibuto, Gaza province. Her household is made up of seven people. The head of the household is her husband who is a mineworker in South Africa. He has been away for twelve years. Clementina's family settled in Maputo city in 1982 because of RENAMO's[14] armed attacks. Although her husband has been away for a long time Clementina still waits for his instructions concerning the day-to-day running of family affairs. This has made Clementina's life somewhat difficult in terms of being able to go out and pursue an economic livelihood for her family back home. Because of cultural beliefs that do not permit her to make any decision without her husband's consent, she cannot go anywhere. In the city of Maputo she is involved in small business (Maputo, 20 July 2005).

For the people interviewed (both men and women) a long migration was linked with masculinity.

> Abílio was born in 1943 in Inhambane province (Southern Mozambique). He is a former mine labourer in South Africa and is now involved in carpentry to support his family of ten people. Two of his unmarried daughters have lived in Johannesburg since 1995 and they left their children with him. However, Abilio has three sons who still live with him and are not able to get a decent job. Abílio feels ashamed of these sons because instead of them going to Johannesburg as the sisters did they only know how to get young girls pregnant and leave the children in his care. *'My sons still children because they are not migrating to the mines as the sisters did. What kind of men do I have?*Abílio asked (Maputo, 21 July 2005).

The empirical evidence to attest this assumption is insufficient to reach precise conclusions on the issue. However, it is still of some significance to have a boy or a young adult who goes to the mines either on a temporary or a permanent basis to prove his masculinity. It is a shame if some males do not leave their place of origin, as Abílio said. Some women's life histories will clarify to what extent they had to 'overthrow' their male counterparts in the process of migration. Women who migrate can tell how difficult life is in rural areas and why they decide to move independently. Surely this freedom of movement constitutes a new feature, which to some extent has impacted on men's masculinity since they stay at home and no longer 'obey; the saying 'here you are not a man unless you travel to the city'. Nowadays, although it is against the social norms (Maputo, Men's and Women's Focus Group discussions, July 2005), women can decide to move in response to specific pressures and can leave their place of origin without needing the consent of the man's family. This situation seems to be new in Mozambique although it has been common in Latin America and Asia for years (Chant 1998).

> Clara Matsimbe, born in 1960 in Maqueze, Gaza province (Southern Mozambique), is a mother of two children (she had eight children, but six of them died), She decided to move to the city of Maputo because she was abandoned by her former husband. The reason for that was a belief among the husband's relatives that she is bewitched because she 'ate' her own children. As an unskilled woman Clara decided to run some businesses. Initially she worked for a former neighbour in Maqueze. For about three years Clara was dependent on a friend of hers. From 2001 she started to settle up her business, which was selling second-hand clothing. Even though it is not a profitable business, she says she can afford to feed the two living children (now seventeen and fifteen years) and the parents who she left at home (Maputo, 20 July 2005).

Another example came from Alegria (year of birth unknown), a peanut vendor in the streets of Maputo.

> Alegria fled from her homeland (Inhambane province) and from her family because her husband went to South Africa for five years and she had not received news from him. She does not feel sorry for leaving her son because she had to feed the family and look for more opportunities in the big city. Alegria knows that in her community of origin her name is connected with misbehaviour (an easy life) and prostitution but she does not care because she now has her own life (Maputo, 20 July 2005).

The literature has emphasized the issue of men's migration as being a particular rite of passage. However, with the impact of the global economy, the independence of Mozambique and the subsequent policy of women's emancipation, it seems that women's migration is no longer a social crime, and neither can migration be a rite of passage. Migration is a survival strategy for women (Raimundo 2002) as shown through the involvement of women in the informal economy and their success as entrepreneurs. Migration used to be a man's road to masculinity, and the man who failed to fit into this framework was not considered macho.

Feminization of Migration and Impact on Family and Men's Masculinity

This section discusses the impact of the feminization of migration on men's masculinity and on the family. In the absence of giving women their identity in the family and their traditional role as family caregivers this new form of migration tends to affect the family children as well as the men's domain (Maputo, Men's

Focus Group discussion, 22 July 2005) and to a lesser extent men's masculinity (Maputo life history, 20 July 2005). The migration of women, especially mothers, has impacted negatively on the school performance of their children. Their husbands do not perform well in their duties as mothers because *'the task after the family belongs to women. Allowing a wife or married woman to migrate is the same as being a widower'* (Maputo, Men's Focus Group discussion, 22 July 2005), and it is unthinkable to have a man following his wife because they are not 'baskets'. However, in the women's focus group discussion it was argued that although it was recognised that a feature of the man's identity was feeding the family, the women had to do so because of economic constraints. Women do not feel that they are taking a man's characteristics or are wearing the trousers, as men say.

> Nowadays what is important is to have someone who can feed the family. Being women we have duties toward our children. Men do not care if they abandon their family, especially children. We women are really concerned for our children. We have to move in order to find something to feed them. We work hard for the money. For that we have to move because in the rural area there is no way of getting money (Maputo, Women's Focus Group discussion, 23 July 2005).

One married man had to follow his wife from the city of Beira (Sofala province) because he had a precarious contract job in his place of origin. Because the wife got a well-paid job in the city of Maputo he had no choice but to follow her. He did not feel 'naked' in his masculinity.

> It was not the case since the decision came from within ourselves. The decision for migration depends on the contractual situation of each one of us. It is good to migrate when you have the guarantee of job or a long contract. It does not matter who gets a job, a woman or a man. It all depends on the opportunities. I feel that masculinity is not defined according to the tasks given by societies for men or women. This definition must change once we are facing changes in the economy that forces everybody to be involved in a paid job' (Maputo, individual interview with a male, 20 July 2005).

However, this interviewee (who did not want his name quoted) emphasized the fact that it depends on economic situation of the husband. If he gets a secure job it is quite hard to follow the wife.

> In terms of an unmarried or abandoned women there is no way of preventing them to migrate since they become "men" once they become breadwinners. I do not think that society can condemn them because of this, although in the recent past migrant women were linked with things such as prostitution and mental illness (Maputo, individual interview with a male, 20 July 2005).

Conclusion

This study has attempted to show that men's migration can be used as a feature of masculinity. However, that migration in Mozambique as well as in other African countries has impacted on women at home (in her place of origin) by adding to her roles traditional duties that were previously performed by men, such as managing household finances and supervising labour in the family field. For years migration was considered and reserved for men since it was the way to gain money to cope with household duties. Colonialism and capitalism exacerbated the imbalances between rural and urban areas, impelling people to move. The colonial system created a need for a cheaper labour force. It was under colonization and capitalism that the issue of manhood gained a certain importance. There was the sense in Southern Mozambique that the only one able to migrate was a man, and only the male had the duty of feeding the family. However, led by changes in the global economy by the late 1970s trends of migration have changed over subsequent decades. Recent empirical evidence from a variety of settings tends to show an increase in the independent migration of rural women to urban areas. Mozambique, as a country in Southern Africa, is no exception. Urban growth in Mozambique, fuelled by rural–urban migration, has been one of the fastest in the region. However, very little systematic research has been conducted on rural–urban migration in Mozambique, and specifically on the gender patterns of that migration. The literature on migration that exists emphasizes the role of men as breadwinners, and little research has been done in terms of the growing number of females who have 'overcome' men as traditional migrants and on how this relates to men being macho within the household. By focusing on a rural and urban area, this study has attempted to discuss how women's migration affects men's masculinity, and concludes that nowadays migration cannot be used as a rite of passage because of the increase of females in the process, either as having manhood features because of the high rates of unemployment, or having no need to differentiate between who should or not migrate. Only specific opportunities can determine who should or should not migrate.

Notes

1. Address for correspondence: Eduardo Mondlane University, Faculty of Arts, Department of Geography, P.O. Box 257, Maputo, Mozambique. E-mail: inesmacamo@yahoo.co.uk
2. 'De la Masculinite en Afrique du Nord' and 'The Masculine Representation of Masculinity in Morocco'. Unpublished papers presented at 2005 CODESRIA Gender Institute on Contemporary Masculinity in Africa, Dakar, June–July 2005 (the translation from French into English it is my own).
3. Sending or departure is the area where migrants are from.
4. Receiving or arrival is the area where migrants go or the destination.
5. Recent census population results undertaken in the Republic of Mozambique after independence.

6. Mozambique attained independence on 25 June 1975.
7. The nickname that people of Southern Mozambique call the city of Johannesburg, South Africa.
8. Frente de Libertação de Moçambique (Mozambican Front Liberation). The government party that has been ruling the country since 1975.
9. Communal villages.
10. 'L'Etat Moderne Africain et le Patriarcat Public'. Unpublished paper presented at 2005 CODESRIA Gender Institute on Contemporary Masculinity in Africa, Dakar, June–July 2005.
11. Mukhero woman or woman. This name came from a corrupted English phrase, 'May you carry me this bag?' which in the Shangana and Ronga national languages spoken in Maputo and Gaza provinces, Southern Mozambique sounds like 'Mukherro' (Sadaca Novela, President of Mukhero Association, 2 August 2005).
12. The elected president of Mozambique (December 2004).
13. A weekly Mozambican newspaper.
14. Resistência Nacional de Moçambique (Mozambican National Resistance). A guerrilla movement that for sixteen years (1976–1992) fought against the FRELIMO government.

References

Adepoju, A., 1995, 'Migration in Africa', in J. Baker and T. A. Aina, eds., *The Migration Experience in Africa*, Uppsala: Nordiska Afrikainstitutet, pp. 87–108.

Aina, T. A., 1995, 'Internal Non-Metropolitan Migration and the Development Process in Africa', in J. Baker and T. A. Aina, eds.. *The Migration Experience in Africa,* Uppsala: Nordiska Afrikainstitutet, pp.41–53.

Anderson, K. J. and Accomando, C., 2002, 'Real Boys? Manufacturing Masculinity and Erasing Privilege in Popular Books on Raising Boys', *Feminism and Psychology*, (SAGE, London), Vol. 12, No. 4, pp. 491–516.

Araújo, M. G. M., 1999, 'Cidade de Maputo, Espaços Contrastantes: Do Urbano ao Rural'. *Finisterra*, Vol. XXXIV, No. 67–68, pp. 175–90.

Brown, B. B., 1980, 'The Impact of Male Labour Migration on Women in Botswana', *South African Labour Bulletin*, Vol. 6, No. 4.

Brown, L. A. and Sanders, R. L., 1981, 'Toward a Development Paradigm of Migration, with particular reference to Third World Settings'. In *Migration Decision-making: Multidisciplinary Approaches to Microlevel Studies in Developed and Developing Countries*, New York: Center for Cultural and Technical Interchange between East and West, Inc., pp. 149–85.

Brydon, L., 1989, 'Gender and Migration'. *In Women in The Third World: Gender Issues in Rural and Urban Areas,* Edward Elgar Publishing, Aldershot, pp. 121–33.

Brydon, L., 1995, 'Gender and Migration', in *Women in the Third World: Gender and Household in Rural and Urban Areas,* Edward Elgar Publishing, Aldershot, pp. 121–33.

Byron, E., 2002, 'Detasseling. A Midwest Rite of Passage, Faces Extinction', www.migration.ucdavis.adu /rmn/more.plp

Cadernos de História de Moçambique, 1980, Universidade Eduardo Mondlane, Maputo.

Chant, S., 1991, *Women and Survival in Mexican Cities: Perspectives on Gender Labour Markets and Low-income Households,* London: Manchester University Press.

Chant, S., 1992, 'Migration at the Margins: Gender, Poverty and Population Movement on the Costa Rica Periphery', in S. Chant, ed., *Gender and Migration in Developing Countries.* London: Belhaven Press.

Chant, S., 1998, *Households, Gender and Rural–Urban Migration: Reflections on Linkages and Considerations for Policy*, London University Press.

Chant, S. and Radcliff, S. A., 1992, 'Migration and Development: The Importance of Gender', in S. Chant, ed., *Gender and Migration in Developing Countries*, London: Belhaven Press.

Covane, L. A., 1996, 'Migrant Labour and Agriculture in Southern Mozambique with Especial Reference to Lower Limpopo Valley, 1920–1992'. Unpublished PhD dissertation, Institute of Commonwealth Studies, University of London.

Das Neves, J. M., 1998, 'Economy, Society and Labour Migration in Central Mozambique, 1930–c. 1965: A Case Study of Manica Province'. Unpublished PhD dissertation, School of Oriental and African Studies, University of London.

De Vletter, F., 1998, *Sons of Mozambique: Mozambican Miners and Post-Apartheid South Africa*, Migration Policy Series No. 8. Southern African Migration Project. Cape Town.

De Vletter, F., 2000, 'Labour Migration in South Africa: The Lifeblood for Southern Mozambique', in David A. MacDonald, ed., O*n Borders: Perspectives on International Migration in Southern Africa*, New York: St Martin's Press, pp. 46–70.

Dialmy, A., 2005, 'De la Masculinité en Afrique du Nord'. Unpublished paper presented at 2005 CODESRIA Gender Institute on Contemporary Masculinity in Africa, Dakar, June–July

Direcção Nacional de Estatística, 1981, *Resultados do Recenseamento Gerald a População*, Maputo

Dodson, B., 2000, 'Women on the Move: Gender and Cross-border Migration to South Africa from Lesotho, Mozambique and Zimbabwe', in David A. MacDonald, ed., O*n Borders: Perspectives on International Migration in Southern Africa*, New York: St Martin's Press, pp. 119–47.

Dodson, B., 2001, '"Discrimination by Default?" Gender Concerns in South African Migration Policy', *Africa Today,* Vol. 48, No. 3, pp. *73–90*.

Fawcett, J. *et al.*, 1984, 'Urbanization, Migration, and the Status of Women', in James Fawcett, Siew-Ean Khoo and Peter C. Smith, eds., *Women in the Cities of Asia: Migration and Urban Adaptation*, Boulder, CO: Westview, pp. 3–35.

Gill, R., 2001, *Rethinking Masculinity: Men and their Bodies*, London School of Economics and Political Science.

Gould, W. T. S., 1995, 'Migration and Recent Economic and Environmental Change in East Africa', in J. Baker and T. A. Aina, eds., *The Migration Experience in Africa,* Uppsala: Nordiska Afrikainstitutet, pp. 122–48.

Gugler, J. and Ludwar-Ene, G., 1995, 'Gender and Migration in Africa South of the Sahara', in J. Baker and T. A. Aina, eds., *The Migration Experience in Africa*. Uppsala: Nordiska Afrikainstituitet, pp. 257–68.

Hanlon, J., 1986, *Beggar your Neighbours – Apartheid Power in Southern Africa*, London: Catholic Institute for International Relations; Oxford: James Currey; Bloomington: Indiana University Press.

INE, 1999, *II Recenseamento Geral da População e Habitação, 1997: Resultados Definitivos*, Maputo.

Kimmel, M., 2004, 'Global Masculinities: Restoration and Resistance', in *Gender Policy Review*, www.ucm.es/into/rqtr/biblioetca/masculinidade/Global % 20masculinity.pdf

Knauder, S., 2000, *Globalisation, Urban Progress, Urban Problems, Rural Disadvantages – Evidence from Mozambique, Aldershot:* Ashgate.

Lubkemann, S., 2000, 'Situating Wartime Migration in Central Mozambique: Gendered Social Struggle and the Transnationalization of Polygyny', Unpublished PhD dissertation, Brown University.

Mouiche, I., 2005, L'Etat modern africain et le patriarcat public'. Unpublished paper presented at 2005 CODESRIA Gender Institute on Contemporary Masculinity in Africa, Dakar, June–July.

Muanamoha, R. C., 2000, 'Dinâmica do crescimento populacional no período pós-independência em Maputo',in Jochen Oppenheimer and Isabel Raposo, eds., *Urbanização acelerada em Luanda e Maputo: Impacto da Guerra e das transformações sócio-económicas (décadas de '80 e 90'), textos para discussão*, Lisboa, pp. 11–19.

Oberai, A. S., 1987, *'Migration, Urbanisation and Development'*, Paper 5, Geneva: International Labour Organization.

O'Connor, A., 1983, *The African City*, London: Hutchinson.

Oucho, J., 2001, 'Does Migration Foster or Stifle Development? Inaugural lecture delivered at the University of Botswana, Gaborone, October.

Parnwell, M., 1993, *Population Movements and the Third World*, London: Routledge.

Raimundo, I. M., 2002, 'From Civil War to Floods: Implications for Internal Migration in Gaza Province'. Unpublished MA dissertation, University of the Witwatersrand, Johannesburg.

Ricca, S., 1989, *International Migration in Africa: Legal and Administrative Aspects*, Geneva: International Labour Organization.

Savana, 2005, 'Os Homens de Guebuza'. *17 de Fevereiro de 2005*, No. 1.

Smith, P., *et al.*, 1984, 'The Migration of Women to Cities: A Comparative Perspective', in James Fawcett, Siew-Ean Khoo and Peter C. Smith, eds., *Women in the Cities of Asia: Migration and Urban Adaptation*, Boulder, CO: Westview, pp. 15–35.

Thadani, V.N. and Todaro, M., 1984, 'Female Migration: A Conceptual Framework', in James Fawcett, Siew-Ean Khoo and Peter C. Smith, eds., *Women in the Cities of Asia: Migration and Urban Adaptation*, Boulder, CO: Westview, pp. 36–59.

Todaro, M., 1976, *Internal Migration in Developing Countries: A Review of Theory, Evidence, Methodology and Research Priorities*, Geneva: International Labour Organization.

Todaro, M. 2000, *Economic Development*, New York: Addison-Wesley Longman.

Ulick, T. and Crush, J., 2000, 'Gender, Farmwork and Women's Migration from Lesotho to the New South Africa', *Canadian Journal of African Studies*, Vol. 34, No. 1.

UNDP, 1998, *Mozambique: Peace and Economic Growth – Opportunities for Human Development*, Maputo.

UNDP, 1999, *Mozambique: Economic Growth and Human Development. Progress, Obstacles and Challenges*, Maputo.

UNDP, 2000, *Education and Human Development: Trajectory, Lessons and Challenge for the 21st Century*, Maputo.

UNDP, 2001, *Mozambique: Gender, Women and Human Development: An Agenda for the Future*, Maputo.

Wright, C., 1995, 'Gender Awareness in Migration Theory: Synthesizing Actor and Structure in Southern Africa', *Development and Change*, Vol. 26, No, 4, pp. 771–92.

12

'Lifting the Cloak on Manhood' Coverage of Xhosa Male Circumcision in the South African Press

Lilian N. Ndangam

Introduction

> In South Africa's liberal and non-racial society, black Africans need to decide whether black traditional customs, such as circumcision – and cultural practices as a whole – remain a critical hallmark to being African.

> Sicelo Fayo, *The Herald*, 12 January 2005

Periods of change such as the post-apartheid dispensation in South Africa offer the possibility of marginalized discourses to gain influence (Epstein 1998). For Epstein (1998), the formation of new versions of masculinity is a key part of reshaping post-apartheid South Africa. However, as the above quotation illustrates, the initiation rite performed by some black ethnic groups is not only evidence of how marginalized masculinities in South Africa have been and are being (re)constituted. Aspects of Black African masculinities have emerged as a site where the anxieties, insecurities and uncertainties about the post-apartheid socio-political transformation in South Africa are projected, negotiated and defended.[1] As a source of information for many people, media coverage of this ritual serves as a useful site where particular cultural definition of masculinity (Craig 1992) in contemporary South Africa can be understood and analysed.

As part of the 2004 National Arts Festival (NAF) in Grahamstown, South Africa, an exhibition called 'Initiation as a Rite of Passage' by artists Thembinkosi Goniwe and Churchill Madikida used photographs, video and songs to explore the subject of male circumcision and initiation ceremonies. The exhibition displayed photographs of young initiates wrapped in white blankets, with their faces painted in white clay and standing next to an initiation hut. A more graphic illustration at the exhibition included a portrait of a naked man with blood around his genitalia. Other aspects of the exhibition included outfits worn by initiates during and after the ceremony, objects used during initiation ceremonies, and artefacts from different parts of Africa where male initiation is practised.

This public display of a rite of passage often shrouded in secrecy became a source of controversy during the festival, provoking media coverage and intense public debate about the initiation ritual for young Xhosa boys. For some, public display of the practice broke a taboo on the secrecy of the ritual, which is not supposed to be seen by women and children. Xhosa traditional leaders felt the exhibition undermined the secrecy and symbolic meaning of the rite, while some parents thought it could potentially scare children from undergoing the rite. Interestingly, Thembinkosi Goniwe has recently defended his work as a critical reflection of media intrusion into the private and sacred aspects of the ritual, which has turned these into both a spectacle and a consumable (Goniwe 2005).

In addition to the comments pages of the guest book accompanying the exhibition, varied opinions about the exhibition were expressed in the local, provincial and national media. Subsequent media coverage of initiation – what columnist Jimmy Matyu describes as 'a sensitive "annual debate" on circumcision' – has variously reported on deaths in initiation schools, forced and botched circumcisions, and efforts to regulate the practice. Both the debate over the NAF exhibition and subsequent coverage are indicative of an ongoing public debate about the practice of initiation by some of South Africa's ethnic groups. The discursive representation of this ritual in the South African media offers an interesting opportunity to explore the constitution and reinterpretations of masculinity within popular discourse.

As significant sources of information and knowledge, newspapers are epistemological sites where, among other things, insights on gender, gender identities and gender relations can be garnered (Taylor and Sunderland 2003). Scholarship on masculinity and the media has documented how men are represented in sports (Sabo and Jansen 1992; Trujillo, 1991), advertising (Barthel 1992; Strate 1992), crime (Consalvo 2003) and lifestyle magazines.[2] While these studies provide valuable insight and contribute to theoretical discussion on the links between media representation and cultural meanings of masculinity, they largely focus on masculinity in America and Europe, with little systematic attention paid to representations of black African masculinity in the media.

Based on coverage in two regional daily publications, this study outlines the media story of Xhosa initiation ceremonies so far. Within that analysis, it discusses the representation of masculinity that emanates from this mediated gaze on the black African male body. This study argues that the public discourse on initiation is one arena where the complexities of change and transformation in post-apartheid South Africa are played out. Analysing the representation of men in various media texts and genres is not only important in understanding how masculinity is defined in the media but is significant in developing theoretical insights about 'the relationship between these sites and gender, the gender order, the cultural differences, identity and identification, the subject, experience, and reality in late capitalism' (Hanke 1998: 183). Regrettably, this sphere of analysis has not received consistent attention in African scholarship, given the social sciences' bias for data obtained from first-hand observation. This notwithstanding, it should be emphasized that the ways in which masculinities are conceptualized, articulated and debated in the media have crucial implications for the ongoing struggles for gender equality in South Africa. An analysis of media coverage of initiation ceremonies, therefore, offers insights into the patterns of contemporary projections of aspects of black African masculinity and the modes in which these masculinities express themselves.

The study is divided into three sections. First, a brief overview of the circumcision ritual – *ulwaluko* – is provided in order to locate its significance within Xhosa culture. The analysis draws on insights from cultural theory and masculinity studies that have used the concept of 'the gaze' to articulate modes of power and regulation in discourse and social relations. Of importance is the view of the body as a site where meanings of being masculine are constantly being ascribed, contested and validated (Ervo and Johansson 2003; Flannigan-Saint-Aubin 1994; Siedler 2003; Tuana *et al.* 2002). Specifically in the case of South Africa, where initiation ceremonies are culturally specific to certain black ethnic groups, press reporting is implicitly a gaze on black African masculinity.

Circumcision and Initiation

For the past two decades, female genital cutting has come under intense scrutiny from feminist scholarship, international media and gender activism. The discourse often dominated by 'anti-female genital mutilation' (FGM)[3] perspectives is itself fraught with tensions between those who condemn the practice as barbaric and oppressive to women and those who assume a cultural relativist position that calls for an appreciation of the cultural relevance and specificity of the practice (for more on this debate, see *Feminist Theory (2004)*, Vol. 5, No. 3). Male circumcision and discourses surrounding it have received far less attention. This relative inattention is perhaps indicative of a culturally sanctioned secrecy and normality surrounding the ritual in many societies where it is practised. This secrecy notwithstanding, anthropological studies and literary texts have documented the processes and meanings of the rite in different cultures.

Traditional circumcision (*ulwaluko*) is widely practised among the Xhosa who occupy the Eastern Cape Province of South Africa. For the Xhosas and many other ethnic groups that practise it, the initiation rite is an essential component of the transition to adulthood. It entails groups of male children between the ages of 15 and 25 undergoing a period of seclusion 'in the bush' together (Meintjes 1998).[4] The initiation season in the Eastern Cape variously takes place in June/July and November/December, each year. Meintjes (1998: 7) notes that initiation 'was traditionally regarded as an educational institution where initiates were taught about courtship, negotiating marriage and social responsibilities and conduct'. Circumcision entails the surgical removal of the foreskin of the penis. In Jewish and Muslim societies, this usually takes place a day or seven days after the birth of the male child. However, for the Xhosa and many other African societies, circumcision is part of a series of rituals that make up the rite of passage for adolescent boys. While the removal of the prepuce is the central part of this rite, initiation refers to the series of rituals that precede and follow this.[5] These rituals include the seclusion period and the coming-out ceremony to mark the return of the initiates.[6] Meintjes (1998) notes that during the seclusion period, initiates' diet and fluid intake are restricted for the first eight days. Initiates are not allowed to drink water, and only hard food is consumed (Ngxamngxa 1971). Other restrictions imposed on initiates during seclusion include not quarrelling or speaking ill of others (Schweiger 1914, cited in Ngxamngxa 1971) and not contacting married women (Meintjes 1998). The cutting of the prepuce (done without an-aesthetic), followed by the period of seclusion, is viewed as demonstrating brav-ery and instilling endurance and discipline in initiates. The bulk of the seclusion period is used to teach initiates how to be proper men in accordance with societal and cultural expectations. On leaving the bush, the hut where the initiates lived during the initiation, clothing worn during the initiation period and other artefacts used during the rite are all burnt. This is a symbolic act to signal the parting with the past. Huge feasts are organized to welcome the initiates when they leave the initiation school. The presentation of gifts to the *amakrwala* (new men or recently circumcised men) and advice from older men is part of the coming-out ceremony. 'In the admonitions the initiates' new status as men is stressed, the duties which they have to assume and behaviour expected of them towards wives, in-laws, and the tribal authorities' (Ngxamngxa 1971: 191).

Collectively, the above three rituals render initiation a rite of passage from boyhood into adulthood (Ngxamngxa 1971). Young boys acquire a new status in society after initiation. This includes the right to attend and speak at male gatherings in the communities, to inherit property and to marry. In spending weeks of seclusion together and enduring the pain of circumcision, the initiation ritual is also viewed as creating a lasting bond between cohorts of young men. Initiates are precluded from discussing the intricacies of this rite with non-initiates.

The centrality of this rite of passage is also reflected in other societies where it is practised. Among the Gisu of Uganda, male circumcision during initiation (*imbalu*) is a ritual that enables boys to both prove their manhood and validate it on behalf of the entire community (Heald, n.d.). Heald (n.d.: 48) suggests that among the Gisu, circumcision is also a rite of emancipation as a circumcised man 'has the right to inherit a portion of his father's land and he should also be provided with the cattle he needs to marry'. In other cultures, circumcision is not only a rite of passage through which adolescent boys acquire a new social status, but it is a source of entitlement for their fathers. For the Luhyia of Western Kenya, where bullfighting is a prominent ritual and pastime, only families with male children can own a bull. More importantly, it is the circumcision of the first son that grants the father a special title as well as the right to own a bull and subsequently participate in village bullfights (Egara Kabaji, personal communication, 20 June 2005).

The significance of this rite of passage is equally reflected in African literary texts. Both Camara Laye's reminiscing on his childhood in Guinea in *The African Child* and Ngugi wa Thiong'o's main character in *The River Between* provide an insight into circumcision and its significance to the individual and the community. In the latter, Ngugi wa Thiong'o articulates the centrality of the ritual in the lives of young boys, through the following description of his central character as he is about to undergo the ritual:

His penis had shrunk in size and as Waiyaki looked at it, he wondered if it really belonged to him. Waiyaki was not alone. All along the banks the other initiates sat, waiting for the 'surgeon'. All his life Waiyaki had waited for this day, for this very opportunity to reveal his courage like a man. This has been the secret ambition of his youth (wa Thiong''o 1965: 45).

In Camara Laye's Guinea, initiation is viewed as a rebirth where childhood innocence is abandoned in favour of being man. After undergoing initiation, a boy's father gives him a hut of his own. He stops sharing a hut with his mother.

Evidently, in societies where it is practised, adult male circumcision is inextricably linked to notions of manhood and masculine identity. The ritual serves as an enactment and validation of manhood.[7] It renders the male body a defining component of male subjectivity that reaffirms, endorses and celebrates a man's identity within that particular society. Such is the centrality of this aspect of social identity that those who avoid the ritual through personal choice risk stigmatisation and even forced circumcision,[8] while some will go to extreme attempts to attain manhood particularly when other factors (such as health or age limits) have prevented them from 'going to the bush'.[9] The penis being its principal focus, circumcision is an important arena where particular cultural meanings of masculinity come to be articulated and epitomized. Saco (1992: 24) describes 'masculinity as signs, where masculinity is regarded as one of the subjectivities that make up social identities'. For the Xhosa man, the circumcised penis is integral to his masculine identity. It is a cultural asset that grants him status among men and the community in general. Men who do not undergo the initiation ceremony are called *'inkwenkwe'* (a derogatory term meaning boy).

Talking Men, Talking Bodies

Critical studies of men, particularly those grounded in social constructionist theories of the body, offer a useful theoretical starting point for the current analysis. Scholars have suggested that the body is at the centre of the discourse on masculinity (Flannigan-Saint-Aubin 1994; MacMullan 2002). In fact Connell (1995: 52–3), in discussing the bodily presence in accounts of gender, suggests that 'the physical sense of maleness and femaleness is central to the cultural interpretation of gender. The body is unavoidable in the understanding of and construction of masculinity. Masculine gender is (among other things) a certain feel to the skin, certain muscular shapes, tensions, certain postures and ways of moving, certain possibilities in sex.' This bodily presence, Connell argues, is what is integral to individual and collective histories, social processes and 'a possible object of politics' (Connell 1995: 56). Male bodies together with culture-specific practices are substantively under scrutiny in the public discourse of circumcision and initiation rituals. This is because newspapers, like magazines, 'have the potential both to maintain and to affect cultural values and norms in society' (Taylor and Sunderland 2003: 169). For instance, *Men's Health* magazine explicitly focuses on male bodies, endlessly scrutinizing, problematizing, shaping and celebrating them; while specialist muscle-building magazines validate and celebrate the hard body as a male body (Johansson 2003).

However, in *The Men and the Boys*, Connell (2000) suggests that masculinity is not inherent in the male body but is a social definition referring to the characteristics of male bodies. 'If the body complies with the social definition it is easier for the meanings to take hold; and sometimes the body cures the social definition' (Connell 2000: 76). The circumcised penis is integral to the cultural definition of the male body in Xhosa culture. It is one way of ensuring that the male body complies with the cultural ideal of Xhosa manhood.

Studies on male bodies usefully provide a framework for understanding men's relationships with their own and other men's bodies, sexualities and masculine abilities (Ervo and Johansson 2003). Scholarship in this area has variously examined the relationship between gendered bodies and gendered power (Whitehead 2002) and theorized on the relationship between men's minds and their bodies (Siedler 2003). While a growing corpus of research within cultural and masculinity studies has concerned itself with the body and embodiment, lacking in the literature is scholarship on circumcised male bodies. Perhaps there is in this absence an implied assumption of what the penis looks like; and that such a penis is natural and possibly universal. But as Njambi (2004: 283) has argued, 'bodies do not exist in a vacuum; they are made and negotiated through everyday rituals and performances that can be simultaneously acceptable and problematic'. This cultural construction of the body deconstructs its biological given, rendering the body a site where meaning is constantly constituted, contested and configured. Media representation of male initiation is one sphere where the cultural definition of the body in post-apartheid South Africa is debated. Although this study examines this discursive representation in the media, it equally acknowledges, as Hearn and Melechi, (1992: 217) have argued, that 'processes of representation and signification are not limited to the formal media and institutional forms of communication; they exist in all forms and instances of social practice'.

Gazing at Black African Men

The circumcision debate in the South African media offers an opportunity to explore how popular media gaze on initiation represents black African masculinity within popular discourse. The power and meaning of looking is embedded in many cultures and is evidenced in everyday speech and/or behaviours. In the English language the expression, 'if looks could kill' is used to describe circumstances when outrage and anger are articulated through a particular visual and facial expression. Critical theorist Dani Cavallaro defines the concept of gaze as 'the sense of sight and the dynamics of looking in the genesis of social identities… It is primarily about the consequences of how we use the sense of sight' (Cavallaro 2001: 140). As a way of looking, the gaze is distinct. For instance, dictionary definitions of words that variously refer to a form of looking include: glance, glimpse, observe, peek, peruse, observe and voyeurism. Cavallaro also makes a distinction between different modes of looking: 'seeing registers sensation of light, shapes and colours, whilst observing entails looking carefully in order to obtain detail' (p.131).

The gaze is therefore more than a look. It is ideologically looking and looking culturally to make and or ascribe meaning. Ideologically speaking, meaning is ascribed through particular perspectives that can be coloured by race, gender, class, sexuality or a combination of these. Consequently, 'when we gaze at something, we are not simply "looking". The gaze probes and masters. It penetrates and objectifies the body' (Cavallaro 2001: 131). The objectification inherent in the process of gazing renders the gaze biased and powerful.

Feminist-influenced scholarship has extensively applied the concept of the gaze to show how women and men's bodies have been objectified. Whitehead (2002: 195) expands on this by employing the concept of 'panoptic gaze' in discussing the scrutiny of the male body. For Whitehead, such a gaze comes with a set of moral, social and cultural codes or assumptions that ascribe values on the body and different values to different bodies. The media is a cultural space where the gaze operates. Through journalistic processes and routines that determine news, particular discourses and sources become privileged over others. This offers an opportunity to legitimate the gaze. In a post-apartheid multiracial South Africa, the discourse of initiation takes an additional racialized dimension given that it is mainly practised by black African ethnic groups such as the Xhosa, Pedi, Sotho and Venda. Consequently, the discourse on male circumcision is usually a gaze at black African masculinity and traditional customs.

Whitehead (2002) suggests the gaze is not simply directed at its subject, but the subject of the gaze comes to regulate his or her own body in the knowledge and presence of the authoritative gaze. Such regulation in South Africa is evidenced not only in the rejection of the initiation ritual by some Xhosa men but also by specific government legislation aimed at ensuring safety and preventing deaths during initiation ceremonies (for instance, the Traditional Circumcision Act, the Traditional Circumcision Schools Act, and the Application of Health Standards for Traditional Circumcision Act, enacted by the Eastern Cape provincial legislature).

Both Cavallaro (2001) and Whitehead (2002) cite Foucault's understanding of the gaze, which linked the dynamics of gazing to the operations of power. This power is defined and legitimated by privileging particular perspectives over others. By implication, those without access to the media, whether as sources or readers, lack the power to define and shape discourses. The public discourse on initiation is one sphere where the complexities and nuances of change and transformation in post-apartheid South Africa are played out. In fact, Morrell (2005: xi) has recently suggested that 'in a society so rapidly changing and with established power relations being challenged (in gender and race terms, if not exactly in social class terms) it is to be expected that constructions of masculinity will change as well'. Media representation of circumcision and initiation rites in South Africa is one area where contemporary constructions of masculinity can be garnered.

What perspectives are played out in media discourse on circumcision? What are the characteristics of men embodied in representation of initiation ceremonies and circumcision? The next section answers these questions by examining initiation-related news stories, editorials, comments and letters to the editor appearing in *The Herald* and *The Daily Dispatch*. Both papers are regional broadsheet dailies published in the Eastern Cape Province, with circulations of over 30,000.[10] To reflect coverage of both initiation seasons in the province, stories appearing between July 2004 and February 2005 were analysed. The aim was to identify the nature of coverage from the province rather than ascertain the differences in coverage between both papers. Where necessary, coverage in other local and regional newspapers is referred to.

The analysis employed discourse analytic techniques to explore the discursive representation of black African masculinity that emanates from the mediated gaze on initiation in the Eastern Cape Province. Discourse analysis provides an approach to analysing text by seeking out the relationship between language use and the social structure, particularly power relations. The emphasis in discourse analysis is 'looking for patterns in the texts, for both consistency and differences in the content and forms of accounts, for shared features, and for the function and consequences of accounts' (Potter and Wetherell 1987: 161). A significant feature of qualitative research of this nature is the emphasis on interpretation – the analysis of implied meanings in texts. As an analytical framework, discourse analysis relies on linguistic categories within texts in order to permit the researcher to source the construction of power relations within texts and to see what ideologies are dominant in such texts. It is therefore a useful tool for exposing patterns of unequal power relations embedded in media text (Taylor and Sunderland 2003: 172). Specifically, the following discourse structures identified by van Dijk (1988, 2001) were employed: semantic macro-structures (topics), implicit and indirect meanings, and the analysis of context. Such an interpretive framework usefully grounds an understanding of the relationship between language use and social structure, particularly power relations.

Secrets, Tradition and the Making of Real Men

A continuing thematic focus in press reports is of initiate deaths during different circumcision seasons, and the hospitalization of many other initiates following complications from circumcision wounds. The recurrent deaths of initiates only serve to bring the rite of passage under scrutiny. Examples of headlines include: 'Initiate dies of blood poisoning' (*Daily Dispatch*, 8 July 2004); '50 initiates in EC hospitals' (*Daily Dispatch*, 16 July 2004); 'Circumcision school deaths under spotlight' (*The Herald*, 12 July 2004); 'Botched circumcisions cut deep into budget' (*The Herald*, 29 September 2004); 'Seriously ill initiates end up in hospital' (*Daily Dispatch*, 9 December 2004); and 'Campaign to safeguard Xhosa initiates' (*The Herald*, 28 January 2005).

   Although these headlines capture the context within which much of the debate about circumcision occurs, they simultaneously serve two purposes. On one hand, the headlines indirectly threaten the centrality of this practice to Xhosa culture by foregrounding the attendant risks that come with the ritual. On the other hand, the headlines (almost recurrent in each circumcision season) indicate the extent to which this cultural practice is essential to Xhosa masculine identity and how cultural ideals are scripted on bodies (MacMullan 2002). The following editorial in *The Herald* reflects how these two discursive positions operate:

> Certainly a certain amount of water deprivation has always been part of the initiation process. But this must be carefully monitored to ensure the health of the youngsters, whatever else they might have to go through in the arcane but essential progress from boyhood to manhood. But parents and indeed the wider community are entitled to guarantees that the youngsters will be given proper care during this time [...] We want our youngsters to grow up to be real men in every sense of the word. (*The Herald*, 8 December 2004)

The observations on 'water deprivation' and 'whatever else they might have to go through' at once admit to the health risks of the initiation rite. However, the editorial simultaneously underscores the centrality of the ritual by historicizing it as 'the arcane but essential progress from boyhood to manhood' and emphasizing the importance of young boys growing up be 'real men in every sense of the word'. This mythologizing informs much of the defence of the practice by traditional leaders and some sections of the press.

The Herald's columnist Jimmy Matyu described initiation as 'an ancient ritual from time immemorial' (24 February 2005). In his regular column, Matyu defended the practice by ridiculing the cultural stigma that comes with being uncircumcised or being circumcised in a hospital.

The stigma that comes with being circumcised by means other than initiation in the bush is also reflected in the position of traditional leaders. After the death of an initiate from blood poisoning, Andile Siko, secretary of the Buffalo City Traditional Circumcision Association (BCTCA), told the *Daily Dispatch*: 'taking the initiate to hospital was not the solution because he might be ostracised' (*Daily Dispatch*, 8 July 2004). Similarly, following reports indicating an increase in hospital circumcisions, the chairperson of the Eastern Cape House of Traditional Leaders, Chief Ngangomhlaba Matanzima, likewise discouraged this trend, arguing that hospital circumcisions did not make men of boys: 'People have different ways of taking this, but we need to look into what is tradition and what is not. When someone performs the operation outside the initiation school system they cannot claim to be men' (*Daily Dispatch*, 10 July 2004). From this discursive position, the need to be men in the eyes of society is emphasized and reinforced by the threat of stigma and ostracization. State regulation of the practice through instituting age limits and 'rescuing' ill initiates by taking them to the hospital is seen by some traditionalists as sanitizing the ritual. The result of such a discourse is the perpetuation and sustenance of an idealized manhood. Regardless of a man's age, an uncircumcised Xhosa man is still considered a boy.[11] Real men (*amadoda*) are those who can stand the pain of having their prepuce removed without anaesthesia, and who shun the sanitized environment offered by modern medical facilities. The overt pain of circumcision in the bush is perceived as both a reflection and embodiment of male power and bravery. This heroic ideal is worth striving for to the extent that many die in the process, and any attempt to intervene to stop pain and disease is castigated ('"Nurse" slain for taking ill initiate to hospital', *The Herald*, 1 May 2005). In some instances, where boys have undergone the culturally sanctioned initiation in the bush, being referred to hospitals following complications arising is perceived as adulteration and a sign of weakness – not being man enough.[12] Those who die in the process pay the ultimate price for trying to be men in the eyes of society.[13] Some undertake self-mutilation as a means of attaining this culturally idealized manhood,[14] while others discovered to have avoided going to the bush are circumcised against their will ('Man, 48, forcibly circumcised', *Daily Dispatch*, 11 November 2004). Still others, for whom the cultural image remains elusive, try to buy themselves into it:

> Let us not forget some of those who went to hospitals to avoid the pain to manhood are customarily ostracised in our society and not treated as 'amadoda' (men). I have seen these people, buying with a bottle of brandy this manhood qualification or the right to call their peers from the bush by names. A humiliating experience. I and other elders have in the past had the task of intervening in an almost volatile situation where a man who was circumcised in a hospital, found himself facing an angry group of initiates who wanted to harm him or repeat the operation on him (Jimmy Matyu, *The Herald*, 2 February 2005).

This traditionalist position, which seeks to conserve the practice, thrives by drawing on and deploying a specific cultural and historical repertoire of what it means to be a man in Xhosa society. Yet, the recurrent deaths of initiates during the circumcision season demonstrate that not all men are capable of attaining this ideal even though there is the constant struggle to experience and subsequently be included in the ideal, if not benefit from its privileges. The circumcision ritual and its discursive representation in the media serve to foreground and reinforce the cultural significance of the penis (Izugbara 2005). The result is the establishment and perpetuation of hierarchies of men and manhood whereby the bush-circumcised man is privileged over others (uninitiated and hospital-circumcised men). Nevertheless, the following letters to the editor demonstrate that these hierarchies of manhood remain contested.

> It is a myth that the initiates undergo extensive manhood training which is supposedly missed by those circumcised in a modern manner. Most of us acquire our manhood skills from our fathers and uncles. It is naive and too opinionated to hold the view that a bush circumcised man is better nurtured and therefore more of an essential asset to society than a modern circumcised man. It is misleading the youth, imprisoning their minds and indeed it is a stone age concept (Dr Z.M. Nazo, *Daily Dispatch*, 28 October 2004).

> After all it is not the physical operation that makes individuals better men.

> Real men are moulded and prepared at home in a family environment before their passage in the bush (Mzi Mahola, *The Herald*, 18 January 2005).

Another aspect of media discourse is the 'unwanted' exposure that comes with the mediated gaze into a sacred and secret rite.

During the controversy over the exhibition at the National Arts Festival in Grahamstown in July 2004, the Xhosa House of Traditional Leaders described the exhibition as 'degrading black humanity and exposing secret practices to women and children'. A spokesperson of the traditional leaders described it as 'a clear manifestation of complete ignorance and a lack of understanding of the fundamental rituals that underpin this important custom' (*Daily Dispatch*, 8 July 2004). A reader writing to the local Grahamstown newspaper described the exhibition as a case of voyeurism. People were making a public spectacle out of a practice which should stay out of public gaze: '… I consider the idea voyeuristic. I think it is bad enough that youths at these camps are allowed to stand viewing cars passing, while they are still wearing the special clothes and are obviously still in camp. I feel it will be better if they stayed mysteriously out of sight' (*Grocott's Mail*, letters, 13 July 2004). However, in an article headlined 'Lifting the cloak on manhood', which reviewed the exhibition, the daily festival newspaper *Cue* quoted the Anglican Archbishop of Grahamstown, Thabo Makgoba: 'Initiation is not a cult. The secrecy is just because we have not learned to communicate issues of sexuality and manhood. But we need to open up about these things' (*Cue*, 4 July 2004).

Both positions reflect the socially sanctioned secrecy about the ritual and the contestations over the nature and consequences of secrecy about cultural practices. For the archbishop, the secrecy is only evidence of historical silences around sexuality, whereas for many advocates of the practice, the secrecy of the ritual is integral to maintaining its mysticism. Similar observations on the secrecy surrounding initiation are also evident in literary texts. In Camara Laye's *The African Child*, where the author describes his experience of growing up in his native Guinea, he details his experience of the initiation he undergoes in Kouroussa – a ritual about which he expresses a degree of ambivalence. Whereas description of the ritual exposes readers to some of the details of the rite of passage, the author is careful to emphasize the secrecy surrounding the practice: 'And we had to tell nothing of what we learned to women or to the uninitiated; neither had we to reveal any of the secret of circumcision. That was the custom' (p. 108). He explains that while the visible part of the ceremony was familiar to the uninitiated, '… the important, the essential part of the ceremony remained a secret'. hence prospective initiates 'only had a vague notion of how it was carried out', and that the operation was painful (Camara 1979: 93). Nevertheless, he later admits that 'the teaching we received in the bush, far from all prying eyes, had nothing very mysterious about it; nothing, I think, that was not fit for ears other than our own' (p.107). Camara Laye's views epitomize the paradox of emphasizing the secrecy surrounding initiation in literary texts and other media that are themselves available to a diverse audience composed of both men and women, the initiated and the uninitiated.

As the *Cue* headline indicated, the exhibition had lifted the lead on a particular feature of manhood in South Africa. It had made visible that which was both sacred and secret. However, for those who advocate 'opening up' about such rites, there is no place for secrecy in contemporary South Africa. In a discussion of the social, political and cultural production of secrecy around child rape in

South Africa, Posel (2005) succinctly outlines four structures of secrecy and how these operate. These are useful in understanding the secrecy/visibility dualism in the public discourse on initiation. She suggests the following modalities of secrecy. Firstly, through a combination of denial, self-deception and a retreat from full knowledge by those who make up and keep the secret, secrecy becomes a combination of knowing and refusing to know. In this respect, secrecy is a mode of knowledge. Secondly, by immersing in and thriving on various political, social and cultural repertoires of disclosure and non-disclosure, secrecy is also a mode of speech. Thirdly, secrecy can also serve as a site of shame and stigma. Here, the modality of secrecy operates through perceptions of shame and stigma that inform the need to avoid exposure. In this case, keeping things hidden becomes a means of forestalling public censure. Lastly, secrecy structures itself as a site of power. This is rooted in power relations and the configuration of interests and norms shaping them (Posel 2005: 41–2).

These modalities of secrecy are simultaneously evident in the debate about male circumcision during Xhosa male initiation ceremonies. On the one hand, are those who want to illustrate what has been in existence but remained invisible to majority of the public. On the other, others maintain and defend the secrecy of the practice as a means of ensuring its sacredness. In the latter position, public visibility through exhibitions and in subsequent media reporting provokes anxiety about the consequences of such exposure to initiates, the ritual itself and consequently on masculine identity. For with such exposure (to women and Others), not only come (uncomfortable) knowledge and awareness of the potential dangers of circumcision during initiation, but a challenge both to the centrality of initiation in the construction of masculine identity within Xhosa culture and to the authority of traditional leaders (most of whom defend the practice). As one member of Xhosa royalty indicated during the controversy surrounding the NAF exhibition: 'children who have not gone for initiation will be scared to go when they see this' (*The Herald*, 8 July 2004). Thembinkosi Goniwe suggests that the anxiety of conservative Xhosa men over the public scrutiny accompanying media coverage also reflects the 'continuing resistance and struggle of Xhosa men against forces reminiscent of colonialism, missionaries, apartheid and modernity' (Goniwe 2005: 82).

A counterview, which runs concurrently with the traditionalists' position, is that which advocates regulation of the practice. This position is explored in the next section.

Regulation and Modernization

The Eastern Cape provincial government's attempts to stem the deaths of initiates has so far included passing legislation to regulate the practice (including setting age limits and licensing traditional surgeons), inspecting initiation schools and taking ill initiates to hospitals, and closing down illegal initiation schools. However, government regulation has sometimes been met with resistance owing to the stigma associated with hospital circumcisions. In July 2004, government officials were stoned in Luthuthu village in the course of inspecting initiation schools.[15]

The counterview to that which advocates the retention of the practice is most evident in reports of initiate deaths and botched circumcisions that have resulted in mutilations. Proponents of this position include the government, some medical professionals and journalists, as well as families whose children have died from complications arising from circumcision. The recurrence of more deaths, sometimes hidden by the fear of stigma, has only served to heighten state intervention. But the modernization discourse is itself fraught with colonialist undertones. Government actions are frequently reported in language reminiscent of crime and deviance, with initiates and traditional surgeons assuming the problematic position of criminals, and initiation discursively positioned as a crime or deviance. In press reports, government intervention in initiation schools is described as a 'crackdown' or 'raid'. For example: 'police are cracking down on illegal traditional surgeons following a series of unlawful circumcision rites in the past few days. More arrests are expected as police intensify their raids' (*The Herald*, 6 July 2004). The subtext of deviant men, criminals and breaking the law operates within a broader discursive characterization of initiation as a deviant practice that is evident in much of the modernist position.

Following the death of two initiates during the winter initiation season, the Eastern Cape's provincial spokesperson for health described the deaths as resulting from barbarism: 'We strongly encourage the community to assist the department of health to put an end to this barbaric behaviour which causes unnecessary deaths' (*The Herald*, 12 July 2004).

Characterizing initiation as barbaric implicitly casts black masculinity as 'savage, deviant, dangerous and barbaric' (Gqola 2005: 83). It draws on and reflects powerful colonialist discourse of African customs as primitive. A primitive and Stone Age practice has no place in modern society. In an opinion column, *The Herald*'s assistant editor questions the utility of the practice in contemporary South Africa by foregrounding a racial discourse:

> A resolution of the matter lies not in the outcome of the current debate on whether the African custom of circumcision should be retained or abandoned.
>
> Rather, it is to be found in a resolution as to whether black Africans in South Africa wish to continue defining themselves in the context of 'blackness'. Clanship, a historic form of collectivism that was a cornerstone for the development of the traditional African black family in South Africa until the mid-60s – and through which African customs, including

circumcision of boys, was properly undertaken and managed – is no longer a viable proposition in 2005 onwards. […] That resolution, however, needs to recognise and accept that contrary to what conservatives would have us do, black teenage boys' circumcision as a symbol of transition to manhood no longer has any rational African significance in the absence of its inherent components, such as collective/clanship management (Sicelo Fayo, *Herald* Senior Assistant Editor, 12 January 2005).

Fayo's views reflect a major theme underpinning much of the debate about the regulation of the rite of passage. As a practice undertaken by black African ethnic groups, the debate in the media epitomizes the contestations over identities, social positions, power and belonging in post-apartheid South Africa.

The following quotation from a member of the National Arts Festival Committee concerning the 'Initiation as a Rite of Passage' exhibition draws attention to the Westernization aspects of the debate:

We're looking at our heritage. A lot of these exhibitions are part of South Africa coming to understand its roots, to understand that everything we've got here has got to be protected because we're being invaded by cultures from elsewhere. But it has also brought into the public domain questions such as 'Shall I go through with this as a Westernised person living in Soweto or must I make my child go through this?' And that's a debate which must be answered by people within that group and culture (Andrew Vester, in *Grocott's Mail*, 9 July 2004).

Vester's position, while calling for a critical examination of the place of circumcision within contemporary South African society and its protection from 'invasion' by other cultures, also epitomizes the nature, power and operation of the Westernized white and colonial gaze that probes the non-Westernized 'group and culture'.

Whitehead (2002) has equally reflected on the politicization of black male bodies in America. His argument that such a politicization emerges from the black male body being contested and being stereotyped as racially and sexually symbolic of both power and resistance is valid in understanding aspects of this debate in South Africa. Both Fayo and Vester draw on a particular discursive repertoire where Western is modern and non-Western is 'Other' – primitive and barbaric. The subtext here is that the position of circumcision in modern and Westernized Soweto (used as a metaphor for Black South Africa) is questionable. Modern and Westernized people do not undergo such a rite. And Westernized black people should be modern. From this discursive position, the hegemony of white masculinity evident under apartheid is articulated, reaffirmed and naturalized by constructing black African masculinity as deviant and barbaric. By bringing attention to black African men and problematizing the specific cultural practices that shape some black male bodies, hegemonic masculinity is reinforced as the dominant masculinity.

Interestingly, what remains missing in much of the media reporting is the voice of the initiate. It is rendered invisible by the journalistic routines of news gathering and editing, which result in the privileging of authoritative (elite) voices over others, and the culturally sanctioned secrecy and discretion expected of initiates. Their presence is only acknowledged through their being subjects of the discourse and photographs often accompanying press coverage. A consequence of this symbolic invisibility is the privileging of competing voices that claim to speak (authoritatively and culturally) for the black male initiate (and prospective initiates) even when these voices contradict and oppose each other. The dominance of men (politicians, traditional leaders, doctors and newspaper columnists) as news sources and opinion formers in the discursive representation of the initiation in the media also speaks to the gendered nature of the debate: only men have the authority to speak about men's practices. Gqola (2005) points out that this particular bias is a dangerous way of policing culture. It is particularly problematic when evidently men's practices and performances of manhood have consequences on both men and women as a community.

Conclusion

As in literary texts, one sphere where the uninitiated come to learn about this rite of passage is the media, particularly in visual and print media. In focusing on the discursive representation of male initiation rites in the Eastern Cape's regional media, this study has outlined how male circumcision as an aspect of certain African masculine identities is socially constructed in popular discourse. It has demonstrated how the circumcision debate serves as a metaphor for gazing at black African masculinity in the current social transformation in post-apartheid South Africa. Coverage brings into focus and sometimes into conflict issues of male identity, race, ethnicity, traditional institutions (chiefs, traditional surgeons) and state institutions (hospitals, the law). Consequently, press reporting is characterized by dualisms such as tradition/modernity, secrecy/visibility civilized/ primitive, African/others (white European).[16] These dualisms reflect the operation of multiplicity of gazes. At the same time, they construct and reinforce a meta-narrative of black African men as strong, brave and capable of standing pain (cutting of the prepuce without anaesthetic). Whitehead (2002: 197) suggests 'the power of the gaze lies in its multiplicity, for it is through these multiple gazes that the paradoxes of embodied masculinity become apparent, as much for those who gaze as for those who are gazed upon'. The multiple gazes on the black African male body evidenced here celebrate and valorize (masculine bravado) at the same time as they challenge, stereotype and denigrate (African barbarism and primitivism). It assumes this position through the centrality of the circumcised

black penis in the cultural definition of a particular African masculinity. The onto-
logical importance given to initiation is such that many die in the process of
attaining the cultural ideal of manhood. The black male body therefore becomes
a site on which fears; insecurities and uncertainties about current socio-political
transformation are projected, negotiated and defended. The result is that black
African male body is not only a site of enculturation, but also a site of contestation
over culture and over masculine embodiment in post-apartheid South Africa.

While public visibility of such a sacred and secret rite through exhibitions and
in subsequent media reporting provokes anxiety about the consequences of such
exposure, the media gaze simultaneously reconstitutes the phallus as the essence
of masculinity. Particularly, it emphasizes and reinforces the central position of
the circumcised penis in the construction of masculine identity of particular black
African cultures. The circumcised penis emerges as the significant factor in
distinguishing between masculinities in contemporary South Africa and hierarchies
within black masculinities.

Given the limitations of the current sample size (urban-based, English
broadsheets), the analysis is by no means a reflection of coverage in the broader
South African media. An examination of non-English language media would
further illuminate the issues discussed here, by pointing to differences or similarities in perspectives and voices.

Besides the circumcision of young boys, virginity testing – a custom practised
by the Zulus – has been another area of contestation and public debate, as in the
case of SABC2's programme *The Big Question*, 30 July 2005. In addition, in a
Sunday Times article, Zulu king, Goodwill Zwelithini, reportedly described the
passing of the Children's Bill, which set the age limit for virginity tests at 18, as an
infringement on culture ('Uproar as state moves to ban virginity testing', *Sunday
Times*, 10 July 2005).

Notes

1. See *Masculinity and Men's Lifestyle Magazines*, ed. Bethan Benwell (2003).
2. Given the controversy that surrounds this topic, the word 'mutilation' is frequently
   used by those who approach the subject from a position of advocacy. Scholars, who
   caution for an unbiased position, label the practice as Female Genital Cutting (FGC).
3. According to current government regulation, the acceptable age for circumcision is 18.
   Parental consent is required for the circumcision of boys under 18.
4. Despite this distinction, the literal translation of the Xhosa word *ulwaluko* is
   'circumcision'. Consequently, media coverage and political discourse utilize the word
   circumcision to refer to the entire ritual.
5. Authors cited by Ngxamngxa vary in their estimates of the seclusion period from three
   to six months among the Xhosa, to three or four months among the Fingo, and three
   to twelve months for the Thembu respectively.

6. Cross-cultural similarities in the significance of this rite have also been identified in Papua New Guinea. See Gilbert Herdt, *Rituals of Manhood* (Berkeley: University of California Press, 1982); and David Gilmore, *Manhood in the Making: Cultural Concepts of Masculinity* (New Haven: Yale University Press, 1990).
7. 'Man, 48 forcibly circumcised' (*Daily Dispatch*, 11 November 2004).
8. 'Boy, 15, does own "ritual"' (*Daily Dispatch*, 10 July 2005).
9. Figures are based on Audit Bureau of Circulation (ABC) statistics available in June 2005. *The Herald* is published in Port Elizabeth and *The Daily Dispatch* is published in East London.
10. When 58-year-old pensioner Velile Ngxingo was released from jail in May 2005, his priority upon being released was to 'become a man': 'I am tired of being a boy! I have been left behind by young boys who have been circumcised' ('Paroled pensioner circumcised at last after a lifetime in prison', *The Herald*, 2 June 2005)
11. In January 2005, 19- year-old Dontsa Lwane, committed suicide after receiving medical attention at a hospital for complications arising from his circumcision in the bush ('Brothers in double tragedy after initiation', *Daily Dispatch*, 10 January 2005).
12. The death of many initiates is no deterrent for advocates of the practice or prospective participants. Camara Laye expresses a similar view in *The African Child*: 'I knew perfectly well that I was going to be hurt, but I wanted to be a man and it seemed to me that nothing could be too painful if by enduring it, I was to come to a man's state. My companions felt the same; like myself, they were prepared to pay for it with their blood' (p.94).
13. Twenty-seven initiates in Qumbu in the Transkei reportedly circumcised themselves using razor blades in 2004 ('3 more initiates die, mob stones officials', *Daily Dispatch*, 13 July 2004).
14. '3 more initiates die, mob stones officials' (*Daily Dispatch*, 13 July 2004).
15. Njambi (2004: 283) identifies similar dichotomies in public discourse on the female genitals, e.g. 'science/superstition; medical knowledge/tradition; healthy bodies/unhealthy bodies; normal sexuality/abnormal sexuality; civilized/barbaric; modernity/backwardness; expert/non-expert; educated/ignorant'.

References

Barthel, D., 1992, 'When Men Put on Appearances: Advertising and the Social Construction of Masculinity', in S. Craig. ed., *Men, Masculinity, and the Media*, Newbury Park, CA: Sage, pp. 137–54.

Benwell, B., 2003, *Masculinity and Men's Lifestyle Magazines*, Oxford: Blackwell Publishing and The Editorial Board *Sociological Review*.

Cavallaro, D., 2001,. *Critical and Cultural Theory*, London: Athlone.

Connell, R. W., 1995, *Masculinities*, Cambridge: Polity Press.

Connell, R. W., 2000, *The Men and the Boys*, Cambridge: Polity Press.

Consalvo, M., 2003, 'The Monsters Next Door: Media Constructions of Boys and Masculinity', *Feminist Media Studies*, Vol. 3, No. 1, pp. 27–45.

Craig, S., 1992, *Men, Masculinity and the Media*, Newbury Park, CA: Sage.

Epstein, D., 1998, 'Marked Men: Whiteness and Masculinity', *Agenda, Vol.*. 37, pp. 49–59.

Ervo, S. and Johansson, T., 2003, *Bending Bodies: Moulding Masculinities,* Volume 2. Aldershot: Ashgate.

Flannigan-Saint-Aubin, A., 1994, 'The Male Body and Literary Metaphors for Masculinity', in H. Brod and M. Kaufman, eds., *Theorising Masculinities*, Thousand Oaks, CA: Sage.

Goniwe, T., 2005. 'A Neglected Heritage: The Aesthetics of Complex Black Masculinities, Thembinkosi Goniwe in Conversation with Pumla Gqola', *Agenda*, Vol. 63, No. 2, pp. 80–94.

Gqola, P. D., 2005, 'A Neglected Heritage: The Aesthetics of Complex Black Masculinities, Thembinkosi Goniwe in Conversation with Pumla Gqola', *Agenda*, Vol. 63, No. 2, pp. 80–94.

Hanke, R., 1998, 'Theorizing Masculinity With/In the Media', *Communication Theory*, Vol. 8, No. 2, pp. 183–203.

Hearn, J. and Melechi, A., 1992, 'The Transatlantic Gaze: Masculinities, Youth, and the American Imaginary', in S. Craig, ed., *Men, Masculinity and the Media*, Newbury Park, CA: Sage, pp. 215–32.

Izugbara, O., 2005, 'Hypothesis on the Origin of Hegemonic Masculinity', *Sexuality in Africa Magazine*, Vol. 2, No. 1, pp. 13–14.

Johansson, T., 2003, 'What's Behind the Mask? Body Building and Masculinity', in S. Ervo and T. Johansson, eds.,*Bending Bodies. Moulding Masculinities*, Vol. 2. Aldershot: Ashgate.

Laye,C., 1979. *The African Child*, trans. J. Kirkup, London and Glasgow: Fontana Books.

MacMullan, T., 2002, 'Introduction', in N. Tuana, W. Cowling, M. Hamington, G. Johnson and T. MacMullan, eds., *Revealing Male Bodies*, Bloomington, IN: Indiana University Press, pp. 1–16.

Meintjes, G.,1998. *Manhood at a Price: Socio-Medical Perspectives on Xhosa Traditional Circumcision*, Grahamstown: Rhodes University.

Morrell, R., 2005, Foreword, in G. Reid and L. Walker, eds., *Men Behaving Differently: South African Men Since 1994*, Cape Town: Double Storey.

Ngxamngxa, A. N. N., 1971, 'The Function of Circumcision among the Xhosa-speaking Tribes in Historical Perspective', in E. J. de Jager, ed., *Man: Anthropological Essays Presented to O. F. Raum*, Cape Town: C. Struik.

Njambi, W. N., 2004, 'Dualisms and Female Bodies in Representations of African Female Circumcision: A Feminist Critique', *Feminist Theory*, Vol. 5, No. 3, pp, 281–303.

Posel, D., 2005,'"Baby Rape": Unmaking Secrets of Sexual Violence in Post-apartheid South Africa', in G. Reid and L. Walker, eds., *Men Behaving Differently: South African Men Since 1994*, Cape Town: Double Storey.

Potter, J. and Wetherell, M., 1987, *Discourse and Social Psychology: Beyond Attitude and Behaviour.* London: Sage.

Sabo, D. and Jansen, S. C., 1992, 'Images of Men in Sport Media: The Social Reproduction of Gender of Gender Order', in S. Craig, ed., *Men, Masculinity and the Media*, Newbury Park, CA; Sage, pp. 169–84.

Siedler, V. J., 2003, 'Men, Bodies and Identities', in S. Ervo and T. Johansson, eds., *Bending Bodies: Moulding Masculinities*, Volume 2. Aldershot: Ashgate, pp. 77–91.

Strate, L., 1992, 'Beer Commercials: A Manual on Masculinity', in S. Craig, ed., *Men, Masculinity and the Media*, Newbury Park, CA: Sage, pp. 78–92.

Taylor, Y. and Sunderland, J., 2003, 'I've Always Loved Women': The Representation of Male Sex Workers in *Maxim*', in B. Benwell, ed., *Masculinity and Men's Lifestyle Magazines*, Oxford: Blackwell and The Editorial Board of *Sociological Review*.

Trujillo, N.,1991,'Hegemonic Masculinity on the Mound: Media Representations of Nolan Ryan and American Sports Culture', *Critical Studies in Mass Communication*, No. *8, pp.* 290–308.

Tuana, N., Cowling, W., Hamington, M., Johnson, G., and MacMullan, T., 2002, *Revealing Male Bodies*, Bloomington, IN: Indiana University Press.

van Dijk, T., 1988, *News as Discourse*, Hillsdale, NJ: Lawrence Erlbaum Associates.

van Dijk, T., 2001, 'Multidisciplinary CDA: A Plea for Diversity', in R. Wodak and M. Meyer, eds., *Methods of Critical Discourse Analysis*, London: Sage, pp. 95–120.

wa Thiong'o, N., 1965, *The River Between*, London: Heinemann.

Whitehead, S. M., 2002, *Men and Masculinities*, London: Polity Press.

13

Ordre masculin, violences politiques et initiatives féminines pour la paix au Congo-Brazzaville de 1991 à 1999

Raïssa Edwige Koutouma Nsona

Introduction

Les années 1990 sont des années tout à fait particulières dans l'histoire du monde en général, de l'Afrique et du Congo en particulier. Le monde, qui avait évolué depuis la fin de la Seconde Guerre mondiale sur la base de la bipolarité Est-Ouest, va connaître une remise en cause à la fin des années 1980 et au début des années 1990. En effet, le bloc Est, c'est-à-dire soviétique, éclate en 1990 pour les raisons suivantes liées à la fois à son évolution politique et économique interne : crise économique de plus en plus aiguë, contestation ouverte du système communiste par des intellectuels et hommes de sciences comme Soljenitsyne et Sakharov ; mise en œuvre par Mikhaïl Gorbatchev d'un programme de réformes économiques et politiques appelé la *Perestroïka* et sur le plan de la politique internationale par l'adoption de positions résolument nouvelles. La crise atteint son apogée notamment avec la chute du mur de Berlin (en novembre 1989).

Ces événements conduisent à la démocratisation des pays de l'Est qui entendent désormais rejoindre le camp de l'Ouest dit camp du monde « libre », caractérisé par le respect des libertés fondamentales et démocratiques et des droits de l'homme. Le vent de la démocratisation s'étend rapidement en Afrique et débouche sur la fin du système de parti unique et le début des processus de démocratisation.

En Afrique, les femmes et les jeunes vont jouer un rôle capital dans ces processus (Tedga 1991). La prise de conscience politique des femmes du monde en général et africaines en particulier est inséparable de l'environnement internationale qui militait en faveur de son émancipation. En effet, au niveau des Nations Unies et de ses institutions spécialisées, de nombreuses conventions avaient été prises pour favoriser l'intégration réelle des femmes au développement et leur participation plus visible aux activités politiques : Convention sur les droits politiques de la femme (1953), Convention sur l'élimination de toutes les formes de discrimination à l'égard des femmes (1979), Protocole facultatif à la Convention sur l'élimination de toutes les formes de discrimination à l'égard des femmes (1999), Convention interaméricaine sur la prévention, la sanction et l'élimination de la violence contre les femmes (1994). La conférence de Beijing tenu en 1995 a été en fin de compte l'aboutissement de toutes les actions menées en faveur de la femme sur le plan international.

Au Congo-Brazzaville, en 1992, au lendemain des premières élections démocratiques de l'après conférence nationale, tenue à Brazzaville du 25 février au 10 juin 1991, les nouvelles autorités politiques créèrent, au sein du nouveau gouvernement, un ministère à l'Intégration de la femme au développement. La création de ce ministère fut un fait nouveau dans le champ politique congolais. En effet, c'était la première fois, depuis l'accession du pays à la souveraineté internationale, qu'un ministère avait pour vocation la prise en charge totale des questions spécifiques des femmes, et comme perspective, son intégration réelle au processus de développement du pays. Ce fait apparemment insignifiant, était en réalité une avancée considérable sur le chemin de la reconnaissance effective des droits des femmes congolaises. Il témoignait au moins de trois choses. D'abord du fait que les nouvelles autorités n'étaient pas restées insensibles aux luttes menées jusque là par les femmes et particulièrement au rôle qu'elles ont joué pour la convocation et la tenue de la conférence nationale. Ensuite du fait qu'il était désormais impossible aux pouvoirs publics congolais de ne pas prendre en compte le poids démographique et par conséquent politique des femmes, mais surtout le rôle déterminant qu'elles jouent sur le plan économique aussi bien dans les campagnes que dans les villes où les hommes, traditionnellement chefs de famille, sont désormais incapables d'assumer leur rôle du fait de la crise économique[1]. Enfin par ce geste, les nouvelles autorités congolaises entendaient s'engager dans la voie de la remise en cause des pesanteurs sociales et historiques qui avaient maintenu jusque là les femmes dans un état de sujétion. L'ordre social, essentiellement masculin, s'était donc traduit jusqu'ici par des violences multiformes à l'endroit des femmes. Sa remise en cause nécessitait une refondation de la société sur de nouvelles bases qui impliquait l'intégration de la femme au développement.

Malheureusement quelque temps après la mise en place de ce premier gouvernement, le Congo est entré dans une grave crise politique. Celle-ci s'est manifestée, pendant près de dix ans, de 1992 à 2002, par des guerres récurrentes qui ont désorganisé la vie congolaise. Les milices des principaux partis politiques, qui ont essaimé à travers le pays, ont été essentiellement constituées par des jeunes chômeurs, des diplômés sans emploi, des « déflatés » de la fonction publique, des enfants vivant dans les rues, etc. Les actes de violence de ces jeunes miliciens se sont révélés comme l'expression d'une masculinité en panne, c'est-à-dire comme des actes posés par des gens désormais incapables d'assumer les responsabilités dévolues au sexe masculin selon les schémas traditionnels : l'homme est le soutien et le protecteur de la famille, celui qui travaille, qui apporte de l'argent à la maison, qui épouse une femme, etc. Au cours de ces dix dernières années, bien des hommes ont donc été perturbés par une grave crise d'identité. Ils ne savent plus comment se définir pour susciter l'admiration et l'estime ; ils ont le sentiment d'être socialement et économiquement rabaissés. Face à cette profonde crise d'identité, la majorité de ces hommes, surtout les pauvres, les sans emplois et les déscolarisés se sont tournés vers la violence et la guerre. Si les hommes se sont révélés comme les organisateurs des violences de la période post-conférence nationale, les femmes au contraire ont été les premières et les principales victimes de celles-ci. Elles ont en effet subi des viols, des pillages, des assassinats, bref des violences de toutes sortes. Une étude récente sur la situation psychologique des anciens déplacés du département du Pool installés à Brazzaville, dans des sites créés par le gouvernement, permet de mesurer les conséquences des différentes guerres sur les Congolais (Loupé 2005). L'auteur, qui a travaillé sur un échantillon de 204 personnes adultes dont 152 femmes et 52 hommes âgés de 25 à 60 ans, a établi les réactions traumatiques de ces personnes pendant les événements et les réactions actuelles après les conflits. Sur les 152 femmes interrogées, 54 ont déclaré avoir perdu leurs maris du fait des tueries. 159 des 204 personnes interrogées, ont présenté, lors de l'enquête en 2002, des symptômes de stress post-traumatique et d'autres symptômes associés : modification caractérielle, troubles de l'humeur et de conduite (évitement, retrait et fuite). Les traumatismes ont concerné les personnes des deux sexes comme le témoigne les propos de cet enseignant :

> Cette guerre m'a beaucoup bouleversé sur le plan moral et financier… car j'ai presque tout perdu […]. J'ai une image négative de toutes les milices. Les « Cobras » comme les « Ninjas »[2] ont pillé, saccagé, tué, violé […]. À présent, quand ça tire, je sens la diarrhée, je suis beaucoup émotionné, j'ai peur. Je déteste la guerre ! (Loupé 2005 : 44-46).

Il ressort de cette étude que les événements survenus en République du Congo depuis 1993 ont laissé des séquelles importantes chez les Congolais des deux sexes résidant dans les régions du sud-ouest. Sur les plans social et professionnel, l'ampleur des séquelles psycho-traumatiques a disqualifié bon nombre d'adultes pour des activités professionnelles, notamment agricoles. Les paysans des départements ayant connu la guerre se sentent désormais incapables de retravailler la terre, découragés par la dévastation de leurs plantations ou bétails par les différentes milices. Sur le plan familial, les différentes guerres ont détruit la dynamique familiale de nombreux foyers à tel point que beaucoup de séparations et de divorces ont été enregistrés.

Pourtant considérées comme des êtres faibles, de par leur nature, ce sont pourtant les femmes qui, les premières, se sont levées pour demander aux politiciens, c'est-à-dire aux hommes qui ne trouvaient pas de solution à la crise, d'arrêter la guerre et de revenir à la paix. Les Congolaises ont porté, avec vaillance, à bras le corps, l'idéal de paix. Leurs initiatives ont permis de créer les conditions qui ont favorisé les négociations entre les différents protagonistes et le retour à la paix.

Dans cette recherche axée sur les masculinités contemporaines en Afrique, nous avons donc choisi d'analyser les violences politiques qui ont marqué la vie politique congolaise de 1992 à 1999, c'est-à-dire de la première crise socio-politique née à la suite du changement des alliances politiques à l'Assemblée nationale, Jusqu'aux accords de cessation des hostilités entre les milices se réclamant de l'opposition politique en exil et le gouvernement de Denis Sassou Nguesso issu de la guerre civile de juin 1997. Ces violences politiques constituent en réalité les nouvelles formes par lesquelles se sont exprimées au Congo les masculinités. Les femmes congolaises y ont opposé leurs initiatives de paix. Nous entendons dans une première partie faire une interprétation théorique de l'ordre masculin dans les sociétés en général et dans celle du Congo en particulier. Dans un second temps nous indiquons comment cet ordre a marqué l'histoire de la démocratisation au Congo au point de se matérialiser par des violences politiques inédites dans l'histoire récente du pays. La dernière partie recense les initiatives féminines pour la paix comme réponse aux violences politiques.

L'ordre masculin : un ordre de violence à l'endroit des femmes (essai d'interprétation théorique)

Il faut entendre par le concept « ordre masculin », la domination exercée par les hommes sur l'ensemble de la société. Cette domination, qui s'exerce particulièrement sur les femmes, dure depuis l'Antiquité. Tous s'accordent à admettre que dans l'histoire de l'humanité, l'oppression de la femme est la première de toutes les oppressions, avant même celle des classes qui est apparue avec l'esclavage, et celle des races avec les impérialismes d'Athènes et de Rome dans l'Antiquité, puis avec le colonialisme occidental dans les époques moderne et contemporaine (Garaudy 1981).

L'oppression de la femme est inséparable du sexisme, c'est-à-dire ce mode de comportement et de pensée qui attribue à un sexe des qualités et par conséquent des privilèges supérieurs à ceux de l'autre sexe. Les tenants de la domination masculine ont de tout temps cherché à justifier les disparités entre les deux sexes en s'appuyant sur des considérations d'ordre religieux, économique ou autres. Il apparaît de plus en plus, aujourd'hui, au regard des travaux réalisés dans les domaines de la masculinité et du genre[3], que ce sont surtout les considérations d'ordre politique notamment de pouvoir, qui sont les plus déterminantes. Celles-ci sont analysées à la lumière des deux courants qui dominent la recherche dans ces domaines : le courant biologiste et le courant culturaliste. Nous développons ces deux courants plus loin dans notre travail.

Du point de vue religieux, l'Ancien Testament, puis l'Église chrétienne, nés dans des sociétés patriarcales, ont fourni un arsenal de justifications à la thèse fondamentale de la soumission de la femme à l'ordre masculin. Le livre de *la Genèse* nous donne deux récits différents de la création de l'humanité. Dans le premier, nous trouvons cette belle formule où Dieu créa l'humanité indivisiblement masculine et féminine : « Homme et femme il les créa » (*Genèse* 1 : 27). Dans le deuxième récit (*Genèse* 2 : 21-23), la femme apparaît tardivement après les animaux, sous la forme d'une cote superflue d'Adam, avant d'être la première coupable du péché (*Genèse* 3). Selon ce deuxième récit, la femme a été créée pour servir d' « aide » à l'homme. Saint Paul confirme cette tradition misogyne en indiquant : « L'homme n'a pas été créé à cause de la femme, mais la femme à cause de l'homme » (Corinthiens I, 11 : 9). Les enseignements de Paul relatifs à ces rapports entre l'homme et la femme ont dominé la pensée des pères et docteurs de l'Église. Dans l'Église catholique, les femmes ne sont pas admises à la prêtrise, comme si une infériorité spirituelle pesait sur elles, et cela en flagrante contradiction avec la parole suivante de Paul :

> Il n'y a plus ni Juif ni Grec, il n' y a plus ni esclave ni libre, il n'y a plus ni homme ni femme, car vous tous, vous êtes un en Christ-Jésusé (Galates 3 : 28*).*

Tous ces sophismes ne doivent rien à l'Évangile, mais aux préjugés d'une société patriarcale.

Les marxistes ont cherché à expliquer la domination de la femme par l'homme en se fondant sur l'organisation du travail et de l'économie. Engels dans *Les origines de la famille, de la propriété privée et de l'État* (1881) et Marx dans *l'Idéologie allemande* (1846) avaient souligné que la première division du travail est celle entre l'homme et la femme. Dans une économie de subsistance, c'est-à-dire, où ce qui est essentiel à la vie quotidienne est produit dans la famille, la répartition des tâches (surtout dans les campagnes) s'est faite selon les sexes. Ces tâches sont peu différenciées et complémentaires. La situation de la femme, dans ce contexte économique, n'est pas alors très inférieure à celle de l'homme. C'est plus tard que commença le déclin du statut des femmes. L'historienne Régine Pernoud estime que c'est à partir du XIVe siècle que commença la dégradation du statut social de la femme en Europe occidentale[4]. Elle exprime cet amenuisement du rôle de la femme en Europe en ces termes :

> La place de la femme au sein de la société semblait … s'amenuiser dans la proportion où la puissance du bourgeois s'étendait (Pernoud 1980 : 5).

À ce sujet, les juristes évoquent au XIVe siècle la loi salique interdisant aux femmes d'accéder au trône de France (Latour et alii 1995). Au cours de ce siècle, l'université de Paris intente des poursuites contre les femmes médecins sous prétexte qu'elles n'ont point de diplômes, alors qu'en réalité on les empêche de les obtenir. La violence symbolique à l'endroit des femmes se poursuit, car un arrêt du Parlement de Paris du 28 juin 1593 interdit aux femmes toute fonction dans l'État. La conséquence de ce processus va être l'apparition de deux mondes : un monde public, masculin où règne la force et la violence symbolique à l'endroit des femmes, et un monde privé, domestique réservé aux femmes. Cette dichotomie sphère publique et sphère privée a perduré jusqu'à l'époque contemporaine. Elle explique tous les combats qui ont été menés, à travers le monde par les femmes et les hommes de bonne volonté, pour l'accession des femmes à plus de droits politiques. Les différentes conventions internationales relatives aux droits spécifiques de la femme dont nous avons faits mention plus haut en sont une illustration.

Toutes les dominations (de classe, de race, de propriété, etc.) présupposaient la domination primordiale de l'homme sur la femme. Les femmes athéniennes, bien que citoyennes, étaient exclues de la *politéia*, c'est-à-dire de la participation à la vie politique de la cité. Le rôle exclusif de la femme était de faire les enfants et de gérer la maison. La situation de la femme n'était guère meilleure à Rome. Pas plus que l'esclave, la femme n'existait pas dans le droit romain. Ses rapports avec ses parents ou avec son mari étaient de la compétence de la « maison » (*domus*, en latin) dont le père, le beau-père ou le mari sont les chefs tout puissants. Le code napoléonien qui, au début du XIXe siècle, s'inspira profondément du droit romain, consacra la totale subordination de la femme. Il fallut attendre l'ordonnance du général de Gaulle du 21 avril 1944 pour que les Françaises deviennent électrices et éligibles dans les mêmes conditions que les hommes. Le 29 avril 1945, les Françaises se rendirent pour la première fois aux urnes en France.

L'évolution de l'humanité depuis la fin de la Seconde Guerre mondiale a entraîné des bouleversements, non seulement dans les domaines de la politique et de la vie économique en accordant une place de plus de plus importante à la femme, mais aussi du point de vue de l'heuristique. En effet, dans le domaine de la recherche, de nombreuses universités anglo-américaines, canadiennes et européennes ont intégré dans leurs cursus universitaires des enseignements relatifs au genre et à la masculinité. Historiquement les Men's Studies (études sur la masculinité) ont été précédées par les Women's Studies (études sur le féminisme).

La question fondamentale qui traverse les études sur la masculinité est de savoir si cette dernière est une donnée biologique ou une construction idéologique (Badinter, 1992 : 41). Les travaux de nombreux chercheurs indiquent que la question oppose les partisans du déterminisme biologique aux culturalistes.

Les premiers indiquent d'abord que c'est la biologie qui définit l'essence masculine et féminine. Ils indiquent ensuite que tous les comportements humains s'expliquent en terme d'hérédité génétique et de fonctionnement neuronal (Badinter 1992 : 42).

Les seconds encore appelés constructivistes, contestent le rôle premier de la biologie. À leurs yeux, la masculinité n'est pas une essence, mais une idéologie qui tend à justifier la domination masculine. Ils s'appuient sur les travaux de l'anthropologie sociale et culturelle, de l'histoire et de la sociologie (Badinter 1992 : 48). Selon les culturalistes, il n'y a pas un seule modèle masculin. La masculinité diffère selon les époques, les classes sociales, les races et les âges de l'homme ; elle n'est donc pas une donnée statique. Elle est en réalité une construction. C'est ce que développent dans leurs travaux respectifs Abdessamad Dialmy (2005), Ibrahim Mouiche (2005).

Il convient de rappeler, en accord avec les auteurs du *Dictionnaire critique du féminisme,* qu'en sociologie et anthropologie des sexes, masculinité et féminité désignent

> les caractéristiques attribuées socialement et culturellement aux hommes et aux femmes. Masculinité et féminité existent et se définissent dans et par leur relation. Ce sont des rapports sociaux de sexe, marqués par la domination masculine, qui déterminent ce qui est considéré comme « normal » – et souvent interprété comme « naturel – pour les femmes et les hommes » (Hirata et alii 2004 :77).

Quelles sont les spécificités qui ont permis l'instauration et la pérennisation de l'ordre masculin en Afrique et au Congo ?

L'ordre masculin trouve ses fondements en Afrique et au Congo dans un ensemble de traditions dont les traces sont encore visibles dans l'Afrique contemporaine[5]. Dans l'Afrique et le Congo pré-coloniaux, tout a été organisé selon les sexes et les classes d'âge. L'éducation et la formation traditionnelles n'y ont pas échappé (Moumouni 1998). Les rites d'initiation y ont joué un rôle de premier plan. Il y a d'abord les rites de puberté obligatoires, propres aux garçons et aux filles, qui permettent le passage de l'âge d'adolescence à l'âge d'adulte. Les rites féminins sont liés à l'apparition des menstrues et sont tournés vers les rôles domestiques de la femme, notamment la procréation et la gestion quotidienne du foyer. Les rites masculins, qui mettent en exergue la force physique et l'endurance, ont pour mission de préparer l'adolescent à assumer son rôle de chef de famille. Il y a ensuite les rites d'initiation aux grands mystères, ouverts aux adultes par cooptation. Les hommes entrent dans ces ordres qui sont nécessaires pour gérer politiquement la cité et assurer sa sécurité et sa stabilité (Eliade, 1959 ; 1965). Au Congo, par exemple, on citera les ordres suivants : l'ordre des hommes-léopards (*Ngo*) chez les *Teke* au Sud ou des hommes caïmans (*Andzimba*) chez les *Mboshi* au Nord. Aujourd'hui encore les ordres initiatiques masculins continuent à marquer la vie congolaise. La guerre civile de juin à octobre 1997 a été, en filigrane, une guerre entre deux leaders politiques (Pascal Lissouba d'une part et Denis Sassou

Nguesso d'autre part) appartenant à deux obédiences différentes de la Franc-Maçonnerie, le tout sous-tendu par des intérêts pétroliers et financiers (Verschaves 1998). Il convient de préciser que la Franc-Maçonnerie ne doit pas être confondue avec les rites initiatiques traditionnels. Elle a été introduite au Congo sous la colonisation et n'intéresse en réalité que les élites. Ce sont ces élites qui ont pris le relais des anciens administrateurs coloniaux et qui travaillent avec les réseaux maçonniques au niveau international. Même si sur le plan local les loges maçonniques disent suivre un rite africain (comme le rite équatorial pour le cas du Gabon et du Congo), il n'en demeure pas moins que les membres de ces loges reçoivent des directives des anciennes métropoles, en conformité avec les intérêts de ces dernières. L'échec de la réunion des francs-maçons congolais ballottés à Pointe-noire en 1997, en pleine guerre civile congolaise, entre les intérêts de la France à travers sa compagnie pétrolière Elf Congo et ceux supposés du Congo représentés par le gouvernement de Pascal Lissouba, est une illustration patente de cet état de fait.

Les grands mystères féminins conduisent généralement à la prêtrise traditionnelle. Ces femmes prêtresses deviennent des médecins traditionnels, des devineresses voire des gardiennes des secrets du pouvoir incarné par le mari-chef (ce fut le cas de la reine téké Ngalifourou décédée en 1957).

Malgré leur infériorité physique et le poids des traditions, les femmes n'ont pas pour autant été absentes des cercles des décisions. Au Congo, par exemple, de nombreuses femmes ont été des chefs de clans et ont dirigé avec maestria les personnes placées sous leur autorité. L'histoire de l'Afrique centrale nous donne des exemples référentiels des femmes qui ont joué un rôle de premier plan sur le plan politique : Anne Nzinga d'Angola ; Kimpa Vita (Béatrice du Congo) ; Ngalifourou du Royaume téké (Ki-Zerbo 1972). Dans le but d'arrêter les guerres récurrentes, au cours de la période 1992-1997, de ramener et d'instaurer une paix durable au Congo, le Comité national des femmes pour la paix (CNFP) a mené des actions en directions de femmes des principaux protagonistes de la vie politique congolaise : mesdames Jocelyne Lissouba et Antoinette Sassou Nguesso. Ces actions ont permis des résultats significatifs que nous indiquons dans la section III de ce travail (Ondziel 1995 ; Rapport national sur l'évaluation de la mise en œuvre des plates-formes d'actions de Dakar et Beijing 10 2005).

Quels sont les stéréotypes sociaux traditionnels issus de ces différents rites sociaux et quels sont leurs conséquences ?

Ces rites se traduisent dans la vie quotidienne des Congolais, aujourd'hui encore, par un certain nombre de comportements sociaux observables aussi bien chez les hommes que chez les femmes. Il est par exemple strictement interdit à un homme de s'adonner à des activités culinaires (comme piler les feuilles de manioc, les courges ou les noix de palme)[6], de laver les habits et surtout les sous-vêtements de son épouse, d'avoir certains types de relations sexuelles considérés comme non traditionnels, comme par exemple le cunnilingus. Cela entraînerait une malédiction pour ce dernier et altérerait sa virilité. La virilité apparaît ici comme l'expression collective et individualisée de la domination masculine. Les attributs sociaux de la virilité (la force, le courage, la capacité à se battre, etc.) sont appris et imposés aux garçons par le groupe des hommes au cours de leur socialisation, pour qu'ils se distinguent hiérarchiquement des femmes. Les femmes, quant à elles, acceptent certains interdits comme les interdits alimentaires qui ne se justifient pas du point de vue scientifique, mais essentiellement par l'égoïsme des hommes. L'idéologie masculine dominante réserve en effet certains aliments considérés comme meilleurs aux hommes.

Dans les sociétés congolaises traditionnelles, où l'activité économique principale était l'agriculture, la division du travail a été faite elle aussi selon les sexes. Les travaux les plus durs, notamment l'abattage des arbres, revenant aux hommes, physiquement plus forts.

Dans une société où la femme était confinée aux travaux subalternes et à la procréation, la tendance, au moment de la colonisation, fut de scolariser prioritairement les garçons. Cela s'est traduit par une faiblesse numérique des femmes scolarisées. La conséquence à long terme a été une faible présence des femmes dans les administrations et dans la politique. À la Faculté des Lettres et des Sciences Humaines de l'Université de Marien Ngouabi au Congo-Brazzaville, par exemple, on ne note que sept femmes (trois maîtres-assistantes, quatre assistantes) sur un effectif de 120 enseignants. Le nombre d'étudiantes baisse rapidement après la licence. Au cours de l'année académique 2003-2004, par exemple, sur les 2742 étudiants inscrits à la Faculté des Lettres, on ne dénombrait que 840 étudiantes. La situation n'est guère élogieuse sur le plan politique : 11 femmes députés sur les 115 députés à l'Assemblée nationale, et 9 femmes sénateurs, dans la législature actuelle. L'ordre masculin a si profondément imprégné la mentalité des Congolais et des Congolaises que lors des dernières élections présidentielles de 2002, Angèle Bandou, la seule femme candidate n'avait obtenu que 27 849 voix sur les 1 222 611 exprimées, soit 2,32 % des suffrages exprimés.

Quel a été l'impact de la démocratisation actuelle du Congo dans la remise en cause de la situation ci-dessus décrite ?

Démocratisation, masculinité et violences politiques au Congo

La démocratisation du Congo, comme nous l'avons indiqué plus haut, a débuté en 1991 avec l'organisation de la Conférence nationale souveraine (2 février-10 juin 1991). Cette conférence qui a regroupé quelque 1100 délégués représentant les partis politiques et les structures sociales (les associations diverses, les ONG, les syndicats et les confessions religieuses) a posé les bases pour la création d'un nouvel espace politique marqué par la démocratie. De 1991 à 1997, la vie politique congolaise s'est articulée autour de trois partis politiques : le Parti congolais du travail (PCT), ex parti unique de Denis Sassou Nguesso, l'Union panafricaine

pour la démocratie sociale (UPADS) de pascal Lissouba et le Mouvement congolais pour la démocratie et le développement intégral (MCDDI) de Bernard
Kolélas. Dans la perspective d'accéder au pouvoir, ces partis ont été amenés à
conclure entre eux des alliances. Lors du deuxième tour de la première élection
présidentielle post-conférence nationale en 1992, le PCT et l'UPADS ont conclu
un accord de gouvernement qui a permis l'élection de Pascal Lissouba opposé à
son challenger Bernard Kolélas. Le non respect dudit accord par l'UPADS a
conduit le PCT à quitter l'alliance UPADS-PCT pour conclure une nouvelle alliance avec le MCDDI. Celle-ci a entraîné automatiquement un changement de
majorité à l'Assemblée nationale.

En effet le changement de camp, à l'Assemblée, des députés du Parti congolais du travail (PCT), précédemment allié à l'Union panafricaine pour la démocratie sociale (UPADS), parti au pouvoir mais non majoritaire à l'Assemblée nationale, renforça le camp de l'opposition. Cette dernière vota alors une motion de
censure le 28 octobre 1992. Celle-ci entraîna la démission du premier gouvernement démocratique post-conférence nationale. Exerçant son pouvoir de dissolution prévue par l'article 80 de la Constitution du 15 mars 1992, le président de la
République a prononcé la dissolution de l'Assemblée nationale, avec pour conséquence l'organisation de nouvelles élections législatives anticipées. La décision présidentielle a provoqué de vives réactions dans le camp de l'opposition.

Les violences politiques récurrentes ont donc démarré au Congo-Brazzaville
après le vote de la motion de censure. L'opposition (désormais composée par le
PCT, le MCDDI et d'autres petits partis) a aussitôt fait dresser des barricades
dans les quartiers sud de Brazzaville, fief électoral du Mouvement congolais pour
la démocratie et le développement intégral (MCDDI). Les deux grandes familles
politiques (la « Mouvance présidentielle » c'est-à-dire l'ensemble des partis soutenant avec l'UPADS l'action de Pascal Lissouba et l'opposition) se sont alors organisées en mettant en place des milices privées[7] et en acquérant massivement des
armes de guerre. Quels sont les enjeux, les rôles et stratégies de chacune des
alliances en présence ?

Il convient d'indiquer qu'au Congo les alliances ne se fondent pas sur des
bases idéologiques ni sur des projets communs de société, mais essentiellement
sur des intérêts conjoncturels ou d'opportunité des leaders : les adversaires d'hier
devenant subitement de nouveaux alliés (Goma-Thethet 2005 ; Fall 2000). Ainsi
lors de la période de transition (du lendemain de la Conférence nationale aux
élections présidentielles de 1992), le gouvernement et le Parlement de transition
ont été dominés par les Forces du changement (alliance des partis politiques opposés au PCT lors de la Conférence nationale) dont le chef de fil était Bernard
Kolélas. Tout au long de la Transition, cette alliance a tiré à boulets rouges sur le
PCT de Denis Sassou Nguesso et l'Alliance nationale pour la démocratie (AND)
forgée autour de l'UPADS de Pascal Lissouba. En rompant, en 1992, l'alliance

conclue avec l'UPADS, le PCT révéla sa volonté de revenir au pouvoir par tous les moyens quitte à pactiser avec l'ennemi d'hier c'est-à-dire le MCDDI de Bernard Kolélas. L'enjeu principal pour les nouveaux alliés et principalement pour le PCT était donc la prise et la conservation du nouveau pouvoir pour éviter des poursuites judiciaires aux anciens dignitaires du pouvoir de la période du parti unique. Pour revenir au pouvoir leur stratégie était simple : renverser le pouvoir de Pascal Lissouba grâce au vote d'une motion de censure par la nouvelle majorité parlementaire. Pour renforcer cette disposition constitutionnelle, la nouvelle alliance avait prévu d'exercer une pression tous azimuts sur le président de la République : agitation sociale par le biais des grèves afin de paralyser les administrations publiques, instrumentalisation de la violence politique avec la création de milices armées.

Les élections législatives anticipées se sont déroulées dans des conditions de fraudes et d'irrégularités. Cette situation a entraîné des affrontements fratricides qui se sont traduits par des viols, des assassinats, des déplacements de populations, bref par des violations des droits de l'homme. Les affrontements qui se sont déroulés dans les quartiers sud de Brazzaville et accessoirement dans la région du Pool (fief électoral de Bernard Kolélas) et les régions du Niari, de la Bouenza et de la Lékoumou (fiefs électoraux de Pascal Lissouba) ont opposé les partisans des deux leaders politiques sus-nommés regroupés dans des milices.

Les milices ont été, dans leur quasi-totalité une affaire d'hommes. Ce sont en effet ces derniers qui ont subi la formation nécessaire, généralement dispensée par des éléments de la force publique proches des leaders politiques, et qui sont allés au « front » c'est-à-dire sur les champs de bataille qui ne sont autres que les quartiers ou les régions habités par les partisans des partis adverses. Il y avait parmi les miliciens des jeunes femmes. Celles-ci, dans la plupart des cas, ont été cantonnées à des tâches non guerrières comme la cuisine, le renseignement des positions adverses ou le transport des munitions, notamment des grenades plus faciles à dissimuler dans des pagnes. Rarement elles sont allées au « front ».

Si les soldats et les miliciens sont essentiellement des hommes, les décideurs politiques, c'est-à-dire ceux qui ont décidé du déclenchement des hostilités sont eux aussi des hommes. Tout se passe comme si les femmes n'existent pas. L'enrôlement des gens dans les milices armées résulte dans la plupart des cas de la colère de ces derniers face à l'incapacité de l'État ou des hommes politiques à satisfaire les attentes juvéniles. Les leaders de l'opposition, s'appuyant sur des considérations messianiques et ethniques mobilisent les jeunes, leur faisant miroiter des lendemains meilleurs une fois qu'ils seront au pouvoir (Ossébi 1995). Selon leurs intérêts spécifiques, les leaders politiques ont donc créé les conditions de prolongation et d'intensification des conflits armés en appelant au recrutement d'hommes et de garçons s'identifiant à leur discours politique (Ossébi 1998). Ils ont ainsi créé les conditions d'une masculinité violente. L'hebdomadaire catholique, *la Se-*

maine Africaine, sous la signature d'Argus, qualifie ces hommes politiques de délinquants de la démocratie (Argus 1996).

Les comportements des individus, ceux des autorités gouvernementales, ceux des groupes ethniques et des groupes sociaux au cours de ces guerres récurrentes ont attiré notre attention : actions paramilitaires organisées, capture et emprisonnement des personnes dans des prisons privées, capture et viol de femmes ou humiliation des parents contraints d'effectuer des rapports incestueux. Des enquêtes menées, par l'ONG Médecins sans frontières (MSF), auprès des femmes des quartiers sud de Brazzaville ou de la région du Pool, après la guerre de Bacongo de 1998, ont révélé que de nombreuses femmes revenant à Brazzaville après s'être réfugiées dans les forêts, ont été victimes de viols collectifs (communément appelés « Viêt-Nam »[8]) par les cobras, milices au service des autorités gouvernementales. Les violences perpétrées par les hommes sur les femmes nous ont conduit à inscrire notre réflexion dans la nouvelle vague de recherche sociale et scientifique sur les hommes et les spécificités masculines qui est apparue dans le monde depuis ces dix dernières années.

Dans la plupart des sociétés, la violence est culturellement masculinisée. Comment la masculinité a-t-elle été reliée à la violence dans le cas du Congo ? Elle a eu des causes multiples parmi lesquelles : la dépossession, la pauvreté, la convoitise, les considérations ethniques, la conception de « l'honneur », etc. Elle s'est nourrie de situations diverses (politiques, économiques, socioculturelles et historiques). Les moyens de la violence (les armes privées, l'armement militaire et les compétences militaires) sont entre les mains des hommes et non des femmes. Les troupes (les soldats et les miliciens) qui allaient au front et écumaient les quartiers étaient constituées essentiellement d'hommes. Du reste, la formation du soldat associe couramment la virilité à la brutalité et considère la peur et la sensibilité comme des caractéristiques féminines.

Ces quelques informations tirées de l'expérience congolaise, nous amènent à présent à voir les initiatives de paix prises par les Congolaises pour faire face à ces violences politiques nées avec la démocratisation.

Les initiatives féminines pour la paix comme réponse aux violences politiques.

Bravant le climat d'insécurité qui régnait à Brazzaville, le ministère délégué chargé de l'Intégration de la Femme au développement, organisa du 13 au 18 décembre 1993, le Forum national de la Femme. Ce forum qui avait pour principal objectif d'évaluer les stratégies prospectives d'action de Nairobi (1985) en vue de préparer la cinquième conférence régionale africaine sur les Femmes de Dakar 1994, a rassemblé les femmes venues de toutes les régions administratives et de tous les partis politiques. Il a été l'occasion de mener une réflexion sur les problèmes de sécurité à Brazzaville et à l'intérieur du pays. C'est ainsi qu'un Appel de la paix fut lancé le 15 décembre 1993, appel qui demanda aux protagonistes de la crise l'arrêt immédiat des violences qui endeuillaient le pays.

Dans le même temps, des délégations de femmes se lancèrent à la rencontre des autorités politiques, administratives, militaires et religieuses afin de transmettre le message de paix du forum. Les déléguées interpellèrent d'abord les femmes, pour dénoncer leur silence complice et coupable. Elles interpellèrent ensuite le chef de l'État en tant que garant de l'unité nationale et chef suprême des Armées, les membres du gouvernement en tant que gestionnaires de l'État et garants du bien être des populations ; les parlementaires dans leurs responsabilités d'élus, représentant des populations martyrisées, les leaders politiques dans leur idéal de serviteurs du peuple. Elles interpellèrent enfin les religieux afin qu'ils pèsent de tout leur poids charismatique dans la résolution du conflit, les sages des différentes régions du pays pour révéler les mécanismes traditionnels de règlement des conflits, la société civile pour l'amener à s'investir dans la bataille pour la résolution du conflit et l'instauration d'une paix durable, les jeunes afin qu'ils prennent conscience de leur avenir hypothéqué.

À cette occasion, les délégations ont rappelé d'une part aux leaders politiques leur rôle dans l'éducation de leurs militants en général et particulièrement de la jeunesse, et d'autre part aux femmes, leur rôle traditionnel d'éducatrice à la paix.

L'initiative des femmes fut jugée salutaire par les autorités qui avouèrent leur incapacité à régler le conflit, compte tenu du climat de méfiance qui régnait dans la capitale.

La réaction favorable des responsables politiques à l'action des femmes a encouragé celles-ci à poursuivre leur objectif de pacification. Elles mirent en place un comité ad hoc de suivi de l'Appel du 15 décembre 1993. Ce comité organisa le 22 décembre 1993 une marche pacifique pour protester contre le redoublement de la violence à Brazzaville. La marche se termina au palais présidentiel où les femmes remirent un second message de paix au chef de l'État, Pascal Lissouba, qu'entouraient pour la première fois depuis le déclenchement du conflit, les membres de l'opposition et de la « Mouvance présidentielle ».

Profitant de la période des fêtes de fin d'année, Le comité s'est lancé dans une grande campagne d'apaisement des esprits auprès des citoyens congolais traumatisés par la guerre. Aussi a-t-il organisé le 26 décembre 1993 une tribune télévisée réunissant autour d'une même table les trois présidents des groupes parlementaires les plus influents, représentant les partis politiques en conflit. L'objectif de cette tribune était de rapprocher les protagonistes par le dialogue.

Pour légitimer leurs actions, les femmes transformèrent le 30 décembre 1993, le comité ad hoc en une organisation non gouvernementale dénommée : Comité national des femmes pour la paix (CNFP). Le CNFP s'assigna deux objectifs prioritaires : à court terme, le rétablissement de la paix ; à moyen et long terme, le maintien, la consolidation et la promotion de la paix par l'éducation à la paix en vue d'instaurer l'unité et la concorde nationales, seuls gages d'une paix durable. L'initiative du comité a servi de détonateur pour la paix, en secouant la conscience des autorités politiques, administratives, militaires, religieuses et des autres composantes de la société civile. Elle a permis la création d'une commission ad hoc parlementaire de paix, le message de paix de la conférence épiscopale du Congo, les messages de paix de plusieurs autres associations, la marche pacifique des fraternités religieuses la naissance de plusieurs associations, en faveur de la paix et de l'unité nationale telles que le Comité National des Femmes pour la paix (CNFP), le Comité National des Droits de la Femme (CONADF), l'Association Congolaise de Lutte contre les Violences faites aux Femmes et aux filles (ACOLVEF), les Messagères de la Paix, le Mouvement pour la Paix des mamans chrétiennes catholiques de l'Afrique Centrale (MOPAX), Génération sans frontières et l'Association de lutte contre le tribalisme.

De décembre 1993 jusqu'à la tenue, en décembre 1994, du Forum national de la culture de la paix organisé conjointement par le gouvernement congolais et l'Unesco, le CNFP a poursuivi ses activités de pacification en mettant l'accent sur la prévention des conflits, notamment par la détection des situations pré-conflictuelles. Il a rencontré tour à tour : les autorités traditionnelles de toutes les régions du pays, la Conférence épiscopale, les parlementaires, l'État-major mixte (armée, gendarmerie et police), le Premier ministre (chef de gouvernement), l'ancien chef de l'État (Denis Sassou Nguesso) à Oyo (ville située à 400 km au nord de Brazzaville), Mme Antoinette Sassou Nguesso (épouse de l'ancien chef de l'État), Bernard Kolélas (président du MCDDI et de chef de l'opposition), Mme Jocelyne Lissouba (épouse du chef de l'État en fonction) Christophe Moukouéké (secrétaire général de l'UPADS, président de la « Mouvance présidentielle »), le président de l'Assemblée nationale, etc.

Ce déploiement d'activités en direction des différentes personnalités sus-indiquées a permis des résultats significatifs parmi lesquels la participation de Denis Sassou Nguesso, de Bernard Kolélas et de chefs traditionnels comme le Makoko (roi de Téké) et le Maloango (roi des Vili) au Forum national pour la culture de la paix. La présidente du CNFP, Madame Julienne Ondziel, fut élue au poste de vice-présidente dudit forum. Le CNFP profita de cette grande rencontre pour faire une déclaration dans laquelle il identifia les obstacles à l'instauration d'un dialogue inter-communautaire et fustigea le détournement des fonds affectés au développement au profit des dépenses somptuaires et militaires. Dans cette déclaration il émit quelques propositions :

- la mise en place par les institutions internationales des mécanismes en vue d'une réglementation de vente et d'achat d'armes conventionnelles assorties de mesures coercitives ;

- l'organisation par les leaders politiques d'une table ronde pour faire la paix en présence de la société civile ;

- la promotion par l'État de la participation de la femme à la gestion de la cité, particulièrement aux mécanismes de règlement des conflits ;

- la réinsertion sociale par l'État des personnes sinistrées lors des conflits ;

- le démantèlement des bandes armées et le ramassage des armes ;

- la distribution à tous les participants d'une affiche servant de support à la campagne d'apaisement des esprits conçus par le CNFP ;

- la distribution de tee-shirts dans le cadre de l'éducation à la paix portant les écrits suivants : « Je milite pour la paix » (CNFP 1994).

En marge des assises de ce forum, une concertation a réuni le 20 décembre les personnalités suivantes : le président de la République, l'ancien chef de l'État, le chef de l'opposition, le chef de la « mouvance présidentielle », la reine Ngalifuru et les roi Makoko et Maloango. Cette concertation a été sanctionnée par un communiqué portant sur la mise en place d'un comité chargé de faire des propositions sur la réorganisation de la force publique et la réhabilitation des services judiciaires.

L'engagement de tous les participants au forum a permis l'adoption de plusieurs textes d'importance parmi lesquels, une déclaration sur la prévention des conflits et la consolidation de la paix et un plan d'action pour la culture de la paix.

De 1994 à juin 1997, le Congo, grâce à l'action conjuguée des femmes, des hommes de bonne volonté épris de paix et de la communauté internationale, a connu une relative période de paix et de stabilité. On peut signaler en effet la signature du Pacte pour la paix le 24 décembre 1995. Mais les appréhensions de l'opposition et du gouvernement en place, face aux futures échéances électorales prévues en août 1997, conduisirent progressivement à une dégradation de la paix qui déboucha le 5 juin 1997 à une nouvelle et grave crise. Celle-ci s'est transformée en une véritable guerre civile qui s'est poursuivie jusqu'en 2002 et dont les conséquences ont été désastreuses pour le pays, tant sur le plan matériel qu'humain.

Les principales responsables du CNFP et bon nombre de ses militantes s'étant réfugiées à l'étranger, l'ONG s'est trouvée momentanément affaiblie. Jusqu'aux accords de cessation des hostilités entre les milices de l'opposition et le gouvernement, l'action des femmes a semblé comme en hibernation. Le CNFP a repris ses activités et poursuit avec de nombreuses organisations féminines, apparues depuis la fin de la guerre, le combat pour la paix qui passe par l'égalité entre les personnes.

Aujourd'hui, on pourrait se demander quel a été finalement le véritable rôle des femmes et du CNFP quand on sait qu'il y a eu, malgré l'immense travail abattu entre 1993 et 1997, un regain des violences au Congo-Brazzaville entre 1997 et 2002 ? A notre avis, ce rôle ne saurait être minimisé. Les femmes congolaises ont fait, avec les moyens qui étaient les leurs, tout ce qui était nécessaire pour pacifier ce pays et l'engager dans la voie d'une paix durable. Malheureusement leurs moyens et capacités ne pouvaient leur permettre de faire face à des situations dont les tenants et les aboutissants échappaient en réalité aux Congolais comme l'ont mis en exergue Verschaves et Mabeko Tali (Verschaves 2000 ; Mabeko Tali 1997).

Conclusion

Le féminisme contemporain a ouvert d'importants débats sur la problématique des genres et de la paix. Aujourd'hui, les recherches portant sur les problèmes liés à la masculinité et leur mise en rapport avec le travail pour la paix sont au cœur de ces débats. Les recherches dans ce domaine sont relativement nouvelles en Afrique et précisément au Congo-Brazzaville. Comme nous l'avons vu dans cette étude, la violence qu'expriment les hommes ne s'enracine pas dans la biologie mais dans les impératifs de la société. L'expérience de la vie politique congolaise depuis les premières élections démocratiques post-conférence nationale nous a révélé que la violence a été instrumentalisée pour accéder au pouvoir et conserver celui-ci. Cette violence s'est exercée de façon indistincte aussi bien sur les hommes que sur les femmes. Mais ce sont les femmes qui ont été les plus grandes victimes ; c'est sur elles que les violences masculines se sont exercées plus fortement. Ce constat nous a fait comprendre que la lutte pour mettre un terme à la violence des hommes envers les femmes et à la violence interpersonnelle parmi les hommes et développer une culture de la paix nécessite un changement de comportements. Cette lutte passe nécessairement par l'éducation et la formation. Dans le cas du Congo-Brazzaville, par exemple, il est indispensable de continuer les politiques et les initiatives actuellement appliquées pour réduire la violence (multiples campagnes des ONG), promouvoir le désarmement par le ramassage des armes (notamment avec le Programme de désarmement, démobilisation et réinsertion sociale des anciens miliciens avec le concours du PNUD), accroître l'égalité économique et politique entre les femmes et les hommes, combattre la discrimination sous toutes ses formes en luttant concrètement contre la pauvreté, promouvoir la créativité et les manifestations culturelles et les œuvres d'art liées à la paix et diffuser les idées et les techniques d'une culture de la paix. C'est dans cette optique que le Comité national des femmes pour la paix (CNPF) a organisé en 2003, sur l'ensemble du territoire national un concours sur la chanson de la paix. Il a ainsi produit 2500 cassettes audio, 7 cassettes vidéo et 4 compact disc. Ces produits ont été par la suite utilisés dans les campagnes de sensibilisation de la population en vue de l'intériorisation des valeurs relatives à la paix (CNFP 2003 : 3).

Toutes ces initiatives démontrent les capacités des femmes congolaises à s'investir dans les problèmes de paix. Dans leur rapport national sur l'évaluation de la mise en œuvre des plates-formes d'actions de Dakar et Beijing + 10, les ONG et associations féminines congolaises indiquent qu'après avoir réalisé des actions visant l'arrêt des hostilités, le rétablissement et le maintien de la paix durant les trois guerres fratricides (décembre 1993 ; 5 juin 1997 et 18 décembre 1998), la société civile congolaise poursuit, depuis que la paix est globalement retrouvée, sa mission de consolidation de la paix. Ces actions se résument comme suit : marches ; interpellations des pouvoirs publics, des leaders politiques et des autorités religieuses, correspondances adressées à des personnalités d'envergure internationale comme Nelson Mandela et Toumani Touré, messages radiotélévisées, séminaires de formation et de sensibilisation, exécution d'un projet d'éducation à la culture de la paix, prise en charge médicale et psychologique des femmes victimes des violences, assistance juridiques desdites femmes, distribution de dons et aides (Rapport national sur l'évaluation de la mise en œuvre des plates-formes d'actions de Dakar et Beijing 10, 2005). La création très récemment du Centre de la femme en politique traduit la volonté des femmes congolaises d'investir le champ politique congolais, de ne pas le laisser aux seuls hommes.

Notes

1. On consultera avec intérêt la communication de Sœur Bibiane Tshibola Kalengayi, une religieuse de Kinshasa, sur le rôle des Kinoises dans l'avènement de la démocratie au Zaïre de Mobutu, faite au colloque *Écriture et démocratie. Les francophones s'interrogent*, organisé à Paris les 18 et 19 février 1993 par le Centre Wallonie-Bruxelles (Centre Wallonie-Bruxelles, 1993).

2. Lors des différentes guerres civiles, les trois grands partis politiques, l'Union panafricaine pour la démocratie sociale (UPADS) de Pascal Lissouba, le Parti congolais du travail (PCT) de Denis Sassou Nguesso et le Mouvement congolais pour la démocratie et le développement intégral (MCDDI) de Bernard Kolélas ont eu chacun leur propre milice : *les Cobras* pour le PCT, *les Ninjas* pour le MCCDI et les *Zoulous* précédemment appelés *Aubevillois* puis *Cocoyes* pour l'UPADS.

3. En 1992, Élisabeth Badinter a, dans son travail sur la masculinité, donné une bibliographie sur les travaux réalisés dans les universités du Nord (Badinter, 1992).

4. Elle lie cela à l'évolution du pouvoir économique des bourgeois. Ces derniers entendent en effet ajouter à leur pouvoir économique tous les autres pouvoirs sociaux et politiques.

5. Amina Mama (1992) et Fatou Sow (2005) sont parmi les chercheures africaines qui ont choisi comme champ de recherche la question de genre en Afrique.

6. Un Congolais, cuisinier de profession, effectuera toutes les activités culinaires traditionnellement attribuées aux femmes à son lieu de travail, mais n'osera pas le faire chez lui pour rester un « vrai » homme à la maison.

7. Il s'agit des *Cobras*, des *Ninjas* et des *Zoulous* dont nous avons déjà fait mention.

8. Le terme Viêt-Nam, selon les *Cobras* désigne les viols collectifs qui étaient perpétrés par les soldats américains sur les Viêt-namiennes.

Références

Argus, 1996, « Les délinquants de la démocratie », *La Semaine Africaine*, n° 2073 du jeudi 30 mai, p.7.

Badinter, Élisabeth, 1994, *XY de l'identité masculine*, Paris : Odile Jacob.

Baudoux, Claudine, Zaidman, Claude, 1992, *Égalité entre les sexes. Mixité et démocratie*, Paris : L'Harmattan.

Breines, Ingeborg, Connel, Robert et Eide, Ingrid (dir.), 2004, *Rôles masculins, masculinités et violences : perspectives d'une culture de paix*, Paris :UNESCO.

Centre Africain pour la Femme, 1998, *Réunion ad hoc du groupe d'experts / forum sur le leadership des femmes en matière de paix : les femmes et le processus de paix : les processus en ce qui concerne l'Afrique*, Johannesburg (Afrique du Sud).

CNFP, 1994, *Déclaration au forum national pour la culture de la paix*, Brazzaville (document inédit).

CNFP, 2003, *Rapport annuel des activités réalisées par le CNFP 2003*, Brazzaville (document inédit).

Centre Wallonie-Bruxelles, 1993, *Écriture et démocratie. Les francophones s'interrogent*, Bruxelles : Éditions Labor.

Dayras, Michèle, 1995, *Femmes et violences dans le monde*, Paris : L'Harmattan.

Dialmy, Abdessamad, 2005, *Problématique théorique de la masculinité*, papier présenté à l'Institut sur le genre du CODESRIA 2005, Dakar : CODESRIA.

Eliade, Mircea,1959, *Naissances mystiques : essai sur quelques types d'initiations*, Paris : Gallimard.

Eliade, Mircea, 1965, *Le sacré et le profane*, Paris : Gallimard.

Fall, Ismaïla Madior, 2000, *La transhumance politique : modalités et impact sur le processus électoral.* Essai d'explication théorique, Dakar : CODESRIA

French, Marilyn, 1992, *La guerre contre les femmes*, Paris : L'Archipel.

Formation de formatrices pour la transformation des conflits fondée sur une perspective genre : Renforcement des capacités des femmes oeuvrant pour le retour de la paix au Burundi, 7- 12 avril 1976.

Garaudy, Roger, 1981, *Pour l'avènement de la femme*, Paris : Albin Michel.

Goma-Thethet, Joachim Emmanuel, 2005, "Alliances in the political and electoral process in the Republic of Congo 1991-1997 ", in Tukumbi Lumumba-Kasongo (Editor), 2005, *Liberal democracy and its critics in Africa. Political dysfunction and the struggle for social progress*, London/ Dakar: Zed Books /Codesria Books, pp. 99-124.

Guillaumin, Colette, 1992, *Sexe, Race et Pratique du pouvoir*, Paris : Côtés–Femmes Éditions.

Hirata, Helena et alii, 2004, *Dictionnaire critique du féminisme*, Paris : PUF.

Ki-Zerbo, Joseph, 1972, *Histoire de l'Afrique noire. D'hier à demain*, Paris : Hatier.

Latour, Patricia et alii, 1995, *Femmes et citoyennes. Du droit de vote à l'exercice du pouvoir*, Paris : Éd. de l'Atelier.

Loupé, Samuel, 2005, *Étude des comportements-problèmes post-conflits dans la vie quotidienne de l'adulte (Cas des réfugiés de la région du Pool à Brazzaville)*, maîtrise de psychologie, Université Marien Ngouabi, Brazzaville.

Mama, Amina, 1992, *Gender violence and Human Rights*, Dakar : CODESRIA.

Mouiche, Ibrahim, 2005, *L'État moderne africain et le patriarcal public*, papier présenter à l'institut sur le genre du CODESRIA 2005, Dakar : CODESRIA.

Moumouni, Abdou, 1998, *L'éducation en Afrique*, Paris : Présence Africaine.

Ondziel, Julienne, 1995, *Réunion du groupe des experts sur la contribution des femmes à la culture de la paix. Contribution du Congo*, Manille, 24-28 avril 1995, document inédit.

Ossébi, Henri, 1995, *Ethnicité, logiques partisanes et crises transitionnelles en Afrique : le cas du Congo*, Dakar : CODESRIA.

Ossébi, Henri, 1998, « De la galère à la guerre : jeunes et « cobras » dans les quartiers nord de Brazzaville », *Politique Africaine*, n° 72, décembre, pp. 17-33.

Pernoud, Régine, 1980, *Les femmes aux temps des cathédrales*, Paris : Stock.

Rapport national sur l'évaluation de la mise en œuvre des plates-formes d'actions de Dakar et Beijing + 10, 2005 (document inédit).

Sow, Fatou, 2005, *Les femmes dans l'exercice de leurs responsabilités politiques en Afrique de l'ouest*, texte présenté le 3 mars 2005 à Dakar, en prélude à la journée internationale de la femme 2005, organisé par le Centre canadien de recherches pour le développement international (CRDI).

Tedga, Paul John Marc, 1991, *Ouverture démocratique en Afrique noire ?* Paris : L'Harmattan.

Verschaves, François Xavier, 1998, *La Françafrique. Le plus long scandale de la république*, Paris : Stock.

* Les livres bibliques cités ici sont extraits de : *La Sainte Bible. Nouvelle version Louis Segond révisée*, Alliance biblique universelle, 1998.

14

Corps et beauté : représentations et enjeux. Socio-anthropologie de la construction binaire : Masculin/Féminin, Le cas de l'étudiante algérienne

Zahia Benabdallah

Introduction

Dans cette modeste étude, nous allons parler du « corps » en tant que phéno-mène social, ajusté par les chercheurs afin de résoudre l'énigme du lien social. Pour ce faire, il serait question de comprendre à travers l'analyse l'achemine-ment de la genèse du concept « corps » en sciences sociales et d'une manière plus pratique, comment à travers la logique des représentations, la concep-tion du corporel s'élabore chez les étudiantes algériennes.

Sociologiquement parlant, le corps tel qu'il est représenté, n'est que le produit d'un imaginaire fertile qui l'introduit à son tour dans une totalité symbolique. Ainsi, la conception du « corps » varie d'un imaginaire à un autre, d'une symbolique à une autre. Dans les sociétés à caractère masculin domi-nant par exemple, l'évaluation corporelle s'effectue de manière distinctive à savoir binaire, selon une répartition genre : Masculin/ Féminin. Étant consi-déré comme sexe faible, le corporel féminin n'est perçu qu'en subordination au masculin, qui est sensé le posséder, le protéger, le surveiller, le marier… et cela selon les conditions et les normes d'une série de représentations indivi-duelles et sociales. Reste à savoir comment le concept « corps » a trouvé son cheminement en sciences sociales et quelles ont été les contributions pionniè-res dans l'insertion et dans la confirmation de ce concept en tant qu'objet d'étude en sociologie? En particulier, chez les universitaires algériennes, quelles sont les représentations et les pratiques de la prise de conscience du corps dans une société qui s'abstient d'entamer des discussions à propos de ce sujet ? Et à partir de quelles demandes le corps social aujourd'hui arrive-t-il à façonner l'image de ses individus ?

Pour le traitement de ces questions, nous proposons deux hypothèses :

1. le « corps » en tant que concept est l'objet d'une multitude de perspectives qui se controversent et qui divergent même au sein d'une même discipline en sciences sociales ;

2. la prise de conscience du corps chez la jeune universitaire est la résultante d'un besoin biologique autant que psychologique et social. Elle n'est que le troisième regard alternatif entre le « soi » et l'autre, entre le féminin et le masculin, entre l'individu et le social.

En vue de réaliser une approche socio-anthropologique sur le « corps » et ses valeurs et afin de bien mener cette recherche, nous nous appuyons sur une méthode qualitative, englobant un aspect littéraire et un autre aspect empirique, où on va travailler sur la représentation et l'usage des techniques du corps à savoir de l'esthétique auprès d'un échantillon composé de vingt étudiantes résidentes dans une résidence universitaire à Oran, issues de différents milieux sociaux, leur âge variant entre dix-neuf et trente ans. Dans le choix de notre étude de cas, le port du voile était un élément de distinction majeur : à égalité, on distingue (10) dix étudiantes voilées et dix autres sans voile. Toutes ces jeunes femmes étaient des célibataires.

Afin de les interroger, on avait procédé par guide d'entretien, élaboré grâce à la technique de l'observation participante dans leur milieu de résidence. Pour cela, il a été convenu avec ces filles d'effectuer nos rencontres le soir, à la fin de la journée, afin que ses dernières soient prédisposées pour tout questionnement. Sujet de recherche, l'observation participante est le fait de « vivre dans »…, de « rester près de »…, « à la disposition de »…. Elle veut dire aussi, regarder de plus près…, s'exposer au regard de tout le monde… ; à leurs commentaires et à toutes les formes du discours social… (Combessie 1998 : 15). Ainsi, cette méthode nous a été de grande aide pour faciliter le contact et pour suivre notre « cas d'étude » jusqu'aux plus délicates questions provocantes sur la vie intime et le vécu esthétique et corporel.

Genèse de la notion du corps en sociologie

Le discours sociologique sur « le corps » représente une grande problématique pour ceux qui travaillent dans ce domaine de recherche. Il existe jusqu'à présent beaucoup de courants et de perspectives qui divergent quant à la genèse de l'insertion de ce concept en sciences sociales. On cherche dans l'histoire ou dans le vécu actuel les éléments qui peuvent soutenir les points de vues et réconforter les argumentations. Le corps, cette bulle du « moi », est aussi un récipient pour tout capital immatériel, irréel ou symbolique à savoir imaginaire. Ainsi, il convient de dire qu'à partir de ce moment, toute représentation calquée par le cerveau n'est qu'une image irréelle propre à la machine qui la produit. De part cet aspect, elle acquiert un caractère personnel et individuel, capable par la suite de se transformer socialement et collectivement.

Pour l'unanimité, beaucoup de chercheurs se sont mis d'accord sur la non-existence d'une définition collective et unique de la représentation du corps, d'autant plus que tout imaginaire est façonné par les conditions de vie de chaque société et par son sens commun. D'autre part, il existe une grande divergence dans le regard au corps et dans son investissement social, que ce soit sur un niveau local ou sur un niveau global, que ce soit à l'interne d'une société ou à son externe, dans le seul groupe ou entre les différentes agrégations.

Le sociologue et le concept « corps »

Sur la base de ce qui vient d'être dit, la représentation du corps ne prend pas une seule image; elle est variable et multiple, ce qui rend le concept corps en perpétuelle révision en sciences sociales. Pour un début, Durkheim ne croyait pas à la faisabilité d'une étude sur « le corps », sociologiquement parlant, car il ne voyait pas en ce dernier un sujet d'étude pour cette science, mais plutôt, il le voyait comme étant un sujet pour les sciences de l'organique et du biologique. Bien qu'il lui accorde une dimension symbolique, il insiste sur le fait que c'est juste un sujet pour la biologie et la médecine (Fournier 2002 : 23).

Contrairement à Durkheim, Max Weber et Marcel Mauss avaient une autre idée relative au corps. Ainsi, ils étaient parmi les premiers chercheurs ayant joué un rôle fondamental dans le traitement phénoménologique du concept « corps » et dans son introduction en sciences sociales, en le subordonnant à la notion de « culture » et à celle de « société ».

Après de multiples recherches en ethnologie et en anthropologie et à partir de ses différentes études sur le mode de vie des sociétés dites primitives, Marcel Mauss est arrivé à constater que ces sociétés utilisent différentes manières pour traiter leurs corps et que ses pratiques sont conditionnées par l'origine de chaque population et sa culture dominante. Ainsi, il remarqua la non-ressemblance de leurs pratiques corporelles; que ce soit en matière d'entretien, d'hygiène ou d'esthétique : leurs façons de faire leurs toilettes, leurs marquages de peaux, leurs manières de se coiffer, de s'habiller et de se maquiller, etc.

À cet effet et en structurant sa perspective à base de notes d'observations, il arriva à faire le lien entre la nature de la pratique et son impact social, entre le mode de vies à mener et l'appartenance sociale et culturelle… en l'occurrence, il déduisait que la notion du « corps » avait la faculté d'illustrer et de définir beaucoup de phénomènes liés au social. Ainsi, il les surnomma : « *les techniques du corps* » *(*Mauss 1967).

Ce concept, Marcel Mauss le définit ainsi : « les techniques du corps sont l'art d'utiliser le corps humain, ou c'est la méthode par laquelle l'individu ou la société utilise son corps d'une manière habituelle » (Des Camps 1986 : 31), n'est pour lui que le résultat d'un savoir-faire, d'un savoir -créer ou d'un savoir-produire. Il considérait qu'il n'y aurait de technique s'il n'y avait pas d'habitudes[1] et que le rapport au corps n'aura de signification que s'il y avait de méthodes pour le traiter et pour l'entretenir.

Perceptions contemporaines du corps

Parmi les travaux pionniers du monde contemporain sur la problématique du corps en sciences sociales, on note ceux de Georges Vigarello, Jean Marie Brohm, Alain Corbin, David Le Breton , Jean-Claude Kaufman, Pierre Bourdieu, Christine Detrez et beaucoup d'autres.

Pierre Bourdieu par exemple voit que « le corps » dans sa signification la plus absolue, n'est que le pur produit d'une totalité socioculturelle, il le considère en tant qu'héritage transmis par la succession historique des civilisations. De son côté, David Le Breton affirme que l'intérêt sociologique de la conceptualisation contemporaine du corps a commencé dès le 16e et 17e siècle, à cause des changements sociaux qui ont caractérisé cette période de l'histoire. Parmi ces changements, il faut citer l'émergence de l'individualisme et son impact sur le vécu corporel.

Dans ce contexte, Le Breton rappelle que « le corps dans la définition contemporaine et à partir duquel la sociologie applique ses méthodes, n'est que la conséquence du recul des traditions populaires et du surgissement de « l'égocentrisme » dans le bloc social, car a priori le rapport au corps traduit la nature du rapport avec le « moi » et ce rapport au « moi » n'est positif qu'à partir du moment où l'auto-valorisation individuelle lui est satisfaisante » (Le Breton 1997 : 29).

Pour certains sociologues l'intérêt porté au « corps » en tant qu'élément d'analyse en sociologie est arrivé à son apogée avec l'apparition des mouvements jeunes et des courants leaders de la fin des années soixante et qui avaient pour principe l'émergence d'une contre-culture par rapport à celle de leurs aînés.

Ayant une empreinte de jeunes, cette nouvelle culture portait en elle les revendications de nouvelles normes et d'une nouvelle logique sociale, que ce soit en matière de styles de vie ou en particularités de codes du comportement : en style d'apparence (tenues vestimentaires, coupes de cheveux, coiffures…), en sexualité et même en goûts alimentaires et musicaux (Travaillot

1998 : 17). A cet effet, le corps, son apparence et ses attributs étaient sujets d'une certaine liberté reendiquée, pour citer la liberté de penser et la liberté d'agir. De ce fait, il en est découlé un énorme stress envers le corps et envers tous ce qui peut être en rapport et en interaction avec lui, d'une manière réelle ou symbolique, que ce soit en représentations ou en pratiques.

Ainsi, à cette période ce changement avait pour conséquence la modification de la nature des rapports et des liens sociaux : entre parents et enfants et entre Homme et Femme. Cependant, ce résultat s'est révélé transgressant tous les interdits pour l'anti- courant conservateur, à savoir celui des parents, et a provoqué un grand conflit entre les groupes sociaux, entre ceux qui l'ont adopté et ceux qui ont voulu assurer le fonctionnement continuel des valeurs et des normes dominantes à l'époque.

Historiquement parlant, comme toute phase transitoire de conflits ou de perturbations, un changement réel s'est installé par l'emportement des mouvements de revendications, en faisant du corps l'hymne du salut. À cet effet, il ne devenait pas juste un souci quotidien pour les jeunes, mais aussi pour toutes les catégories sociales emportées par la vague du changement et sa nouvelle conception.

Prenant par causalité l'extension du temps libre pour l'individu, Hardan et Dumizel considéraient que cette grande attention portée au corps est due à l'extension des jours de congés, de vacances ou des week-ends, causée par la diminution des heures de travail rémunéré, le fait ayant favorisé l'apparition de multiples loisirs dont l'entretien du corps est leurs intérêt numéro un.

D'autre part, Christian Pociello considère que c'est durant les années quatre-vingts que le phénomène du corps s'est accentué le plus, en impliquant toutes les sociétés dans des enjeux à caractères universels : là où il existe un rapport entre l'individu et son « moi » ou, là où existe un rapport entre l'individu et le social. De ce point de vue, il trouve que le stress envers le corps et envers la manière dont il est traité, est devenu une habitude ancrée dans les mœurs et les normes de chaque société pour devenir une part indissociable de sa culture (Pociello 1989 : 153-155).

À son tour, Gay Borde expose une approche genre pour affirmer que ce même stress est la cause directe d'une série de phénomènes qui ont apparu dans les sociétés contemporaines, telles que la mode et l'esthétique. De son point de vue, ces attributs au corps ont contribué d'un côté à renforcer le pouvoir féminin qui les a consciemment instrumentalisé, et d'un autre, ils ont contribué à remettre en cause le rapport avec le masculin. Dans ce contexte, il arrive à dire : « On vit dans une société qui croit à la souveraineté du corps et de l'apparence… et derrière l'encouragement de cette souveraineté, les groupes à domination culturelle et surtout les femmes » (Travaillot 1998 : 2).

Conçue pour les femmes, bénie par les hommes, la mise en valeur du corps avait contribué au surgissement de maintes modifications au sein de l'architecture sexuelle et sociale. En s'infiltrant dans la société moderne par les multiples formes de l'information et de la communication, le féminin était le genre le plus sujet à l'emblème de la bulle charnelle et de son enveloppe externe et devint par la suite porteur d'une certaine identité culturelle, notamment après l'accès qualitatif et quantitatif à la sphère publique par le biais de l'apprentissage et du travail. Cette nouvelle condition sociale, ce fut une grande révolution contre les forces qui ont travaillé à occulter la voix du plus faible par le pouvoir de la domination masculine.

Particulièrement, il faut dire que le monde arabo-musulman vit aujourd'hui un surinvestissement du corps féminin par rapport au passé, tiraillé entre tradition et modernité, entre permis et interdit, entre licite et illicite, il devient un terrain fertile pour toutes controverses, pour tous affrontements et conflits. Ainsi, la question du corps et du pouvoir des apparences se conjugue actuellement à plusieurs temps et à différentes personnes : du singulier et du pluriel, pour la négociation d'un certain statut social.

La mode et l'esthétique ne représentent-elles pas des intérêts plus appropriés aux femmes, à leurs distinction par rapport aux hommes ? Ne contribuent-elles pas à leur épanouissement personnel et collectif ? Ne façonnent-elles pas leurs vécus et n'affirment- elles pas leur identité individuelle et sociale ?

Le phénomène « mode »

Bien que les études sur la mode ne donnaient pas lieu à de sérieuses recherches qu'à partir des années soixante, où quelques travaux embryonnaires apparaissent, le discours sur ce phénomène social n'a cessé depuis lors d'intéresser les scientifiques et les littéraires. Parmi les premiers chercheurs à avoir pensé à faire de la « mode » un thème de réflexion et de recherche en sciences sociales, il faut citer Herbert Bleumer.

Cependant, après de maintes recherches, il est arrivé à déclarer qu'il n'a pas trouvé un grand intérêt dans l'étude de la phénoménologie de ce concept, à part le fait de sa configuration en tant que panneau au sein des sociétés dynamiques (Zdatny 1996 : 24-27).

Toutefois, cette conclusion n'a pas convaincu l'ensemble des chercheurs en sociologie et en anthropologie. En revanche, elle a suscité leur enthousiasme vers d'autres aspects en matière de recherche sur le même thème. Dans ce même cheminement, Marie Louise Robert est arrivée à démonter que bien au contraire, le sujet de « la mode », peut être un très bon élément d'analyse en sociologie, à savoir un bon indicateur sur les conditions de vie des individus et surtout de la femme (Robert : 1996 : 57).

En anthropologie historique, Philippe Perrot s'est intéressé à une étude comparative de deux sociétés occidentales à deux périodes, à savoir le XVIIIe et le XIXe siècle. Progressivement, il a noté une grande marge de distinction en matière d'apparences et en matière du rapport au corps et du rapport au social, ainsi, il voyait cette distinction comme étant un terrain utile pour analyser la situation sociale de l'époque.

La société du du XVIIIe siècle dite société aristocratique, s'est caractérisée par le mode de parité en apparence, que ce soit entre les deux sexes, entre différentes tranches d'âges ou entre différents individus : aussi bien en habillement, en coiffure ou en esthétique générale ... En apparence, en fait tout le monde était pareil (Perrot 1984). La mode de cette époque était telle que les hommes et les femmes, les petits et les grands, les riches et les pauvres se maquillaient, portaient des perruques, de la dentelle, des bijoux, de la fantaisie... le corps dans tout ses dimensions était célébré.

Contrairement à cette société, celle du XIXe siècle s'est distinguée par un mode d'apparence différent : le corps et ses attributs représentaient pour les acteurs sociaux de cette époque un support pour raccrocher leurs identités sociales. La quête de distinction en look était de mise pour dénoncer une certaine appartenance ou une certaine affiliation, soit à un groupe, à une structure ou à une tendance.... En tant qu'échantillon représentatif de cette nouvelle condition de vie, le corps « élite » était parmi les premiers sujets à être distingué et à être identifié par rapport à l'ensemble de la population. A travers le corps, on marque le pouvoir ou la faiblesse, on assure soit sa socialité ou sa marginalité.

Au moment où la parité des apparences a contribué à brouiller les éléments d'analyse entre les catégories sociétales de la première société, dans la deuxième, la mode de distinction en matière d'apparence a participé à l'apparition de nouvelles catégories à identités spécifiques, au sein du domaine professionnel, ainsi que dans la trame de la vie quotidienne.

Représentations sociales du corps

La famille est le premier noyau de la société, de ce fait, elle est la plus importante institution qui contribue à la socialisation de l'individu par la passation des normes, des valeurs, des expériences et des héritages matériels et immatériels, d'une façon diachronique ou synchronique. En sauvegardant ces multiples enseignements, elle veille sur la préparation de générations à perspectives cohérentes et à la formation de groupes à identités collectives.

Dans le monde arabe, la structure familiale est fondée sur la base des liens du mariage. Ainsi, au sein de la structure parentale, se sont les mères qui sont déléguées pour l'éducation et la prise en charge des enfants. À l'instar des pères, se sont elles qui veillent sur leur bonne socialisation en leurs transmettant tout leurs savoir vivre, leurs attention et leur tendresse. Elles sont là pour les préparer pour demain et pour leurs passer les recommandations et les connaissances liées à leurs vécu actuel ou lointain, notamment en ce qui concerne l'utilisation de la première machine humaine, à savoir leur corps.

Cependant, selon de multiples études sur le genre, il faut dire qu'il existe une grande marge de distinction dans l'éducation de l'enfant mâle ou femelle. Remarquablement, la socialisation des filles est plus rigoureuse par rapport à l'éducation du garçon, surtout, dans l'imaginaire et le contact à la chair.

Les germes de l'enseignement du conscient corporel

À partir d'un moment précoce, on prépare la future bonne femme et future bonne épouse, en apprenant à la petite fille les bonnes manières : dans les discussions, dans la façon de se tenir, de s'habiller…. On lui apprend des techniques relatives à l'hygiène, à la propreté, à la démarche, comment elle doit parler, comment elle doit s'asseoir, comment elle doit marcher, comment elle doit se tenir propre... En revanche, son frère en tant que garçon mâle, n'est pas aussitôt censuré. Toute une initiation particulière portante sur le rituel corporel. On commence à attirer l'attention de la jeune fille sur son corps et à semer en elle les valeurs et les normes liées à son existence et à celle de la société, à lui faire remarquer la différence entre le féminin et le masculin, à lui faire comprendre ce qui lui est propre de ce qui lui est impropre, en lui imposant le maintien sous le tutorat des adultes dominateurs.

Selon le travail de terrain et selon les résultats vérifiés par la suite, quel que soit leurs milieux d'origine ou leurs milieux de provenance, à savoir le rural ou l'urbain, le fait de prendre conscience du corps chez la population objet d'étude s'est révélé à un âge précoce. Plus de la moitié des vingt étudiantes interviewées ont déclaré qu'elles se sont rendues compte de leur vécu corporel à un très jeune âge, même avant la puberté et avant même d'avoir leurs premières menstrues. Qualifiant la découverte ou la connaissance du corps progressivement, elles déclarent avoir pris conscience de sa bonne maintenance et de son bon entretien, en matière d'hygiène et en matière d'esthétique, à partir du milieu familiale ou de l'entourage voisinant ou amical. Onze jeunes filles avaient noté leur conscience prématurée par rapport à leurs frères dans l'obligation de porter un œil attentionné à leur corps, à ses organes et à ses mouvements. En envisageant un âge minimal pour la puberté féminine et en prenant en considération les cas présumés, il est à déduire que même avant l'âge de dix ans (10), on peut vivre les premières moments du conscient corporel.

Alors que cinq filles avaient signalé qu'elles n'ont pas réalisé leur appartenance au « moi », au féminin et aux dimensions du corps qu'à partir de leur totale réalisation de l'émergence de leur métamorphose biologique, deux autres avaient répliqué que la révélation et la découverte de leurs corps se sont effectuées à partir de l'instant où elles avaient commencé à prendre leur bain toutes seules.

En nous replongeant dans la littérature, les données de ce qui vient d'être dit trouvèrent une coïncidence chez Pierre Bourdieu qui affirme que la prise de conscience du corps chez la fille commence à se développer et à se réaliser dès son jeune âge, à partir de l'âge de quatre ans, où chacune commence à se comporter selon ce que lui dicte sa génétique, son anatomie et sa structure corporelle (Bourdieu 1991 : 23). Il trouve aussi que la différence entre les deux sexes a pour origine leurs distinctions biologiques et que le fait de se rendre compte de son corps est lié au fait de prendre conscience de son sexe qu'il soit mâle ou femelle.

Pour une deuxième remarque, on avait noté selon tous les entretiens réalisés que la majorité des filles ont ajouté qu'en réalité, la vrai prise de conscience du corps s'effectue réellement avec l'éveil du corps et avec l'éveil de ses organes sexuels, fait déclenché par le début de sa métamorphose biologique et psychologique, où des signes d'ordre visible surviennent pour accentuer le regard et l'intention à son égard. Apparition des poils et des duvets, surgissement de la poitrine et arrondissement des hanches… révèlent la naissance d'une nouvelle identité, d'une nouvelle bulle à connaître et à découvrir. À ce moment crucial de l'existence, il est à citer que si le social proche n'est pas à l'écoute et ne subventionne pas à ses besoins, une quête à l'explication et un appel au savoir va pousser la jeune fille à chercher des personnes pour lui expliquer ce qui lui est incompréhensible. Cependant, même si leurs renseignements et leurs enseignements sont confus et faussés, elle les suivra et s'en servira pour façonner ses goûts et fabriquer ses représentations.

À cette étape de la vie où les sens commencent à être identifiés, à se préciser et à s'accentuer, façonner son corps et son apparence devient un sérieux enjeu social dans le fondement de l'architecture sexuée, dans l'impulsion et la répulsion entre le masculin et le féminin. Avoir un beau corps et une bonne apparence, c'est se présenter, se référer, s'insérer, c'est d'être reconnu et non marginalisé.

En prenant le corps en tant que variable, George Tarabichi nous rapporte que à la base de tout un imaginaire social, une représentation individuelle vient pour enrichir la donnée collective et contribue à la création de l'inconscient populaire : « Dans l'inconscient arabo-musulman, on dit que la guerre est un fait masculin, tandis que la paix est une réclamation féminine ; l'homme est fort, tandis que la femme est faible, on dit aussi que la prison est pour les hommes, mais la maison est pour les femmes » (Tarabichi 1982 : 2).

Ainsi, à base de ces attributions d'ordre sexiste, cette société arrive à faire du corps un support et un facteur de distinction qui hiérarchise les individus selon leur profil sexuel et selon leur validité corporelle. Par la suite, c'est cette même hiérarchisation qui assure la loi du dominé et du dominateur, en impliquant le genre humain dans une logique de stratégie de pouvoir.

En parlant de division sexuelle, George Tarabichi remet en cause la socialisation enfantine dans sa formation et ses orientations, dans ses méthodes d'ancrage et ses modèles de propositions. À cet effet, il discute la culture du jeu, en croyant que la prédisposition de l'enfant dans le choix de son jouet favori, n'est que résultante d'une certaine assimilation au monde des adultes. Dés leurs premiers ages, « les garçons sont attirés par les pistolets et les fusils, tandis que les filles adorent les poupées. En avancent dans l'age, même les préférences de lectures ne sont pas authentique chez l'adolescente que chez l'adolescent : au moment où les garçons préfèrent les histoires et les romans policiers, les filles sont fascinées par les histoires d'amour et les contes de fées » (Tarabichi 1982 : 03). Cependant, il faut dire que dans ce cas, il ne s'agit pas que d'une simple illusion ou d'un simple imaginaire normatif, mais de toute une réalité qui trouve sa justification dans l'existence matérielle et immatérielle des gens, depuis leur création en passant par tous les cheminements de leur vie.

L'entité du corps est minutieusement fabriquée à travers sa biologie, sa psychologie ou son social. Dans cette fabrication, on distingue deux blocs identitaires qui servent à la formation de la totalité sociale, à savoir le masculin et le féminin. Cette bipolarité qu'on vient de citer n'est pas tout à fait indépendante l'une de l'autre, bien au contraire, elle est corrélée, soit par les liens d'intérêt général ou par des intérêts particuliers, soit par les liens du contrat social ou par les liens affectueux d'amitiés ou d'amour. À partir de l'adolescence, phase du déclenchement morphologique et sexuel, les liens de subordination entre le féminin et le masculin commencent objectivement à se tisser. Charme, élégance, beauté… sont à exhiber. Penser sérieusement à son corps à cette étape, c'est penser à son épanouissement pour l'autre et à travers l'autre. C'est aussi penser à son image et à son esthétique, c'est le fabriquer pour trahir et attirer le regard.

Dans le régime patriarcal, la notion de l'honneur est fondamentale pour sauvegarder la condition de la domination masculine. Sous la norme du châtiment et du mérite, « le corps » est le premier lieu de la censure et de la surveillance, notamment le corps féminin. Pour son utilisation, si pour une fois la tradition n'est pas respectée ou ajustée à la norme dominante, il en résulte de graves conséquences qui peuvent être arbitraires, car tout ressourcement représentatif altèrant son groupe d'appartenance est hautement censuré, voire mal considéré. Toutefois, à la moindre transgression, la fille ou la femme se fait basculer à l'autre rive avec les exclues et les marginaux.

Au moment où le discours social sur le corps prohibe toute provocation vulgaire du charnel, toute transgression à cette rigoureuse recommandation devient une transgression au sens commun, une transgression de la tradition et des mœurs, donc de la pudeur. La pudeur qui est une des dimensions de l'honneur est le socle de tout comportement censé être normatif et exemplaire. Pour nous expliquer le rapport au corps dans un contexte maghrébin, Farid El-Zahi[2] nous évoque l'appréhension de l'usage même du vocabulaire corporel, comme étant un vocabulaire à connotation sexuelle (El-Zahi : 1999). Car le fait d'évoquer le corps, c'est évoqué son mouvement, sa gestuelle, ses sens, ses désirs et ses attentes… c'est évoqué le tabou que le social veille sur son occultation.

Dans la conception arabe, en subordination à la notion de l'honneur, la pudeur joue un rôle majeur dans la structuration du lien social. Il relève du déshonneur qu'une parente qu'elle soit mère, fille, sœur ou même une cousine éloignée soit mal perçue par les gens du voisinage ou même de toute la société à cause d'un comportement contre-mœurs. Ainsi, ce sentiment du déshonneur a amené beaucoup de familles à chercher des solutions même les plus rudes pour essayer de se racheter auprès de leurs groupes d'appartenance, l'expression utilisée dans cette condition est « laver son honneur ». Beaucoup d'histoires présumées être du déshonneur ont terminé par des crimes ou à la moindre des choses, par un bannissement définitif de la collectivité. Un corps féminin non contrôlé, représente un danger, une atteinte non seulement au masculin, mais aussi à l'ensemble de son genre.

Démontrer ou faire du charme, séduire, forniquer, porter léger, porter court, trop farder… on croit que tous ses élément liées au corps féminin, forment une atteinte à la pudeur de part leurs liaisons avec le sexuel, lieu interdit de toute pratique illégale. Cependant, toute emprunte collée ou affichée, induit sa partenaire dans un monde de dévergondées, de prostituées, de mauvaise mœurs, des sans pudeur, donc des femmes sans hommes qui les commandent et qui les protègent : celles qui sont pour tout le monde, pour n'appartenir à personne.

Dans ce sens, l'identité féminine dans le monde arabe est construite conjointement sur un aspect corporel défini préalablement, comme sur l'aspect mental soumis aux normes sociétales. À la base de cette binarité, la représentation du rapport entre masculin et féminin remet en cause à perpétuité le rapport au corps. L'homme admire la beauté féminine, mais de l'autre côté, il l'occulte pour avoir le droit individuel du bénéfice. Il abuse d'elle, il l'instrumentalise, puis il la condamne pour afficher une position, une conformité après avoir satisfait un manque et assouvit un besoin. Cette ambivalence que vit l'homme dans sa conception du corps, relève t-elle vraiment de l'éthique, de la religion, de la norme, ou est-ce que c'est juste un usage vicieux au nom du sacré?

À partir des données de terrain, dix-neuf (19) étudiantes de notre échantillon qualitatif avaient répliqué sur la question en disant que l'Islam en tant que religion, n'a rien à voir avec la construction totale de la notion du corps chez les musulmans. Selon leurs points de vue, l'Islam traite cette notion d'une manière claire et à égalité entre femmes et hommes, chacun dans son genre d'appartenance, en prenant en ligne de compte les intentions et les conditions des individus, c'est plutôt son interprétation qui est différemment codée et qui donne lieu par la suite, à une lecture controversée et à des comportements distinctifs. L'Islam n'interdit pas la sexualité, n'interdit pas l'esthétique, mais interdit plutôt leur mauvais usage. Cette position est illustrée par maintes passages et textes dans le coran et la tradition du prophète Mohamed (la Sounà). Depuis « Dieu est beau et aime la beauté », à « il n'y a pas de pudeur en religion (science) », passant par les recommandations au propos des femme : « je vous conseille de bien traiter les femmes »…, la religion musulmane n'absente pas le corps et elle ne le marginalise pas, elle essaye de le sauvegarder contre toute les formes de l'abus.

Corps : enjeux et représentations du beau

La conception masculine de la beauté féminine n'est pas juste une conception liée à une appréciation extérieure d'un corps ou d'une apparence physique ; elle inclut aussi l'aspect moral et éthique de la personne. À cet effet, même si la femme porte en elle les signes du beau, elle n'est pas tout à fait valorisée juste sur ce point.

Beauté intérieure, jugement extérieur

Dans les sociétés à caractère patriarcal, à savoir les sociétés du monde arabe, parmi les références appréciées chez une femme, il y a sa fragilité et sa sagesse. Fatma Ait Sabah nous cite que la passivité et la soumission à l'homme sont parmi les qualité les plus appréciées chez une femme, car c'est des qualités qui incarnent la perpétuité de la domination masculine (Ait Sabah 1982 : 42). Dans son livre *La femme dans l'inconscient musulman*, elle nous rapporte que l'homme arabe trouve le beau en une femme quand il constate la passivité de ses réactions et sa soumission dans l'application de ses recommandations. Celle qui n'a pas le pouvoir d'exprimer son point de vue et celle qui ne le contredit pas; c'est celle qui plait à ses yeux, c'est celle qu'il peut prendre comme épouse. « L'homme cherche la soumission et la passivité chez une femme, cela satisfait son égocentrisme, son sentiment de supériorité et du pouvoir, non seulement par rapport à elle, mais aussi par rapport à son clan et à son groupe » selon Hanane, 23 ans, d'origine d'un petit village de la wilaya de Mascara, habitant un appartement avec ses parents, ses cinq frères et quatre soeurs.

En la considérant en tant qu'être faible, il se voit le plus fort et cela lui procure un sentiment d'autosatisfaction et d'assurance, selon Wassila, 24 ans, 3ᵉ année licence en Droit. Par contre, s'il aperçoit en elle l'autonomie des prises de décisions et l'expression de l'opinion avec la faculté de le contredire, il se développe en lui une certaine méfiance, une certaine distance à la prendre en tant qu'épouse et de constituer avec elle un projet familial. Pour lui, la cause directe est que cette femme ne représente pas l'image de la femme incarnée par sa mère ou ses soeurs, elle n'incarne pas le modèle féminin, elle ne satisfait pas les représentations qui lui ont été inculquées dés son enfance. Par contre, cette façon d'être lui reflète une situation insécurisante et suscite en lui l'impression de tomber dans le profane, dans l'impure, dans la souillure, si un de ses jours, elle arrivera à le détrôner par la condamnation de son pouvoir de domination et de maîtrise.

Quinze (15) étudiantes de l'échantillon d'étude, dont huit (08) sont des filles voilées, avaient répliqué que si un homme est amené à choisir une femme pour épouse, son choix est fait a priori sur la base de son aspect éthique engendrant la bonne réputation et la bonne conduite, non seulement de la fille, mais aussi de l'ensemble de sa famille. Pour qu'elle soit élue, elle doit être connue par sa gentillesse, sa bonté, sa soumission aux commandements des mâles de sa famille… un modèle qui perpétue la conception traditionnelle du sens commun.

En modernisant les secteurs de la vie par les moyens d'interacculturation globaux, une rénovation en matière de goûts et de préférences arrive à reconstituer et à modeler les représentations et les pratiques des individus. Entre normes durables et critères qui changent, la conception corporelle aujourd'hui inclue pour une grande part le côté éthique ou moral, aussitôt après le côté image et apparence. Une fois que les qualités internes existent, cela ne veut en aucun cas signifier la négligence des qualités physiques, qu'elles soient naturelles ou artificielles, telles que les formes du corps, son teint, la qualité de sa chevelure,… ou son esthétique et son élégance vestimentaire. Dans le monde arabe contemporain, l'intérêt à l'apparence est vivement sollicité et notamment pris en considération pour le choix de la future épouse.

Beauté extérieure, jugement intérieur

La valeur de la beauté féminine dans le vécu arabo-musulman, n'est pas une nouvelle valeur, bien que ce soit une valeur à conception changeante ou relative, elle trouve ses racines dans le passé lointain comme dans l'actualité présente, dans la tradition comme dans la modernité. À cette effet, la structure « du beau » en une femme est une structure bien et tellement ancrée dans les représentations collectives. Dans l'imaginaire, le « beau » est symbole du bon, symbole du généreux, symbole de la santé et de la jouissance, donc symbole de la fertilité, de la nature de la terre et de la religion, où la femme par son corps devient « une déesse ».

L'impact de la beauté dans la société est un impact d'ordre remarquablement élémentaire, où l'image de la beauté féminine représente non seulement un patrimoine culturel et symbolique, mais aussi un mouvement d'ordre pratique et actif. La réalité sociale dans notre présent actuel travaille toujours sur la préservation de son héritage concernant l'image de ses individus et qui est, à vrai dire, sa propre image. Le look ou l'envers du look, tel que vu par Michèle Pagés Delon (1989), qu'il soit fabriqué ou naturel est un critère élémentaire dans la valorisation et la création de la réussite sociale. En ce sens, les femmes sont les plus sujettes à la question où elles sont aussi jugées selon leurs conditions physiques. Selon les entretiens recueillis, 16 cas arrivaient à voir qu'une grande oppression sociale est appliquée aux femmes de différents statuts, si elles ne sont pas conformistes aux modèle proposé par les collectivités locales, en matière du corporel :

> le monde est injuste…je ne sais pas pourquoi, on demande toujours à la femme d'être belle, à prendre toujours soin de son corps et de son apparence, tandis que pour l'homme peu importe son physique et son « look »… on dit que lui est un homme « Rajel »,… lui, il se marie malgré son handicap et sa laideur, tandis que la femme, elle est « M'Râ » : un petit défaut physique la renvoie à un éternel célibat et personne ne voudra d'elle … (Samah, 27 ans, non voilée, 4ᵉ année Chimie).

La possibilité d'accès au marché matrimonial est une possibilité qui dépend du mérite. Chez les familles algériennes, plus que la bonne condition morale et éthique, la beauté féminine est une condition importante dans l'institution du mariage, on dit bien qu'il n'y a de défauts qu'en femmes (El-aib ghir fi n'ssa). Comme si le défaut physique est un problème féminin et non pas aussi masculin. Dans ce sens, la nature du défaut peut être à caractère matériel ou immatériel, physique ou morale. Ainsi, la femme se veut belle et bien éduquée, élégante, mais à bonne conduite. Pour entrer dans la logique de la possession des biens, elle doit être admirée et appréciée dans sa totalité et par référence à un modèle exemplaire. Cette légitimité du choix est renforcée par

une forte demande sociale qui s'appuie à son tour sur une législation individuelle.

Selon cette problématique du mérite, Samia Hassan El Saâti nous rapporte que le goût populaire, dans le choix d'une future épouse, se repose
souvent sur deux principaux critères liés à la beauté du corps : un relatif à la
qualité et à la couleur de la peau et un autre relatif à la bonne corpulence et à
la bonne stature de la femme. Elle dit que : « ainsi, le goût populaire adore la
blancheur de la peau, la finesse du tour de taille. Il admire les jambes de la
femme et ses mollets bien potelés… à vrai dire, il préfère les femmes corporellement rondes (El Saâti 1999 : 223).

Conjointement à cet avis, Malek Chebel note qu'au Maghreb, les rondeurs
des formes, la blancheur de la peau, la longueur de la chevelure et la noirceur
des yeux, sont les principaux éléments qui caractérisent la beauté féminine
dans ces sociétés (Chebel 1996 : 96). Par référence à l'échantillon d'étude, ces
valeurs du corps trouvent une confirmation chez les étudiantes questionnées,
elles avaient citées trois niveaux de l'évaluation du « beau » chez une femme :

- — 1er niveau lié à l'aspect physique du corps : « qu'il soit bien fourni, avec
  d'agréables formes et courbes » ;

- — 2e niveau lié aux particularités du corps notamment le visage : « la finesse
  de ses traits. Ses couleurs : teint blanc, joues rosées, lèvres rougeâtres,
  longs cils noirs… Ses rondeurs : visage rond avec de grands yeux. Et
  surtout la couleur et la qualité de la chevelure ne sont pas négligées ;

- — 3e niveau lié à l'apparence en général, incluant surtout le côté hygiénique
  et esthétique : « la propreté de la femme et son entretien corporel, plus la
  manière avec laquelle elle se met en valeur ».

Premier niveau

Quelle que soit l'origine d'appartenance, selon les représentations de quatorze
(14) interrogées, un corps féminin n'est pas beau s'il n'a pas de rondeurs et de
formes. Pour elles, ces rondeurs sont synonymes de séduction et de charme
et ajoutent une grande touche de beauté à la femme. Elles donnent à la sil-
houette une forme de vie, de mouvement, de flexibilité et de tendresse. En
dessinant un vase au tour de la taille, elles invitent le regard aux profondeurs
du « moi » et du charnel, elles l'enroulent sur un mouvement intérieur/ exté-
rieur. De ses entretiens réalisés, nous relevons deux opinions suivants :

> Moi, malgré qu'ils me disent que j'ai une taille de mannequin, je souhaite
> qu'un de ces jours, j'arrive à grossir et à prendre des formes…, pour
> paraître en tant que femme et non pas en tant que fillette; car je crois
> que les rondeurs sont à la mode, et puis, les hommes n'ont jamais

cesser à s'intéresser et à être attirer par les femmes rondes. Même dans le vocabulaire des jeunes, on retrouve aujourd'hui plein de mots de dragues qualifiant la jeune fille de pleine, de bien portante (M'âmrate, M'rihate, M'lihate)… et je crois c'est pour lui faire des éloges et non pas pour l'insulter (Khadidja, 21 ans, voilée, 3ᵉ année Psychologie).

…Moi, je trouve que certains hommes préfèrent les femmes rondes, parce qu'elles leurs rappellent leurs bonnes mères, ou tout simplement, elles les attirent sexuellement, … donc il y a une sorte d'attachement d'ordre nostalgique où les rondeurs sont synonymes de bonté et de grâce et aussi de sexualité » (Amina, 24 ans, non voilée, 4ᵉ année Droit).

Selon les résultats d'une étude publiée sur le net,[3] un corps charnu revoie directement à une lecture psychologique pour comprendre comment dans une société qui vénère les tailles sveltes, il existe certains individus qui ont une attraction physique envers d'autres types de corps, à savoir, les corps à multiples rondeurs. Cette étude qui arrive à justifier cette problématique, nous éclaire à travers les points suivants :

- les rondeurs adoucissent les traits de la physionomie féminine, elles portent un message de douceur qui sécurise. Elle est belle parce que son corps exprime la douceur ;

- les rondeurs permettent aussi à la femme de se différencier physiquement de l'homme : les hommes entre eux sont des adversaires naturels; ils sont constamment sur la défensive, tandis qu'un homme en présence d'une femme, sait qu'il n'a rien à craindre. Elle est belle parce que son corps exprime la paix et c'est cela qui favorise la domination masculine ;

- les rondeurs stimulent sexuellement l'homme; elles réveillent sa pulsion sexuelle. Elle est belle parce que son corps exprime un message sexuel ;

- un visage rond et éclatant, peut exprimer la joie de vivre, aussi, il donne une douceur à l'expression du visage et montre que la femme est en bonne santé, qu'elle est douce et d'une bonté pareille à celle des bonnes mamans.

Deuxième niveau

Se caractérisant par un teint méditerranéen, qui tire vers le bronzé, les Maghrébins optent plutôt pour une peau claire. Ainsi, ce contraste est parmi les qualités et les valeurs de la beauté féminine. Être blanche de peau, signifie être désirée dans les représentations populaires, c'est aussi un signe de bonté et de noblesse, comme c'est un signe de richesse et d'une certaine appartenance sociale. Une autre explication, qui nous vient d'une des 12 filles qui ont montré leur préférence des peaux blanches, reporte que c'est un critère d'originalité, car tout ce qui est rare est précieux et ça devient admirable pour son originalité.

Il est vrai que l'être humain est toujours en quête de ce qu'il n'a pas, de ce qu'il ne possède pas. Si certains préfèrent les blondes, il se peut que d'autres préfèrent les femmes brunes ou de teint foncé. Suivant une logique de goûts, le choix d'une épouse selon les critères de son teint, devient un élément irrationnel adopté par une mentalité collective. N'est-ce pas que les goûts et les couleurs ne se discutent pas ?

Troisième niveau

L'hygiène du corps joue un rôle très important dans la vie des individus ; un corps bien propre et bien entretenu représente non seulement les qualités d'un comportement individuel, mais aussi d'une démarche de civilisation, quelle que soit la condition de ce vécu : intime ou public. La femme est propre pour elle, c'est une évidence, mais elle est censée l'être pour les autres aussi : pour tout le monde et surtout pour l'homme avec lequel elle va partager sa vie. Une femme ne se fait pas respecter quand elle laisse aller son hygiène et quand elle délaisse son entretien corporel. Une tache apparue sur ses vêtements, fait d'elle une malsaine, une misérable, une dingue, une femme non valable et non intéressante. Il est conçu qu'une vraie femme, c'est une bonne ménagère et si celle-ci n'arrive pas à gérer le ménage de son corps, elle n'arrivera jamais à gérer le ménage de son foyer, du couple. Elle ne sera pas une bonne épouse pour son mari, ni une bonne maman pour ses enfants. En plus, elle suscite le dégoût et l'insécurité.

L'hygiène corporelle joue un rôle important dans les relations amoureuses. Un corps bien entretenu est beau, car attirant et désirant. Il ne laisse pas le regard indifférent. En cette matière, il nous est rapporté de la tradition arabe que les musulmans depuis plusieurs siècles avaient un regard très attentionné au corps, surtout en matière d'hygiène et de propreté. Telles sont les recommandations pour entrer en contact avec le sacré et le divin. En terre d'Islam, l'entretien du corps prend deux dimensions : une qui relève du rituel en référence au religieux et une autre qui relève de la technique en référence au social. Cette deuxième dimension est construite à base du respect de l'autre, de l'humain. À travers son corps, on se fait aussi respecter et perdurer le sentiment affectif. À ce propos, Mahmoud El Istanbouli, dans son livre sur les liaisons amoureuses, nous dit : « l'hygiène et l'entretien du corps sont les meilleurs outils de la séduction pour la femme; car le nez est comme l'œil, très sensible et très sélectif. S'il arrive à détecter une bonne odeur ou une mauvaise odeur, il travaille directement sur la transmission du sentiment d'appréciation ou de mépris de cette sensation olfactive au cœur » (El Istambouli 1986 : 103). Ainsi, les femmes s'entre-conseillent en disant :… « Fais attention à ce que ton mari voit en toi ou sente en toi quelque chose qui lui déplairait ».

Conclusion

En terme de conclusion, il faut dire que les hypothèses de travail se sont pertinemment vérifiées par l'éclairage de la littérature et le questionnement du terrain. On retient que :

- le corps est un grand sujet de débats dans les travaux de beaucoup de chercheurs en sciences sociales, il est l'objet d'un grand discours controversé. En matière de démarche anthropologique, il devient un bon élément d'analyses du patrimoine social, qu'il soit symbolique ou matériel ;

- la prise de conscience du corps chez la jeune fille universitaire est une dimension non seulement liée au développement biologique, mais aussi conjointement au vécu social et psychologique. Si le biologique est lié au fait de mûrir et de se métamorphoser corporellement à partir de la puberté, le social est lié à sa prédisposition à partir des modes de socialisation familiale et institutionnelle. Ainsi, ce sont deux dimensions du vécu corporel qui travailleront par la suite sur la structuration de sa psychologie du savoir et de l'identité ;

- la beauté féminine, en tant que norme liée aux représentations collectives et individuelles, est a priori le résultat d'un capital culturel matériel et immatériel lié aux goûts et aux préférences des individus. Elle est la valeur du distinctif, du rare et du symétrique. En milieux sociaux appartenant au monde arabo- musulman, elle est censurée et ajustée selon un modèle subordonné à l'image de la domination masculine ;

- le but le plus important de la mise en valeur du corps par l'entretien et l'esthétique chez les étudiantes universitaires, se construit par rapport à la nature d'un besoin social qui se justifie par l'appréhension de l'exclusion et de la marginalisation, notamment lorsqu'on provient d'un milieu ou d'une origine sociale différent, à savoir non civilisé. De ce fait, l'esthétique de l'apparence devient un excellent moyen pour se faire voir et entendre, pour créer des zones de communication et d'échanges et surtout, pour accéder au marché matrimonial par la conquête du monde de la masculinité.

Le corps dans l'abstrait évoque une problématique du moi et de l'autre, du beau et du charnel, une démarche à double sens et à sens inverse : du passé, du présent et du futur. Cependant le capital corporel est un patrimoine et une tradition qui se fait respecter même chez les petits groupes porteurs et vecteurs de modernité et de changements. Ainsi, la beauté, l'esthétique de l'apparence, du look, des formes, des couleurs, de la morale de l'éthique... deviennent des attributs au corps par lesquels, il se définit et se redéfinit d'une manière synchronique et diachronique, entraînant la société globale dans des enjeux à caractère universel.

Notes

1. Ou selon le concept employé par Bourdieu « Habitus ».
2. Farid El Zahi est chercheur dans un centre universitaire à Rabat
3. http://www.3.sympatico.ca/rondes/horbau. htm

Références

Ait Sabah, Fatma, 1982, *La femme dans l'inconscient musulman, Désir et pouvoir*, Paris : Éditions les Sycomures.

Bourdieu, Pierre, 1991, « Sexe, catégorie sociale », *Revue de recherche en Sciences Sociales : Masculin/ Féminin*, n° 83.

Chebel, Melek, 1996, *Le livre de la séduction*, Paris : Éditions Payot et Rivages.

Combessie, Jean Claude, 1998, *La méthode en sociologie*, Alger : Éditions Casbah.

Des Camps, Marc Alain, 1986, *L'invention du corps*, Paris : PUF.

El Istanbouli, Mahmoud, 1986, *Touh'fatou El-Arouss*, Beyrout : Éditions El Maktab El Islami, 6e édition.

El Saâti, Samia Hassan, 1999, *Sociologie de la femme, vision contemporaine de ses principaux propos*, Le Caire : Éditions Fikr Al Arabi (version en arabe).

El Zahi, Farid, 1999, *Corps, l'Image et le Sacré en Islam*, Rabat (Maroc) : Éditions Afriquiya El Charqu'.

Fournier, Martine, 2002, «Le corps emblème de soi », *Revue des sciences humaines*, n° 133.

Le Breton, David, 1997, *La sociologie du corps*, Paris : PUF.

Mauss, Marcel, 1967, *Manuel d'ethnographie*, Paris : Payot.

Pagés Delon, Michèle, 1989, *Le corps et ses apparences-L'envers du look,* Paris : l'Harmattan, collection Logiques sociales.

Perrot, Philippe, 1984, *Le travail des apparences ou transformation du corps féminin du XVIIIe au XIXe siècle*, Paris : Seuil.

Pociello, Christian, 1989, *Structure et évaluation des loisirs sportifs dans la société française de 1975 à 1995*, Paris : Éditions Université de Paris.

Robert, Mary Louise, 1996, « Prêt à déchiffrer, la mode de l'après guerre», *Revue du mouvement sociale*, n° 174.

Tarabichi, George, 1982, *Est / Ouest : Masculinité/ Féminité : étude sur la crise du Genre et de la civilisation,* Beyrouth : Éditions Taliâ, 3ᵉ édition (le livre est en arabe).

Travaillot, Yves, 1998, *Sociologie des pratiques de l'entretien du corps*, Paris : PUF.

Zdatny, Steven, 1996, « La mode à la garçonne de 1900 à 1929 », *Revue trimestrielle : Le mouvement Social*, fondée par Jean Maitron, Éditions Atelier, n°174, janvier- mars.

CPSIA information can be obtained
at www.ICGtesting.com
Printed in the USA
LVHW041131251119
638400LV00003B/307/P